SKYE &
THE INNER HEBRIDES
INCLUDING MULL

KATIE FEATHERSTONE

www.bradtguides.com

Bradt Guides Ltd, UK
The Globe Pequot Press Inc, USA

Bradt GUIDES
TRAVEL TAKEN SERIOUSLY

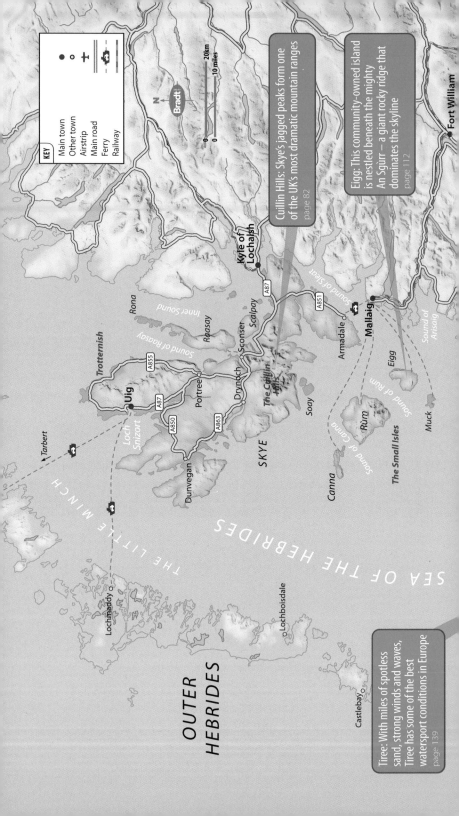

KEY
● Main town
○ Other town
✝ Airstrip
⛴ Ferry
▭ Railway

20km
10 miles
0
0

N

Bradt

Fort William

Cuillin Hills: Skye's jagged peaks form one of the UK's most dramatic mountain ranges
page 82

Eigg: This community-owned island is nestled beneath the mighty An Sgùrr – a giant rocky ridge that dominates the skyline
page 112

Tiree: With miles of spotless sand, strong winds and waves, Tiree has some of the best watersport conditions in Europe
page 139

Kyle of Lochalsh

A87

A851

Sound of Sleat

Armadale

Mallaig

Sound of Arisaig

Eigg

Rona

Inner Sound

Sound of Raasay

Raasay

Scalpay

Sconser

Trotternish

A855

Uig

A87

Portree

Drynoch

The Cuillin Hills

SKYE

A850

Loch Snizort

A863

Dunvegan

Soay

Rùm

Sound of Rum

Muck

The Small Isles

Canna

Sound of Canna

Tarbert

THE LITTLE MINCH

OUTER HEBRIDES

Lochmaddy

SEA OF THE HEBRIDES

Lochboisdale

Castlebay

Lismore: A low-lying island steeped in history, from Tirefour's well-preserved Iron Age broch to the ruins of 13th-century Achadun Castle
page 185

Duart Castle: Learn about the archipelago's tumultuous clan history while exploring this dramatically positioned fortress
page 166

Easdale: One of the tiny Slate Islands, which roofed the world, Easdale is the smallest inhabited island in the Inner Hebrides
page 199

Ben More: Bag a Munro by climbing Mull's highest mountain — on a clear day there are views across the whole of the Inner Hebrides
page 164

Oronsay Priory: This historic Augustinian priory can only be reached at low tide, when the natural causeway from Colonsay is exposed
page 211

Loch Gruinart RSPB Reserve: Come to watch 37,000 geese return to Islay in October, or listen for the distinctive call of elusive corncrakes at other times of the year
page 232

Islay whisky: Drink a dram of Islay's famous peaty whisky — with ten working distilleries on the island you'll be spoilt for choice
page 213

Loch Linnhe

Oban

Lismore

Kerrera

Lochaline

Lochaline

A884

Sound of Mull

Tobermory

Loch Tuath

Treshnish Isles

Arinagour

Coll

Scarinish

Tiree

MULL

Loch na Keal

Ulva

A848

Salen

Craignure

Lochbuie

A849

Ross of Mull

Iona

Fionnphort

Seil

The Slate Islands

Finn of Lorn

Garvellachs

Luing

Scarba

Sound of Jura

Inverlussa

A846

Jura

Port Askaig

Port Ellen

Islay

A846

The Oa

A847

Laggan Bay

Portnahaven

Scalasaig

Colonsay

Oronsay

Lochgilphead

Tarbert

Taynuilt

Kennacraig

A83

Gigha

Kintyre

SKYE & THE INNER HEBRIDES
DON'T MISS...

PUFFINS
From May until August, watch puffins nesting on Sanday or the Treshnish Isles PAGES 124 & 171
(HM/S)

SPECTACULAR QUIRAING LANDSLIDES
Take in panoramic views as you hike the Quiraing loop on Skye PAGE 70
(DK/S)

THE SMALL ISLES
Explore the Small Isles' dramatic, volcanic landscapes. Pictured: Rùm from Eigg's An Sgùrr PAGE 116
(JD/VS)

PICTURE-PERFECT SETTLEMENTS
Taste island specialities or pick up local crafts on your wanderings through the towns and villages of the Inner Hebrides. Pictured: colourful Tobermory PAGE 154
(SV/S)

GEESE MIGRATION
Visit Islay in mid-October to witness over 30,000 geese returning to the island PAGE 10
(SS)

SKYE & THE INNER HEBRIDES
IN COLOUR

above (NH/S) Skye's pretty capital Portree is the Inner Hebrides' most populous settlement PAGE 60

below left (KF) The landscape of Jura is dominated by its three rocky Paps, which provide great hiking opportunities PAGE 242

below right (SBP/S) Whisky is the mainstay of Islay's economy – there are ten distilleries across the island PAGE 213

The small passenger ferry between Point on Lismore and mainland Port Appin only takes 10 minutes PAGE 187

above left
(EQ/S)

A ferry operator's dog rides between Seil and Luing in the Slate Islands PAGE 195

above right
(KF)

Local culture and history is preserved in the islands' excellent heritage centres and small museums. Pictured: Skye Museum of Island Life PAGE 72

right
(FB/S)

Highland dancing, pipe bands and Herculean feats of strength all feature in the islands' Highland Games and summer fèis events PAGE 46

below
(JSH/A)

Katie Featherstone is a freelance writer focusing on the west coast of Scotland, where she lives, and Iceland, where she's been working as a seasonal mountain hut warden since 2017. While the first edition of this book was also her first published work, she now writes hiking routes and walking guidebooks for Cicerone and *Trail* magazine; has had articles and features published in *The Guardian*, *The Independent*, *The Great Outdoors* magazine, *Hidden Europe*, *Coast* magazine and *Scottish* *Islands Explorer*; and works for the American publisher *Frommer's* on their whole-country guidebooks. In her ever-dwindling spare time, she still occasionally spills her heart on to an increasingly neglected blog w featherytravels.com, and procrastinates by oversharing on social media; you can follow her on Facebook, Twitter (or 'X', if we must) and Instagram: featherytravels.

British Library Cataloguing in Publication Data
A catalogue record for this book is available from the British Library

AUTHOR'S STORY

Having holidayed around the Inner Hebrides every year since I was born, I spent my first decade of adulthood getting as far away from the UK as possible, writing a lot and trying to learn how to use a camera. Sometime around Christmas 2016 I reconsidered and decided that, actually, I found hiking in horizontal rain more exciting than lying under palm trees – and haven't been able to shake the idea since.

This is a second edition of my first book. I always strive to do a good job, but the first time round was a particularly desperate experience: I began by researching wildly in as much detail as I physically could, scouring old books, pouring over Historic Environment Scotland's map (w canmore.org.uk) and questioning locals relentlessly. On each island, I drove down every side road, poked my head into countless en suites, and tramped around the countryside looking for ancient monuments, beaches and beautiful views, living mostly on chocolate digestives. At some point, I realised I'd done enough research to write a book ten times longer than this one, and that *somehow* I needed to battle this information on to the page.

I've approached this second edition with more confidence, revisiting the islands like old friends and asking for help from the human ones I made along the way. As ever, I hope this guide does a service to the Inner Hebrides and helps people discover what makes each island unique.

Second edition published November 2024
First published 2020
Bradt Travel Guides Ltd
31a High Street, Chesham, Buckinghamshire, HP5 1BW, England
www.bradtguides.com
Print edition published in the USA by The Globe Pequot Press Inc,
PO Box 480, Guilford, Connecticut 06437-0480

Text copyright © Katie Featherstone, 2024
Maps copyright © Bradt Travel Guides Ltd, 2024; includes map data © OpenStreetMap
contributors; contains Ordnance Survey Data © Crown copyright and database right 2024
Photographs copyright © Individual photographers, 2024 (see below)
Project Manager: Samantha Fletcher
Cover research: Pepi Bluck, Perfect Picture

ISBN: 9781804691809

Photographs AWL Images: PhotoFVG (PF/AWL); Alamy.com: jeremy sutton-hibbert
(JSH/A); Dreamstime.com: Shaiith (S/D); Katie Featherstone (KF); Mary-Ann
Featherstone (MF); Shutterstock.com: 4 season backpacking (4/S), Captblack76
(C/S), Daniel_Kay (DK/S), EQRoy (EQ/S), Erni (E/S), Francesco Bonino (FB/S),
HedvikaMichnova.jpg (HM/S), Inspired By Maps (IBM/S), Jamie Harwood (JH/S),
Kevin Standage (KS/S), Kraft_Stoff (KrS/S), Mark Caunt (MC/S), Mark Medcalf (MM/S),
Martin Prochazkacz (MP/S), mountaintreks (m/S), Nataliya Hora (NH/S), Nicol Nicolson
(NN/S), RJ1990 (R/S), SergeBertasiusPhotography (SBP/S), Stefano_Valeri (SV/S), stewart
dawber (SD/S), Thomas Lukassek (TL/S); SuperStock.com (SS); Visit Scotland: Airborne
Lens (AL/VS), John Duncan (JD/VS), Kenny Lam (KL/VS), Paul Tomkins (PT/VS)
Front cover The Cuillin Hills on Skye (PF/AWL)
Back cover Above left: Portnahaven on Islay (KL/VS); below left: white-tailed eagle near
Mull (JH/S); right: Kilt Rock (TL/S)
Title page Left: Iona Abbey (KrS/S); above right: picturesque Mull (SS); below right: a
Highland cow on Skye (S/D)

Maps David McCutcheon FBCart.S. FRGS

Typeset by Ian Spick, Bradt Travel Guides, and Geethik Technologies, India
Production managed by Gutenberg Press; printed in Malta
Digital conversion by www.dataworks.co.in

Paper used for this product comes from sustainably managed forests, and recycled and
controlled sources.

Acknowledgements

I'd like to thank the staff and freelancers at Bradt Guides whom I worked with in 2019 and 2020: Sue Cooper, Rachel Fielding, Emma Gibbs, Anna Moores, David McCutcheon, James Lowen and Claire Strange. This time round, I need to thank Claire again, along with my editor Samantha Fletcher for all her help. On the subject of Bradt, thank you to Mark Rowe, author of *Outer Hebrides*, for his general encouragement and suggestion of the title, *Skye and the Inner Hebrides*, for this new edition; additionally to Emma Gibbs, my old editor and author of the new *Scotland's North Highlands*, for her ongoing moral support.

Thank you to prolific walking guidebook author Peter Edwards for his admirable patience and camaraderie, and to both him and Fiona Rintoul for their covert investigative work around Skye.

To all those island residents and business owners who invited me to stay, eat or join activities; provided me with information and encouragement; or sold me a child single bus ticket at the age of 32 – this book would not exist without your support.

Thank you to all my family and friends for their help with the first edition and for putting up with me while I continue to do this work despite my own better judgement: Mary-Ann Featherstone, Jenny and Nick Bowman, Pauline Short, Janet and Rod de Maine, Bryony Welburn, and particularly my dad, Nick, for whom I wrote this book.

Finally, and most of all, thanks to my husband, Dan, for everything you do.

FEEDBACK REQUEST

At Bradt Guides we're aware that guidebooks start to go out of date on the day they're published – and that you, our readers, are out there in the field doing research of your own. You'll find out before us when a fine new family-run hotel opens or a favourite restaurant changes hands and goes downhill. So why not tell us about your experiences? Contact us on ☎ 01753 893444 or e info@bradtguides.com. We will forward emails to the author who may post updates on the Bradt website at w bradtguides.com/updates. Alternatively, you can add a review of the book to Amazon, or share your adventures with us on social:

f X ◎ BradtGuides & featherytravels

Contents

MAP LIST

Introduction

Splintering off Scotland's west coast, the Inner Hebrides make up a loosely scattered archipelago including all the islands from Skye in the north to Islay and Gigha in the south; they stretch as far west as Tiree and cut into the mainland to the east, with Lismore and Kerrera sitting in the Firth of Lorn. From the edge of the Atlantic to more sheltered sea lochs, 20 islands are covered in this book, but these are just the places with visitor accommodation and regular boat services; there are countless other islands of varying sizes within the archipelago.

Surrounded by miles of intricate coastline, with vast swathes of wilderness between the villages inland, the Inner Hebrides are a haven for wildlife and a particularly important habitat for coastal birds and marine mammals. Sightings of seals are almost guaranteed, while even luckier or more patient visitors have a chance to spot otters, basking sharks and even minke whales.

Following Scotland's Scottish Outdoor Access Code, well-prepared walkers have infinite possibilities on the islands. Large areas of each map are uninhabited and there is a high likelihood of being able to enjoy Mull's dramatic rock formations or Jura's Paps without the interruption of another person in sight.

The islands' modern-day charms and gentle demeanour give little indication of their turbulent past: Irish monks and Viking invasions, the creation of the Lords of the Isles' kingdom and subsequent clan warfare. These long-lost civilisations left behind ruined castles, intricate carvings and crumbling chapels, sprinkling the islands with fascinating archaeology.

The 19th-century Clearances hit the Inner Hebrides hard and the bumpy road to recovery through the 20th century and into the 21st is still far from over. Reclaiming an identity, through cèilidh dances and music, their native Gaelic language and traditional industries, remains an ongoing struggle but, despite having fewer than 20,500 people living across the whole region, each of the islands retains a distinctive history, character and culture. Pious Iona, Islay with its whisky and Canna, where the village shop still has an honesty box, all support their own unique communities. Whichever islands you choose to visit, you can be sure to feel a world apart.

ACCESSIBILITY Sights, accommodation, places to eat and drink and shops marked ♿ indicate that they are wheelchair accessible and that any available toilets are suitable for people with disabilities.

AUTHOR'S FAVOURITES Finding genuinely characterful accommodation or that unmissable off-the-beaten-track café can be difficult, so the author has chosen a few of his favourite places throughout the country to point you in the right direction. These 'author's favourites' are marked with a ✳.

PRICE CODES Throughout this guide we have used price codes to indicate the cost of those places to stay and eat listed in the guide.

Accommodation The following codes are used to give a general indication of price bracket. They are based on the cost of one night in a double room, two people in a dorm or two sharing a tent in high season, and include breakfast where it is offered. You are likely, however, to find large seasonal discounts, reductions for single travellers or for longer stays. For self-catering properties, rather than giving a price code, the cost of a week during high season is used instead to avoid confusion.

Luxury	£££££	£220+
Upmarket	££££	£130–220
Mid-range	£££	£100–130
Thrifty	££	£60–100
Budget	£	up to £60

Restaurants The following categories are used in this book to indicate the cost of an average main meal.

High end	£££	£25+
Mid-range	££	£15–25
Cheap	£	up to £15

MAPS

Keys and symbols Maps include alphabetical keys covering the locations of those places to stay, eat or drink that are featured in the book. Note that regional maps may not show all hotels and restaurants in the area: other establishments may be located in towns shown on the map. Additionally, Mountain Bothies Association bothies (page 44) mentioned in the book are also shown on the maps, marked with a (⌂).

Grids and grid references Several maps use gridlines to allow easy location of sites. Map grid references are listed in square brackets after the name of the place or site of interest in the text, with page number followed by grid number, eg: [56 D4].

Part One

GENERAL INFORMATION

THE INNER HEBRIDES AT A GLANCE

Location Islands off the west coast of Scotland

Neighbouring regions Outer Hebrides, Argyll and the Highlands

Size/area A combined landmass of 1,594 square miles

Climate Mild oceanic climate; plenty of wind and rain; Skye winter averages 6°C, summer averages 15°C

Population 20,000

Main towns Portree, Tobermory, Bowmore

Economy Agriculture, tourism, fishing, whisky distilling

Languages English and Scottish Gaelic

Religion Christian: mainly Church of Scotland, Free Church of Scotland and other Protestant denominations. Increasing numbers of inhabitants are atheist or agnostic.

Currency Pound sterling (Scotland has its own banknotes, but English notes are also accepted)

Exchange rate US$1 = £0.75; €1 = £0.84 (Sep 2024)

International telephone code +44

Time GMT (end Oct–end Mar), GMT+1 (end Mar–end Oct)

Electrical voltage 230V

Weights and measures Road signs in miles; elsewhere both metric and imperial units are widely used

Flag Debatably, the UK's Union Jack. Scotland's flag is the 'St Andrew's Cross' or 'Saltire', which has a white cross diagonally set on a blue background. Some islands also have their own flag such as Tiree's Bratach Thiriodh, which depicts ears of barley forming a sun on a green background.

National sports Highland Games, football, rugby, shinty

Public holidays The same as mainland Scotland: 1 January (New Year's Day), 2 January, Good Friday, early May bank holiday (first Monday in May), spring bank holiday (last Monday in May), summer bank holiday (first Monday in August), 30 November (St Andrew's Day), 25 December (Christmas Day), 26 December (Boxing Day)

1

Background Information

GEOGRAPHY

Looking at a map of Scotland, the Inner Hebrides crumble off the west coast at a point where the mainland appears so intricately broken by lochs and shoreline that it is often difficult to tell which parts of land are islands and what is attached. This is a scattered archipelago, spanning 150 miles north to south and around 50 miles east to west. While over 20 of the islands are inhabited, a countless number have no human residents at all; from Scarba, at 6 square miles, to hundreds of rocky islets that are left to nature as some of the UK's most precious areas of wilderness.

Spread across a combined landmass of 1,594 square miles (4,130km²), the definition of the Inner Hebrides is somewhat hazy even to the people who live there. During the course of researching this book, I was often asked by residents which islands was I going to include. Does Seil still count as an island even though it is only separated from the mainland by the tiniest, bridged channel and, in that case, what about Skye? This guidebook includes both Seil and Skye, as well as all the inhabited islands up the Firth of Lorn into Loch Linnhe, where the Hebridean definition gets a little stretched.

Scattered as they are, the islands are defined by the stretches of water surrounding them. For centuries these seas would have been impassable for most inhabitants and in high winds that can still be the case today.

The most northerly of the islands is Skye, separated from the Outer Hebrides by the Little Minch, while more temperate Islay and Gigha are the most southerly. The other islands are spread out between them: some, like Seil and Kerrera, so close to the mainland that they are almost still part of it; while, in the far west of the region, low-lying Coll and Tiree are exposed to the full force of the Atlantic Ocean.

GEOLOGY

With craggy coastlines and sandy beaches, rough moorland, mountains and fertile glens, one of the Inner Hebrides' greatest delights is the sheer variety of its landscapes. To understand them better, it is necessary to look at the islands' geology, which varies greatly across the archipelago.

The oldest rocks in the region (as well as in the UK) are those of Lewisian gneisses, which take their name from Lewis in the Outer Hebrides and date from around 2,500 million years ago, during the Archean Eon. These can be found on northern Raasay, Rùm, Coll, Tiree, Iona and the southeastern coast of Skye's Sleat Peninsula.

Also on the Sleat Peninsula, northeastern Rùm and Raasay are layers of red Torridonian sandstones, sedimentary rocks that settled around 1,000 million years ago. Around Ord and the head of Loch Slapin on Skye there are also a variety of sedimentary rocks from the Cambrian and Ordovician periods, deposited in a shallow sea around 550 to 450 million years ago.

In contrast, but from a similar time period, the Slate Islands (unsurprisingly, perhaps) were formed from metamorphic slate; the export of the characteristic blue-grey slates once held up the economy of these islands.

More sedimentary rocks were deposited by rivers and shallow seas during the Mesozoic Era (around 245 to 90 million years ago). These are of particular interest for the evidence they left behind of life during the Triassic, Jurassic and Cretaceous periods: Jurassic dinosaur footprints can be seen at An Corran on Skye (page 70); and on Camas Mòr on Muck (page 128), layers packed with fossilised shells are exposed on the foreshore. Sedimentary rocks from this period can also be found on Raasay, Eigg and Rùm.

The Palaeogene Period (66 to 23 million years ago) left signs of volcanic complexes from a time when northwest Europe began to split from North America, creating the North Atlantic. Arguably the most dramatic mountain range in Britain, the Cuillin Hills (page 82) on Skye are remnants of the roots of one such early Palaeogene volcanic centre.

Over the last 2 million years, the main geological activity across the Inner Hebrides has been the shaping of existing rocks and landscapes by moving ice. Various ice ages have swept across Scotland, the most recent of which peaked about 18,000 years ago. After their creation as volcanic complexes, both the Skye and Rùm Cuillin were later eroded by the build-up and withdrawal of glaciers. On Jura, Sgriob na Caillich (page 244) is thought to be a medial moraine, a narrow strip of debris deposited between two streams of the Devensian ice sheet as they collided. Trotternish Ridge in northern Skye continued to see landslides long after the disappearance of the glaciers, resulting in amazing rock formations such as the Storr (page 68) and Quiraing (page 70).

The islands' geology has resulted in often dramatically different ecosystems and undoubtedly affected human communities and industry. Rùm, with its savage peaks, and waterlogged Jura have always had relatively small populations as vast swathes of their land are simply uninhabitable. In contrast, Lismore is based on metamorphosed limestone and particularly fertile; this has affected life on the island for both wildlife and people. Islay's peat bogs have long been harvested for fuel and used in the process of whisky making, while quarrying has taken place on most islands in the region: slate on the Slate Islands (page 194), iron ore on Raasay (page 95), limestone on Lismore (page 191) and pink Ross of Mull granite (page 172) are just a few examples.

CLIMATE

The islands' proximity to the Atlantic Ocean gives them a mild oceanic climate with cool temperatures. In winter, the north of Skye averages around 6°C, whereas temperatures for Islay and Gigha are closer to 8°C; in summer, Skye sees averages of 15°C and the more southerly islands are a degree or two warmer than that. Tiree is known as one of the sunniest places in the UK, but there is nothing to protect you from the savage Atlantic winds there. Apart from on the loftiest peaks, the islands generally receive very little snow and they are said to be kept warmer by the Gulf Stream; none of this is a great comfort in the long winter months, however, in the face of howling winds and biting rain.

Thought to be already affecting the behaviour of certain species of wildlife, there are major concerns about how **climate change** will impact the future of the Inner

Hebrides. Warmer temperatures, rising sea levels and even more unpredictable weather would make the islands increasingly inhospitable for both wildlife and human inhabitants.

NATURAL HISTORY AND CONSERVATION

Many different parts of the Inner Hebrides are recognised as unique and protected under various conservation areas. Loch na Keal National Scenic Area, which is protected from 'inappropriate' development because of its exceptional landscapes and coastline, covers much of western Mull and all the small islands out to the Treshnish Isles. Launched in 2019, Argyll Coast and Islands Hope Spot (w argyllhopespot.scot) includes the north and east of Jura, the Slate Islands, Lismore, Kerrera and the Sound of Mull; it is said to be rivalled only by St Kilda in terms of biodiversity in Scotland. There are two RSPB reserves on Islay (pages 232 and 229), one on Coll (page 138) and almost the entirety of Rùm is run as a nature reserve by NatureScot. Countless other small reserves, such as Ballachuan Hazelwood (page 199) on Seil, protect specific locations and species.

HABITATS AND HIGHLIGHTS Like many isolated islands, the Inner Hebrides have developed their own very specialised ecosystems. Although, excluding deer and goats, they are generally low in species of land mammal, this is over-compensated with birds and marine wildlife. The occasional arrival of invasive hedgehogs and non-native species is something of a mystery, which raises much confusion and can cause a great deal of damage. The Tiree machair complex is particularly noteworthy as one of the few examples of rabbit-free machair in Scotland; elsewhere, such as on Canna, you can immediately see the erosive damage of their burrowing.

Sandy beaches and the machair Machair is a Gaelic word for a fertile low-lying grassy area. It is used to describe the habitat formed as strong wind blows crushed shells up from the shore and this sandy base is colonised by grasses and plants.

PLASTIC POLLUTION

Aside from climate change, the biggest human-inflicted environmental threat to species in the Inner Hebrides is undoubtedly plastic pollution. The archipelago's exposed beaches, in a prime location to receive accidental unbiodegradable litter from Scotland, Ireland and the Atlantic Ocean, have a new haul of debris dumped on them with every storm. Although some of this is everyday food packaging, bathroom waste and balloons, the depressing majority comes from the fishing industry. Nets, plastic straps, fish boxes, floats and buoys are a common sight on the islands' shorelines; the once scenic additions of round glass floats or fraying rope made from biodegradable materials such as heather have changed to plastic tangles, perfectly designed to trap fish and equally destructive to birds and larger marine mammals such as whales, who can eat it by mistake. The visible evidence of this problem is only the tip of the proverbial iceberg; microplastics, tiny scraps that can be eaten by small fish and enter the food chain, are said to be as omnipresent as 26 million pieces per square mile.

Consider collecting litter when you visit beaches and disposing of it when you find a large enough public bin.

One of the least common habitats in Europe, the calcium-rich shell sand supports a fragile ecosystem, parts of which can easily be destroyed by careless boots or, significantly worse, off-road driving. On sandy beaches, curlews, oystercatchers, ringed plovers and other wading birds feed at the water's edge and nest further up the tide line. With relatively small numbers of land predators, ground-nesting birds are common and successful.

Rocky shorelines and cliffs On rocky coasts, the area between high and low tide lines supports a fascinating array of species. Small fish and prawns get caught in rock pools, while sea urchins and starfish cling to the rocks. By carefully investigating under thongs of seaweed, you can discover sheltering crabs, frilly sea slugs and colourful shellfish. The coastline of the Inner Hebrides is fringed by an intricate network of peninsulas and partially protruding rocks, which form sanctuaries for wildlife including otters and seals. Protecting their eggs from potential land and sea predators, including humans, cliffs can host huge colonies of nesting seabirds: guillemot, fulmar, kittiwake, shags and gulls; puffins nest in a couple of specific places on the Treshnish Isles (page 171) and Sanday (page 124).

Kelp forests The kelps are a set of large, brown seaweeds, which grow exceptionally fast and can reach lengths of up to 260ft in the right conditions. Providing the coast with some degree of protection in storms, kelp forests are both food and shelter for many marine creatures. A strong, claw-like 'holdfast' anchors each plant on to a rock; the tiny caves and tunnels created by this feature typically host between 30 and 70 different species per plant.

The high seas With fierce currents, crashing waves and Corryvreckan whirlpool, the seas surrounding the Inner Hebrides do not always feel like a habitable environment but, despite depleted fish stocks, the area is still an excellent place to spot the UK's largest and most exciting species: whales, dolphins, basking sharks and large numbers of seals.

Peat bogs The Inner Hebrides are rich in peat bogs. Peat is formed as the ground becomes waterlogged and plant matter is unable to decompose properly. Although it only supports a small number of species, mostly sphagnum bog mosses, cotton grasses and some small carnivorous plants such as sundew, as well as birds such as merlin, golden plover and dunlin, this habitat is of global environmental importance for its ability to trap huge quantities of carbon. The carbon dioxide that is absorbed and converted by plants during photosynthesis is trapped under anaerobic conditions beneath the water and stored underground for an infinite length of time.

Accumulated peatland also provides an unusual opportunity to examine the entire history of an ecosystem's development; as a form of archive, it stores pollen grains and plant remains (macrofossils), making it possible to reconstruct an idea of past landscapes and climatic periods; in the case of UK peatlands, this is as far back as 10,000 years.

Farm and croft land When managed sympathetically, something that the RSPB and other organisations are working hard to promote, low-intensity farming and smaller-scale crofts can work alongside wildlife. Islay's choughs (page 212), for example, feed on insects and larvae found under cowpats. Corncrakes are only found in small pockets of the mainland, but changes in farming methods have increased populations in certain parts of the Hebrides where they stay between April and September before migrating to Africa for the winter. Towards the end of April into the beginning of May, Coll (page 129) is one of the best places in the UK to hear their distinctive 'crex-crex' call. Whether they are appreciated or not, barnacle and white-fronted geese swamp farmers' fields every autumn, the most dramatic display being found on Islay (page 212).

Woodland The Inner Hebrides are not known for their forests, but there are some magical exceptions including the woodland around Craignure on Mull (page 166), near Inver on Raasay (page 100) and Bridgend Woods on Islay (page 222). Ancient woodland – those that have existed since before 1750 – supports a unique variety of delicate lichens, ferns, fungi and even the elusive pine marten in places. Native broad-leaved trees are the perfect habitat for many small birds including redstart, wood warbler and tree pipit and although evergreen conifer plantations are generally considered to be less scenic, especially when they have to be felled, they do support good populations of the certain species that thrive, siskin and goldcrest for example.

Lofty peaks The Skye Cuillin are the Inner Hebrides' (and arguably the UK's) most imposing mountain range, with 3,254ft Sgùrr Alasdair being the highest peak; Jura, Rùm, Mull and Islay all have substantial hills and most of the islands have some variation in altitude. These peaks are important habitats for golden eagles and, in the case of Rùm, Manx shearwater, which arrive in their thousands to breed. On Mull in particular, you might see golden and white-tailed or sea eagles flying together. It is important not to publicise their nesting sites online, as unfortunately there is still a threat of sabotage and a black market for eggs.

FLORA AND FAUNA *with James Lowen*
Among visitors with even a smidgeon of interest in nature, few depart the Inner Hebrides anything other than wowed. The waters between the islands are arguably the UK's finest for spotting whales and dolphins, while rocky coastlines and interpolating bays are frequented by otters and seals. Boat trips offer a near-guarantee of close views of white-tailed eagle, while the closely related golden eagle soars on uplifts of air above. Feathered throngs of geese and seabirds delight in winter and summer respectively, while the latter season can be one of plenty for colourful orchids, rare bumblebees and stunning butterflies and moths.

Land mammals The most iconic mammal inhabiting the Inner Hebrides is one that blurs the boundaries between land and water: the **otter**. Equally at home in lochs, ditches and seaweed-strewn, rocky bays, this member of the weasel family is rather common on many islands. Seeing it is another matter, usually requiring either persistence or luck. Early morning and late evening are best, particularly – for coastal animals – on an incoming tide. Chances are highest on calm days, when it is easier to spot the distinctive V-shaped furrow made by a swimming otter. Tiree (including Loch Bhasapol), Mull (Calgary Bay), Skye (Milovaig) and Rùm (Kinloch) are probably your best bets.

Rivalling the otter for top spot is **red deer**, the UK's largest wholly land-dwelling mammal, which inhabits several islands. Typically, animals spend the summer on high moorlands, but descend to the lowlands in winter. The most exciting time of year to see them is autumn, when males engage in 'rutting' – a visceral, antler-clacking display of dominance that decides which individuals secure the rights to sire that year's offspring. Jura is thought to mean 'deer island', and perhaps 5,000 individual deer live there, while the red deer of Rùm have been studied intensively since 1953 – one of the longest-running and most comprehensive studies of any animal anywhere in the world.

The most obvious land mammal on Islay and Tiree is the **brown hare**, while **mountain hares** have been introduced to islands including Mull, Skye and Raasay. The latter is less rangy than the more familiar brown hare, with shorter ears. Mountain hares on Mull, at least, originated from Ireland, which makes them **Irish hares** – a subspecies that originally colonised Ireland during the last Ice Age.

Other mammals were also introduced to the islands, including **goats**, which now roam in feral herds, and **hedgehogs**, which inhabit lowland grasslands and machair. Meanwhile, the opening of the Skye Bridge has enabled **pine martens** to cross from mainland Scotland on to Skye. They have now spread throughout the south and west of the island. Less clear is how pine martens reached Mull during the Noughties. The most plausible theory suggests that the original arrivals were stowaways aboard timber-laden ships.

Marine life Like otters, seals confuse the distinction between land and marine mammals. But whereas the otter is essentially a landlubber that may feed at sea, the UK's two seals are fundamentally sea-dwelling creatures that come ashore to breed and lounge. Both **grey seal** and **harbour** (aka **common**) **seal** are readily seen around the coasts of many islands. Distinguishing the two can be difficult. Grey typically has a Roman nose on a flat head, unlike the rather squished-in face and round head of harbour. One of the UK's largest colonies (or 'rookeries') of grey seal is on the Treshnish Isles. Good places to see harbour seal are the southeast coast of Islay, and the bays of Vaul and Salum on Tiree.

According to mammal expert Richard Moores, 'the seas of the Inner Hebrides, being rich in food, are undoubtedly one of Britain's best areas for watching whales and dolphins'. Even more excitingly, they are relatively easy to see thanks to regular boat trips organised by local companies. Scotland's most common species, **harbour porpoise**, occurs year-round and is particularly abundant in the sounds of Mull and Jura. A small resident pod of **bottle-nosed dolphins** inhabits waters around Mull and has become a firm favourite among tourists. This species – the quintessential dolphin – tends to stick close to shore; favoured spots include Tobermory and Dervaig bays.

Waters between Mull, Coll and Tiree can be good for seeing **common dolphins** during the summer (until mid-August). According to the Hebridean Whale and Dolphin Trust (HWDT), sightings have increased 20-fold since 2004. Coll and the Small Isles are best for the thickset **Risso's dolphin**, which is most frequently seen in autumn. The Small Isles also offer the greatest chance of **orcas** (aka **killer whales**). A single pod is known from the area, and scientists have tracked it widely through the waters of west Scotland.

If you have never seen a whale, you can do no better in the UK than join a vessel exploring the seas of the Inner Hebrides. A highlight of summer boat trips in the deep waters around the Small Isles, Mull or Coll is **minke whale**, which can be 30ft long and weigh 10 tonnes. Typical views can be frustratingly brief – a quick roll of the back and a flash of dorsal fin as the whale surfaces to breathe – but occasional animals amaze by performing acrobatic leaps out of the water.

The second-largest fish in the world's seas – behind only the whale shark of tropical waters – is the **basking shark**. The Inner Hebrides is one of the best places *anywhere* to see this marine behemoth. Seen from above water, the telltale signs are

While I was on Mull, I managed to interview Karl Stevens from the Hebridean Whale and Dolphin Trust (HWDT) about their project, the Hebridean Whale Trail (w whaletrail.org). Visibly brimming with enthusiasm, he was a great champion for Scotland's marine mammals.

'We just want people to know that they should look,' Karl said, impulsively glancing over his shoulder to the window out on to Tobermory Harbour from our table in the bakery. 'Even if they just sit for an extra 5 minutes; it's about slowing people down. These islands are one of the best places in Europe for land-based marine mammal watching, but not many people realise that yet.'

Karl went on to explain how a quarter of the world's whale and dolphin species are found off the west coast of Scotland. Resident populations of bottle-nosed dolphin can be seen in Tobermory Harbour itself and the region is one of the best places to see porpoise in Europe. Coll and Tiree are known for their basking sharks and minke whales, especially between April and October, before the basking sharks move to deeper waters and minke whales migrate further south. Each year a very lucky few people manage to see killer whales.

The Hebridean Whale Trail, stretching between Cape Wrath (the most northwesterly point of mainland Scotland), St Kilda (in the Outer Hebrides) and Arran, encompasses the Inner Hebrides and aims to make cetacean spotting as accessible as possible. To report your sightings, you can download the Hebridean Whale and Dolphin Trust's app or create an account on their website (w whaletrack.hwdt.org).

Even more excitingly, there is a possibility to join the team on board the *Silurian* (w hwdt.org/silurian), receiving training in marine research and sailing, to work alongside the HWDT crew as a field biologist.

an equilateral dorsal fin, followed a few feet later by a smaller isosceles triangle – the tail fin – piercing the calm sea. Observations start in May, peak between June and August, and end in October. Waters around Tiree and Coll appear to be the shark's favourite, although the Small Isles and west of Mull are also good. Boat trips enable close views but animals can often be seen from land too.

Birds There is only one contender for the title of the Inner Hebrides' most famous bird: the **white-tailed eagle**. Following six decades of absence from the UK, the island of Rùm was selected as the location for a groundbreaking reintroduction programme. Not only did this return the 'flying barn door' to the country, but it has also boosted the local economy: eagles are thought to contribute £4.9–8 million annually to the coffers in Mull. You have a chance of spotting a 'sea eagle' along the coastlines of any island, but Mull and Skye are arguably the best, with perhaps 15 pairs on the latter. On the former, Loch na Keal is probably the best spot: eagles sit for hours on Scarisdale Rocks. On Skye, you could do worse than taking a boat trip from Portree, which run each morning with captains proffering fish to hungry raptors.

Skye, Mull and Islay are among the best islands for **golden eagle**. Seeing this large raptor, which looks longer-winged and longer-tailed than its heftier relative, typically involves scanning the skyline through binoculars. Good areas to search are Glen More (on Mull) and the Cuillin (Skye). Whatever you do, make sure you don't mistake a **buzzard**; birdwatchers and locals alike dismissively call these 'tourist eagles' in view of over-eager misidentifications. Other predatory birds for which it is worth keeping an eye out include **hen harriers** (especially on Islay), **merlins** (particularly Coll), **peregrines** (along coasts or near concentrations of ducks) and **short-eared owls** (in moorland glens).

Wintering geese are an internationally renowned feature of Islay, Tiree and Coll, where vast flocks can fill field and sky alike. Alongside perhaps 4,000 **Greenland white-fronted geese**, over 30,000 **barnacle geese** throng on Islay. Few birds' names have such a curious etymology as this piebald waterbird. For several hundred years, it was believed to grow underwater in goose barnacle shells attached to driftwood before emerging on to land in autumn. Nowadays, there is conflict between the geese and Islay residents. NatureScot runs an 'adaptive goose management scheme' for damage to pasture and crops caused by browsing geese – and, in 2015, authorised an annual cull that saw 8,200 barnacle geese shot across the following three winters. However, in subsequent years the number of culled birds has dropped off significantly. Annual numbers are determined by early-season counts, which has led to no geese being shot over the winters of 2021–22 and 2022–23 due to bird flu, and only a few hundred in 2023–24.

The sea is a good place to look for other large birds. Duck such as **eider** and **red-breasted merganser** are present year-round, being joined in winter by **scaup** and the globally threatened **long-tailed duck**. Three species of diver feed offshore during the colder months with one, **red-throated diver**, moving to moorland lochans on Jura, Islay and Skye in order to breed.

The Hebrides harbours plenty of true seabirds, which congregate in discrete breeding colonies on long-favoured cliffs. The commoner species, which you could equally well bump into while on a ferry or boat trip, include **fulmar**, **shag**, **guillemot** and **razorbill**. The UK's largest seabird, the **gannet**, is routinely seen feeding offshore, as are **kittiwakes** (a rapidly declining and now globally threatened gull) and **Arctic terns** (the avian world's most extreme migrant). The suave-looking **black guillemot** – colloquially known as 'tystie' – is a Scottish speciality; Port Askaig (Islay) is a particularly good place to bump into one. **Puffins** nest on the Treshnish Isles, while the mountains of Rùm host the world's largest colony of **Manx shearwaters**, meaning this ocean wanderer can be easily seen in surrounding waters. The UK's southernmost **Arctic skuas** – an aerial pirate that harries other seabirds to release their catch – breed on Jura.

Two species of grouse inhabit upland areas of certain islands. **Red grouse** favours heather-rich moorland while its mountaineer cousin, **ptarmigan**, frequents stony

GROUND-NESTING BIRDS

In May and June, beaches with pebbles and sand can be nest sites for seagulls, terns, oystercatchers, ringed plovers and other wading birds. During the spring and summer, grassland, moorland, heather and peat habitats might hide the nests of game birds such as pheasants and grouse, as well as snipe and small birds like skylarks, meadow pipits and lapwings.

Birds will usually alert you to their presence with plenty of noise – and sharp-beaked Arctic terns and predatory skuas are likely to dive-bomb if you get too close – but look where you step and keep dogs on a lead during nesting time as they can disturb birds off their nests and even eat the eggs.

If you are walking on an RSPB reserve, it's best to check their specific recommendations as these might vary throughout the year.

AVIAN FLU

Since summer 2021, Highly Pathogenic Avian Influenza (HPAI) has been devastating UK wild bird populations. To prevent the chance of spreading the disease further, don't touch any sick or dead birds, and keep dogs away from them. To report dead wild birds, please use the government's online reporting system or call their helpline (w gov.uk/guidance/report-dead-wild-birds; ☎ 03459 335577). Additionally, you are asked to make a separate report to the British Trust for Ornithology (w bto.org/our-science/projects/birdtrack) to help assess population impacts. If you're on a nature reserve, such as those run by the RSPB, please also tell staff.

ground at higher altitudes, notably in the Cuillin (Skye). Lowlands, particularly seasonally flooded grasslands and (on Tiree and Coll) machair, are nationally important for breeding waders. **Lapwings, oystercatchers** and **redshanks** are the most prominent, attracting attention with their strident cries, but the diligent should also be rewarded with **curlews, dunlins** and **snipes**.

Occupying similar terrain, but usually concentrated in dense cover such as iris beds or hayfields, is the **corncrake**. This odd-looking and rare rail arrives in April to spend the summer on fortunate islands (Coll, Tiree, Iona and Islay). A reclusive bird, it is usually detected by voice – a loud, double-note rasp uttered incessantly day and night. Tiree's thriving population comprises one-third of the UK quotient – testament to years of conservation-sensitive farming from local crofters.

Another charismatic feathered creature sought by visiting birdwatchers is the **chough**. This red-billed ragamuffin is a crow essentially restricted to Britain's western coast, where it probes soft turf for invertebrates. An unabashed aeronaut, groups float in the wind before dive-bombing the ground, only to pull out at the last moment. Islay is the best place to see it. **Rock doves** also occur here – and more widely along clifftop grasslands and sea cliffs. This is the wild ancestor of the ubiquitous feral pigeon that blights our cities – an avian indication that you are treading through wilderness.

Other animals Among life in cold blood, the **common toad** is relatively uncommon and poorly distributed, whereas the **common frog** is widespread and increasingly frequent. **Palmate newts** are a feature of acidic watercourses, including on Mull. **Adders** – our sole venomous snake – are regularly encountered in sheltered moorland on Islay, Mull and Skye.

The islands are rather too windy for visitors to readily see butterflies, but calm sunny days can see flower-rich meadows and machair come alive with these winged wonders. **Small tortoiseshell, green-veined white, small heath** and **meadow brown** are common and widespread. On the dunes, **grayling** sit with their wings snapped shut, their superbly camouflaged form revealed only when you tread too close and flush them into the air. **Small pearl-bordered fritillary**, a blaze of orange embroidered with black, is a feature of damp grasslands during June and July. **Common blue** – the males of which are scintillatingly neon – adorns the machair, and migrant **painted lady** and **red admiral** add variety in certain summers.

Excitingly, the Inner Hebrides is host to some of the UK's rarest butterflies and moths. As its name suggests, the gorgeous **marsh fritillary** resides in damp grassland on parts of Islay (such as The Oa), Jura and Mull. Adults nectar at the lilac-bloomed devil's-bit scabious from mid-May to mid-July, while the caterpillars build large, easily noticeable webs during August and September. The **pearl-bordered fritillary** has declined dramatically across the UK, and now only a single colony remains in this region – in southern Mull.

This same island is graced by some remarkable and very scarce day-flying moths. In spring, **narrow-bordered bee hawk-moths** buzz over flowers like tiny hummingbirds. Come June and July, two dramatic and very localised species of black-and-red burnet moth buzz around wild thyme-covered coastal grassland. In the UK, **slender Scotch burnet** is known only from a handful of sites on Mull (notably Glengorm) and Ulva, while **transparent burnet** occurs at several locations on Mull, plus Lismore and north Jura. Other famous day-flying Hebridean moths include the Barbour-green **forester**, the bizarre **belted beauty** (whose female is flightless and rather resembles a raisin covered in belly fluff), the caramel-coloured and decidedly scarce **dew moth**, the stunning, pink-fringed **clouded buff** and the dramatic **emperor**, whose wings display eye-like spots to terrify wannabe predators.

The Inner Hebrides host a small range of dragonflies and damselflies, which typically hawk, flurry and fluster around freshwater pools, particularly in boggy areas. The mightiest – indeed the largest in the UK – is the **golden-ringed dragonfly**, which scuds scarily in search of inattentive prey. A couple of steps down in size are the darters and chasers. The **four-spotted chaser** is the first to emerge, on the wing from late May. In July and August, it is followed by the striking **black darter** and **common darter** of a Scottish-exclusive form known as 'Highland' darter. Damselflies are the smallest and weediest of the lot – with the **blue-tailed damselfly** being widespread but the **common blue damselfly** favouring large lochs.

Nine species of bumblebee thrive on the flower-festooned machair and pastures of Tiree and Coll, where they provide the indispensable ecological function of pollination. **Moss carder bee**, with its burnt-orange upper body and yellow lower body, is a striking and common sight. But the star is the **great yellow bumblebee** – a large, bright-yellow insect that has declined by 80% nationwide in the last century. Another machair speciality is the **short-necked oil beetle**, thought extinct in the UK until 2008 but which is now known to be doing well on Coll. This beetle is a rather gruesome parasite. Once the eggs have hatched, larvae wiggle on to vegetation then hitch a lift on a passing solitary bee. Upon being transported to the bee's nest, the larvae both eats its host's eggs and devours the protein-rich pollen brought back by the adult, before emerging as an adult beetle the following spring.

Plants Conservation body Plantlife has identified eight distinct 'Important Plant Areas' on the Inner Hebrides, a notable density for a relatively small landmass. One of the richest is Ardmeanach Peninsula (Mull), which supports 400 species of plant, including nationally scarce species such as **hairy stonecrop**, **alpine cinquefoil** and **mountain avens**. Small lochs on Coll and Tiree support one of the UK's most important populations of **slender naiad**. The machair of those two islands, plus Colonsay, bursts into bloom in May and reaches its peak in July. Spring's primroses cede to the sun-yellow of **buttercups**, **bedstraw** and **trefoils** which, in turn, are supplanted by the whites, blues and purples of **pansies**, **vetches**, **ragged robin** and **gentians**. Steep basalt sea cliffs on Eigg support **roseroot**, **sea campion** and alpine-arctic species such as **yellow saxifrage**, **Arctic sandwort** and **alpine willowherb**.

Perhaps the most readily appreciated plants of the Inner Hebrides are its orchids. Tiree, Coll, Islay and Mull are probably the best islands for these showy plants. **Heath spotted**, **northern marsh** and **heath fragrant orchids** can be locally abundant.

On meadows, you can easily see **greater butterfly orchid** and **common twayblade**, but a sharp pair of eyes will be needed to spot the smaller **frog orchid** and **small white orchid**. Damp upland areas are the domain of **bog orchid** and the tiny **lesser twayblade**. But perhaps the most desirable of all Hebridean orchids is **Irish lady's-tresses** – a delicate ivory whirl of a plant. For this you must head to Coll, Colonsay or Oronsay – and be prepared to search diligently. Not all the natural specialities of the Inner Hebrides are as showy as bottle-nosed dolphins or white-tailed eagles…

ARCHAEOLOGY AND PHYSICAL HISTORY

Although there is an astounding wealth of archaeology across the Inner Hebrides, the majority of it requires a little perseverance to discover and some imagination to appreciate. There are some notable exceptions: impressive medieval castles such as the restored Duart on Mull (page 166) and Dunvegan on Skye (page 80), as well as more ruinous and atmospheric structures like Raasay's Brochel (page 100), Gylen on Kerrera (page 192) and Lismore's Castle Coeffin (page 190); religious buildings including the impressive Oronsay Priory (page 211) and the heavily restored Iona Abbey (page 177); plus Islay's Finlaggan (page 223), once the central power base for the Lords of the Isles.

Anyone with an interest in archaeology or history should familiarise themselves with the incredible map provided by Historic Environment Scotland (w canmore. org.uk/map/about; select 'view all sites on the map' and zoom in on the area of interest). Keen archaeologists or detectorists will most likely be aware of Scotland's Treasure Trove policy (w treasuretrovescotland.co.uk), which states that any portable finds are subject to claim by the Crown. Artefacts should be reported directly to Treasure Trove unless they include human remains, in which case, the police should be made aware immediately.

HISTORY

There seems to be a common assumption that because the Hebrides are on the edge of our current civilisation they must have been among the last places to be settled. Looking at the types of archaeological evidence present, this theory is quickly blown out of the water, but more recent documentation also proves the islands were not always at the fringes; their surrounding waterways often put them central to control of the nearby Scottish mainland.

PREHISTORY
Mesolithic era Around 11,500 years ago, the glaciers of the last Ice Age melted away and the Mesolithic era began as humans were able to live in the Inner Hebrides. From c9,000–3,000BC, hunter gatherers roamed the islands, predominantly leaving traces of their presence behind in middens or as arrow heads.

Neolithic era This era (c4,000–2,000BC) marked the adoption of farming. People began to settle on the islands, leaving behind burial sites in the form of cairns and cists, as well as mysterious standing stone monuments.

The Bronze and Iron ages
The development of metalworking technology marked the beginning of the Bronze Age around 2,000BC, which then ran into the Iron Age (800BC–AD100). The Inner Hebrides has many roundhouses from these periods and, from the Iron Age, a collection of brochs.

The Picts From AD100 onwards, the Picts – a civilisation that spoke an early Celtic language called Pictish – inhabited western and northern Scotland, including the northern islands of the Inner Hebrides. A transitional era between archaeology and history, our knowledge of this mysterious civilisation is predominantly informed by carved stones and later writings.

DÁL RIATA AND THE CONVERSION OF THE PICTS The Scots, or Scotti, of Dál Riata were a Gaelic-speaking, Irish kingdom who emigrated across to modern-day Scotland's western seaboard at an unknown date in the centuries before the year AD500. During this time, monks from Ireland – including the famous St Columba and his contemporary St Moluag – established religious centres on Iona and Lismore and began the somewhat unclear process of converting the Picts to Christianity. By the 8th century, Dál Riata's empire extended from Ardnamurchan to the Mull of Kintyre and included the islands from Coll and Tiree to Bute and Arran, with possible colonies on Skye and Raasay too. There is evidence of some struggle between the Picts and the Scots of Dál Riata, but it seems to have been a gradual takeover by the Scots. By 843, Kenneth, son of Alpin, had become king of the Picts as well as Dál Riata and the Picts faded away into history.

From the middle of the 7th century, there were three ruling family groups: Cenél nÓengusa (kindred of Oengus) on Islay; Cenél nGabráin governed Kintyre, Cowal and Bute (possibly also Gigha, Jura and Arran); and Cenél Loairn had Lorn, Colonsay, Ardnamurchan, Mull, Coll and Tiree. This was the beginning of the Kingdom of Scotland, with Argyll deriving from the Gaelic *Airer Goidel* (coastline of the Gael).

THE NORSE For obvious geographic reasons, the islands stretching from Shetland around the western coast of Scotland were among the first and most affected by Viking invasions. Their advanced shipbuilding techniques and maritime skills far outmatched any existing power in the area. With Ireland, the Isle of Man and Norway all being part of the Norse kingdom, the Hebrides were far from the remote and scattered hideaway we imagine today and instead part of a busy nautical highway. As early as 795, Skye was attacked and, from this time onwards, Iona was subject to numerous raids and massacres (though somehow a small community of zealous monks persisted until the 11th century).

The Norse used the Hebrides as stepping stones, relatively inconsequential parts of an ever-expanding movement across England, Ireland, mainland Europe, Russia, Iceland and eventually as far as North America.

For most individual Norsemen, it was a very different story. Along with the generally accepted pillaging, many so-called Vikings were not warriors but farmers and fishermen, searching for fertile lands to inhabit. The density of Norse names for settlements decreases the further south in the region you look while the proportion of them referring to topographical features rather than farms increases, suggesting that they did not settle for long. Although there is endless historical debate, it seems relatively conclusive that there was more intermingling than previously assumed. Crosses carved and buried among Viking graves, recordings of Irish-Norse names and the simple fact that both Norse and Gaelic existed simultaneously all the way through until the 13th century show that the relationship between cultures was more nuanced. During this period, a title of Lord or 'King' of the Isles developed, an unspecific and complicated title that echoed on until the end of the 15th century, long after the influence of the Norwegian crown had faded, and one that is actually still held by the Prince of Wales.

Although Norse dominion strengthened through Godred Crovan's establishment of a dynasty covering the Hebrides and the Isle of Man, his granddaughter later went on to marry Somerled of Argyll and thus the power of his genetics outlasted that of Norwegian control in the region.

Somerled, the Lord of Argyll, was a new breed of sea king with appropriately mixed heritage: part Gaelic, part Norse. He died while invading the mainland in 1164, but his influence in the Hebrides was monumental and his ancestors continued to rule the western seaboard as 'Lords of the Isles' until 1266, when the Kingdom of Scotland took the Hebrides and Isle of Man under the Treaty of Perth.

CLAN RULE The Lords of the Isles continued as a crown dependency of Scotland until the latter half of the 15th century when a series of ill-advised power scuffles forced the King of Scotland to remove their lands. Other clans such as the MacLeods, MacDonalds and MacKinnons increased their hold on the islands and retained their power until the 18th century. With the Treaty of Union in 1707, the Inner Hebrides became part of the new Kingdom of Great Britain, but their remote location allowed them to continue much as before. However, after several clan chiefs came out in support of the Jacobite rebellions in 1715 and 1745 (attempts by James Francis Edward Stuart and his son Charles Edward Stuart – Bonnie Prince Charlie – to regain the British throne), their autonomy was diminished.

POPULATION GROWTH AND DECLINE IN THE 18TH AND 19TH CENTURIES The kelp industry (in which the ash of seaweed kelp – rich in iodine and alkali – is used in the production of glass) boomed in the 18th century and up until the end of the Napoleonic Wars in 1815. In combination with grain being sold at high prices and the introduction of the potato from the mid 18th century, the islands' populations continued to grow until the 1820s. The subsequent decades, however, were filled with misery and famine as the grain market collapsed owing to cheaper imports, kelp ceased to be profitable, fish stocks failed and potatoes caught a blight, causing failed crops and mass hunger. Many people left the islands by choice, but many more were forced out in the infamous Clearances as tenants were replaced by more profitable sheep.

Between 1820 and 1900, the population of the Inner Hebrides was cut in half, with all islands affected and some, such as Rùm and Muck, losing their entire populations. People left to try and make a living in other parts of Scotland, or were given 'assisted passage' as far as Canada, Australia and the United States. While some reportedly prospered, others died of disease or were unable to scratch a living in foreign lands; without the technology to communicate, whether they survived or not would never have been known to those who were left behind. The Inner Hebrides are littered with the remains of these lost communities' settlements, with the descendants of the people that used to inhabit them scattered across the globe.

The Clearances are a dark period of history for Scotland's Highlands and islands, but also more complex than the popular narrative suggests. As a general overview, the old, traditional landowners, often the clan families, became more integrated with society elsewhere in the UK and less involved with their tenants. This mingling also introduced them to ways of life they were previously unexposed to: building fashionable houses, sending their children away to expensive schools, paying large expenses for their sons' army careers and travelling more – all of which put a strain on their finances. Although crofters' rights were eventually established after the Battle of the Braes (page 55) and the investigation under the

Poverty and the Clearances (page 15) forced large percentages of each island's population to find a life for themselves elsewhere, whether this was in other parts of Scotland, the UK or as distantly as the USA, Canada and Australia. For members of this diaspora who are looking to find out more about their families, individual island heritage centres should be a first port of call. Many of these centres hold an archive or are at least likely to have knowledgeable volunteers to point you in the right direction where information is available.

Scotland Births Deaths and Marriages (w sctbdm.com) is a free resource for researching genealogy and Scottish family history.

Napier Commission in 1886, populations on the islands continued to dwindle until recent decades when some of them have slowly begun to recover.

THE WORLD WARS Like all of the UK, the Inner Hebrides were gravely affected by both World Wars. War memorials and military graveyards, found all across the region, are sombre reminders of how many lives were lost. A number of disastrous shipwrecks off the islands' treacherous coastlines resulted in heroic rescue attempts from the islanders and their involvement in the traumatic process of retrieving and identifying the bodies of those who did not survive; the enormous American Monument on Islay (page 229) is a visible testament. In the north, Raasay became the unlikely location of a prisoner of war camp, as well as mining iron ore needed for submarines (page 95). Used as a base for military communications (page 130) during World War II, Tiree is the Inner Hebridean island that's possibly the most visibly altered by its military past.

THE INNER HEBRIDES TODAY While island populations are still only a fraction of their pre-Clearances numbers, gradual improvements to transport links, increased amenities and the Scottish Land Reform Act of 2003 – which made it easier for communities to buy out the land they live on – have given island residents more control over their lives. According to Brendan O'Hara, who represents the Scottish National Party in Argyll and Bute, 'physical and digital connectivity and depopulation' remain among his constituents' major concerns, with bad road conditions and a lack of high-speed broadband being the most frustrating topics. Although job prospects have increased (see opposite), a seasonal imbalance between the abundance of work and availability of affordable housing still make it hard for young people to settle. Many islanders have multiple jobs to support themselves. While the coronavirus pandemic, a rise in UK living costs and disruption within the CalMac ferry service have seen some businesses close their doors, an increase in domestic tourism has – in many instances – allowed others to spring up and fill the gaps.

GOVERNMENT AND POLITICS

Split between the two councils, which also include far greater swathes of the mainland, it is difficult to talk generally about politics in the Inner Hebrides. Highland council includes Skye, Raasay and the Small Isles, as well as a huge area of northwestern Scotland, while Argyll and Bute encompasses all the islands further south. While mainland Argyll and the more southerly Hebrides seem to work cohesively, facing a lot of similar issues. Skye's high number of visitors sets it apart from much of the Highlands and many inhabitants believe they would be better served with more autonomy or by joining the Outer Hebrides.

At Scotland's independence referendum in 2014, both areas reflected the national vote by voting against independence (Argyll and Bute 58.52%, Highland 52.92%). In the UK-wide general elections between 2015 and 2019, the Scottish National Party (SNP) held the constituencies of Argyll, Bute and South Lochaber, and Inverness, Skye and West Ross-shire (part of Highland council). But in 2024, while the SNP held the former, the latter was lost to the Liberal Democrats. When, in 2016, the UK voted to leave the EU in another historic referendum, every council area in Scotland had voted in vain to remain in the EU. The resulting 'Brexit' process has impacted Inner Hebridean communities, who previously relied on EU infrastructure funding, seasonal staff and access to markets for food products including lamb, beef, fish and whisky. Whether on a business or a personal level, the increased cost of products imported from the EU is also felt more heavily in the Highlands and Islands region, where delivery was already more expensive and complex than within the rest of the UK.

On a more localised level, decision-making processes vary greatly between islands. One factor that comes into this system of management is land ownership. Large areas of land across the Inner Hebrides are still privately owned, as they have been for centuries, and although crofting laws allow tenants more rights and security than they had back in clan times, several of the same families have retained ownership throughout many generations (most notably, the MacLeods of Dunvegan who still own large parts of Skye). Since the economic troubles in the 1800s, the majority of islands and areas of land have been split or sold to new owners. Eigg, Gigha and more recently Ulva have been bought by the communities themselves, whereas in other places people have come together to organise their own development programmes for local improvements: South Islay Development (w southislay.co.uk), the Tiree Community Development Trust (w tireetrust.org. uk) and the Isle of Canna Community Development Trust (w theisleofcanna.com) are notably successful examples of this, but there are many others.

ECONOMY

Although tourism is ever growing in the Inner Hebrides, traditional industries such as crofting, fishing and whisky distilling continue. While the global whisky market is slowing, plans for new Islay distilleries continue to go ahead. Crofting and fishing continue to be a struggle here, though some entrepreneurs have created successful businesses off the back of these traditional employments by offering boat trips, accommodation on their crofts or through selling high-quality produce.

Much of the available work is part time, meaning that many people have more than one job or supplement their income with a small side business. Owing to tourism, the majority of work also falls over the summer, meaning that many people either try to earn their annual salary in under five months or travel elsewhere to find jobs in the off season. The unreliability of tourism is a problem, brought to the forefront of people's minds during the Covid-19 pandemic, but even more so is a lack of accommodation for the necessary workforce during summer months, compounded by it being more profitable to let property to visitors. It is not at all uncommon to see caravans and mobile homes hidden around the back of hotels; more often than not, this is staff accommodation.

FISH FARMS

The Inner Hebrides has over 70 active marine aquaculture sites. Once hailed as a sustainable solution to lessen any further impact on the UK's severely depleted fish stocks, certain aquaculture sites, particularly salmon farms, have subsequently come under scrutiny for a different set of environmental concerns. According to a report from the Scottish Environment Protection Agency in 2018, almost one out of every five salmon farms in Scotland failed to meet statutory environmental standards and there are a variety of associated problems.

Open-net pens placed in sheltered coastal waters close to the shore can hold tens of thousands of fish. Although this system is 'good' for the farmed fish themselves, allowing water to flow freely around them, extreme levels of pollutants are also uncontained, suffocating the underlying seabed in faeces and uneaten food and releasing chemical treatments and medicines directly into the surrounding waters. Intensive farming of any sort makes animals susceptible to disease and parasites, most commonly in this case sea lice, which are a health risk not only to the farmed fish themselves, but also to nearby wildlife; wild salmon and sea trout are particularly at risk. Adding further concern, in the species reassessment released in December 2023 by the IUCN's Red List of Threatened Species, the main UK populations of Atlantic salmon were reclassified as endangered.

Nets are also a danger to other species, particularly predators such as seals, dolphins and porpoises that can become entangled while attacking seemingly easy pickings. To try and prevent this problem, as well as the resulting damage to nets and loss of fish, Acoustic Deterrent Devices (ADDs) are used by salmon farms to try and scare away predators with noise. Seemingly a neat solution, an output of over 179 decibels is enough to deafen porpoises, dolphins and whales, driving them away from their feeding grounds and potentially causing them to starve. Licensed shooting of seals is also used to protect farmed fish.

Although the environmental consequences seem damning, the stable source of employment and job creation by fish farms is enticing and, in some cases, essential in order to provide a livelihood for young people wishing to remain on the islands. Closed containment systems, which put a physical barrier between farmed and wild fish and the wider environment, can be used as an alternative to solve many of the issues associated with open-net salmon farming.

According to the Office for National Statistics, 76.7% of people of working age in Highland are classed as 'economically active', while the figure is 72.5% for Argyll and Bute council areas.

While some businesses were unable to survive the Covid-19 pandemic or have since closed due to rising costs, tourism to the area seems only to increase in popularity, providing more opportunities for new accommodation, food, shopping and activity providers. Crofting, farming and fishing all face new challenges due to increased costs and Brexit, which can be felt more keenly than elsewhere in the UK due to the high proportion of residents relying on these industries. Delays to the provision of replacement ferries for the CalMac fleet have also had a knock-on effect for local people, visitors and businesses due to decreased services and reliability. The economic picture varies across the region, with some of the larger islands having more jobs than people in the workforce and others struggling to provide enough viable opportunities for residents to make a living.

PEOPLE

The inhabitants of the Inner Hebrides are a diverse mix of long-standing residents, people who have moved there for work, and visitors who have fallen in love with an island and decided to move there permanently. Whereas the statistics for the entirety of Scotland suggest that 62.4% of people identify their nationality as 'Scottish only', in Argyll and Bute this figure is reduced to 57.4% and in Highland 61.5%. Looking at the islands more specifically, the picture is complicated and not as you might expect: in the south of Mull only 31.8% identify as only Scottish, 39.4% on northeast Coll and 41% on Iona; on the other hand, in Portree it is 71.6%, Gigha 66.9% and northern Islay 63.7%. The majority of those who do not see themselves as purely Scottish are from other parts of the UK, particularly England.

POPULATION Just over 20,000 people currently call the Inner Hebrides home. Half of the archipelago's population live on the biggest island, Skye, which is 639 square miles (1,656km²), and around another 6,500 are split between the second and third largest islands, Mull and Islay. However, aside from those three islands, geographical size and population have very little correlation here, with the fourth largest island (Jura) having fewer than 300 inhabitants and Tiree, the sixth largest island, home to more than 700 inhabitants; Seil, which ranks 16th in size, has more than 500 inhabitants.

Although each island has its own 'capital', Skye's Portree, with fewer than 3,000 residents, is the largest town in the archipelago; Tobermory on Mull is the second biggest settlement, home to around 1,000 people. The vast majority of townships are no bigger than English hamlets, with few houses and no amenities at all.

LANGUAGE

Apart from in the Outer Hebrides, the council areas of Argyll and Bute and Highland have the highest percentage of Scottish Gaelic speakers in Scotland: somewhere between 1% and 10%. Once widely spoken across the region, with the disintegration of traditional communities in the 18th and 19th centuries Gaelic fell out of fashion with the ruling classes and began to decline. Although it seems unlikely that the language will ever recover to its previous strength, Gaelic culture has been making a revival in recent years and is celebrated in festivals, music and through various centres of heritage and education; see page 265 for some common Gaelic words and phrases. Visitors should have no trouble making themselves understood in English, but strong regional accents can take some time to tune in to.

RELIGION

Christianity, mainly Church of Scotland, Free Church of Scotland and other Protestant denominations including Baptist, is still by far the main religion, although the number of people who do not identify as religious has also increased in recent years. Across Scotland the percentage of people who state their religion as Christian is around 50%; in the Highland council area it is closer to 54%, whereas it rises to nearly 70% in Argyll and Bute, with some of the islands even higher. Around a third of people identify as Church of Scotland across the country, but this number rises to 40% in Argyll and Bute and as high as 60% on Tiree. However, the numbers of Roman Catholics are generally much lower than across the rest of Scotland.

EDUCATION

Having enough resident children to support a primary school is a matter of much concern in many rural communities, but even more so on the islands; ask almost anyone who they would like to move to their island and they will most likely say that they need young families or couples who are likely to have children. Although island-based primary schools are seemingly idyllic, with a wealth of interesting local trips and small class sizes, the majority of islands (excluding Islay, Mull, Skye and Tiree) do not have a large enough population or enough funding to support a secondary school. While some children do a weekly ferry commute, staying on the mainland Monday to Friday, other families decide against this; one of the main causes of island depopulation is that when children reach the age where they would otherwise have to go away and board, the whole family decides to move to the mainland with them. Parents may return once their children are fully fledged, but a lack of housing makes this difficult and there is usually a notable lack of teenagers and people in their twenties on the islands. Improvements in technology, including remote learning and work-from-home employment, are making gradual improvements in the options for young adults.

CULTURE

With long, dark winters, dramatic weather and historically isolated communities, each of the islands has its own distinct culture. While some subtleties might not be apparent to a first-time visitor, architectural differences set the islands apart and their residents' creative work is represented across a huge variety of disciplines and styles.

ARCHITECTURE Tiny houses nestled in dramatic scenery are synonymous with Scotland and the Inner Hebrides have no lack of these. Mull, Skye, Eigg and Canna are a photographer's dream in this respect, but by far the most striking examples of traditional buildings are Tiree's blackhouses. Low, whitewashed buildings, some of which are still thatched, but now more frequently seen with contrasting black felt roofs, these dwellings were built with double dry-stone walls, packed with earth and without chimneys, so smoke was supposed to simply drift up through the thatch. Once home to both animals and people, they might look romantic now but would have been a cramped and eye-watering abode, particularly challenging through the long winter months. While most complete blackhouses are still in use, or rented out as holiday cottages, the Skye Museum of Island Life (page 72) gives visitors a chance to see how blackhouses were traditionally lived in.

Colourful or whitewashed seaside villages are another iconic sight, with Mull's Tobermory being the most famous example, but Portree is also cheerfully decorated, with each house different from the next. Portnahaven, with its rows of small white cottages and grey slate roofs, could have been taken straight off the pages of a children's picture book, while there are countless other examples on the Slate Islands, Coll and Gigha.

Modern architecture is uncommon, with An Turas (page 143) being the most obvious example, and the islands' most striking buildings are often either ruined castles or churches; arguably the prettiest examples of the latter can be found in Dervaig on Mull (page 162), Canna (page 120) and the round church overlooking Bowmore (page 219).

ART The Inner Hebrides have a long and varied artistic tradition. During the time of Columba (page 14), Iona was a great centre of learning, producing a specific style of decoratively carved cross and possibly Ireland's gloriously decorative national treasure, the Book of Kells, a couple of centuries later. The majority of medieval art remaining on the islands is carved into stone as West Highland grave slabs, depicting warriors, swords and crosses, each stone telling the story of the person it commemorates.

Duart (page 166) and Dunvegan (page 80) castles are brimming with invaluable artwork; portraits of clan chiefs and tumultuous seascapes preserved for generations to come. In 1831 J M W Turner was commissioned by Sir Walter Scott's Edinburgh publisher to illustrate the *Poetical Works of Sir Walter Scott*, a job which took him to Loch Coruisk (Loch Coriskin) on Skye and Fingal's Cave on Staffa, two spectacular locations, made only more dramatic in Turner's interpretation.

These days, the island art scene is thriving and the majority of islands have at least one gallery; real enthusiasts could spend a whole holiday on Skye discovering them and still manage to miss a few. While there are a few established exhibition spaces to be found in the islands' main villages, the majority are hidden down long farm tracks, in somebody's shed or taking up the best room in the house. Despite these impromptu settings, the quality of work displayed is usually very impressive, representing the islands' high concentration of artists who've either grown up inspired by their surroundings, or moved to the Inner Hebrides especially.

CRAFTS Craft shops are perhaps even more prevalent than art galleries, and often likely to be a coalition of several craftspeople. Knitting and weaving are perhaps some of the most highly regarded crafts on the islands and buying something made from local wool is one of the best ways you can support the local economy. There are only a few small, family businesses and individuals creating woven goods on Skye and Islay, but in some ways this allows more creative freedom; the pedal-powered loom at Skye Weavers (page 76) is a great example. Knitting and crochet are more widespread, with a locally made warm woolly hat being one of the most treasured and practical souvenirs you can find.

LITERATURE With plenty of space to think, an emotive setting and everyday battles with the forces of nature, it is perhaps unsurprising that the Hebrides have been home to an array of writers or the setting for their work. House of Lochar (page 207) are a small publisher and bookseller based on Colonsay, who specialise in local interest books.

Martin Martin's book *A Description of the Western Islands of Scotland* (1703) and Samuel Johnson's *A Journey to the Western Islands of Scotland* (1775), which describes his 83-day journey through the Hebrides with his younger friend James Boswell, describe the islands from an outsider point of view, recording their perceived peculiarities as remote and obscure fringes of the map. Many of the places they describe are still recognisable.

Published in 1949, the most famous novel to come out of the Inner Hebrides was *Nineteen Eighty Four*, which George Orwell wrote mostly at Barnhill, in the wilderness north of Jura (page 246), little changed to this day.

CHILDREN'S LITERATURE, FILM AND TV

The islands have inspired countless children's stories, many of which have beautiful accompanying pictures.

The intricately illustrated story books by Benedict Blathwayt, who has spent most of his life on Mull, are a feast for imaginative children. I grew up reading *Tig and Tag*, the adventures of two Scottish blackface sheep, but he has other books such as *Bear's Adventure* (set in Tobermory), *Ferry* and *Little Seal*, aimed at children aged three to five.

Despite the somewhat repetitive theme song, the CBeebies TV series *Balamory* had a very devoted following. Set somewhere strikingly similar to Mull's Tobermory (and filmed there; page 152), children aged between three and five might be excited to see the colourful harbour in real life.

Katie Morag is the title character in a series of illustrated children's books set on Struay, a fictional island inspired by Coll where the author and illustrator Mairi Hedderwick has lived for long periods. Katie is a determined and independent child, perfectly at home on the island. The books are aimed at children aged five to eight, and a TV series was made for CBeebies in 2013–15 (and still shown on repeat).

Successful Scottish writer and illustrator Debi Gliori created both *The Tobermory Cat*, set on Mull, and *A Hebridean Alphabet*, detailing all the things you might hope to see in a day on one of the islands. They are aimed at children aged around five to seven.

The Hill of the Red Fox by Allan Campbell McLean, for children aged from ten to younger teenagers, is a spy thriller written in 1955. Living in the time of the Cold War, the 13-year-old protagonist gets entangled in a dangerous situation while on his long summer holiday on Skye.

The Secret of Kells is a beautifully animated film directed by Tomm Moore. Although it is set in Kells, Ireland, the Viking invasions of the Hebrides are central to the story as 'master illuminator' Brother Aidan arrives with the Book of Kells, or Book of Iona, after the Vikings attacked his monastery on Iona. It is a gentle film, aimed at children, but adults with an interest in illustration, animation or Celtic mythology are also likely to enjoy it.

Of course, historically, the main language on the islands was Gaelic. The seminal poet Sorley MacLean (1911–96) grew up on Raasay. His immensely popular poem *Hallaig*, published in 1954, reflects on the Clearances, referring to a deserted township (page 99) on the island's southeast coast.

MUSIC AND DANCING Local pipe bands, bards and Gaelic choirs still exist on many of the islands. While certain groups, such as the Isle of Skye Pipe Band (page 62) have a long-standing tradition, others have formed in recent years as part of an ongoing cultural revival. Modern cèilidhs are traditional social gatherings, with Gaelic folk music, usually held in village halls and other community buildings. They are organised more formally than the old spontaneous gatherings, but will generally include amateur performances of traditional music, singing and dancing. Visitors are welcome, especially if they join in with the dancing.

To find local events once you have arrived on the islands, buy a copy of the local paper or news sheet. The frequency of concerts and celebrations dramatically increase during the island fèis (festival; page 46).

In classical music, *The Hebrides*, also known as *Fingal's Cave* after the famous rock formation on Staffa (page 171), is an overture written by the German composer Felix Mendelssohn in 1830. The iconic 'Skye Boat Song', written in the 1870s about Flora MacDonald and Bonnie Prince Charlie (page 15) and more recently adapted for recital on bagpipes, is one of Scotland's most easily recognised tunes.

Perhaps the best-known musicians to come from the islands in recent years are the Celtic rock band Skerryvore, who were formed on Tiree in 2004, taking their name from the majestic lighthouse visible from the south of the island. Runrig, an earlier band of a similar genre, formed on Skye in 1973.

TV AND FILM While the islands provide a scenic backdrop for several films and TV series, their most popular on-screen appearances are undoubtedly in British nature documentaries. The BBC's *Hebrides – Islands on the Edge* (2013) was a popular series, while the islands also regularly feature on the BBC's *Springwatch*, *Autumnwatch*, *Winterwatch* and *Coast*. *Scotland's Sacred Islands With Ben Fogle* visited Islay, Jura and Skye in its second series (2023), with a mixed reception from islanders themselves.

SPORT

Sport is a big deal on the islands and, whether it is the local team's 'at home' rugby match or the annual Highland Games, fans and supporters will usually show up in force. The biggest Highland Games in the region is held near Portree at the beginning of August (w skye-highland-games.co.uk), but there are other events on different islands throughout the summer (page 47). A team game played with sticks and a ball, shinty, is a traditional Highland game, which has some comparisons to hockey or lacrosse; it's more popular on Skye than the islands further south.

2

Practical Information

WHEN TO VISIT

As with any destination, but possibly more than most, your impression of the Inner Hebrides will be greatly affected by the weather. Beautiful and unspoilt in sunshine, it suddenly becomes all too apparent when it rains that the smaller islands are severely lacking a coffee shop. To add to the adventure, seasonal conditions are totally impossible to predict in advance, with clear bright days in winter being just as possible as whole weeks of rain in July. Then there's also daylight hours: the summer solstice on 20 June sees 18 hours of daylight on Skye while the shortest day of the year (21 December) lasts for just 6 hours and 37 minutes. With the right mindset, clothing and interests, any time of year can be enjoyable, but there are a few general trends to bear in mind.

SPRING (MARCH TO MAY) As hours of daylight increase around March and the year opens out into spring, the islands begin to emerge from their winter slumber. Although few visitors take advantage of these months, they are arguably the most rewarding. Temperatures are still relatively low in March, but April, generally known in the UK for its showers, is actually often a sunny time on the islands. Even if it rains, you will see a wonderful show of wildflowers, as well as many species of birds returning from their winter migration. The midges don't tend to come out in force until around 20 May, making spring a good time to avoid them.

One downside of coming early is that seasonal attractions, cafés and places to stay do not generally open until the middle of April and sometimes stay closed until June; that said, it is a perfect time to visit the most popular natural attractions, such as Skye's Old Man of Storr, as the majority of visitors will not arrive until the summer.

Seabirds start nesting on the cliffs in March, but the few places with breeding puffins are best visited from the beginning of May until August.

SUMMER (JUNE TO EARLY SEPTEMBER) Most people visit the Inner Hebrides in summer and there are several enticing reasons to follow suit. Nights are at their shortest in late June and the following couple of months are the best time to see basking sharks and marine mammals such as porpoise, dolphins and minke whale.

Summer is also the main time to attend festivities including fèis events of traditional Gaelic arts and culture (page 46), Highland Games, agricultural shows and other local traditions. Accommodation generally needs to be booked in advance and the most popular attractions are likely to be busy but, if you get off the beaten track or just walk a little further, you'll likely find that the majority of places are still free to explore in solitude.

AUTUMN (MID-SEPTEMBER TO NOVEMBER) The summer stretches into September before starting to fade away into autumn, with a higher likelihood of storms and temperatures beginning to drop. With geese returning in their thousands, stags rutting and broad-leaved trees in their golden and copper finery, autumn is a great time for nature lovers.

Many places close in October, their owners catching up with creative projects or maintenance work; this can make it increasingly difficult to find places to eat out or to visit indoor attractions. Accommodation options are more limited, but those that do stay open often cut their rates significantly.

WINTER (NOVEMBER TO FEBRUARY) Many outdoor activities start to become unfeasible in November and December, with short hours of daylight, snow on high mountaintops and unpredictable weather. Although the long winter nights are perfect for being cosy by the fireplace, in clear weather the cold nights are also great for stargazing; with so little light pollution, the sky puts on an incredible display and it's sometimes even possible to see the northern lights (page 28).

Christmas and Hogmanay (New Year's Eve) are festive celebrations with hearty food and drink, best spent at home with family or at the local pub.

If not before, almost everywhere closes in January and February, and the now seemingly endless winter drags on with storms, freezing temperatures and occasional, glorious respite. Few people choose to visit at this time of year, but those that do often have the feeling of having an island to themselves.

HIGHLIGHTS

With the greatest joy coming from accidental otter spotting, strolling across empty expanses of sand and finding hidden archaeology among overgrown heather, the Inner Hebrides is really a region to discover your own highlights. That said, there are of course some things that shouldn't disappoint.

All the islands have great wildlife-watching opportunities, but excursions to see **puffins** in the Treshnish Isles (page 171) or Sanday in the Small Isles (page 124) at the right time of year are undoubtedly one of the most guaranteed and rewarding experiences. Witnessing **34,000 geese returning to Islay** around early to mid-October (page 233), visiting the teeming **seabird cliffs on Colonsay** (page 210) or the **Manx shearwaters on Rùm** (page 109) are welcome reassurances about the natural world.

Mountaineers will find their best options in **Skye's Cuillin**, but hikers and hill-walkers will love **Ben More on Mull** (page 164), **Jura's Paps** (page 242) and the huge nature reserve of **Rùm** (page 105). On Coll and Tiree particularly, visitors are spoilt for choice over **deserted sandy beaches**, but Islay, Mull, Gigha and Colonsay all have more than their fair share.

Islay is known primarily for its **whisky** and visiting some of its distilleries will undoubtedly be a highlight for enthusiasts. Skye's **Portree** (page 60) has the best variety of places to eat and drink, while colourful **Tobermory** (Mull; page 154) is a fun place to spend an afternoon whatever the weather.

The restored splendour of the imposing fortress of **Duart Castle** (page 166) and **Iona Abbey**, with its connection to Columba and huge collection of carved medieval grave slabs (page 177), are some of the most interesting and impressive historical sites across the islands. Equally important, but slightly less well known, are the **priory on Oronsay** (page 211) and Islay's **Finlaggan** (page 223). Traces of prehistory are never far away, with mysterious sites such as **Lochbuie stone circle** (page 167) and **Fingal's Limpet Hammers** (page 210).

SUGGESTED ITINERARIES

If I can convey one message through this book, it is that these islands should not be rushed and, while they are all different, you will get more enjoyment from a two-week trip to just one or two islands than you possibly could from trying to visit seven within the same period. That said, the smaller and more accessible islands – the Slate Islands, Lismore, Kerrera and Gigha – can be visited on short trips of **a couple of days**.

One week could easily be spent on any of the islands, but you could also visit a couple in the same area: some of the Small Isles; the Slate Islands and Lismore; Islay and Jura or Colonsay; or Coll and Tiree.

Two weeks will give you enough time to relax and explore some of the large islands like Skye, Mull or Islay at a more leisurely pace. Within two weeks, you could also comfortably visit all of the Small Isles or hopscotch from Oban to Colonsay to Islay and then over to Jura.

Those who have **longer than two weeks** and want to explore more of the region should first look at the map of ferry connections (page 31) and see which islands are linked together. Unlike the Outer Hebrides, which are essentially strung out in a long chain, travelling between the Inner Hebrides is a stop-start affair that involves multiple trips to the mainland.

Visiting every island in this book at a relaxed pace takes around **three months** (trust me) and should ideally be planned to coincide with the seasons: Skye is much further north than Gigha, for example, and gets cold earlier in autumn and warms up later in spring.

TOURIST INFORMATION

There are few **tourist information offices** in the Inner Hebrides, but many islands have community centres or shops that provide an unofficial service. Most individual islands or smaller groups also have their own websites.

Visit Scotland w visitscotland.com. Scotland's national tourist board runs 3 iCentres in the Inner Hebrides: Portree on Skye (Bayfield Hse, Bayfield Rd IV51 9EL; ℡ 01478 612992), Craignure on Mull (The Pier PA65 6AY; ℡ 01680 812377) & Bowmore on Islay (The Square, Main St PA43 7JP; ℡ 01496 305165). There's also one nearby on the mainland, in Oban (North Pier PA34 5QD; ℡ 01631 563122). These information centres offer free advice, maps & leaflets. Staff are usually knowledgeable locals & will help you book tours & find transport & accommodation where possible, although it is often better to do most of this in advance if your trip depends on it.

Wild About Argyll w wildaboutargyll.co.uk. Lots of inspiration & information about the Inner Hebridean islands that fall under the county of Argyll.

MAPS Mapping Great Britain since 1791, **Ordnance Survey** (w ordnancesurvey. co.uk) have occasionally been known to confuse Gaelic, Old Norse and English place names, but remain an infinite source of information. They are now also available digitally and can be purchased from the Ordnance Survey website. For driving, long-distance cycling and trip planning, the OS Landranger series of 1:50,000 scale maps should be detailed enough, but if you are walking, mountain biking or travelling off-road, you will find the Explorer 1:25,000 scale more useful. OS maps are now available on- and offline in the form of a paid subscription app (w ordnancesurvey.co.uk/shop/os-maps-online.html), which can be very useful for day walks.

Do be wary that phones and Scottish weather are not always compatible, and for longer hikes in wilderness areas it's important to have backup in the form of a GPS or paper map and compass.

Harveys Maps (w harveymaps.co.uk) work particularly well for the Skye Cuillin, as they are designed specifically for walking with easy-to-read colours and clear contour lines, plus, most importantly, they are waterproof.

As well as online, you can often buy locally relevant maps from shops on the islands themselves, as well as at Waterstones in Oban (page 259) and specialist book and map shops such as Stanfords (w stanfords.co.uk) in London and Bristol. It is always best to call ahead to check the shop has the particular map you need in stock.

The free online resource **Walkhighlands** (w walkhighlands.co.uk) covers thousands of walks across Scotland, with route descriptions and marked maps covering everything from easy strolls to real mountaineering.

TIDES Tide times can be estimated at w tides.willyweather.co.uk, but it is always best to check with someone once you arrive, as there can be local differences to account for.

WEATHER The islands are known for their tendency to experience all four seasons in one day; while it is always a good idea to check the weather forecast, it's also sensible to keep waterproofs and a spare woolly hat on hand at all times. The wind direction can give some indication as to which parts of the coastline will be more exposed or sheltered on that particular day. For the best weather forecasts, check w metoffice.gov.uk, BBC Weather (w bbc.com/weather) or w xcweather.co.uk.

AURORA FORECASTS In winter months, it's worth keeping an eye on aurora forecasts. The Glendale App (w aurora-alerts.uk) is a trusted resource, as is AuroraWatch UK (w aurorawatch.lancs.ac.uk).

TOUR OPERATORS

Although the Inner Hebrides are easy to navigate independently, those who are not confident driving on single-track roads, want to meet like-minded people or have the hassle removed from trip planning might prefer to opt for a tour. Day trips and guided walks are best found more locally, but the following companies offer multi-day trips across several islands.

If it is simply **trip planning** and organisation you require, there are various self-drive or self-guided options, whereas other companies offer the added reassurance, information and entertainment provided by a guide.

The majority of **boat trips** can be found in the individual island chapters: there are quick seal-spotting excursions, trips to uninhabited islands such as the Treshnish Isles and Staffa (page 171) or out to Skerryvore lighthouse (page 142), as well as whale-watching excursions.

There are also **small-scale cruises**: far from the stereotypical image of enormous ships docking in too-small harbours, these companies offer trips for between six and 50 people.

TRIP PLANNING
McKinlay Kidd ☎ 01412 609260; w mckinlaykidd.com/scotland. Offers various self-drive, car-free & guided tours, including island-hopping, as well as the option of tailor-made trips.

Rabbie's 01312 263133; w rabbies.com. Small-group minibus trips. Depart from Glasgow, Edinburgh & Inverness.

Roaming Scotland m 07967 595662; w roamingscotland.com. Multi-day trips in the Small Isles, Mull, Iona, Islay, Jura, Colonsay & Skye, including short hikes & ancient sites. Departing from Edinburgh, Glasgow or Stirling (elsewhere by arrangement with private groups).

Scottish Routes w scottishroutes.com. Minibus whisky tours with multi-day trips to Islay, departing from Edinburgh.

BOAT TRIPS AND COASTAL WILDLIFE WATCHING

Arisaig Marine 01687 450224; w arisaig. co.uk. Trips out to the Small Isles, with the aim of seeing wildlife en route, & some trips have time ashore. Departing from Arisaig.

Basking Shark Scotland m 07975 723140; w baskingsharkscotland.co.uk. Multi-day diving & snorkelling trips, with a possibility to snorkel with basking sharks & seals, see puffins & watch white-tailed eagles, depending on the season. Departing from Oban & Coll.

Coastal Connections m 07919 615210; w coastal-connection.co.uk. Personalised private day-tour charters to any of the islands between Muck & Islay. Based in Oban.

Minch Adventures m 07437 670212; w minchadventures.co.uk. Trips to the Small Isles & Skye, 4x4 access to Rùm, drop-off to remote

hiking locations & luxury seafood lunches. Based in Mallaig.

Selkie Explorers m 07827 888321; w selkie-explorers.com. Sailing adventures around the Small Isles & further afield on a small boat carrying max 9 passengers, including crew. Trips depart from Mallaig or Eigg.

SMALL-SCALE CRUISES

Hebridean Island Cruises 01756 704704; w hebridean.co.uk. The *Hebridean Princess* carries 48 passengers in 30 luxury cabins. Trips all over the Hebrides for 4–10 nights, departing from Oban.

The Majestic Line 01369 707951; w themajesticline.co.uk. Small-group or private tours on retired fishing boats & custom-built vessels, with options covering most of the Inner Hebrides. Departing from Oban.

Provident Sailing m 07549 935222; w providentsailing.co.uk. Classic sailing adventures scheduled annually, with 4 cabins accommodating 8–10 guests. Regular trips around parts of the Inner Hebrides, as well as further afield. Departing from Oban.

St Hilda Sea Adventures 01631 564121; w sthildaseaadventures.co.uk. Cruises have fewer than 12 passengers aboard a former tall ship, Norwegian ferry, rescue ship or cruising lifeboat. Options include sailing around Islay, Jura, Mull, Skye, the Small Isles & the Slate Islands, with wildlife watching & distillery visits. Departing from Oban.

RED TAPE

The Inner Hebrides are part of the UK, so visitors should follow the same procedures as entering the UK elsewhere; check specifics before travelling at w gov.uk/visit-uk-holiday-family-friends. Visitors from the EU, EEA, Switzerland, the United States, Canada and Australia do not need a visa for holidays of up to six months.

While many countries have **consulates** based in Edinburgh or Glasgow, their main embassies are in London; all major nations are fully represented by embassies or High Commissions (for Commonwealth members). A full list of contact details can be found at w gov.uk/government/publications/foreign-embassies-in-the-uk.

GETTING THERE AND AWAY

The Inner Hebrides range from relatively remote to quite accessible depending on your choice of destination. While it might take 4 hours to reach Tiree from the mainland, or you could have to wait a couple of days to catch a ferry to Canna, driving across to Seil or Skye takes a matter of minutes. In all cases, the journey should be considered a part of your trip, as mainland Argyll and the Highlands are beautiful parts of Scotland and ferry journeys provide great wildlife-watching opportunities in the open sea.

Note that it's not necessary to have a **car** to visit the Inner Hebrides, but – with the exception of Skye and Seil where some buses run directly over the bridge – in order to reach the islands by public transport you will generally have to change and get on to the ferry on foot.

BY BUS AND TRAIN The best place to check all public transport routes and times within Scotland is w travelinescotland.com.

Most visitors travelling by bus or train from elsewhere in the UK, including from Edinburgh or London, are likely to have come through **Glasgow**. Buses leave from Buchanan Bus Station for Kennacraig, Tayinloan, Oban, Fort William (where you can change for Mallaig) and Portree (Skye), with the most useful operators being Citylink (✆ 01413 524444; w citylink.co.uk), West Coast Motors (✆ 01586 552319; w westcoastmotors.co.uk) and Stagecoach (✆ 03452 418000; w stagecoachbus.com).

Trains to Oban, Mallaig, Arrochar and Tarbet (the last two for bus connections towards Kennacraig and Tayinloan) leave from **Glasgow Queen Street**. Times and fares can be checked via w scotrail.co.uk.

The journey from Glasgow to Oban by both bus and train takes just over 3 hours (costing around £30 on the train and between £17 and £26 on the bus), with departures every couple of hours throughout the day. Travelling to Mallaig takes just over 5 hours with only a couple of departures each day and the possibility of needing to change in Fort William. By both train or bus the journey is likely to cost around £40.

It takes just over 3 hours to reach Kennacraig, for connections to Islay, by Citylink bus and costs around £24, whereas travelling to Tayinloan (for Gigha) adds a further 30 minutes and a couple of pounds more; there are departures a few times a day.

If you know your travel plans, it is usually worth booking tickets in advance; some companies offer a discount and buses can sometimes be fully booked on the day.

Travelling between mainland port towns on public transport can be a longer process than you might hope. Transport routes are set up on the assumption that passengers will be travelling in and out of port towns to/from the islands rather than between towns and, although there are connecting routes, there are usually several changes to make.

BY BRIDGE Skye and Seil can be accessed on foot, bus or car over a bridge. Kyleakin on Skye is connected to Kyle of Lochalsh on the mainland, while Seil is connected to the mainland by the 'Bridge Over the Atlantic' across Clachan Sound. At the time of writing, both of these crossings were free, but there is always some talk of reinstating the toll for the Skye Bridge, so that would not be an entirely surprising development.

BY FERRY The word 'ferry' in the Inner Hebrides may refer to anything from a six-seat, independently run passenger boat to a multistorey car ferry. The vast majority of services are run by **CalMac** (✆ 0800 066 5000; from outside the UK: +44 1475 650397; w calmac.co.uk). Nuances and exceptions within the ferry network are explained in the 'Getting there and away' sections of each chapter in this book, but it's important to know that while both vehicle and foot passenger tickets can be bought in advance or when you embark on most routes, it's strongly

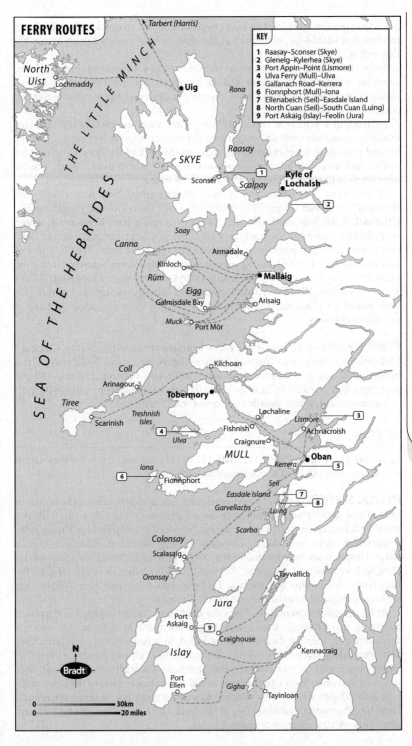

FERRY ROUTES

KEY
1 Raasay–Sconser (Skye)
2 Glenelg–Kylerhea (Skye)
3 Port Appin–Point (Lismore)
4 Ulva Ferry (Mull)–Ulva
5 Gallanach Road–Kerrera
6 Fionnphort (Mull)–Iona
7 Ellenabeich (Seil)–Easdale Island
8 North Cuan (Seil)–South Cuan (Luing)
9 Port Askaig (Islay)–Feolin (Jura)

Tarbert (Harris)

North Uist
Lochmaddy

THE LITTLE MINCH

Uig

Rona

Raasay

SKYE

Scalpay

Sconser · 1 · **Kyle of Lochalsh**

· 2 ·

Soay

Canna

Kinloch

Rùm

Eigg

Galmisdale Bay

Muck · Port Mòr

Armadale

Mallaig

Arisaig

SEA OF THE HEBRIDES

Kilchoan

Coll

Arinagour

Tiree

Scarinish

Treshnish Isles

Ulva · 4

Tobermory

Lochaline

Fishnish

Craignure

Lismore · 3

Achnacroish

Iona · 6

Fionnphort

MULL

Kerrera · **Oban** · 5

Seil

Easdale Island · 7

Garvellachs · 8

Luing

Scarba

Colonsay

Scalasaig

Oronsay

Tayvallich

Jura

Port Askaig · 9 · Craighouse

Kennacraig

Islay

Port Ellen

Gigha · Tayinloan

N

Bradt

0 — 30km
0 — 20 miles

advised to pre-book vehicles on many routes as they fill up quickly. Bicycles travel for free, but should be mentioned at the time of booking (there's an option for this online).

Before you travel, check for any service updates on your route online (w calmac. co.uk/service-status), download CalMac's app or sign up for text updates – sailings can sometimes be amended, diverted or cancelled due to adverse weather conditions or vessel issues.

Arriving in a vehicle at the larger ferry ports, there are usually staff in high-visibility jackets who will direct you into the correct lane; on less busy routes the normal procedure is generally to just drive to the back of the queue and wait for further instruction. While the larger ports also have staffed ticket offices, smaller ones are unmanned, so tickets can be bought on board.

Of the main port towns and villages, **Mallaig** (page 260) serves the Small Isles and Skye; **Oban** (page 257) serves Mull, Coll, Tiree, Colonsay and Lismore; **Gallanach Road**, just south of Oban, has ferries to Kerrera; **Kennacraig**, which is really little more than a shed ferry terminal in a large car park, serves Islay; and ferries to Gigha leave from **Tayinloan**. To reach the Slate Islands, you will first have to travel to **Seil;** for Raasay there are ferries from **Sconser** (Skye); the main Jura ferry leaves from **Port Askaig** (Islay); to Iona from **Fionnphort** (Mull); and to Ulva from **Ulva Ferry** (Mull; page 179). Minor crossings and options for inter-island travel are explained within the 'Getting there and away' sections of the island chapters.

BY AIR Hebridean Air (✆ 08458 057465; w hebrideanair.co.uk) fly to Islay, Colonsay, Coll and Tiree from Oban (page 257). These flights, on a small BN2B aircraft, run between one and five times a week and usually cost between £30 and £80 per passenger. You can also fly to Islay from Glasgow with **Loganair** (✆ 01496 302361; w loganair.co.uk), which usually costs between £120 and £140.

HEALTH

In an **emergency** call ✆ 999 or 112. **NHS 111** (✆ 111) can help if you have an urgent medical problem and you're not sure what to do.

MEDICAL SERVICES Access to non-emergency medical services on the islands is limited and many places do not even have a pharmacy. For peace of mind, you should stock up on any medication you regularly need before your trip. The majority of islands do have some form of doctors' surgery, district nurse or community nurse. Hospitals are only located in Portree (page 63) and Broadford (page 89) on Skye, in Bowmore on Islay (page 222) and in Mull's Craignure (page 166); on the mainland you can also find them in Lochgilphead, Oban and Fort William, but serious or specialist cases are often flown to Glasgow.

Although this apparent lack of services might seem intimidating, it is important to realise that although health care might not come in a form that you are accustomed to, there is always a plan of action in place: well-trained community first responders are on call nearby, dispensing doctors can prescribe medicine where pharmacies are not available and health professionals generally have more time to spend on each patient than you would find in busier parts of the UK; brand-new defibrillators are also now attached to walls in many places across the islands. Note, too, that prescriptions are free in Scotland. Dentists are few and far between, often only offering emergency appointments.

DRINKING WATER You can happily assume that all water from kitchen taps is drinkable unless otherwise indicated. In special cases it may come reddish-brown from the tap; this is just caused by the water running through peat underground and is nothing to be concerned about.

For hikers, water from small streams in the hills is generally safe to drink as long as you are able to check far enough upstream to be sure that there is not a dead sheep or deer near the water; to be safe you can use a filtration system or tablets.

HARMFUL OR IRRITATING CREATURES Scotland does not have any large predators to worry about, but it is important to know how to deal with certain bites and stings. In the extremely unlikely event that you or a companion experience a severe allergic reaction, call ✎ 999 straight away and they will help you decide what to do next. Signs of a severe allergic reaction include: swelling of your lips, mouth, throat or tongue; difficulty breathing or breathing very fast; a tight throat or struggling to swallow; blue, grey or pale skin, lips or tongue; confusion or dizziness; and loss of consciousness.

Ticks The most dangerous creature on the islands is actually the tiny tick. This small, blood-sucking parasite starts out as an almost invisible black dot and then grows as it fills itself with blood. Alone, it is no more than an irritation, causing itching and at worse an infection, but the problem is that the minuscule arachnids have now contracted Lyme disease and can occasionally pass this on to human hosts. Saying that, most ticks are harmless and simply need to be removed.

Ticks usually bite in late spring and summer, but are becoming more prevalent in winter due to climate change. The best way to prevent getting bitten is to avoid moving through undergrowth with bare skin brushing the plants. Although it isn't very fashionable, tucking your trousers into your socks will stop them from climbing up your legs; boots are better than trainers for the same reason. Spend a moment checking yourself when you get back from a walk so you can remove the tick quickly if you find one.

Ticks should ideally be removed complete, and as soon as possible, to reduce the chance of infection. You can use special tick tweezers, which can be bought in good travel shops; or failing this, with your fingernails, grasp the tick as close to your body as possible, and pull it away steadily and firmly at right angles to your skin without jerking or twisting. Applying irritants (eg: Olbas oil) or lit cigarettes is to be discouraged as a means of removal since they can cause the ticks to regurgitate and therefore increase the risk of disease. Once the tick is removed, if possible douse the wound with alcohol (any spirit will do), soap and water, or iodine. If you are travelling with small children, remember to check their heads, and particularly behind the ears, for ticks. Spreading redness around the bite and/or fever and/or aching joints after a tick bite imply that you have an infection that requires antibiotic treatment. In this case seek medical advice.

Midges These tiny biting flies do not carry disease in Scotland or generally have any lasting effect, but they can be unbearably annoying. Especially troublesome when there's no wind to blow them away, they are common around marshy ground, bodies of water, dense undergrowth and forests. Although the relentless clouds are worst in late July and August, midges can come out as early as the middle of May and stick around until September.

There are various repelling sprays and creams, but your best defences are clothing and trying not to be outside around dusk, when they usually come out in force. Bizarrely, Avon's oily Skin So Soft moisturising spray is used as a repellent by Royal Marine Commandos as well as some locals.

Adders Black and brown, with a zigzag and diamond pattern, adders are Scotland's only venomous snake. Although they are not aggressive, they can bite when they feel threatened or are accidently trodden on. Common on heather moorland, look out for them on sunny summer days when they might be basking in the sun; if you are walking through undergrowth, it can be a good idea to hit the plants in front of you with a stick to alert them of your presence. In the unlikely event that you get bitten, try to remember what the snake looked like as doctors will need a positive identification before they can administer an antidote, stay calm and still, loosen any constricting jewellery or clothing and call ⟍ 999 immediately. Bites are usually painful, but not deadly.

Jellyfish and other sea creatures Most stings from British sea creatures are not dangerous and can be treated without the help of a medical professional. While weaver fish, sea urchins and jellyfish are all relatively common in the Inner Hebrides, the likelihood of getting stung is very low because the seawater is cold enough for most people not to stay in for long without a wetsuit. Wearing water shoes will protect you against weaver fish and sea urchins as well as sharp rocks. If you are stung, rinse the affected area with seawater, remove any spines from the skin using tweezers, soak the area in water as hot as can be tolerated for at least 30 minutes (a clean cloth soaked in hot water can also be used) and finally take regular-strength painkillers. Seek medical attention if you have continuous severe pain, or if you have been stung on your face or genitals.

SAFETY

In terms of both residents and visitors, the Inner Hebrides are very safe. Many inhabitants do not even bother to lock their doors and if any criminal activity was to take place then the culprits could not get very far before being stopped at the ferry terminal; in many places, the honesty box shop is still a workable business model.

DRINK DRIVING AND TRAVELLING AT NIGHT Drink driving can still be a problem in the Inner Hebrides. Scotland's low alcohol limits (page 40) apply just as rigorously on the islands, but the rural and isolated nature of some communities can mean that some people, whether locals or distillery-visiting holidaymakers, feel that the law may be more flexible than elsewhere. Police checks occur with increasing regularity, particularly around festivals and events, but it is also important to drive, cycle or walk along roads with extra care at night.

OUTDOOR EMERGENCIES To reach **Mountain Rescue**, just call the normal emergency number (⟍ 999 or 112) and ask for 'police, mountain rescue'. Do the same to call the **coastguard** and simply ask for 'coastguard'. You can also contact 999 via SMS text message, which might be easier in areas of poor network coverage, but it is easier for the emergency services if you have registered your phone in advance (w relayuk.bt.com/how-to-use-relay-uk/contact-999-using-relay-uk.html); this service should only be used when a phone call is not possible.

The best way to avoid getting into trouble in the first place is to be well prepared and understand your own capabilities. Land- and seascapes that appear gentle in photos can turn out to be much more severe with the addition of Scotland's famously relentless weather. If you are unsure of your ability or a total beginner, don't try a new outdoor sport without being accompanied by a more experienced and trustworthy friend or guide.

Though **walking** is the most accessible activity on the islands – and one which many people can enjoy with appropriate clothing and a little forward planning – **navigation** becomes vital when hill-walking inland. Map-reading skills and a compass, along with the possible addition of a GPS device, are essential.

When **swimming in the sea**, it is important to be aware of rip tides. If you find yourself being dragged out, do not fight the current, but swim out sideways, parallel with the shore, to escape. Another obvious hazard can be waves. You should be able to tell if the sea looks too rough to swim in, but even on calmer days you can hurt yourself by being pushed on to the rocks at the side of a bay. Only very confident swimmers who are used to similar conditions should swim out of their depth when alone at the beach.

Kayaking and other small craft can be safe on lochs or in sheltered bays, but the open sea is a serious endeavour only suitable for those with experience or with a guide.

WOMEN AND LGBTQIA+ TRAVELLERS

Although discrimination exists in the Inner Hebrides the same as anywhere else in the UK, it is unlikely to affect your trip. Women should not fear walking alone through towns at night and LGBTQIA+ travellers are unlikely to raise eyebrows.

Akin to most parts of the country, there can be no guarantees against occasional drunken wolf whistlers on a Friday night outside the pub, but this uncouth behaviour is looked down upon by the community. Should you ever feel unsafe, don't be afraid to explain the situation to any member of staff or other local person and they will most likely take you under their wing. Period protection is widely available in even the smallest community shops, but the range of products on offer is generally more limited than in larger Scottish towns.

TRAVELLING WITH A DISABILITY

Although things tend to move slowly in the Hebrides, communities are now making a real effort to be inclusive of people with disabilities. Sights, accommodation, places to eat and drink and shops marked ♿ indicate that they are wheelchair accessible. CalMac ferries offer a 25% discount on the price of a vehicle ticket for Blue Badge holders from EU countries, as well as arranging for you to park near the lift on larger ferries for hassle-free embarkation. Support dogs are also welcome in all passenger areas.

There is some form of wheelchair-accessible accommodation on most of the islands but, whatever your disability, it is always a good idea to phone ahead and explain your specific needs. Many places that are not officially adapted are still keen to try to accommodate or assist guests with disabilities in any way possible.

Unfortunately, properly wheelchair-accessible attractions are few and far between. Those islands that do not normally allow cars will usually make an exception for Blue Badge holders if it is possible to bring a car over on the ferry. You can borrow an 'off-road' wheelchair for use on beaches or grass on Tiree (page 141) and Islay (page 218).

An ever-growing resource for those who use wheelchairs is w euansguide.com, and the Visit Scotland website (w visitscotland.com/accommodation/accessible) is a good way to search for accessible accommodation. In addition, many of the individual island websites will be able to help you find suitable options.

The UK's gov.uk website (w gov.uk/government/publications/disabled-travellers/disability-and-travel-abroad) has a downloadable guide giving general advice and practical information for travellers with a disability (and their companions). The Society for Accessible Travel and Hospitality (w sath. org) also provides some general information, while specialist UK-based tour operators that offer trips to the Inner Hebrides include Disabled Holidays (w disabledholidays.com).

TRAVELLING WITH CHILDREN

The Inner Hebrides is an excellent place to visit with children. There might not be such a wide-range of organised activities and attractions as available elsewhere, but the islands are the perfect setting to make your own fun. The majority of island accommodation is child friendly, but self-catering and camping options usually offer more freedom and value for money for families.

Children old enough to make sensible choices outdoors can enjoy a level of independence that has often been lost elsewhere. Swimming in the sea and scrambling on rocks are part of the adventure, but are always riskier if done alone; with patchy or non-existent phone signal, it isn't always easy to keep in touch.

Indoor activities for children can be a little trickier to find across the islands, but Tobermory (page 154) is a rewarding destination, as is Port Charlotte's Islay Nature Centre (page 232); budding palaeontologists should visit the Staffin Dinosaur Museum (page 70).

TRAVELLING WITH A DOG

Well-behaved dogs can have a great holiday in the Inner Hebrides: they travel free on ferries and are even allowed to sit inside with their owners in certain parts of the ship; dogs are a talking point with locals throughout the islands; and there are plenty of places that they can run around. Special care needs to be taken around livestock (page 49) and ground-nesting birds in the spring (page 10).

WHAT TO TAKE

You can expect local shops, on all but the least-populated islands, to have basic essentials of food, cleaning products and toiletries, but if you have a preferred brand, it would be a good idea to pick up supplies on the mainland. With a few exceptions in Portree and Tobermory there are very few places to buy clothing or shoes, so it is always best to bring what you need with you.

At any time of year, wet or muddy ground usually means that without sturdy footwear you can't go anywhere outside of towns and villages without getting sopping wet feet. Waterproof hiking boots are recommended, though if you only plan on doing short walks wellies or rubber boots will also work. Regardless of your plans, a waterproof jacket is essential and anybody doing any walking will also want waterproof trousers. Putting aside their dubious fashion credentials, waterproof ponchos do not seem to work well in wind.

In general, the Inner Hebrides are places to wear practical and comfortable clothing; getting on and off ferries is not simple in high heels, and light, floaty dresses are likely to fly up in the wind, revealing your underwear at unfortunate moments. You can, of course, take a nicer outfit for evening meals out, but it is unlikely anyone will look twice if you don't.

Unlike many other places in Europe, the UK uses a 13-amp plug with three rectangular prongs arranged in a triangle. Coming from elsewhere, you will need an adaptor – it's advisable to buy one of these in advance of travelling out to the islands as they can be hard to get hold of.

Good binoculars are essential for wildlife enthusiasts, while the pocket version will always be useful to get a closer look at seals, a distant otter or eagle. Photographers will benefit from a high-quality zoom lens and tripod.

Those partaking in moderate **day hikes** should come prepared with:

- An OS map or Harvey map of the area (page 27)
- A compass and the ability to use it and/or GPS device and extra batteries
- Food, including a little extra, and filled water bottle or bladder
- Small first-aid kit
- Fully charged mobile phone (keep in flight mode to save battery)
- Waterproof jacket and trousers
- Walking boots
- Walking trousers
- Quick-drying T-shirt
- Micro-fleece/mid-layer warm top suitable for hiking in
- Gloves (preferably rainproof)
- A warm hat (whatever you are comfortable in; wool stays warmer when wet)

Optional extras:

- Gaiters (for protection against adders)
- Walking poles
- Thin neck warmer or scarf to pull over your face and protect against wind chill

Multi-day hikers in summer and shoulder seasons should add the following:

- A hiking backpack
- A strong tent – take some extra strings, pegs and gaffer tape for emergencies
- Sleeping bag – look at the comfort rating (not the extreme rating) and be sure that it can go lower than 5°C in summer or to −5°C in spring or autumn
- Cooking equipment: a small gas stove, several lighters and matches (protected from water), a pot, sharp knife and spoon at least
- Dry bags to keep your clothes and sleeping bag safe (several strong plastic bags are also workable)
- Waterproof bag cover (might come with your bag)
- Roll mat
- A charged power bank
- Wool/wool-blend socks (at least two pairs)
- Thick, warm jumper in wool/fleece or a down (type) jacket (for sitting down in the evenings)
- Hiking trousers (one or two pairs depending on quality of waterproof trousers)
- Long-sleeved base-layers
- Underwear
- Torch
- A strong needle and thread/dental floss for emergency fabric repairs

- Basic and minimal toiletries including hand sanitiser
- Suncream

Optional extras:

- A wind-breaker jacket
- Long thermal underwear (for evenings, sleeping or even while hiking)
- Binoculars
- Insect repellent (the best protection against midges might just be to hide in your tent)

Only those with experience hiking in winter mountain conditions with ice or snow should attempt to do so, as this requires an additional set of skills and equipment.

MONEY AND BUDGETING

Pound sterling is the only currency accepted on the islands and, although Scotland has its own banknotes, both standard British and Scottish versions are accepted. Excluding the largest and most populous islands, most places in the Inner Hebrides do not have their own bank. **ATMs and bank branches** are few and far between, but people with UK bank cards can withdraw cash at post offices. Some shops offer cashback with a purchase or have a fee-paying ATM of their own, but this isn't guaranteed. It is therefore always a good idea to take out some cash on the mainland before travelling.

UK bank cheques are occasionally accepted, but it feels like only a matter of time until this dies out. It probably does not need mentioning but travellers' cheques are now an outdated system and extremely unlikely to be recognised.

Accommodation can usually be paid for online in advance, but otherwise it is worth noting that B&Bs probably will not have a card machine on site, whereas hotels, larger campsites and hostels usually will. Similarly, restaurants will nearly always take cards, but cafés and small shops sometimes only take cash.

BUDGETING Wild camping (away from roads or settlements, in line with the Outdoor Access Code; page 44) is free. Campsites usually cost around £15 per person per night, so by sleeping in a tent combined with cycling, hitchhiking, walking or taking buses, and eating basic food from grocery stores, it would be possible to get by on about £20 a day or even less for the very determined.

Dorm beds are generally around £25, so without carrying camping equipment the bare minimum rises to around £35 a day; the sporadic placement of hostels means this sort of trip will require some planning and booking in advance.

A couple wanting a private room in a cheaper B&B will struggle to find anything less than £80 per night in most places and often the cheapest option is nearer £100; unfortunately single people will usually still be paying at least £60. Considering most B&Bs will not have anywhere to cook, you will probably want to eat out at least once a day, making the total at least £120 a day for a couple or £80 a day for a single person.

The mid-range of B&Bs, hotels and restaurants will probably bring a couple up to £170–220 a day, but this can be dramatically reduced by renting self-catering accommodation and cooking your own food.

Luxury, high-end accommodation and places to eat may or may not exist depending on which island you are visiting; Skye has by far the widest range in this price bracket, with Islay coming in second for its accommodation, but lagging behind with top-end restaurant choices.

Eating and drinking out is comparable to elsewhere in the UK. You will usually find that prices seem cheap in comparison with Edinburgh or London, but are generally more expensive than other rural parts of Scotland. In a pub, a main course will cost £9–20, a pint of beer around £4.50, while a dram of whisky upwards of about £4. A sandwich and hot drink from a café will set you back around £7.

The price of groceries is comparable to any small corner shop or village store in the UK. General examples include: a loaf of bread £1.60; a pint of milk about 85p; and a Mars bar 85p.

A souvenir shop will usually sell postcards for around 80p or a T-shirt for about £25. Fuel is generally about 10p a litre more expensive than on the mainland; a litre of petrol costs around £1.47.

GETTING AROUND

BY CAR Almost all roads in the Inner Hebrides are paved and, excluding a few good stretches on Skye and a couple on Mull and Islay, the vast majority are single track. The condition of the roads is a point of much contention among locals who are accustomed to driving on narrow roads, but resent the inconvenience and damage caused by pot-holes.

You can generally expect the quality of roads to decrease in accordance with the size of the population and proximity to the mainland: although single track, Seil's roads are smooth and painless, whereas those on Skye's northern Waternish Peninsula, the west coast of Mull and towards the north of Raasay are more dubious.

Jura deserves a special mention for its only substantial road: the A846. The classification as an A road should not confuse visitors into assuming it will be well maintained – the northern section sees grass growing in the middle and in places the sides are so sunken that a small car is likely to occasionally graze the road with its undercarriage.

Driving on single-track roads The only friction that regularly occurs between residents and visitors regards driving on single-track roads. Many good drivers coming from elsewhere in the UK or abroad will not have much previous experience driving on roads like this, but for locals it is second nature.

Single-track roads are those that are only wide enough for one car at a time; passing places dotted along the way allow vehicles to get past each other. You should always pull into a space on your left-hand side, unless you are passing a particularly large and difficult-to-manoeuvre vehicle, such as a lorry or a tractor with a trailer, in which case it's occasionally necessary to pull over to the right. Use your indicators in advance to avoid any confusion.

It is important to use the passing places for allowing both oncoming traffic to pass you and cars from behind to overtake you. If somebody is driving behind you, you should pull in at the nearest convenient opportunity and let them overtake. With oncoming traffic, by far the least stressful way to use the passing places is to pull in first and wait for the other car to pass. (This usually provides a good opportunity to admire the view.)

Flashing headlights is often used by locals to indicate that they have stopped to let you pass, but it is worth noting that this effect can be accidentally replicated by a car with its lights on driving over bumps in the road.

2

Across the Inner Hebrides, with the exceptions of Skye and Mull, it is often still customary to wave at other drivers as you pass them. This need not be more than a casual upright stretching of your fingers from the steering wheel, but is appreciated as a friendly gesture.

Hazards As well as driving on single-track roads, there are a few more hazards encountered when driving on the islands that visitors may not be used to. Sheep, cattle, deer and other animals frequently wander on to the road; slow-moving tractors, quad bikes and bicycles are common; and pot-holes or obstacles such as fallen branches or minor flooding might not be dealt with as quickly as elsewhere. If you come across unaccompanied farm animals on the road, drive slowly and carefully towards them, which usually gets them to move. Sheep are not particularly bright and it can be tempting to use your horn, but this tends to make them panic even more.

To reduce the risk of an accident, reduce your speed more than usual as you approach corners, minor junctions and turnings, so you are not taken by surprise. Although you may feel pressured to increase your speed by a hurried local driving behind you, it is always better to find somewhere to pull in and let them pass.

Parking Official car parks can be rather few and far between on the islands, and the unspoken 'common sense' rules about where parking is allowed are not always immediately obvious to visitors (myself included). Blocking passing places, gates or any kind of access is never allowed for obvious reasons.

Mull and Islay tend to have adequate if not explicitly marked car parks. The most popular tourist sites on Skye are sometimes overcrowded; in these cases, it is really frowned upon to park off the edge of the road, as heavy traffic destroys the ground quickly and ruins the area for everyone. On smaller or less populous islands, the parking situation is a little more ad hoc. In some very quiet places, it might be possible to park on ground by the side of the road, but be careful not to do so in front of houses or on fragile habitat such as machair (page 5). If you are unsure, simply ask any local and they will usually be very happy to explain.

Drink driving Scotland's drink-driving limits were reduced in 2014 and are now significantly lower than elsewhere in the UK; even one drink could be enough to put you above the limit. The cut-off measurements are: 22mcg of alcohol in 100ml of breath; 50mg of alcohol in 100ml of blood; and 67mg of alcohol in 100ml of urine.

Fuel The majority of islands that allow visiting cars also have some form of filling station, with the notable exceptions of the Slate Islands and Raasay; in these cases, make sure you fill up before heading over. Note that fuel is often slightly more expensive than on the mainland.

Campervans Driving a small campervan around the islands is a real taste of freedom, but single-track roads can be a lot more difficult to negotiate in large vehicles. One idea to alleviate this headache is to bring or hire bicycles; leaving your campervan in a campsite for the day, you can then explore baggage-free and without having to worry about getting stuck. Campervan drivers on Skye should visit the community-run campsite Camping Skye (page 87), who are happy to provide information on road conditions across the island. Some of the smaller islands, such as Lismore, are particularly unsuitable for large vehicles and it is worth contacting a campsite in advance to ask for their advice.

Larger campsites and a few special community-run facilities allow you to dispose of toilet waste. These are all mentioned in the island chapters, and it is worth checking there is one in advance, as not all islands will have one.

Parking up for the night is a delicate issue and should be done with care. It is kinder to both residents and nature to use campsites, where they are available. Contrary to popular belief, the Scottish Outdoor Access Code (page 44), which allows wild camping in tents, does not apply to vehicles. If you are camping outside of campsites, make sure that you are well away from houses and somewhere where your vehicle is not causing any obstruction. Be sure not to park in passing places (whether for an hour or a night) and be aware as you drive that traffic might be stuck behind you – pull over when you can, even if that makes your journey slower.

Car hire You can hire cars locally on Skye, Mull, Islay and Tiree (see the island chapters for details), plus in Oban from Hazelbank Motors (℡ 01631 566476; w obancarhire.co.uk) and Lochgilphead and Campbeltown from Kintyre Hire (℡ 01586 554480; w kintyrehire.com).

It is important to ask about a spare tyre, as this is not standard on all models and it can truly ruin a holiday to have to wait for one to be delivered from the mainland. Also think carefully about ground clearance; the very smallest cars are not always easy to drive on more remote roads or those in poor condition. Personally, I did all the research for the first edition of this book in a little VW Polo, but I also managed to burst four tyres and scraped the bottom of the car on numerous occasions.

Electric car charging points Public charging points are springing up around the Inner Hebrides, but check the current situation on w greenerscotland.org/greener-travel/greener-driving/charge-point-map before planning any travel with an electric car.

BY TAXI All the region's larger islands and some of its smaller ones have privately run taxi services, but these do not exist everywhere and often have limited availability. It's always worth arranging a journey in advance if your trip relies on it. Listings are included within the specific island chapters.

BY BUS With a little forward planning, a holiday or trip around some of the Inner Hebridean islands by bus is perfectly possible and allows you the extra luxuries of being a little higher above the ground and not needing to watch the road, so you can relax and enjoy the scenery.

Bus services on the islands, though usually reliable, comfortable and convenient where they exist, have limited routes and timetables. Generally, schedules work around school times rather than the arrival of ferries, so there might be some wait between connections. On Sundays, services are dramatically reduced and often do not run at all.

Bus companies and fares vary from island to island. On Skye, Portree to Broadford (with Stagecoach) takes 40 minutes and costs £6.30; on Mull, Craignure to Tobermory (West Coast Motors) takes 50 minutes and costs £6.70; and on Islay, Bowmore to Port Ellen (Argyll and Bute Council/Islay Coaches) takes 25 minutes and costs £3. There are usually significant reductions on return tickets.

BY FERRY Routes between islands are more limited and less frequent than those between the islands and the mainland, making it impossible to explore the whole archipelago without intermittently visiting the mainland; fortunately, Argyll and the Highlands are both beautiful parts of Scotland, so this is really no hardship.

That said, it is possible to travel between some of the islands: Coll and Tiree; Islay to Jura and Colonsay; between some of the Small Isles; Seil to Easdale and Luing; Skye to Raasay; and Mull to Iona and Ulva.

For general information about ferries and routes, see page 30 and the map on page 31.

BY BICYCLE Cycling is a cheap, sustainable and healthy way to get around the islands. Apart from certain places on Skye, roads are rarely busy and, assuming the weather co-operates, it is a good way to see the scenery and wildlife. Most of the islands, keen to reduce traffic, welcome cyclists and often have at least one place offering bike hire; this usually costs about £25 a day, with reductions for longer periods and children. Bikes are carried for free on CalMac ferries, but should be mentioned at the time of booking.

When you are cycling on single-track roads, pull over into left-hand passing places or the side of the road to let cars pass.

HITCHHIKING Hitchhiking on the islands is as safe as it ever can be. Basic precautions such as talking to the driver briefly before you get in the car and not travelling at night still apply, but the main consideration is probably how long you might have to wait before someone is actually driving the way you're heading. It's noticeably easier to catch a ride on the smaller islands and west coast mainland than it is on Skye.

ACCOMMODATION

Accommodation in the Inner Hebrides is a wonderfully Scottish experience. You can stay in a homely B&B and be treated to a full Scottish breakfast with eggs from the back garden; sit by a roaring fire in a country house hotel; or rent an old crofter's cottage on a secluded stretch of coastline.

The quality of accommodation in each price bracket is generally very high, with the biggest 'problem' usually being slow Wi-Fi connection. In high season, many types of mid-range or higher-end accommodation will have a minimum two-night stay. Whereas some places close completely over winter, others will offer substantial discounts.

Excluding camping in your own tent, accommodation needs to be booked in advance during high season. On Skye in particular there are stories of people starting to look for somewhere to stay in Broadford and travelling all the way up to Trotternish without finding anywhere to sleep; a costly and upsetting mistake to make.

For an explanation of the accommodation price codes used in this guide, see page viii.

HOTELS Only around half of the islands featured in this book have a hotel. Far from impersonal chain establishments, hotels in the Inner Hebrides are distinctly individual, often owner-managed and run with great pride.

For those seeking old-fashioned Scottish luxury – high-ceilinged banquet halls, huge log fires and free-standing baths deep enough for wallowing – a scattering of high-quality accommodations have been established in buildings once called 'the big house'. These manor houses were once home to the laird, his family and their servants, but have since been made into hotels, providing employment for local people and a second life for historic buildings.

Other high-end hotels are more modern, often stunningly situated with panoramic views and serving excellent food. Generally, all hotels have rooms with en-suite bathrooms, offer breakfast and the option of eating dinner on site.

BED AND BREAKFASTS Alongside self-catering, B&Bs make up the bulk of accommodation in the Inner Hebrides. Although the majority of them are in part of somebody's home, most are professionally managed, spotlessly clean and serve a hearty breakfast. The kitchen is not usually for guest use, but most B&Bs provide tea- and coffee-making facilities in your bedroom.

Owners are often keen to share their local knowledge and favourite spots. At the very top end, they might be similar to hotels, but smaller and more personal, with luxurious finishings and glorious views. Most B&Bs cost between £80 and £120 a night; these do not fall in the 'luxury' bracket, but are generally clean, comfortable and serving a filling fried breakfast. Some of the true hidden gems fall under £80, simply because the building is too old to be modernised with en suites and the owner does not feel they can charge anything more.

GUESTHOUSES The definition of a guesthouse is somewhat obscure. Generally speaking, they are bigger than B&Bs, less likely to be in the owner's home and possibly with a lower staff presence. Accommodation is normally in private rooms rather than dormitory style, and there is unlikely to be a kitchen for guests' use.

HOSTELS AND BUNKHOUSES The difference between hostels and bunkhouses in the Inner Hebrides is very unclear. Originally, bunkhouses were more rudimentary converted farm buildings, with the word 'hostel' inferring a few more amenities and a higher level of comfort, but these distinctions do not really apply any more. These types of accommodation have predominantly shared dorm rooms but might have some affordable private rooms. They will also have a shared kitchen and bathrooms.

Even islands with a very small population, like those in the Small Isles, seem to have a bunkhouse, the best of which have a relaxed communal space and are sometimes in stunning locations.

Hostels and bunkhouses are often the best choice for independent travellers, and those who are looking to save money and meet new people. Older travellers should feel just as welcome to stay in them as twenty-somethings.

The Covid-19 pandemic hit this style of accommodation badly, with some providers closing completely or converting the space into standard self-catering.

SELF-CATERING PROPERTIES Self-catering accommodation, where you rent an entire house or apartment, falls into a distinctly different category from hotels, B&Bs and hostels. Although you can sometimes book properties for a couple of nights during low season, it is more usual to have to book a whole week. For family holidays or groups of friends, this style of accommodation provides all the freedom and flexibility of having your own home. Often in more remote and scenic locations, you can find everything from a modernised blackhouse or old crofter's cottage to modern buildings with plenty of glass to show off the view.

All self-catering accommodation should have a kitchen and most will have free laundry facilities. You will not generally see much, if anything, of the owner, and can consider the house your own for the duration of your stay.

CAMPSITES Campsites in the Inner Hebrides range from very basic but picturesquely positioned pieces of land with little more than clean running water and toilets, to large holiday park sites with hardstanding areas for caravans, laundry facilities and electric hook up. Some motorhome-specific spaces have opened in recent years; these aim to cater for an increased number of visitors travelling in this way, and might lack toilet facilities on the assumption that people have their own. The majority of campsite staff are helpful and knowledgeable about the local area.

CARAVAN PARKS, GLAMPING AND PODS This is camping for people without their own tent or campervan. Ranging from insulated caravans with a small bathroom, kitchen and heating, to wooden shell 'pods', which may be nothing more than a dry place to put your own bedding, it is important to check exactly what facilities are provided in advance. Semi-permanent tents such as yurts and tipis also fall under this category. Location is particularly vital here: as tourism has increased in Scotland, pods have sprung up as a quick way to provide accommodation without the complication of having to apply for planning permission. While waking up in a wooden hut on the shorefront can be invigorating, the same cannot be said for the edge of a 'busy' road, so it is a good idea to check the finer details before booking anything.

WILD CAMPING The Scottish Outdoor Access Code (w outdooraccess-scotland. scot) applies to people camping in tents or with bivvy bags rather than vehicles. It states that individuals or small groups may camp freely for less than three nights, as long as they are not disturbing local people or farm animals, and that they should be well out of sight of buildings or roads and away from enclosed fields. Care should be taken not to disturb deer stalking or grouse shooting and, most importantly, campers should 'leave no trace' of their campsite, litter or fires. Human waste should always be buried in an adequate hole and kept well away from water sources.

MOUNTAIN BOTHIES ASSOCIATION Official bothies in remote locations are cared for by volunteers from the Mountain Bothies Association (w mountainbothies.org. uk). These are disused buildings or houses that have been repaired or converted into free accommodation for passing walkers and hikers. Anyone is welcome to use them, but the same 'leave no trace' rules as wild camping are also very important here as guests rely on each other to keep the building and surroundings in a good condition. Some bothies have particular access rules as detailed on the website, but groups of six or more are never permitted and you should not stay longer than a couple of nights. Bothies are no longer a well-kept secret and you should embrace the idea of sharing with strangers and prepare to meet new friends.

EATING AND DRINKING

LOCAL PRODUCE AND SPECIALITIES Although there is more to Scottish cuisine than **haggis**, first-time visitors to Scotland should try to forget their preconceived notions and be prepared to try it. Traditionally held together in an animal's stomach, the tasty filling contains sheep's heart, liver and lungs, minced onion, oatmeal, suet, pepper and salt along with other spices. Unlike other depressing meat substitutes, vegetarian haggis is remarkably tasty; it usually includes beans, pulses and nuts in addition to the usual non-meat ingredients.

Look out too for **Cranachan**, a delicious dessert made from oats, cream, whisky and raspberries. For breakfast, **porridge** is a must; medium-ground oats are preferred and serving suggestions range from just a pinch of salt to sugar and a tot

Highland cattle and blackface sheep are synonymous with the Scottish landscape and are, conveniently, often more willing to oblige for photos than more skittish wildlife species. Of course, farmers do not keep these animals around to be cute. Highland cattle, Luing cattle (page 201) and Aberdeen Angus, all bred predominantly for beef, and blackface sheep, recognisable by their curled horns, black faces and legs, are hardy breeds able to withstand ferocious Scottish storms, low temperatures and snow.

Keeping these robust animals allows farmers to make use of difficult land in the hills or along coastlines that would otherwise be impossible to cultivate. The conditions animals are kept in are the epitome of free range and you will often encounter them in dubious positions on the edges of cliffs or occasionally, unfortunately, as a woolly mess below.

Buying local beef and lamb supports more traditional crofting and farming methods, which have a much lower impact on the environment than industrial-scale operations elsewhere: animals are predominantly grass fed and buying local saves on emissions produced in transport and helps preserve a valued way of life by providing important jobs for people in the community.

Of course, there are other ethical arguments against eating any meat at all, but this has to be some of the most guilt-free beef and lamb on the planet.

of whisky. The square **Lorne sausage**, usually made from beef, can be tried on the CalMac ferry, if not before.

Local **seafood** and **venison** are some of the islands' most luxurious abundances. You can also find free-range eggs, homemade jams or chutneys and other fresh produce sold from people's gateways and other unexpected places. Mull is particularly rich in honesty box shops, despite being one of the bigger and more frequently visited islands, and the excellent Mull and Iona Food Trail (w mullandionafood.co.uk) helps visitors locate these hidden gems, as well as great restaurants where you'll find local produce on the menu.

EATING OUT Thirty years ago you'd have been lucky to find a fish and chip shop on most Scottish islands, but the Inner Hebrides are starting to gain international recognition for their quality ingredients and handful of exceptional restaurants.

Loch Bay (page 76), on Skye's Waternish Peninsula, currently holds the Inner Hebrides' only **Michelin star**, but a further three restaurants are listed in the Michelin guide, all on Skye: The Three Chimneys (page 76) and Edinbane Inn (page 76) in the northwest; and Scorrybreac (page 62) in Portree. Of course, the Michelin Guide is not the be-all and end-all of fine dining, and many of the smaller islands also have excellent places to eat, with the wild northwest of Mull deserving a special mention. There are also many relaxed mid-range restaurants and cosy pubs serving good food along the lines of hearty venison pies, local seafood and Aberdeen Angus steaks.

The variety of **vegetarian and vegan food** available on the islands is dramatically increasing every season. Many places are also beginning to offer gluten-free options and are usually happy to work around allergies wherever possible; in these cases it is usually a good idea to phone and ask in advance.

Fish and chip shops and vans can still be found in some of the larger townships, often serving Scottish specialities such as battered haggis or black pudding, and sometimes their vegetarian alternatives. Thankfully the fabled battered Mars bar does not often appear on the menu.

Cafés across the islands serve increasingly good coffee, with a couple of artisan coffee shops dotted across the region. More homely establishments also sell inexpensive freshly baked cakes and sometimes light lunches such as soup or sandwiches. Homemade pastries and pies, usually made with plenty of butter, are generally good value and delicious where available.

For an explanation of the eating out price codes used in this guide, see page viii.

DRINKS Many people travel to Scotland especially because of their love of whisky, and if you appreciate a peaty dram then there is no more rewarding destination than Islay, which currently has ten working distilleries (page 213) and plentiful evidence of others starting up soon. Many of the distilleries run tours, which allow you to see the inner workings of the process and try a few 'samples' along the way.

Jura, Skye, Raasay, Mull and Tiree also all have their own whisky distilleries, so a grand tour of the Inner Hebrides or several shorter trips, with the aim of visiting them all, would be an interesting plan for enthusiasts.

Newer on the scene are artisan gins, craft ales and even rum; while The Isle of Eigg Brewery claims to be Scotland's first co-operative brewery. You can try all of these, as well as whiskies, in local pubs and restaurants. In the 1970s, an Englishman visiting an island pub would have had difficulty ordering his normal pint of bitter and may have had to refer to it as 'a pint o' heavy', or maybe a 'half and a half pint' to be understood. These days drinks at the bar are international, but it is always worth asking the bartender if they serve anything local and they might even give you a little backstory about where it is made.

PUBLIC HOLIDAYS AND FESTIVALS

While winters are quiet apart from Christmas and Hogmanay, the summer is filled with sporting events like the Highland Games, agricultural shows and music or cultural festivals. These range from very small-scale individual village traditions to those that are internationally renowned.

PUBLIC HOLIDAYS

1 January	New Year's Day
2 January	New Year Holiday
Friday before Easter Sunday	Good Friday
First Monday in May	May Day
Last Monday in May	Spring Holiday
First Monday in August	Summer Holiday
30 November	St Andrew's Day
25 December	Christmas Day
26 December	Boxing Day

FESTIVALS AND EVENTS Where applicable, each island chapter has its own events section, where you can find details of annually held festivals, celebrations and other local traditions.

Fèis Simply meaning 'festival', fèis events are lively celebrations of Gaelic culture originating in Ancient Ireland. Including Highland dancing in traditional dress, music (such as piping, fiddles, flute playing, tin whistles and Gaelic singing), sports, theatre and other performances, these festivities are held in different parts of Scotland on different dates. The following are particularly well-established annual fèis events in the Inner Hebrides, which welcome visitors:

May   Islay's Fèis Ìle (page 217) centres largely around the whisky distilleries and is an extremely popular event with accommodation booked up to a year in advance.

July   Fèis Eige (Eigg; page 105); Fèis Thiriodh (Tiree; page 139); and Fèis an Eilein (Sleat, Skye, page 59; ten days of events).

Highland Games
A long-held tradition, surviving from clan times or even earlier, spectators are welcome to cheer participants in 'heavy events', including hammer throwing, tossing the caber, and the shot. There are also often 'light events', such as running, cycling and tug of war. The festive atmosphere is kept alive with Highland dancing and music in the form of pipe bands and other performances with traditional instruments.

The biggest event of this type in the region is the Isle of Skye Highland Games in Portree (page 59), held in August; another is held in Tobermory on Mull in July (page 155), while in the same month the Small Isles Games is hosted by a different island each year (page 105).

Agricultural shows
These annual events give farmers the opportunity to present their finest sheep and cows, including majestic Highland breeds of course. There may also be competitions in horseriding and dog showing, as well as baked goods, vegetables, flowers and crafts. They are family events, which are likely to have some children's entertainment, such as a bouncy castle or games.

The following have been running for some years and welcome visitors: in July, Lismore Agricultural Show (page 187) and Tiree Agricultural Show (page 139); and in August, Bunessan Show in Mull (page 155) and Islay Show (page 217).

Christmas and Easter
These Christian celebrations are usually celebrated at home with family or in church. If you are staying on the islands at either time and would like to join the celebrations, check what services are being held in the local church. There might also be events for children such as Easter egg hunts.

Hogmanay
This celebration of the new year is held on 31 December and possibly derives from a Norse winter solstice, and also incorporates parts of the Gaelic celebration of Samhain. The turn of midnight is referred to as 'the bells' and there are a great many localised traditions, but the practice of first-footing, starting immediately after midnight, is common; the first person to cross the threshold in the new year brings symbolic gifts and luck to the household. You're more likely to come across this tradition by accident, though Hogmanay celebrations are held in many local pubs, hotels and restaurants, as well as outside in the form of fireworks and other festivities. Have a look on local noticeboards to see if any events are taking place while you're there.

SHOPPING

With the exception of the Co-op, which has grocery stores on all of the bigger islands, the Inner Hebrides are a stronghold of independent shops. You will not find anything resembling a shopping mall, there are no national chain clothing shops and many places still close for lunch. All of this is not to say that there is nothing to buy – far from it.

ARTS AND CRAFTS Anything handmade from local wool is likely to be high quality, as well as supporting a struggling, traditional industry. Knitted jumpers, warm hats and gloves are obvious favourites, but you can also buy hand-loom woven scarves and throws, and even sheep skins.

You might be more surprised to find the elegant work of silversmiths and, in some parts of the Inner Hebrides, particularly on Skye, it feels like there is a tiny art gallery on every corner; discovering local artists and craftspeople is one of the best rainy-day pastimes you can find.

More modestly, a host of independent craft shops sell unique gifts or souvenirs, everything from homemade natural toiletries and candles to postcards from local wildlife photographers.

FOOD AND DRINK It was not so long ago that the process of food shopping on the islands involved pointing out cans of peas to a lady standing behind a counter; often only one type of bread was available: a depressing white sliced 'Scottish Loaf' from Mother's Pride. Although there are a few surviving examples from this time, the majority of local grocery stores have now been modernised. Considering that most of the islands have a population size barely large enough to be considered a village elsewhere in the UK, the quality and variety of their stock is quite remarkable and buying groceries in local stores is a great way to support the islands' communities.

You can often buy unpackaged seasonal vegetables and local free-range beef and lamb or venison from the surrounding hills. Freshly caught seafood is also a real highlight.

ARTS AND ENTERTAINMENT

Individual island websites, community noticeboards and local newspapers are a great way to find out what's on. Cèilidhs (community events with organised dancing) are still an integral part of society and are regularly held as celebrations across the region. Many islands also have their own pipe band, which usually perform at larger events. This is a long and proudly held tradition harking back to clan times.

The Screen Machine (w screenmachine.co.uk), a fantastic mobile cinema, visits many of the islands. Mull also has its own theatre (page 157).

Local pubs often offer weekly, monthly or occasional traditional music nights; although the bagpipes are an acquired taste, they rarely feature, and you are more likely to come across the fiddle, tin whistle, accordion or singing.

OUTDOOR ACTIVITIES

With huge swathes of wilderness and seemingly endless miles of rugged coastline, the Inner Hebrides can feel like a giant adventure playground for those with the right expertise and equipment. Visitors who lack experience or can't bring their own kit also have ever-increasing opportunities to try new sports with a guide or to rent out equipment to use independently. You can hire a paddleboard on Colonsay (page 205), hire mountain bikes on Eigg (page 113) or go kayaking with a guide along the coast of Skye (page 91) for example. With miles of sandy coastline, a good swell and strong wind, Tiree is world famous for its watersports (page 142) and has great options for lessons and equipment hire.

For adults and children who love horses, there is nothing quite comparable to the thrill of cantering along the beach or trekking across open moorland. There are opportunities to join a group trek on Mull (page 161), Tiree (page 142) and Skye (page 77).

WALKING AND HIKING Slowly and on foot is arguably the best way to explore the Inner Hebrides. Moving quietly, you will notice wildlife and nothing can make you feel as connected with the landscape as getting a wet foot in a bog. You must be totally independent as nothing is waymarked and in many places there isn't even a path.

Scotland's Land Reform Act of 2003 gives everyone rights of access over land and inland water throughout Scotland, as long as they abide by the Access Code (w outdooraccess-scotland.com). These rights are known as the 'freedom to roam' and trust that people will respect landowners and others as well as the environment itself. In the Inner Hebrides, the majority of restrictions revolve around deer stalking (particularly on Jura, page 241, and Islay, page 219).

The Inner Hebrides have 13 Munros, Scottish mountains with a summit height of more than 3,000ft (914m), 12 of which are in Skye's Black Cuillin (page 82); these

WALKING AROUND LIVESTOCK

Walk or drive almost anywhere in the Inner Hebrides and you are likely to see either sheep or cows. Although they will generally just ignore you, there are a couple of things that are worth being aware of.

Sheep are particularly vulnerable while they are pregnant or with small lambs. This time in the spring, usually April or May, is called 'lambing' and extra care needs to be taken around them. 'Worrying' is a term used for disturbing sheep, making them get up or attempt to run away. Sadly, this can cause them to lose their lambs or even die. Worrying most commonly happens when sheep are chased by a dog and can actually happen as early as November when the ewes first become pregnant.

Farmers and crofters are understandably tetchy about the issue and generally ask that dog walkers go around fields with pregnant sheep or small lambs in them where possible. If it is impractical to go around the whole field, keep dogs on a short lead and walk as far away from the sheep as you can, giving them at least 15yds of space. If there is somebody available to ask, it is always preferable to do so.

The same advice applies to **cows**, but remember that cows can also be aggressive when they have calves and there are sometimes bulls roaming free. At any time of year and regardless of whether you have a dog or not, it is always best to keep your distance so as not to disturb them, but there is no need to be frightened. Always avoid getting between a cow and her calf as this can cause distress; if they begin to approach you, move away calmly as cows are more likely to get excited and chase you if you run.

If you find an animal in distress, maybe stuck in a fence or obviously suffering in some way, inform a local person, who is likely to know the farmer. Sheep occasionally get stuck on their backs, which is a very unnatural position for them and may ultimately result in their death; if you encounter this, the most helpful thing to do is to calmly approach and roll the sheep back over.

are generally considered to be the hardest of the Munros to 'bag', in some cases only accessible to serious mountaineers or rock climbers. In this case even good hikers should consider hiring a guide.

Mull's Ben More (page 164) is the final Munro in the archipelago and very much easier to climb. For serious hill-walkers, the Paps of Jura and the Rùm Cuillin also have rewarding climbs, while rough multi-day coastal walks can be an exciting challenge on Islay. Increasingly popular and taking in some of Skye's most incredible landscapes, the Skye Trail (page 92) is a 79-mile unofficial long-distance route that traverses most of the island.

SURFING The Inner Hebrides are not a popular destination for surfers. Beaches are unguarded and there can be strong rip tides (page 35), but for those who really know what they're doing, there are enough good waves to make taking a board worthwhile. Alone in the Atlantic with beaches facing every direction, Tiree is unsurprisingly the best place to find surf, but a few other spots are worth bearing in mind: Hogh Bay on Coll; Islay's Laggan, Machir and Saligo bays; the north end of Staffin Bay and Brother's Point on Skye; and occasionally Kiloran on Colonsay. Surfline (w surfline.com) and Surf Forecast (w surf-forecast.com) provide surf reports and forecasts.

OPENING HOURS

Although I've included opening times for almost every establishment in this book, it seems almost inevitable that half of them will have changed by the time you visit. Opening times, particularly out of season, can vary depending on staff availability, the current ferry schedule or whether it happened to be busy that morning. Many shops close for lunch, restaurants stop serving dinner early and small art galleries are generally an extension of somebody's home, so it often just depends on whether they had something else to do that day.

If your plans are relying on something in particular, it is always best to phone ahead. On Sundays, many shops still close, and ferries and buses have dramatically reduced hours.

MEDIA AND COMMUNICATIONS

MEDIA Some islands have their own newspapers, which are a great source of information regarding upcoming events, community projects and local businesses; the news section also gives an interesting insight into island life. Where available, these will be sold in community shops and might also be accessible online.

The *Ileach* (w ileach.co.uk) covers Islay and Jura, while the *West Highland Free Press* (w whfp.com) is a community-based, employee-owned newspaper based in Broadford on Skye. On Mull, you can find the monthly *Round and About* magazine (w roundandaboutmull.co.uk), while Tiree also publishes the fortnightly newsletter *An Tirisdeach* (**f**).

Argyll FM (w argyllfm.com; 106.5, 107.1 and 107.7FM) broadcasts to the west coast of Scotland, while BBC Radio Scotland (w bbc.co.uk/radioscotland; 92.5FM) is the national station. Generally, all British TV channels are available. Anyone learning Gaelic should watch BBC Alba (w bbc.co.uk/alba), a TV channel dedicated to the language, or should tune into Radio nan Gàidheal (w bbc.co.uk/radionangaidheal; 103.5FM).

INTERNET Public-use computers are found in some accommodation, community centres and libraries, but Wi-Fi is more widely available. Most places to stay, CalMac ferries and some cafés do have public Wi-Fi, but it can be slow or temperamental.

TELEPHONE Network coverage for mobiles is sporadic, especially in more rural areas. It's therefore always a good idea to check vital travel information before you leave the safety net of Wi-Fi or network coverage. Thankfully a lot of red telephone boxes are still in operation if you need to make an urgent call.

POST Post offices are widespread, but their opening hours can be extremely limited in more remote locations. Once posted, mail does not usually seem to take much longer to arrive than on the mainland. Visitors are always encouraged to post their postcards from rural post offices, where the threat of closure is a constant worry.

CULTURAL ETIQUETTE

Churches, chapels and graveyards are an integral part of the Inner Hebridean landscape and are often of interest for their historical or picturesque value. Although most locals welcome visitors to look around, be mindful that services might be in progress (usually indicated by cars parked outside) and adopt a suitably sombre demeanour when exploring.

TRAVELLING POSITIVELY

Often cold, windy and wet, somewhat lacking in famous 'attractions' and not always particularly easy to get to, the Inner Hebrides attract a certain type of person. If you're dreaming of deserted beaches, dramatic cliffs and rugged landscapes; of somewhere to disconnect or reconnect; or an honest experience among genuine people – you will not be disappointed. Treat the islands as your home, support the businesses you would like to thrive and enjoy the wilderness whatever the weather; you can always adjust your plans. Most importantly, take your time; only by travelling slowly will you discover the Inner Hebrides' true charm.

2

Part Two

THE GUIDE

3

Skye (An t-Eilean Sgitheanach)

With a mountainous interior dominated by the mighty Cuillin Hills, Skye's more romantic Gaelic name, Eilean a' Cheò ('the misty isle') refers to the lingering clouds that shroud its lofty peaks and cling to the valleys. The sea cuts into the land in the form of long, sheltered lochs, creating five enormous peninsulas and around 400 miles of rugged coastline to explore.

The second largest island in Great Britain, Skye's population of around 10,800 is similar to that of the other Inner Hebridean islands combined and, with the added accessibility of a connecting bridge from the mainland, it also receives a significantly higher number of visitors. There is something to tempt most travellers here, from excellent restaurants to the wealth of outdoor activities; the island is also a haven for creatives, and stumbling across tiny galleries in unexpected places is one of its greatest joys.

While Skye is famous for a few 'honeypot' locations – the Old Man of Storr, the Fairy Pools, Dunvegan Castle, Neist Point and the Fairy Glen in particular – it's still possible to find more magical and atmospheric places elsewhere on the island (particularly if you favour solitude over crowds). The Trotternish and Minginish peninsulas have incredible hiking opportunities, some of which will satisfy even serious mountaineers, and there are plenty of other fantastic places to walk across the island.

Despite the crowds in a handful of places, the vast majority of the island remains wild and is home to some of Scotland's most exciting species, including sea and golden eagles, otters and minke whale, not to mention more plentiful seabirds, seals and mountain hares.

HISTORY

As a huge and somewhat disjointed island, Skye's past is tricky to surmise as a whole. At An Corran near Staffin is a Mesolithic hunter-gatherer shell midden that's thought to be over 9,000 years old, making it one of the oldest archaeological discoveries in Scotland. An Corran has been linked to a site at Applecross (on the mainland) by the tools made of baked Staffin mudstone that were found there. A number of other archaeological sites are visible to casual observers, including Neolithic cairns, such as the one at Rubh' an Dunain (page 84), several Iron Age souterrains and a large concentration of strategically placed dùns and brochs.

The Picts are thought to have inhabited Skye during the late Iron Age, but left little more than a few carvings, the easiest of which to find is the symbol stone Clach Ard at Tote (page 77). The island later came under the control of Dál Riata in the 7th century AD, followed by the Norse who obliterated previous place names, but left little further indication of their presence. The 'Viking canal' at Rubh' an

Dunain (page 84) has been radiocarbon dated to the turn of the 12th century, an unsettled period after the decline of Norse control.

From the 13th century onwards, a turbulent time ensued as the clan families raced to assert their claims on the land; the MacLeods and MacDonalds of Sleat soon emerged as the most powerful people on Skye. Unlike other parts of the Hebrides, where the Lords of the Isles (page 15) dominated between the 12th and 15th centuries, the Lordship was only granted Skye in the 15th century and quickly lost it again a few decades later. Subsequently, Clan MacKinnon rose in status, while Clan MacNeacail and the MacInnes were associated with Trotternish and Sleat respectively. Limited written records document this era and it remains swathed in myths and legends; it is clear, however, that Skye's inhabitants would have been caught up in the feuding of the clans.

The MacLeods and MacDonalds were entangled in the Jacobite uprising of 1745 (page 15). While Norman MacLeod originally supported the Jacobite cause, he later turned to work against it for the government. The MacDonalds of Sleat supported the government during the insurrection, but Flora MacDonald is famous for going against them to help Charles Edward Stuart (otherwise known as 'Bonnie Prince Charlie'), leader of the rebellion and hopeful to the throne, escape. The well-known *Skye Boat Song*, written in the 1870s, is about this adventure.

The 1800s saw the collapse of the kelp market, famine and brutal Clearances, with 30,000 people evicted off Skye between 1840 and 1880. The remains of their houses can be seen across the island. In 1882, the Battle of the Braes saw a rare win for the people: Lord MacDonald tried to evict his tenants, but the sheriff's officer sent to carry out the task was met with forceful resistance and made to burn the eviction notice. Some 50 policemen from Glasgow were sent to restore order, only to be met by twice the number of men, women and children armed with whatever they could find. Five men were arrested, some injured and some fined, but public sentiment was on their side and ultimately their bravery led to the Napier Commission inquiry and the Crofters' Act of 1886 that secured crofters' rights to tenure and to pass their land on to their children. The Battle of the Braes has been called the last land battle fought on British shores.

These days, although traditional industries such as agriculture, fishing and forestry still exist, the mainstay of Skye's economy is tourism.

GETTING THERE AND AWAY

BY LAND There are three routes to Skye from the mainland: the Skye Bridge and the ferries from Mallaig and Glenelg. You can walk, cycle or drive over the **Skye Bridge** [map, page 88] from Kyle of Lochalsh on the mainland to Kyleakin on Skye without charge. (The bridge connects to Skye via the small island of Eilean Bàn.)

There are also **bus** routes: Scottish Citylink (page 30) run services between Uig (Skye) and Glasgow (including Glasgow Airport), Fort William and Inverness.

BY FERRY The CalMac ferry (page 30) from **Mallaig** to Armadale takes around 30 minutes (foot passengers/car £3.20/10.65); there are 60 crossings weekly in summer and 19 weekly in winter, with fewer services on weekends. CalMac also run ferries from Sconser to Raasay (page 96), and between Uig and the Outer Hebrides (Tarbert on Harris and Lochmaddy on North Uist; foot passengers/car £6.85/33.85). Both Outer Hebrides routes take around 1 hour 45 minutes and sail between five and 12 times weekly, depending on the time of year. Book in advance for all routes if you're travelling with a vehicle.

SKYE

The last manually operated turntable ferry in the world, the *Glenachulish*, sails across beautiful Kyle Rhea from **Glenelg** (↖ 01599 522700; w skyeferry.co.uk; ⊕ Apr–mid-Oct regularly 10.00–18.00/19.00 daily; foot passengers/car £3/18).

MOORINGS There are visitor moorings at Kyle Harbour and Portree (w highland. gov.uk/info/1523/transport_and_streets/102/harbours), and at Loch Dunvegan (w lochdunveganmoorings.com).

GETTING AROUND

BY CAR Don't underestimate driving times or the strain of negotiating single-track roads. Whatever your vehicle, you must be competent at reversing it around corners. Many of Skye's minor roads are unsuitable for large campervans, with small passing places, steep undulations or pot-holes.

Car hire is available from Drive Skye (page 89) in Armadale, or Skye Car Hire (↖ 01599 534323; w skyecarhire.co.uk), who are based in Kyle of Lochalsh, but offer drop-off and collection across Skye.

BY TAXI
Armadale Taxis Armadale; m 07398 059048; w armadaletaxisskye.co.uk
BW's Taxi Portree; ↖ 01478 612865; w skye-taxi-tours.co.uk

Gus's Taxis Portree; ↖ 01478 613000; w skye-taxis.co.uk; ♿. Also offers bike transfer & luggage transfer.
Portree Taxi Services Skeabost; ↖ 01478 612444; w portreetaxis.co.uk

BY BUS The following operators run services on Skye. Check w traveline.info for listings of all stops, current timetables and fares. Some of these buses run less often than once a day.

A MacDonald (↖ 01478 611160; cash only)
608: Portree–Fiskavaig
Citylink (↖ 01413 524444; w citylink.co.uk)
915/916: Uig–Kensaleyre–Portree–Broadford–Kyleakin
917: Portree–Broadford–Kyleakin
Stagecoach (↖ 03452 418000; w stagecoachbus.com)
52: Portree–Broadford–Armadale

55: Glasnakillie–Elgol–Broadford–Kyle of Lochalsh
56/56X: Portree–Edinbane–Dunvegan–Glendale (Duirinish)
57A: Portree–'North End Circular' anticlockwise around Trotternish
57C: Portree–'North End Circular' clockwise around Trotternish
58: Portree Town Service
150: Broadford–Kyle of Lochalsh

BY BIKE Cycling is a great way to soak up Skye's scenery, though be aware that some of the roads are much busier than in other parts of the Inner Hebrides and cars drive particularly fast down the A87. Good options include Sleat, Waternish, the Braes and the western parts of Minginish.

Bike hire
Bikes on the Brae [map, page 61] Quay Brae, Portree IV51 9DB; w bikesonthebrae.com; bikes/ e-bikes; £45/70 a day
Skye EBikes [map, page 66] 16 Bornesketaig IV51 9YS; m 07460 633507; w skye-ebikes.com; e-bikes £60/day

Skye MTB Adventures [map, page 88] Church Rd, Kyle of Lochalsh IV40 8DD; ↖ 01599 534731; w skyemtbadventures.co.uk; hardtail mountain bikes £120/week. Car racks & drop-off/pick-up also available.

FESTIVALS AND EVENTS

MARCH

Dunvegan 5km/10km
e racemanagement@skye-events.
co.uk; f DunveganCastle10k.
Running races starting at
Dunvegan Castle.

MAY

Skye Live The Lump, Portree;
w skyelive.co.uk. Music festival
with a varied line-up including
traditional Scottish acts & global
electronic musicians.

JUNE

Isle of Skye Half Marathon Portree;
w skyehalfmarathon.com

JULY

Fèis an Eilein/The Skye Festival
w seall.co.uk. 10 days of music,
performances & events across Sleat.

AUGUST

Isle of Skye Highland Games The
Lump, Portree; w skye-highland-
games.co.uk. Held near the beginning
of Aug, the Highland Games are
the most iconic event on Skye. The
event has taken place every year
since 1877, with the only exceptions
being during the 2 world wars & the
Covid pandemic.

NOVEMBER

Festival of the Small Halls w seall.
co.uk. A celebration of traditional island
life & Scottish musicians spread across
the village halls of Skye & Raasay.

CHRISTMAS AND
HOGMANAY Look out for
possible fireworks & events hosted
by Broadford & Strath Community
Company (w broadfordandstrath.org).

TOURIST INFORMATION AND TOUR OPERATORS

Tourist information is available from Portree iCentre [map, page 61] (Bayfield Hse,
Bayfield Rd IV51 9EL; ☎ 01478 612992; ⊕ 09.30–17.00 Mon–Sat). Skye is a large
island with lots to see and do so, if you are looking to tick off most of the major
sights in a short space of time, booking a tour might be a more relaxing option than
driving. There's also a wide range of options for outdoor activities. Good places
for **boat trips** include Elgol (page 85), Uig (page 69) and Portree (page 63). The
following additional operators are all based on Skye:

MINIBUS AND PRIVATE TOURS

Isle of Skye Wildlife Tours Portree IV51 9LP;
m 07972 260249; w skyewildlife.com. Minibus
tours starting in Portree with the aim of spotting
otters & eagles. Guide Andy is a local expert with
many years' experience.

Skye History & Heritage Day Tours ☎ 01478
611915; w skyehistoryandheritagetours.com. A
choice of trips visiting both famous & lesser-known
historical sites, plus wild-swimming days. Max
4 passengers.

Skye Jeep Tours m 07976 238862;
w skyejeeptours.com. Vintage convertible
jeep tours for up to 3 passengers with
flexible itineraries.

Skye Luxury Tours ☎ 01599 537100;
w skyeluxury.co.uk. Individually designed private
tours in a Jaguar XJ, Range Rover Vogue or luxury
Mercedes people carrier.

Skye Scenic Tours ☎ 01470 552771;
w skyescenictours.com. Starting in Portree,
these minibus day tours visit some of Skye's
best-known sights.

Skyefari m 07871 463755; w skyefari.com. Day
or nighttime 4x4 minibus tours to off-the-beaten-
track locations, with the aim of seeing wildlife.

OTHER OUTDOOR GUIDED ACTIVITIES

Bikes on the Brae (see opposite). Bespoke
bike tours.

Skye Adventure m 07810 660735;
w skyeadventure.com. A wide range
of guided outdoor activities including
climbing, hiking, canyoning & coasteering.
Options available for families.

Skye Guides Skye Basecamp, Lime Park,
Broadford IV49 9AN; m 07769 221500;
w skyeguides.co.uk. Mountain guides for the
Black Cuillin Ridge, plus abseiling, ice climbing,
scrambling, rock climbing & alpine training
courses. Mike, originally from Carlisle, has
many years of experience & is recommended by
local hikers.

Skye MTB Adventures (page 58).
Based in Kyle of Lochalsh; offers guided

mountain bike hire £90/160 half-day/day.
Flexible itineraries.

South Skye Sea Kayak Sleat (page 91)

**WILDLIFE
PHOTOGRAPHY WORKSHOPS**
✳ **Golden Eagle Photography
Workshops** w jamesroddie.com/golden-eagle-
guiding-scotland; ⏲ Jan–May. James Roddie is a
multi-award-winning professional photographer.
His adaptable 1- or 2-day workshops include
a short hill-walk to a remote location popular
with golden eagles, plus advice on photographic
technique, & produce spectacular results. Book
well in advance.

PORTREE AND THE BRAES

Skye's small but bustling capital is clustered around a pretty harbour, at the mouth
of three rivers. Part of the town looks out towards Ben Tianavaig with other houses
hidden behind a small, rounded peninsula called the Lump.

Southeast of Portree, the Braes Peninsula is rural and astonishingly undisturbed
by tourism despite its proximity to the capital. The gentle coastline looks over the
Narrows of Raasay to Clachan and Inverarish.

Although everything seems to be severely up- or downhill, Portree is small
enough to explore on **foot**. While Portree is well served by **buses** (page 58), the
Braes, around 6 miles further southeast, doesn't have good public transport access,
so you'll need your own wheels.

 WHERE TO STAY *Map, opposite, unless otherwise stated*
Although Portree has the widest range of places to stay of anywhere in the Inner
Hebrides, it is not cheap and even dorm beds fall just above the budget category.
Booking in advance is essential in high season. For peaceful self-catering options in
the Braes, see w isleofskye.com/accommodation/self-catering/portree/braes.

Cuillin Hills (39 rooms) Scorrybreac Rd IV51 9QU;
📞 01478 612003; w cuillinhills-hotel-skye.co.uk;
♿. Grand 18th-century building, much extended
& modernised, set in large grounds on the
northern edge of Portree (& thus slightly separate
from the town). It's worth paying extra for a sea
view. **£££££**

The Marmalade Hotel (34 rooms) Home Farm
Rd IV51 9LX; 📞 01478 611711; w perlehotels.
com/marmalade; ♿. Boutique-style hotel in an
attractive 19th-century Georgian house with a
modern extension. Stylish interior incorporates
some original features. Smaller rooms than Cuillin
Hills. **£££££**

Canowindra Bed & Breakfast [56 D4]
(4 rooms) Penifiler IV51 9LG; 📞 01478 613640;

w canowindraskye.co.uk; ⏲ Mar–mid-Oct.
A luxurious B&B with views of the Cuillin. In a
peaceful location, 6mins' drive south from Portree
towards the Braes. **££££**

Viewfield House (13 rooms) 9 Viewfield
Rd IV51 9EU; 📞 01478 612217;
w viewfieldhouse.com; ⏲ Apr–mid-Oct.
A 10min walk south from the centre of
Portree, this old mansion is tastefully
traditional: a real old country house scattered
with antiques, featuring wooden floors strewn
with Persian rugs, gilt-framed oil paintings
& antlers on the walls. Rooms are big, with
brass beds, fireplaces & freestanding bathtubs,
plus views over woodland gardens or to the
sea. **££££**

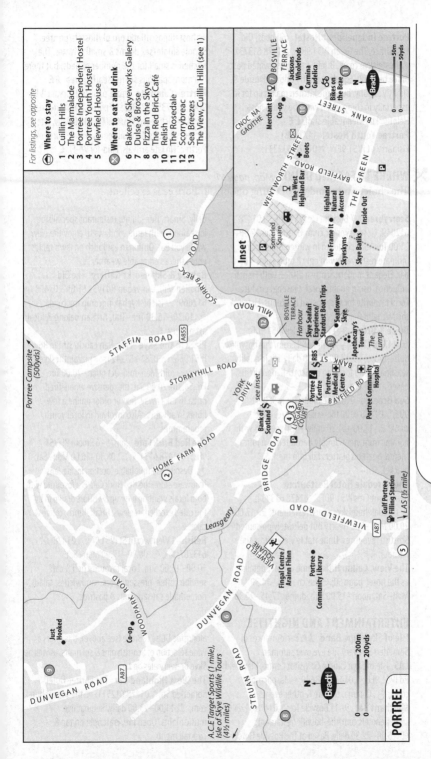

PORTREE

For listings, see opposite

Where to stay
1 Cuillin Hills
2 The Marmalade
3 Portree Independent Hostel
4 Portree Youth Hostel
5 Viewfield House

Where to eat and drink
6 Bakery & Skyeworks Gallery
7 Dulse & Brose
8 Pizza in the Skye
9 The Red Brick Café
10 Relish
11 The Rosedale
12 Scorrybreac
13 Sea Breezes
The View, Cuillin Hills (see 1)

Inset

Somerled Square

We Frame It
Skyeskyns
Skye Batiks

WENTWORTH STREET
The West Highland Bar
Highland Natural Accents
Inside Out

BAYFIELD ROAD
Boots

THE GREEN

CNOC NA GAOITHE
Merchant Bar
Jacksons Wholefoods
Co-op
Carmina Gadelica
Bikes on the Brae

BOSVILLE TERRACE
BANK STREET

Portree Campsite (500yds)

STAFFIN ROAD
A855

SCORRYBREAC ROAD

MILL ROAD

STORMYHILL ROAD

YORK DRIVE

HOME FARM ROAD

BRIDGE ROAD

Leasgeary

WOODPARK ROAD

DUNVEGAN ROAD
A87

Just Hooked
Co-op

A.C.E Target Sports (1 mile), Isle of Skye Wildlife Tours (4½ miles)

STRUAN ROAD

DUNVEGAN ROAD

VIEWFIELD ROAD
A87

Gulf Portree Filling Station
LAS (½ mile)

Fingal Centre / Aralnn Fhinn
Portree Community Library

VIEWFIELD SQUARE

BOSVILLE TERRACE
Harbour
Skye Seafari Experience/
Stardust Boat Trips
Seaflower Skye

Apothecary's Tower
The Lump

Bank of Scotland
LISGARRY COURT

see inset

RBS
BANK ST
Portree iCentre
Portree Medical Centre

BAYFIELD RD

Portree Community Hospital

61

Portree Independent Hostel (60 beds) Old Post Office, The Green IV51 9BT; 01478 613737; w hostelskye.co.uk. Bright-yellow renovated post office building. Equally brightly coloured inside & slightly shabby, but large kitchen makes up for it, especially in comparison with the youth hostel. Helpful, knowledgeable staff. **££**

Portree Youth Hostel (47 beds) Lisigarry Ct IV51 9EW; 01478 612231; w hostellingscotland.org.uk/hostels/portree. Simple single-sex dorms & small privates. The kitchen is small for the number of beds, but there is a more spacious shared seating area. **££**

Portree Campsite [map, page 66] Torvaig IV51 9HU; m 07359 328368; w portreecampsite.co.uk; ⊕ Mar–Oct; reception: 08.00–18.00 daily. Site for tents, c/vans & motorhomes, 1 mile north of Portree. No late arrivals. Paid-for Wi-Fi. **£**

✗ WHERE TO EAT AND DRINK *Map, page 61*

The choice and standard of eating options in Portree is excellent.

Scorrybreac 7 Bosville Tce IV51 9DG; 01478 612069; w scorrybreac.com; ⊕ summer 17.00–21.00 Tue–Sun, reduced in winter. Unimposing, intimate restaurant with only 8 tables plus 4 in bar. Elegant modern Scottish dishes, with French influence, using quality local, seasonal produce. Local favourite for very special occasions. Listed in the Michelin Guide. **£££**

Dulse & Brose 9–11 Bosville Tce IV51 9DG; 01478 612846; w perlehotels.com/the-bosville/dulse-brose; ⊕ 17.00–20.30 daily. High-quality seasonal menu focusing on Scottish ingredients, based at The Bosville Hotel. **££–£££**

Sea Breezes 2 Marine Bldgs, Quay St IV51 9DE; 01478 612016; w sea-breezes-skye. co.uk; ⊕ 17.00–21.30 daily. Fresh seafood with harbourfront view. Simply decorated in nautical theme. Seafood platters fall into the £££ bracket. **££–£££**

The Rosedale Hotel Restaurant Beaumont Cres IV51 9DF; 01478 613131; w rosedalehotelskye.co.uk/restaurant; ⊕ 17.00–20.00 Mon–Sat. Hearty but delicately presented Scottish favourites. Unbeatable view across the harbour. **££**

The View, Cuillin Hills Same contact details as the hotel, page 60; ⊕ lunch noon–14.30 Mon–Sat, noon–15.00 Sun, dinner 17.45–20.30 daily. Smart, fine-dining restaurant specialising in seafood, with large windows to enjoy the view while you eat. Option to eat lunch on lawn tables when there's agreeable weather. **££**

Bakery & Skyeworks Gallery The Old Woollen Mill, Dunvegan Rd IV51 9HG; 01478 612669; w isleofskyebakingcompany.co.uk; ⊕ 10.30–15.30 Tue–Thu. Artisan baking & local art gallery. **£**

Pizza in the Skye Pairc Nan Laoch/Struan Rd IV51 9EG; m 07814 872421; w pizzaintheskye. com; ⊕ mid-Mar–mid-Oct noon–20.00 Tue–Fri, 14.30–20.00 Sat. Inexpensive wood-fired pizza to take away. Text or order online a few hours in advance. Also involved in local youth programmes. **£**

The Red Brick Café Jans, 5–6 Broom Pl IV51 9HL; 01478 613417; ⊕ 08.30–16.00 Mon–Sat; &. Despite its improbable location inside Jans hardware store, the Red Brick Café is a favourite with both locals wanting a fry up & visitors drawn in by the café's excellent reviews. B/fast, lunch, coffee & cake. **£**

Relish 1 Wentworth St IV51 9EJ; 01478 613787; f; ⊕ 08.30–17.00 Mon–Sat, 10.00–16.00 Sun. Local favourite deli & café serving coffee, pressed juices, sandwiches, salads, homemade sausage rolls & pastries. **£**

ENTERTAINMENT AND NIGHTLIFE

Isle of Skye Pipe Band f. Performances in Somerled Sq every Tue eve over summer.

LAS Isle of Skye Candle Co Visitor Centre, Viewfield Rd IV51 9EU; 01478 613649; w lasportrigh. co.uk; &. Cinema, theatre & other events.

Merchant Bar 9–11 Bosville Tce; 01478 612846; w perlehotels.com/the-bosville/restaurant; ⊕ 16.00–22.30 daily. Based at The Bosville Hotel alongside Dulse & Brose (see above), this offers a wide selection of Scottish gins & sgl malts, as well as Skye Brewery ales on tap.

The West Highland Bar The Portree Hotel, Somerled Sq; 01478 612511; w theportreehotel. com; ⊕ 11.00–23.00 daily. Regular live music nights. Open fire, craft beer on tap & cocktail menu.

SHOPPING
Books, arts and crafts
Carmina Gadelica Bank St IV51 9DA; 01478 612585; w skyebooks.co.uk; ⊕ 09.00–17.30 Mon–Sat. An independent bookshop with a good range of local interest books & maps.
Highland Natural Accents The Green IV51 9BT; 01478 611694; w highlandnaturalaccents.com; ⊕ 09.30–17.30 Tue–Sat. High-end textiles.
Skye Batiks The Green IV51 9BY; 01478 613331; w skyebatiks.com; ⊕ 09.30–17.00 Mon–Sat. Interesting Sri Lankan/Scottish-fusion colourful batiks & woven cotton including clothing & smocks, accessories & homewares.
Skyeskyns The Green IV51 9BT; w skyeskyns. co.uk/our-portree-shop; ⊕ check online. The Portree outlet of Waternish-based Skyeskyns (page 78) who make luxury sheepskins & leather, wool & sheepskin homeware & clothing. You can also buy artisan coffee here to drink outside on the decking with a great view.
We Frame It Kings Hse, The Green IV51 9BS; 01478 613788; w we-frame-it.co.uk; ⊕ 10.00–18.00 daily. Work from Scottish/Skye artists & gifts.

Food and drink
Co-ops Bank St IV51 9DA (01478 612855; ⊕ 07.00–23.00 daily;); Woodpark Rd IV51 9HQ (01478 612483; ⊕ 07.00–22.00 daily;). The Woodpark Rd branch is a large supermarket in an industrial estate.
Jacksons Wholefoods Bank St IV51 9EJ; 01478 613326; f; w highlandwholefoods. co.uk; ⊕ 09.00–17.00 Mon–Sat; . An actual co-operative selling health foods, wholefoods & other uncommon groceries. Entrance & bottom floor accessible to people in wheelchairs, but staff can assist with goods upstairs.
Just Hooked Ltd 6 Leasgeary Road; 01478 612288; f; ⊕ 09.00–15.00 Mon–Fri. Fresh fish & seafood.

Outdoor gear
Inside Out The Green IV51 9BY; 01478 611663; w inside-out-skye.com; ⊕ 09.00–18.00 Mon–Sat. Hiking & outdoor shop.

SPORTS AND ACTIVITIES
A.C.E Target Sports Struan Rd (B885) IV51 9EG; 01478 612081; w ace-skye.com. Archery, clay shooting, axe throwing & air rifles. Uses renewable energy. Access along single-track road; may be impassable in winter.
Fingal Centre/Arainn Fhinn Viewfield Rd IV51 9ET; 01478 614819; w highlifehighland.com/fingal-centre. Swimming pool, gym, steam room & sauna. Check online for times.
Seaflower Skye Portree Harbour, Quay St IV51 9DE; m 07342 622727; w seaflowerskye. com. Luxury day-trip sea tours around Skye, Raasay & Rona, departing from Portree. Local seafood lunches.
Skye Seafari Experience 3 Douglas Row, Portree Harbour IV51 9DD; m 07535 312617; w skyeseafariexperience.co.uk. RIB (rigid inflatable boat) trips to Kilt Rock, Raasay & wildlife watching.
Stardust Boat Trips 1 Douglas Row, Portree Harbour IV51 9DD; m 07798 743858; w skyeboat-trips.co.uk. Operating 4 boats from Portree Harbour, this company focuses on wildlife watching around the spectacular scenery of coastal east Trotternish & Raasay.

OTHER PRACTICALITIES
Banks Bank of Scotland (Somerled Sq IV51 9EH; 03457 213141; ⊕ 10.00–16.00 Tue–Thu); RBS (Bank St IV51 9BX; 03457 242424; ⊕ 09.30–16.30 Mon–Tue & Thu–Fri, 10.00–16.30 Wed)
Fuel Gulf Portree Filling Station, Viewfield Rd IV51 9EU; ⊕ fuel pumps 24hrs
Health Portree Community Hospital (Fancyhill, off Bank St IV51 9BZ; 01478 613200); Portree Medical Centre (Fancyhill IV51 9BZ; 01478 612013; w portreemedical.scot.nhs.uk; ⊕ 08.00–18.00 by appointment only); Boots (5 Wentworth St IV51 9EJ; 01478 612100; ⊕ 09.00–17.30 Mon–Sat)
Laundry Portree Independent Hostel (see opposite; coin operated); Skye Laundry (m 07703 645707; w skyelaundry.co.uk; collection & delivery)
Library Portree Community Library, Viewfield Rd IV51 9ET; 01478 614823; w highlifehighland. com/libraries/portree-library; ⊕ 09.10–17.00 Mon–Fri, 10.00–16.00 Sat
Post office 4 Wentworth St IV51 9EJ; ⊕ 09.00–17.00 Thu–Fri

WHAT TO SEE AND DO A stroll along the harbour presents the prettiest views of Portree. If you have been travelling around the islands for some time, the main things to do here are enjoy eating out, stock up on supplies and visit the tourist information centre to help plan your next adventures.

The Braes Rightfully most famous for the Battle of the Braes (page 55), the Braes Peninsula is a peaceful backwater, great for cyclists, wildlife watching and walks.

Camas a' Mhòr Bheòil and An Àird [57 E5] The long curve of **Camas a' Mhòr Bheòil** is one of Skye's best beaches; it has some stone and rocks, but the far end is sandy. Possibly more special than the beach itself is the view across the water to the slopes and points of Ben Tianavaig further north. For those seeking relaxation, the beach might be enough; redshank feed along the northeast shoreline and sheep graze quietly on the grass.

Those with a little more energy could explore the whale-tail-shaped **An Àird Peninsula** (beyond the northwestern end of the beach). At the northern point of the peninsula is Dunan an Aisilidh, a ruinous, galleried dùn that has some similar features to a broch and probably dates from the Iron Age. From this strategic point, you have a spectacular view across the Narrows of Raasay, the stretch of water between An Àird and Inverarish, and infinitely further north through the channel. Look out for the seals that live on Raasay's west coast and maybe even porpoises or dolphins on calm days. In the southeast part of the whale tail are a small series of wonderful caves, bridges, archways and sea stacks. Be very careful all the way along this coastline as drops can appear suddenly. It is a very special place and you are more than likely to have it to yourself.

A grassy path down to Camas a' Mhòr Bheòil and An Àird starts just past the post box in the township of Gedintailor (✪ 57°20'17"N 6°06'50'W). To reach this spot, travel south from Camastianavaig on the B883 until you reach a left turn for an even more minor road marked towards 'Gedintailor, Balmeanach, Peinachorrain'. If you have a car, it's best to find somewhere to park near this turning and walk the remaining 500yds as there is no parking near the start of the path.

THE LUMP

'The Lump' [map, page 61] is a small peninsula south of Portree Harbour, also known as the Meall, Sròn a' Mhill and the Sugar Lump. The coast path, which starts on the left-hand side of Portree Free Church of Scotland, gives ever-changing panoramic views. From the north of the Lump you can look down over Portree Harbour, with an attractive row of houses up on the hill and fishing boats anchored below. A hum of chugging boat engines, seagulls and squawking rooks accompanies you as you follow the coast path until, rounding a corner, everything goes quiet and the bustle of the town is left behind; there are tall, twisted trees, some monkey puzzles and a wonderful view out to Ben Tianavaig.

In the centre of the Lump is a green lawn, which makes a pleasant place for a picnic, and the small Apothecary's Tower. Built in 1829, the tower was originally used to inform passing ships that medical assistance was available, in addition to serving as a dispensary. Climbing to the top gives a splendid view over Portree and, on a clear day, you can just see the Old Man of Storr.

Dominated by the sheer cliffs of Trotternish Ridge, this peninsula has some of Skye's most iconic landscapes – views of the Quiraing and the Old Man of Storr rock formations are used to advertise Scotland around the world – but with attractive townships, endless hiking opportunities, towering cliffs, fossilised dinosaur footprints and hidden archaeology, the area has plenty to detain you beyond its best-known sights. Uig, on the west coast, is the busiest settlement, despite only having a few hundred residents, and has ferry links to the Outer Hebrides.

Compared with other rural areas of Skye, Trotternish is relatively well served with **buses**, but you should still check timetables closely to avoid getting stuck. The peninsula is served by Citylink and Stagecoach services (page 58).

With such dramatic scenery, it's a shame to rush through Trotternish. From strenuous hikes to easy footpaths, there are infinite **walking** opportunities and, for many people, exploring on foot is the most rewarding way to enjoy the landscape. Though the stretch of road between Portree and the Old Man of Storr can be busy, **cyclists** who do not mind the odd hill will love the northern half of Trotternish.

WHERE TO STAY While there are a few B&Bs along Trotternish's ring road, most accommodation is found in Uig which, for a small port town, has a great range of options. With so much to explore, Trotternish is a perfect place to book a self-catering cottage (w walkhighlands.co.uk/skye/cottages_trotternish.shtml).

The Ferry Inn [map, page 68] (3 rooms) Uig IV51 9XP; 01470 542300; w theferryinnskye.com. Stylish, luxury accommodation above a restaurant & bar in a 19th-century building. 2 'bay view' rooms & 1 rear-facing with 'woodland view'. Family business. Min 2-night stay. **£££££**

Glenview B&B [map, page 66] (2 rooms, 1 self-catering studio) Culnacnoc IV51 9JH; 01470 562248; w glenviewskye.co.uk. Across the road from Brothers' Point (page 69), professional chef Simon & his wife Kirsty run this characterful B&B. With the sort of shabby-chic décor boutique hotels aim for but often miss, rooms are spacious &, for those in the B&B rooms, there's a wide range of homemade b/fast options including Simon's granola with fruit compote, home-baked bread, or the full Scottish fry-up with eggs from their own hens. Optional, very reasonably priced early morning Hatha yoga offered, & there's a shop selling naturally dyed yarn next door. **££££**

Uig Hotel [map, page 68] (19 rooms) Uig IV51 9YE; 01470 542205; w uig-hotel-skye.com; ⊕ Feb–Dec; Good 3-star hotel, up the hill to the south of town. Comfortable, nicely finished rooms, some with baths. Split between main hotel & lodge, but staff & quality are the same. Lodge rooms are sea-facing, bigger & newer; it's a 30yd walk from the hotel, but parking is directly in front. **££££**

Woodbine B&B [map, page 68] (5 rooms) On the A855, Uig IV51 9XP; 01470 542243; w woodbineskye.co.uk. Friendly B&B in traditional, whitewashed stone croft house. There is a guest lounge with wood burner. Good value at the bottom of this price bracket. **£££**

The Cowshed Boutique Bunkhouse [map, page 66] (34 beds & 8 pods) Near Uig IV51 9YD; m 07917 536820; w skyecowshed.co.uk; . Modern luxury bunkhouse with good facilities & great views across Uig Bay. Bunks have privacy curtains. Pods sleep 3 adults or 2 adults & 2 children & are furnished with bedding, tiny kitchens & en suite. It's a 35min walk or few mins' drive south of Uig ferry port on the main road. **££–££££**

※ **Dun Flodigarry Hostel** [map, page 66] (30 beds & campsite) Flodigarry IV51 9XB; 01470 552212; w flodigarry-hostel.scot; . Family-run since 1992, this is the best sort of old-school hostel. The large building is spectacularly situated on cliffs above the ocean. Very spacious, well-equipped kitchen, & staff have decades of experience; they offer hiking advice & have wall maps marked with walks in the area. Campers can use the kitchen & there's communal seating inside. **£–££**

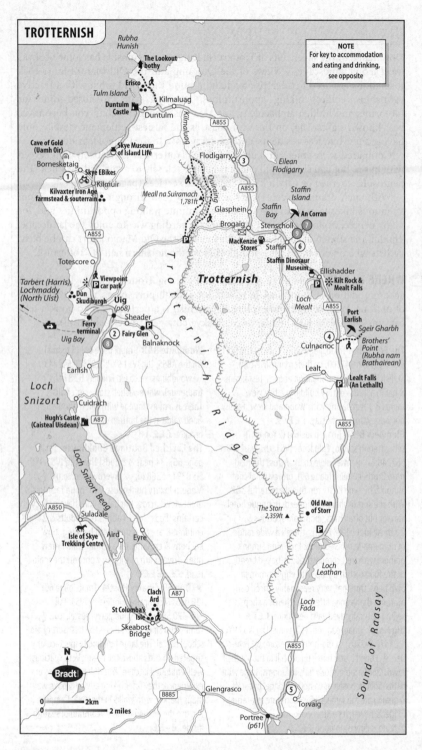

TROTTERNISH

NOTE
For key to accommodation
and eating and drinking,
see opposite

Rubha
Hunish

The Lookout
bothy

Erisco

Tulm Island

Duntulm
Castle

Kilmaluag

Duntulm

A855

Cave of Gold
(Uamh Oir)

Skye Museum
of Island Life

Bornesketaig

Skye EBikes

Kilmuir

Kilvaxter Iron Age
farmstead & souterrain

Flodigarry ③

Eilean
Flodigarry

Meall na Suiramach
1,781ft

Quiraing

Glasphein

Brogaig

Staffin
Island

Staffin
Bay

Stenscholl

An Corran ⑦
⑨
⑥

A855

MacKenzie
Stores

Staffin

Totescore

Trotternish

Staffin Dinosaur
Museum

Ellishadder

Viewpoint
car park

Kilt Rock &
Mealt Falls

Dùn
Skudiburgh

Trotternish

Loch
Mealt

A855

Tarbert (Harris),
Lochmaddy
(North Uist)

Uig
(p68)

Sheader

Fairy Glen

Port
Earlish

Ferry
terminal

② ⑧

Sgeir Gharbh

Brothers'
Point
(Rubha nam
Brathairean)

Uig Bay

Balnaknock

Culnacnoc ④

Earlish

Lealt

Loch
Snizort

Cuidrach

Lealt Falls
(An Lethallt)

Hugh's Castle
(Caisteal Uisdean)

A87

A855

A850

Suladale

Loch Snizort Beag

Aird

Eyre

The Storr
2,359ft

Old Man
of Storr

P

Isle of Skye
Trekking Centre

Loch
Leathan

Clach
Ard

A87

Loch
Fada

St Columba's
Isle

Skeabost
Bridge

A855

Sound of Raasay

Bradt

N

⑤

0   2km
0   2 miles

B885

Glengrasco

Torvaig

Portree
(p61)

TROTTERNISH

For listings, see from page 65, unless otherwise stated

 Where to stay

1 Camus More
2 The Cowshed Boutique Bunkhouse
3 Dun Flodigarry Hostel
4 Glenview B&B
5 Portree Campsite *p62*
6 Staffin Caravan & Camping Site

✕ **Where to eat and drink**

7 Columba 1400 Café
8 The Galley Seafood Café & Takeaway
9 The Hungry Gull

Camus More [map, opposite] Kilmuir IV51 9YS; ☎ 01470 552312; ⊕ May–Sep. Beautiful, peaceful camping with very basic facilities (no shower). **£**

Staffin Caravan & Camping Site [map, opposite] Clachan IV51 9JX; ☎ 01470 562213; w staffincampsite.co.uk; ⊕ Apr–Oct. Modern campsite with electric hook-ups, free showers & shelter for tent campers. **£**

Uig Campsite [map, page 68] Uig IV51 9XU; ☎ 01470 542714; w uig-camping-skye.co.uk. Basic but friendly site for tents & c/vans. Quiet, but next to the ferry. Pet-friendly. **£**

✕ **WHERE TO EAT AND DRINK** As with accommodation, the majority of Trotternish's eating establishments are in Uig. While most of Skye seems to shut down in winter, the presence of the ferry port allows many places in Uig to stay open.

The Ferry Inn [map, page 68] Same contact details as hotel, page 65; ⊕ sittings 18.15, 19.00 & 19.45 Tue–Sat. Elegantly presented tapas-style menu made from local ingredients. Tasteful, modern interior with distressed wood & grey/blue colour scheme. Book in advance online. **£££**

Uig Hotel [map, page 68] Same contact details as hotel, page 65; ⊕ Feb–Dec 07.15–09.45, noon–14.30 & from 17.30 daily; &. Busy restaurant catering for all. A favourite is the venison with dauphinoise potatoes, creamed beetroot, savoy cabbage, pickled brambles & rosemary gravy. Book ahead. **££**

The Galley Seafood Café & Takeaway [map, opposite] Carnbeag, Earlish IV51 9XL; m 07485 133316; ☐; ⊕ noon–20.00 Tue–Sat; &. Fresh seafood, fish & chips, burgers, etc. Good portions

& cheaper than anywhere in Uig for evening meals. **£–££**

Columba 1400 Café [map, opposite] Staffin IV51 9JY; ☎ 01478 611400; w columba1400. com/social-enterprise-cafe; ⊕ 10.00–16.00 Mon–Fri. Modern, bright & spacious café with views across to the Quiraing. Very welcoming, with extensive & affordable menu. Columba 1400 is an award-winning social enterprise & charity, providing leadership training for young people; the café raises funds. Good cause, good food & great view. **£**

The Hungry Gull [map, opposite] Staffin Community Hall IV51 9JS; m 07909 323848; ☐; ⊕ usually Apr–Oct 10.00–16.00 Wed–Sat, but check Facebook. Very popular brunch café by day; sit-down meals or take-aways in the evening, with licensed bar. Great vegetarian haggis. **£**

SHOPPING
Arts and crafts

Uig Pottery [map, page 68] The Pier, Uig IV51 9XX; ☎ 01470 542421; ⊕ May–Sep 09.00–17.30 Mon–Fri, 11.00–16.00 Sat–Sun, Oct–Apr 09.00–17.00 Mon–Fri, 11.00–16.00 Sat. Large shop with working pottery inside.

Food and drink

Isle of Skye Brewing Co (Leann an Eilein) [map, page 68] The Pier, Uig IV51 9XP; ☎ 01470 542477; w skyeale.com; ⊕ 10.00–17.00 Mon–Sat; &. Award-winning craft-ale brewery. Range includes everything from a 7% Cuillin Beast ale to more refreshing IPA, golden ale & lager.

Rankins [map, page 68] Uig IV51 9XP; ☎ 01470 542213; w rankins-skye.co.uk; ⊕ 08.30–18.30 Mon–Sat, 10.00–15.00 Sun; &. Well-stocked, independently owned licensed grocer. ATM.

Staffin Stores Stenscholl, Staffin IV51 9JS; ☎ 01470 562221; ☐; ⊕ 09.00–18.00 Mon–Sat; &. Relatively large & well-stocked community-owned grocery store. Laundry service.

Uig Filling Station & Shop [map, page 68] Ferry port, Uig IV51 9XX; ☎ 01470 542774; ☐; ⊕ 08.00–20.00 Mon–Sat, 09.00–19.00 Sun; hours reduced in winter (check Facebook); &. Quite expensive, but has essentials including alcohol.

For listings, see from page 65

🛏 **Where to stay**

1 The Ferry Inn
2 Uig
3 Uig Campsite
4 Woodbine B&B

❌ **Where to eat and drink**

The Ferry Inn (see 1)
Uig (see 2)

Uig Wood

Rha Falls

Rha

④

N

Bradt

⓪ 0 ——— 200m
0 ——— 200yds

A855

A87

Ⓟ ● Village hall

①

Rankins ●
✉

Uig Wood

Uig Filling Station
& Shop 🛒

Isle of Skye
Brewing Co
(Leann an Eilein) Ⓟ

Ⓟ

③ ● Uig Pottery

● Ferry
ticket office

Pier

Uig Bay

Fairy Glen
(1.3 miles)

A87

Uig Tower
●● ②

Tarbert (Harris),
Lochmaddy (North Uist)

The Cowshed Boutique Bunkhouse (500yds),
The Galley Seafood & Café (1 mile)

SPORTS AND ACTIVITIES

SkyeXplorer Boat Trips w puffinsandwhales. co.uk. Trips around the protected Ascrib Islands to see puffins (May–Jul) leave from Uig Pier, while trips to explore the Trotternish coast, with a chance to see minke whales, dolphins, white-tailed eagles & seals (Aug–Sep), leave from An Corran Beach near Staffin.

Staffin Gym Above Staffin Community Hall IV51 9JS; \ 01470 562221 (Staffin Stores); w tallastafainn.org/gym.html; ⊕ 24hr coded access. Small but well equipped with bikes, rowing machines, treadmills, weights, etc. Community owned. £5/day or £10/month.

OTHER PRACTICALITIES

Bank There's an ATM inside Rankins (page 67)
Fuel [map, page 66] MacKenzie Stores (Stenscholl, Staffin IV51 9JS; \ 01470 562234; ⊕ 09.00–18.00 Mon–Sat, 11.00–14.00 Sun); Uig Filling Station & Shop (page 67)

Post office Brogaig (IV51 9JY; \ 01470 562209; ⊕ 09.00–noon Mon–Sat); Rankins, Uig (page 67; ⊕ 09.00–13.00 Mon–Sat)

WHAT TO SEE AND DO
The southeast coast of the Trotternish Peninsula

The Old Man of Storr and Lealt Falls Travelling north from Portree on the A855, the landscape quickly becomes mountainous and the Storr, the sheer, cliff-edged mountain behind the Old Man of Storr, soon comes into view. Around 4 miles north of Portree, you pass the lovely lochs of Fada and Leathan, before reaching the pay and display car park (£5/day; toilets) for the **Old Man of Storr**. The uphill walk to reach this famous rock pinnacle is just under 3 miles return on a well-maintained path, with an elevation gain of 935ft. Although the route starts (from the car park) on a substantial track, it diminishes into an anarchy of trodden paths, muddy in places and not always particularly clear; sturdy boots and a bottle of water are recommended, along with appropriate clothing for the weather. In high season it is best to arrive early or late to enjoy your visit without the crowds that throng here for most of the day.

As much as I would like to tell you the Storr is over-hyped, it isn't: the 'Old Man' (a somewhat miraculous pointed rock stack) and the surrounding mountain range are incredibly striking. Given just the right amount of mist, clouds shift slightly to reveal different crags, and a dampening silence descends over the area.

Further north is **Lealt Falls** (An Lethallt). A popular stop along the road, there is a large car park here with a wooden platform (♿) in place to give you a great view over the waterfall and canyon. At the bottom of the cliffs, on the shore, are the remains of a 19th-century diatomite works. Skye diatomite is a silica-rich sediment formed by microscopic algae and was of interest for its potential use in the production of dynamite during the 1880s. The iron-roofed construction on the south of the river is a disused salmon fishing station.

Walk: Brothers' Point (Rubha nam Brathairean)

Distance: 2 miles; time: 2 hours; start/end: Culnacnoc; OS Explorer map: 408 Skye – Trotternish & The Storr

Taking in ruined buildings, a rocky shore at Port Earlish and the spectacular headland of Brothers' Point, this is not a particularly strenuous walk, though it would be challenging for someone with a fear of heights. The quiet bay at Port Earlish is worth visiting even if you do not want to complete the whole route.

If you have a car, park it some 150yds north of Glenview B&B (in Culnacnoc), where there is a small car park (⊕ 57°35'05.4"N 006°09'27.7"W). The walk starts opposite the Glenview: pass Brothers' Point Cottages and look out for a wooden sign directing you right, down to the shore. On the left, you will come to Taigh Ruaraidh Dhomhnaill a' Chuirn, the atmospheric ruin of a farmstead at Port Earlish, which has been unoccupied since the late 19th century.

Footprints of sauropods and theropods, older cousins of the T Rex, have been found on the shoreline on the tidal area of Sgeir Gharbh, between Port Earlish and Brothers' Point itself; to get here, turn right when you get down to the shore at Port Earlish and follow the coast. For children, it is a glorious place for rock pooling and there are plenty of indentations that could be dinosaur footprints and might well be, but I must admit that I was not able to positively identify them myself. (Spend some time looking at pictures online first and visit the Dinosaur Museum in Staffin for more information; page 70.) This is a wonderful, rocky bay with inquisitive common seals and a few hazards to be aware of: large waves crashing on the rocks may come up further than you expect and, once you get higher on to the grassy area between the bay and Brothers' Point, there are steep drops down to the rocks below.

Walk around the shore, keeping the sea on your left, until you come to a couple of ruined buildings and can see a way to safely ascend the slope to a broad, grassy platform. From here there is a narrow path beside a steep drop, on the middle ground between the cliffs above and below it. Once you reach the base of the headland, where the twisted form of Brothers' Point stretches out directly in front of you, it is quite obvious that you must follow the small and dubious path, keeping on the left-hand side of the ridge in order to get out to the promontory. This is easier than it looks at the beginning and, once you have climbed up to the highest point, halfway along the peninsula, you will see a wide grassy area leading out to the point itself. From here you can see the Old Man of Storr and Kilt Rock on a clear day. Look out for circular holes, the remains of an obvious quern quarry (✪ 57°35'12.8"N 6°08'16.8"W) in the rocks below around 55yds southeast of the point. Return along the same route.

Northern Trotternish

The northeastern coast At **Kilt Rock and Mealt Falls** is a large car park and a viewing point over the towering cliffs (♿). With dramatic basalt columns, named for their resemblance to the pleats of a kilt, and a narrow waterfall plummeting 196ft down to the sea, this quick stop is a favourite with photographers. Take some time to scan the sea for dolphins, porpoises and other marine mammals.

Nearby is the **Staffin Dinosaur Museum** (Ellishadder; w staffindinosaurmuseum. com; ☉ Apr–Oct 10.00–17.00 daily; adult/child £4/2), a small museum in a traditional cottage with an amazing collection of dinosaur fossils and information. This is also the best place to ask for advice about finding footprints in the area.

Although it is well known that there are dinosaur footprints on **An Corran beach** near Staffin, this fact does not make them any easier to find (roughly ✪ 57°38'13.8"N 6°12'17.4"W). There is an interpretation board at the car park here, but it is worth studying the photo to see what you are looking for, as the map is quite inaccurate. While I was scouring the ground, I was lucky enough to meet a local woman who showed me two ornithopod footprints. To find them, head down the ramp that runs from the car park to the beach; they are about 5yds east (towards the sea) from the lowest boulder on the ramp. The footprints have three toes, each around the same size as a human foot, and are positioned as if the creature was walking towards the sea. They are set into rock, which looks like the fossilised ripples of a sand bed; this rock is covered with green algae, which might make them difficult to distinguish; at times the tide brings up sand, making them impossible to see.

Marginally further north, **Brogaig** and **Glasphein** – two close hamlets with around 50 white houses between them – are nestled at the base of the mighty **Meall na Suiramach** (1,781ft); the eastern slopes of this mountain descend into the landslides known as the **Quiraing**.

Walk: The Quiraing loop

Distance: 4 miles, or 6½ miles with extension; time: 3 hours, or 4 hours with extension; start/end: Viewpoint car park at the summit of the minor road between Staffin and Uig; OS Explorer map: 408 Skye – Trotternish & The Storr

The Quiraing, pronounced 'kirrang', is another of Skye's hotspots, and though the car park (£3/3hrs or £6/6hrs) has recently been extended, it can still be difficult to find a spot. There are more mountain rescue call-outs in this area than in the substantially more dangerous Black Cuillin, so it is not somewhere that should be underestimated. Strong winds are amplified over the plains and up the slopes; the path is a little unclear at times and takes you close to the edge, so check the wind forecast (page 28) first before deciding to set out.

Cross to the north side of the road and take the path, opposite the car park, signposted 'Cuith-Raing'. Follow this surfaced path for about 250yds before taking the smaller, steeper path to your left that heads up Maoladh Mòr. After around 400yds the ascent becomes gentler and the path begins to contour around the hill, with excellent views of Staffin Bay and Staffin Island. Cross over the stile and take the faint path to your right, which begins to climb a grassy slope. Stay on the path closest to the edge; as you get to the top of the hill, small cutaways at the tops of the crags give you amazing views of the spires and rock formations of the Quiraing below. The intermittent path passes by a small cairn on the right; from here it is possible to make a straightforward detour to the trig point at the peak of Meall na Suiramach by turning left.

From the peak, the cliff path winds along the edge for a few hundred yards more before descending with views into the valleys and little lochs; you'll see the imposing rock-walled, flat-topped summit of Leac nan Fionn to the east and the next plateau – Sron Vourlinn – to the northeast. As the boggy path heads downhill and begins to plateau out, you can see small villages near the northernmost point of Skye. On your left are the cliffs of Sgùrr Mòr. Eventually you will reach a stile on the right that crosses a wire fence; climb over the stile and then head down the steep, eroded path to the bottom of the valley. The route then heads south–southeast below the cliffs.

Follow the path as it meanders through the hillocks and rocks at the base of the cliffs on your right; you will come to a cairn and a junction off to your left that you should ignore. Soon you will catch a glimpse of Loch Cleap in the distance. Crossing a stile, you begin to get into the rocky pinnacles that the Quiraing is famous for. Crags begin to appear in the cliffs, which open out to reveal the Needle rock stack up above you. Pass between the cliffs and the Prison, a large rock structure good for rock climbing, listening out for the echo of your footsteps. The path then descends through a boulder field and, keeping right at the junction, starts to climb steadily. Returning to the car park is fairly straightforward from here: just continue along the path, but care should be taken to find sure footing and hand placement in a number of the gulleys, which are sometimes wet, with loose rocks.

The far north The peaceful crofting land in the far north of Trotternish, between Flodigarry and Uig, is a breath of fresh air after the busier roads further south. There are many ruined buildings, some abandoned since the Clearances, as well as rusty barns and current, traditional homes with whitewashed walls and slate roofs.

✳ Walk: The Lookout over Rubha Hunish and Erisco
Distance: 3 miles; time: 2 hours; start/end: Kilmaluag; OS Explorer map: 408 Skye – Trotternish & The Storr
This route leads to and from a former coastguard lookout with spectacular views over the most northerly point of Skye – Rubha Hunish – where, on a calm day, you have a decent chance of seeing marine mammals. The return leg visits the abandoned settlement of Erisco. It is not particularly challenging, but it does cross boggy ground.

Leave the main road at the Kilmaluag phone box (Shulista Road End), where the number 57 bus stops between the tiny townships of Kilmaluag and Duntulm, and turn on to a track called Shulista Road for 50yds. Just before the first cattle grid is the small Rubha Hunish car park (marked on Google Maps).

Cross the cattle grid and follow a sign pointing left that says 'Rubha Hunish 2.5km', taking this path with its occasional white-topped markers northwest along the higher ground above a shallow valley on your left. Out to the west is Duntulm Castle and small, grassy Tulm Island not far offshore. As you continue you will notice the ruined settlement of Erisco down in the valley to your left.

After just over a mile, on an intermittent but relatively easy-to-follow path, you should reach a metal kissing gate (✆ 57°41'41.6"N 006°20'26.1"W); go through this, bear right, then after 440yds go through another metal kissing gate as the path heads into the channel between two low hills (Meall Deas on the left and Meall

Tuath on the right). After around 500yds you will see a small trail leading off to the right; take this up on to Meall Tuath and head north to the Lookout (⊕ 57°42'05"N 6°20'41"W), a small building with big windows.

Inside the Lookout are binoculars and identification charts for whales and dolphins, along with star constellations and an information board about Dave Brown, a wilderness lover, who the Lookout is dedicated to. This building is now a Mountain Bothies Association bothy (page 44) where you are welcome to sleep, but as it is well known among hikers you are unlikely to have it to yourself. There is obviously no rubbish collection here, so as always, please take everything away with you and leave the bothy clean. After you have absorbed the spectacular view over Rubha Hunish, scanned the ocean for dolphins and maybe eaten your sandwiches, return to the kissing gate the way that you came.

From the kissing gate you can make the short walk down to Erisco (⊕ 57°41'35"N 6°20'27"W) where eight ruined but well-preserved cottars' houses are placed along the line of a township enclosure wall. These houses were built by people who had been evicted from elsewhere by Lord MacDonald to make room for sheep; it is known as an 'improvements' settlement and is the best example of one on Skye. After the Crofters' Act of 1886 the inhabitants moved away again, hopefully to better and bigger land. Around the same area are quite a few earlier and more damaged houses with lazy-bed cultivations. These are obviously from an earlier settlement in the same spot, though not much is known about them.

From Erisco, find a slight path that leads 300yds southeast back up to the original track you began on and follow it back to the car park.

The northwest coast The oldest parts of **Duntulm Castle** (⊕ open access) were built in the 14th and 15th centuries; what's left of it sits in a dramatic clifftop position on the west coast, not far from where the ring road starts to head south. This area saw many years of feuding between the MacDonalds (of Sleat) and the MacLeods until it settled as the seat of the MacDonalds in the 17th century. In 1732 Sir Alexander MacDonald was looking for something a bit more comfortable and robbed the stones from Duntulm to build his new residence Monkstadt House, 6 miles further south. There is a place to park at the corner of the road and the castle ruins are a short walk away on a grassy path. Be sure to look down at the sea as an otter lives along this coastline and you might even see porpoises or dolphins. There is also a cairn to Flora MacDonald (page 55) and a great view out to small, lumpy Tulm Island and of the coastline to the north.

Heading further south on the A855, do not miss the **Skye Museum of Island Life** (Kilmuir; w skyemuseum.co.uk; ⊕ Easter–Sep 10.00–17.00 Mon–Sat; adult/child

CAVE OF GOLD (UAMH OIR)

Uamh Oir (⊕ 57°39'36"N 6°24'36"W), meaning Cave of Gold in Gaelic, is a very special place on the northwest coast. Towering basalt columns rise from the sea, similar to those that form Fingal's Cave on Staffa (page 171), but much less frequently visited. Seabirds use the cliffs to nest and gannets, shags, gulls and guillemots fish in the surrounding waters.

A short walk along the coast from Bornesketaig can be navigated with OS Explorer map 408 (*Skye – Trotternish & The Storr*) and is described by Walkhighlands (w walkhighlands.co.uk/skye/caveofgold.shtml). Take extra care on the steep, muddy path down the grassy slope to the cave.

£6/free), which aims to demonstrate how crofters lived and worked in the area. A number of traditional thatched houses are arranged to show a different element of crofting life from around the end of the 18th century. The Croft House, the largest of the group, is set out to represent a home with a kitchen and old-fashioned box bed in the bedroom. There is also a barn, full of agricultural objects; the Weaver's Cottage, depicting a workshop with loom and spinning wheels; a blacksmith's workshop; and the Ceileigh House, which contains old documents and photos of Skye.

Kilvaxter Iron Age farmstead and souterrain (✪ 57°38'26.4"N 6°22'35.1"W; ☉ open access; donation requested; ♿) This 2,000-year-old grass-covered roundhouse and underground tunnel is a great example of a souterrain, and is one that you are actually able to go inside, although you might need wellies and waterproofs.

Walk: Dùn Skudiburgh
Distance: 3 miles; time: 2 hours; start/end: viewpoint car park between Totescore and Uig; OS Explorer map: 408 Skye – Trotternish & The Storr
This is an easy return walk to visit Dùn Skudiburgh, a complex fortification, of which the oldest parts are thought to be prehistoric.

If you have a car, park it at the indicated viewpoint parking (✪ 57°36'07.8"N 6°22'40.5"W) on the corner of the A855, about 600yds south after the sign for 'Totescore' or 2 miles north of Uig, with the postbox and bus stop.

Walk 200yds south along the road from the car park to find a track going off to the right, towards a large green barn. Follow the track and take the left fork at the barn, through the gate on to another wide dirt track that leads west and downhill towards the sea and Scuddaborg Farm.

Just before you get to the farm's gate, take the left-hand turning on to an obvious grassy track; you'll pass an old, rusty plough before heading down to the shore. You will now be able to see Dùn Skudiburgh and the sea stack next to it on your right.

Keep on the sea side of the fence and walk to the base of the hillock and then around it anticlockwise to the north, where the old access route will lead you up to the top of the fort. There are rocky bays on either side that make glorious spots for a picnic and it is also the perfect place to watch the sun set on a long summer evening – just make sure you leave enough time to get back before dark! Unfortunately this shoreline collects quite a lot of ocean plastic. If you can, please take a bit away with you to dispose of properly. Return the way you came.

Uig and southwest Trotternish
Spread around Uig Bay, this small port town has a lot going on, including ferries to the Outer Hebrides (page 55). It is a good place to stock up on supplies, have a pint or get some fish and chips. Note that extra care should be taken on the stretch of road that leads in from the north, being narrow with sharp hairpin bends.

Uig Wood
A band of broad-leaved trees follows Uig Bay 600yds southeast from the village hall; Uig Wood (w woodlandtrust.org.uk/visiting-woods/woods/uig-wood) comprises over 17ha of native woodland around the town, which can be explored on indicated walking paths. The mature woodland provides a valuable habitat for butterflies and interesting lichens; listen out for the distinctive songs of chiffchaffs and other small woodland birds.

From the centre of Uig, another path starts just west of Woodside Farm and leads upstream along the banks of the tumbling River Rha towards **Rha Falls**. Also part of Uig Wood, the trees in the steep-sided ravine are more slender and it is only a couple of hundred yards to the double cascade of Rha Falls.

Uig Tower On the hill south of the town, overlooking the bay, is the folly Uig Tower. This short stone tower was built around 1860 for Major William Fraser who was the owner of Kilmuir Estate. His house, Uig Lodge, was washed away in the great flood of 1877 just after he had organised Skye's last Clearances. Visible from both the bay and the road, it is best observed from a distance as bulls are kept in the surrounding field.

Fairy Glen In the hills east of Uig, between Sheader and Balnaknock, the **Fairy Glen** has become one of the busiest tourist honeypots on Skye. The highlight of this landscape of small hillocks is the rocky protrusion called **Ewan's Tower**; climbing the few yards to the top gives you a good view over the area. The turning to reach the glen is just south of Uig Hotel; it takes about 35 minutes to walk from there, or you can park in the small, dedicated pay and display car park (£2/2hrs) 500yds away from the glen. It's worth visiting in early morning or evening, when the crowds are fewer and parking is easier.

Hugh's Castle (Caisteal Uisdean) This ruined square tower stands guard over the entrance to Loch Snizort Beag. Probably dating from the early 17th century, the ground-floor walls are solid, without any openings apart from some narrow holes in deep embrasures. The castle is best known for its association with Uisdean MacGhilleasbuig Chlerich, the nephew of Donald Gorm of Sleat who, having failed in his plot to murder his uncle and become chief, fled to the Outer Hebrides where he was captured. He died in the dungeon at Duntulm.

The castle is near the few buildings that make up South Cuidrach, just over a mile's walk south of the township of Cuidrach. If you have a car, park it near Cuidrach: either in the disused quarry and walk to the junction where a green sign points left towards 'South Cuidrach 1.5m [miles]', or in the small parking place there if room.

EDINBANE, DUNVEGAN AND THE DUIRINISH AND WATERNISH PENINSULAS

Duirinish and Waternish, the wings forming Skye's northwest, are in some ways the most remote parts of the island. Duirinish's isolation means you might expect it to be the least visited peninsula on Skye, but this has changed in recent years. Neist Point, for example, despite being off the single-track B884, gets more traffic than elsewhere. Meanwhile Waternish, lacking any major tourist attractions, is still peaceful and unassuming.

The main road (the A850), connecting these peninsulas with Portree and Minginish in the south, hosts a few small townships including Edinbane and the more famous Dunvegan. In the latter, the castle – ancestral home of Clan MacLeod – is the most famous and impressive historical building on Skye, but there are a great many other sites in this area that are usually overlooked; the peninsulas are dotted with Iron Age brochs and ruined medieval churches, with carved grave slabs and turbulent histories.

As half the coastline and interior are totally uninhabited, there are infinite opportunities for hiking. Dramatically positioned lighthouses and steep seabird cliffs can be found on the coastal extremities, while sea lochs provide more gentle waters to the interior.

This part of Skye is served by only a few roads, leaving big areas that are inaccessible to **vehicles**. While the A850 has two lanes, the Duirinish and Waternish peninsulas have only single-track roads, some of which have pot-holes and blind summits or corners.

Stagecoach (page 58) run a service between Portree and Edinbane, Dunvegan and Glendale (Duirinish).

🏠 **WHERE TO STAY** There are lots of accommodation options at the top end of the market, but this side of the island is distinctly lacking in cheaper places. For self-catering, see On the Croft, below, or for options in Waternish, see w visit-waternish.co.uk/categories/self-catering.

Greshornish House [56 C3] (10 rooms) Greshornish IV51 9PN; 📞 01470 582266; w greshornishhouse.com. Grand old manor house set in 30 acres, with a cannon in the grounds. Once owned by Kenneth MacLeod, who founded Edinbane (page 78) in the 19th century. Full-size snooker table & lawn games. Rooms all different in size, shape & decoration, but generally large. Master rooms are enormous & regal. Price reduced massively in winter. £££££

Hillstone Lodge [56 B4] (3 rooms) Colbost IV55 8ZT; 📞 01470 517241; w hillstonelodge.com. A modern building with huge windows overlooking Loch Dunvegan. Meticulously decorated with Skye Weavers' tweed & luxurious finishings. Drinks licence. Previous winner of the Taste Award for 'Best B&B on Skye'. Adults only. Min 2-night stay. £££££

The House Over-By [56 B4] (6 rooms) Same contact details as The Three Chimneys (page 76) & run by the same people. The communal areas have dramatic details, including an intricate, boldly coloured stained-glass doorway & enormous, expressive seascapes on the wall. Huge windows allow you to have b/fast or evening drinks overlooking Loch Dunvegan. Dressing gowns, well-stocked minibar, coffee machine, fresh fruit, home baking, fresh milk, mineral water & everything else you might expect from super-luxury accommodation – all reflected in the price. 2 rooms have sea views. £££££

Edinbane Inn [56 C3] (6 rooms) Edinbane IV51 9PW; 📞 01470 582414; w edinbaneinn.co.uk; ⏱ mid-Mar–mid-Oct. Tasteful, modern interior with touches of tartan in muted colour scheme of grey, blue & white. Above a lively restaurant & bar. ££££

Ronan House [56 C3] (3 rooms) 21 Upper Edinbane IV51 9PR; 📞 01470 582449; w ronanhouse.co.uk. A friendly B&B run by locals Ronnie & Anne, with fantastic views across the valley & small village of Edinbane. You would really need a car or bicycle to stay here as it is quite far off the A850. At the lower end of this price bracket. ££££

Kinloch Camping [56 B4] Dunvegan IV55 8WQ; 📞 01470 508009; w kinloch-campsite.co.uk; ⏱ mid-Mar–mid-Oct; reception 09.00–11.00 & 14.30–19.00 daily. Well-run campsite in great location at head of Loch Dunvegan. Free Wi-Fi & phone charging, plus there are tide tables and reports of wildlife sightings. Book online. £

Skye Camping & Caravanning Club Site [56 C3] Edinbane IV51 9PS; 📞 01470 582230; w campingandcaravanningclub. co.uk; ⏱ Apr–Sep. Great spot on the banks of Loch Greshornish; part of a working croft. Tents, motorhomes & c/vans. Inexpensive pods (sleeping 2 adults & 2 children) have minimal furnishings, with own bedding needed, but are right by the water. £

Self-catering

On the Croft [56 C3] (2 cottages, 1 cabin) Nuig Hse, Upper Edinbane IV51 9PR; 📞 01470 582221; w edinbane-self-catering.co.uk. Here you'll find: Tigh Dubh (sleeps 4; ♿), a cosy converted blackhouse; Merman Cottage (sleeps 4), a traditional stone house; & Ewan Bàn, a hand-built wooden cabin. Situated on a magical 12-acre croft, this is a peaceful, green location & feels in many ways like stepping back in time. Handmade wooden furniture, Edinbane Pottery & Skyeskyns throws inside. Helen also offers Shiatsu therapeutic massage or Reiki sessions in a bespoke pod on site. £490–1,333/week.

✕ WHERE TO EAT AND DRINK With the Inner Hebrides' only Michelin star and a number of other celebrated restaurants, foodies are truly spoilt for choice on this part of the island.

Loch Bay [56 B3] Stein IV55 8GA; \ 01470 592235; w lochbay-restaurant.co.uk; ⊕ Mar–Oct Tue–Sat, Nov–mid-Dec Wed–Sat, sittings 18.45 & 19.15. Michelin-starred restaurant in a traditional cottage in this charming harbour village, serving contemporary Scottish food with classic French influences. Tasting menu £145/person. £££

The Three Chimneys [56 B4] Colbost IV55 8ZT; \ 01470 511258; w threechimneys.co.uk; ⊕ lunch Apr–Oct noon–13.45 daily, dinner mid-Jan–mid-Dec 18.30–21.15 daily. Traditional whitewashed building with slate roof & expected number of chimneys. Iconic, top-end restaurant listed in the Michelin guide; choose tasting menu or à la carte. Delicately balanced flavours, high-quality local ingredients, seasonal produce. £££

Edinbane Inn [56 C3] Same contact details as hotel, page 75; ⊕ mid-Mar–mid-Oct 17.30–22.30 Mon–Sat, noon–22.30 Sun (check online for winter bar times). Busy bar &

Michelin-recommended restaurant specialising in local seafood, including Hebridean mussels & squid. Book ahead for restaurant. ££

Greshornish House [56 C3] Same contact details as hotel, page 75; ⊕ noon–16.30 (afternoon tea) & 18.00–20.30 daily. This historic manor house in a remote location serves a market menu, changing each day. Pretty restaurant with fairy lights for evening meals. Afternoon tea, served in a grand dining room or sunny conservatory, needs to be booked 24hrs ahead. ££

The Old School Restaurant [56 B4] Dunvegan IV55 8GU; \ 01470 521421; w oldschoolrestaurant.co.uk; ⊕ 17.00–19.00 Fri–Tue. Light, airy restaurant serving locally caught seafood including langoustines & mussels. ££

Café Lephin [56 A4] Glendale IV55 8WJ; \ 01470 511465; w cafelephin.co.uk; ⊕ Mar–Oct around 11.00–16.00 Mon–Fri. Tea & coffee, light lunches, home baking & local ale. £

ENTERTAINMENT AND NIGHTLIFE Edinbane Inn [56 C3] (page 75; check Facebook for dates & times) hosts traditional Scottish music nights.

SHOPPING
Arts and crafts
Cuckoo Tree [56 B3] 12 Lochbay, Waternish IV55 8GD; m 07796 157067; w cuckootree. com; ⊕ 11.00–17.00 most days (call ahead before making special trip). Art studio & shop of printmaker Denise Huddleston, who creates colourful pieces inspired by local wildlife & scenery.

Edinbane Pottery Edinbane IV51 9PW; \ 01470 582234; w edinbane-pottery.co.uk; ⊕ Easter–Oct 09.00–18.00 daily. Working pottery selling thick crockery in lovely blues & terracotta shades. Dishwasher & microwave safe.

Gilleasbuig Ferguson Rare Books Tigh na Mara, Skeabost Bridge IV51 9NP; \ 01470 532808; w gilleasbuig.co.uk; ⊕ hours vary. Owner is a local history enthusiast & has been collecting rare Scottish books for 15 years.

Hebridean Alpaca Company 1 Lochside, Dunvegan IV55 8WB; \ 01470 52577; w hebridean-alpacas.co.uk; ⊕ Mar–Dec 11.00–16.00 Mon–Sat; ♿. Wool from their own

alpacas, with photos of alpaca faces on labels. Clothes, scarves, hats, gloves & alpaca bedding. In addition to owning 15 alpacas, they also import fair-trade wool.

Raven Press Gallery Colbost IV55 8ZS; \ 01470 511748; ⊕ Apr–Oct 10.00–17.00 Mon–Fri. Incredibly detailed low-grain boxwood prints by Kathleen Lindsley & Nick Carter's photography.

Skyeskyns, Yurt Tea & Coffee [56 B3] 17 Lochbay, Waternish IV55 8GD; \ 01470 592237; w skyeskyns.co.uk; ⊕ 10.00–16.30 daily; ♿. Free guided tour (page 78; note no tours in final 30mins of opening). Showroom & shop with sheepskins, clothing & weaving. Proper coffee & homemade cake in on-site Yurt café (summer only; £).

Skye Weavers [56 A4] 18 Fasach, Glendale IV55 8WP; \ 01470 511201; w skyeweavers. co.uk; ⊕ Apr–Oct 10.00–17.00 Tue–Sat. Bicycle-powered loom, plus shop with woven accessories & soft furnishings.

Food and drink

Fasgadh Stores Dunvegan IV55 8WA; \01470 521432; 🄵; ⏰ 09.00–19.00 Mon–Sat, 11.00–17.30 Sun; ♿. Basic grocery shop.

Fruit & Nut Place Dunvegan IV55 8WA; \01470 521480; 🄵; ⏰ 09.00–16.00 Mon, 09.00–18.00 Wed–Sat. Doesn't look like much from the outside, but this corrugated shed is packed with a great selection of loose, often local fruit & veg, plus eco cleaning products, vegan ingredients & magazines.

Geary Crofts Produce Geary, Waternish IV55 8GQ. Different honesty stall businesses. Eggs, cheese, baking & vegetables when available.

Glendale Shop & Post Office 2 Lephin, Glendale IV55 8WJ; \01470 511266; w glendaleshop.co.uk; ⏰ summer 10.00–19.00 Mon–Sat, winter 11.00–18.00 Mon–Sat. Little shop with basic groceries.

SPORTS AND ACTIVITIES

Dark Sky w visit-waternish.co.uk/dark-skye-viewing. Waternish has been recognised as an exceptional place for stargazing; on a clear night, when the moon is not too bright, you can see the Milky Way & a number of other astronomical features that are often obscured by light pollution elsewhere. The same advantages apply for aurora hunting (page 28).

Divers Eye Stein IV55 8GD; \01470 592219; w divers-eye.co.uk. Various trips including wildlife watching, fishing & landing on uninhabited Isay Island, where there is an abandoned settlement & huge numbers of birds.

Isle of Skye Trekking Centre [map, page 66] Croft 2, Suladale IV51 9PA; \01470 582419; w theisleofskyetrekkingcentre.co.uk. Family-friendly pony trekking across open moorland & through the hills. £35 pp/1hr.

OTHER PRACTICALITIES

Fuel Atholl Filling Station, Dunvegan IV55 8WA; \01470 521487; 🄵; ⏰ 08.00–19.00 Mon–Fri, 08.00–18.30 Sat, 10.00–17.00 Sun

Health The Dunvegan Medical Practice, Health Centre, Dunvegan; \01470 521203; w dunveganmedicalpractice.co.uk

Post offices Dunvegan (IV55 8WA; \01470 521201; ⏰ 08.45–13.00 & 14.00–17.00 Mon & Fri,

08.45–13.00 Tue–Thu, 08.45–12.30 Sat); Edinbane Community Hall (Old Post Office Row IV51 9PW; ⏰ 13.00–15.00 Tue); Glendale Shop & Post Office (see above; ⏰ 11.00–17.00 Mon–Tue & Thu–Sat, 11.00–16.00 Wed); Hallin Post Office (Greenbank, Halistra, Hallin IV55 8GL; ⏰ 10.00–noon Tue); Struan Post Office (Struanmore, Struan IV56 8FG; ⏰ 10.00–12.30 Mon–Sat)

WHAT TO SEE AND DO

The road northwest from Portree For those coming from Portree, the A850, which runs west through the sleepy settlement of Skeabost Bridge, is the usual starting point for journeys into the Waternish and Duirinish peninsulas; aside from a couple of interesting shops (see opposite) and an excellent walk (see below), there's little to detain you here, and most visitors continue straight through to Edinbane or Dunvegan.

Walk: St Columba's Isle and Clach Ard [map, page 66]

Distance: 1¼ miles; time: 1 hour; start/end: Prabost Junction (on the A850); OS Explorer map: 410 Skye – Portree & Bracadale

Steeped in the past and legends as far back as the Picts, this easy, short walk is a must for anyone interested in history or archaeology.

Heading west on the A850 from the direction of Portree, there is a small turning to the right marked to Peinmore, Tote and Prabost, which crosses a cattle grid. The number 56 bus also stops here (ask for Tote). Take the first left almost immediately after the cattle grid and follow the road until you reach Skeabost Bridge, which crosses the River Snizort. Just before is a small footpath to the right, which will take you to the small bridge across to St Columba's Isle (⊕ 57°27'12"N 6°18'21"W).

3

On this small islet, at the point where the river joins the loch, is an ancient burial site and the late medieval foundations of Snizort Parish Church. It is thought to have served as a cathedral church of the Bishops of the Isles, with an even older building having once served the same purpose on this site. The Chapel or 'Teampall' of St Columba is further west, shrouded by a tree, but more complete; this building is thought to be from around the 11th to 13th centuries. According to folk history, 28 Nicolson chiefs are buried here; a 16th-century carved knight slab is the most impressive grave, but it's worth exploring the whole island to find others marked with a skull and crossbones.

To continue to the carved Pictish stone, Clach Ard (✪ 57°27'30.5"N 6°18'05.5"W), return to the bridge the way you came, and then walk about 100yds east until you see an unmarked turning to the left.

Follow this road for about 270yds before taking a turning to the right, which will take you into the back of Peinmore; the road ends at a T-junction where you will find Clach Ard. Erected in its present position in 1880, having previously been used as a door jamb in a cottage at Tote, this 7th-century Pictish symbol stone is one of only a couple found on Skye and generally one of very few archaeological remnants of the Picts. The symbols have been identified as a crescent, V-rod and disc.

To return, head southeast (to your right if you are looking at Clach Ard) along the road and go for about 400yds until you reach another T-junction. Here, turn right again and walk south for around 500yds to reach the starting point.

Edinbane and the Waternish Peninsula

The A850 now bypasses **Edinbane** [56 C3], the biggest settlement along the first stretch of the road, though it is so small that it is easy to enter and leave without ever realising you've arrived. This was not always the case: in the 19th century, having made his fortune in India, Kenneth MacLeod of Greshornish and Gesto (a rival of the MacLeods of Dunvegan) founded Edinbane as a pioneering, self-sufficient model settlement with an inn, mill, school and a hospital, the first on Skye. However, as Portree grew during the 20th century and transport links improved, Edinbane's significance dwindled.

Around 4 miles further along the A850 is the turning for the **Waternish Peninsula** and, on the left a little further on, a car park for the **Fairy Bridge** (✪ 57°28'12"N 6°32'30"W). This modest, flat-topped arch bridge is part of one of many traditions relating to the so-called Fairy Flag (page 81) at Dunvegan. In this tale, a chief of Clan MacLeod married a fairy, but she was forced to leave him after 20 years to return to fairyland; as she left across the Fairy Bridge she gave him the enchanted Fairy Flag as a parting gift.

Stein and around

[56 B3] Stein is Waternish's biggest village, but that isn't saying much. Three small and picturesque rows of white cottages stand overlooking Loch Bay and Beinn Bhreac across the water; a couple of majestic old boats rest by a small jetty and free-roaming chickens peck around the verges of the car park. Note that this is one of only a couple of places to park in Waternish.

Just north of Stein is **Skyeskyns** (page 76; ♿), where you can take a free guided tour of the tannery. Visitors are shown how sheep skins are fleshed on a traditional wooden beam before being paddled in a salty pickle and transferred to a tanning bath; later the leather is oiled, stretched, dried, buffed, trimmed, combed and ironed.

Dùn Hallin

[56 B3] A well-preserved Iron Age broch, Dùn Hallin (✪ 57°32'25"N 6°35'11"W) has magnificent views across to Isay Island and Duirinish. While many

In 1732, Rachel Chiesley (known as Lady Grange) was kidnapped by her MP husband, Lord Grange. His brother, John Erskine, had led the failed Jacobite rebellion of 1715 and Lord Grange himself was sympathetic to the Jacobite cause. After their marriage broke down due to his affairs, Lord Grange feared his wife would expose him. He took her to the Outer Hebrides and claimed that she had died; in fact, she had been left on St Kilda. Somehow managing to communicate with a cousin, she was moved again by Lord Grange – to Skye – before a chance of rescue and spent the final three years of her life on the island under the 'care' of Norman 22nd chief of Clan MacLeod. Here she was kept on Waternish Peninsula, usually in a local house, but possibly, under suspicion of her managing to send out another cry for help, for some time in a cave on Idrigil Point as well. She died in 1745 and her gravestone can be found at Trumpan Church; however, as it wasn't erected until 140 years after her death it is unlikely to mark the spot of her burial, which is thought to be at Kilmuir Cemetery in Trotternish. Far from being a damsel in distress, Rachel Chiesley appears to have been a fiery, determined and unpredictable character. She is portrayed intricately in Margaret Macaulay's book *The Prisoner of St Kilda: The True Story of the Unfortunate Lady Grange*.

of Scotland's brochs are now little more than piles of rubble, Dùn Hallin is a perfect circle: 11 rows of large stone blocks have survived the last two millennia, giving us some indication of how the complete, taller structure must have once been assembled. Readers of this guide have permission to park at Waternish Free Church in Hallin between Monday and Saturday in order to visit the broch, but please only do so if there are two or fewer cars in the car park already. A track (starting at ✪ 57°32'23"N 6°35'58"W) runs to the right-hand side of the church (roughly east), past a telephone box and over a cattle grid; after about half a mile you should be able to see the broch standing on the hill.

Trumpan Church [56 B2] The main road up Waternish ends at Trumpan where the ruin of **Trumpan Church** stands quietly looking across to North Uist. The site of a 1578 massacre, it is a haunting place to visit. The MacDonalds set fire to Trumpan Church in 1578 as part of an ongoing feud (page 114): it was full of Clan MacLeod worshippers at the time. According to folk history, one girl escaped and ran to Dunvegan Castle (she must have been very fit as it is 11 miles) and the heroic MacLeods hastened to Ardmore Bay with their charmed Fairy Flag (page 81) to destroy the invading force. This became known as the Battle of the Spoiling of the Dyke as the bodies were buried in a ditch. Trumpan Church is still roofless and missing large parts of its wall, with one arched doorway remaining. There are some late medieval carved slabs around the graveyard, the remains of a font and several interesting graves. A few yards southwest from the church is **Clach Deuchainn**. This is a prehistoric standing stone, also known as the Priest's or Heaven Stone. According to tradition, if an accused person can find the hole in it with their finger while blindfolded, they are innocent.

Walk: Waternish Point
Distance: 8½ miles; time: 3–5 hours; start/end: Trumpan car park, just opposite the church; OS Explorer map: 407 Skye – Dunvegan/Dùn Bheagan

The route to Waternish Point is a long coastal walk with incredible views, sprinkled with archaeology and with great wildlife-watching opportunities.

Walk back along the road from the car park, for around 500yds to where the road takes a sharp corner.

On your left here at the corner is a gate leading to a track that runs alongside a stone wall. Listen out for the croaking sound of corncrakes in summer as they thrive here. You can follow this track all the way to the end, but after around 2 miles be sure to look out for **Dùn Borrafiach** (✛ 57°34'43"N 6°37'35"W), a well-preserved Iron Age broch that is around 400yds east of the path on your right-hand side; it is one of the best examples on Skye and well worth a detour.

Closer to the end of the track you will pass another broch, **Dùn Gearymore** (✛ 57°35'21"N 6°37'33"W); this is more severely robbed of stones, probably to build the more recent buildings around it, but retains enough detail that you can make out the gallery between its double walls.

Soon afterwards, the small, white **Waternish Lighthouse** that stands on **Waternish Point** comes into view and you can bear left off the track as it veers to the right near two posts, following a very faint path towards the gap in a dry-stone wall. Follow the coast along the clifftops to reach the lighthouse. Keep an eye out for white-tailed eagles and great skuas in particular, but there are many seabirds here, plus a decent chance of spotting minke whales if the sea is calm.

It is possible to continue along the coastline here, though it becomes much more challenging and would require your own assessment. It's much easier to return the way you came.

Dunvegan and around

[56 B4] The village of Dunvegan is most famous for its castle, which bears the same name. The roofless, ruined parish church of **St Mary's**, 400yds east of the village centre, dates from the 18th century. Although St Clement's Church in Rodel on Harris was the main burial ground for the MacLeod chiefs, some are also buried here, in addition to many generations of MacCrimmons, who were hereditary pipers to Clan MacLeod. The most interesting late medieval carved grave slabs here are those near the spiked obelisk, with another example near the entry to the church.

Giant MacAskill Museum (41 Kilmuir Rd, Dunvegan; ☎ 01470 521296; w dunveganmuseums.co.uk/GiantMacAskill.html; ⊕ Easter–Oct 09.30–18.00 daily; adult/concession/child under 14 £2/1.50/free) Set in a traditional thatched cottage, this museum is dedicated to the eponymous Angus MacAskill (1825–63) who, at 7ft 8in (2.36m) still remains the tallest Scotsman to have ever lived. MacAskill was renowned for outrageous feats of strength; the small museum presents some of his achievements and includes a model of the man himself and replicas of his bed, table and a chair. Possibly most amazing is the size of his socks.

Dunvegan Castle (¾ mile north of Dunvegan village; ☎ 01470 521206; w dunvegancastle.com; ⊕ Apr–mid-Oct 10.00–17.30 daily; adult/concession/child/family £16.50/13.50/11.50/37.50 This grand, largely 19th-century castle is built around the remains of a much older one, with elements from as early as the 13th century; the site itself is thought to have been fortified since prehistoric times. A naturally defensive position, above a wall of rock overlooking Loch Dunvegan, the present structure began with a curtain wall enclosing the promontory, parts of which can still be seen. It was originally accessed through the sea gate, which remained the only entrance until 1748 and is still an imposing sight today. The site

DÙN FIADHAIRT

This peninsula takes its name from the Iron Age broch in its centre, where you can still identify some of the intricacies of the construction, including the chambers between walls, steps and lintels. In the southeast you have unrivalled views across the water to Dunvegan Castle and the common seal colony living around the islets in between. In the west, the distinctive MacLeod's Tables on Duirinish Peninsula are visible on a clear day, and to the east, eagles can often be seen flying above the forest by Loch Suardal.

If you have a car, park just before the A863 crosses over the dam on Loch Suardal, 2 miles north of Dunvegan, being careful not to obstruct the gate. It's best to take the OS Explorer map (*407 Skye – Dunvegan/Dun Bheagan*) to help you to easily find your way on to Dùn Fiadhairt Peninsula.

was owned by Clan MacLeod for 750 years; the family's motto 'Hold Fast' certainly seems to have been successful with Dunvegan Castle.

In many ways more interesting than the castle itself are its contents, many of which have associated folk tales or history, including heirlooms such as Sir Rory Mor's drinking horn and the Fairy Flag, a tattered piece of silk, which is thought to have originally come from Asia and is associated with several myths and legends. Another interesting collection relates to the Jacobite rebellion, with a lock of Bonnie Prince Charlie's hair and objects belonging to Flora MacDonald (page 55) including her stays, a type of fully boned bodice worn as underwear.

Coral Beach [56 B3] The road north from Dunvegan leads, after about 4 miles, to the busy car park for one of Skye's most attractive stretches of sand, Coral Beach. From here it's a 1-mile walk to the beach; the route starts (and is signposted) from the western side of the car park and is easy to follow. The beach is formed from dead pieces of maerl, a coralline red algae, which dries out to be white and makes a striking sight in juxtaposition with the seaweedy black rocks along the route.

The Duirinish Peninsula

Duirinish, dominated by MacLeods in all senses, is distinctive for the flat-topped mountains of Healabhal Mhòr and Healabhal Bheag, known as MacLeod's Tables. According to a folk story, when the chief wanted to impress a visitor he would take them to dine on Healabhal Mhòr. If you're a keen hiker, there is a route and map on Walkhighlands (w walkhighlands.co.uk/skye/macleodstables.shtml).

Further exploring in Duirinish should be done with the aid of an OS map and compass; the south is an uninhabited wilderness that only the most intrepid are likely to explore.

Neist Point [56 A4] Neist Point must be one of the most photographed spots on Skye and is definitely the most famous lighthouse in the Inner Hebrides. In summer months drivers should expect to do plenty of reversing on the scenic but tiny single-track side road that leads here. The lighthouse itself is nothing more special than countless others in the region, but its westerly position, at the end of a steeply undulating path, gives the impression of a building at the edge of the world. If possible, visit in the shoulder seasons to avoid the worst of the crowds as, even in the evenings, the car park gets busy with campervans (whose drivers must be much braver than me).

Dùn Beag [56 C4] Though outside the Duirinish Peninsula, the Iron Age broch of Dùn Beag (✦ 57°21'37"N 6°25'33"W) can be easily visited en route to or from Minginish. Just 300yds away from the A863, on the eastern side of the road, this excavated broch is one of the finest examples of its kind in the region. Originally from the late 1st millennium BC, it also shows signs of re-use in the early medieval period. The gallery, cell and stairway can still be seen between the inner and outer dry-stone walls.

MINGINISH AND THE CUILLIN HILLS

The mighty Cuillin, visible on the horizon from as far south as Mull and undoubtably the most impressive mountain range in this region, dominate the landscape of Minginish Peninsula. Any serious mountaineering into the Cuillin will require research and preparation far beyond the scope of this book, but for many people it will be enough just to be in their presence. Peter Edwards's new *Walks in the Inner Hebrides: Skye*, published by Scotland-based Pocket Mountains, provides a good introduction to hiking in the area, while Skye Guides (page 60) are recommended for anyone tackling the Cuillin Ridge.

Accessed down long, winding stretches of single-track road, Minginish also has a couple of Skye's finest sandy beaches and endless lengths of dramatic coastline. Crofting is an integral part of society here, and the majority of people live in the few small settlements that run along the south coast of Loch Harport.

A lack of public transport means that Minginish is difficult to access without a **car or bicycle**. Roads are single track and winding, so journey times can take longer than anticipated. A MacDonald (page 58) run the 307/308 **bus** service between Portree and Fiskavaig several times a day from Monday to Friday.

WHERE TO STAY Minginish is the best place on Skye to find budget accommodation, which helps make it a great destination for hikers and people who love the outdoors. While Glenbrittle is positioned among the Cuillin, staying somewhere along the road that leads out to Portnalong maintains a good balance between a dramatic backdrop and some of the comforts of civilisation.

Sligachan Hotel, Self-catering & Campsite [57 D5] (21 rooms, 3 self-catering properties & campsite) Sligachan IV47 8SW; ☏ 01478 650204; w sligachan.co.uk, sligachanselfcatering.com, sligachancampsite. com; ☺ Apr–Sep. Though these pose as separate businesses, they are all owned by the same family & within walking distance of each other. The setting would be idyllic if it wasn't on the edge of a busy road; the Cuillin make a spectacular backdrop & there's a river tumbling down into Loch Sligachan. Built in the 1930s, the hotel is one of the island's oldest coaching inns & also has its own small mountaineering museum, as well as a restaurant, 2 bars & a micro-brewery (w cuillinbrewery.com). The whole place is understandably busy with hikers & holidaymakers as it is the perfect spot from which to start exploring the Cuillin. Self-catering £350–600/ night, min 3-night stay; camping **£**, hotel **£££££**

Taigh Ailean Hotel [57 C5] (5 rooms) Portnalong IV47 8SL; ☏ 01478 640271; w taighailean.scot; ☺ Apr–Oct. Owners Johnny & Katie, originally from England, are a welcoming couple & involved with the local community. All rooms are clean & nicely furnished. Comfortable guest lounge with open fire, books & games. Min 2-night stay. Dogs welcome. **££££**

The Old Inn B&B & Bunkhouse [57 C5] (5 rooms & 24 beds in bunkhouse) Carbost IV47 8SR; ☏ 01478 640205; w theoldinnskye.co.uk; ♿. Pleasant en-suite private rooms on B&B basis, plus a simple bunkhouse with great views across the loch & good kitchen facilities. **£–££££**

Skyewalker Hostel [57 C5] (27 beds) The Old School, Portnalong IV47 8SL; ☏ 01478 640250;

w skyewalkerhostel.com; ⊕ Apr–Oct. 2-, 3- & 4-person rooms & garden huts with shared kitchen & bathroom facilities. Set in a 5-acre garden with giant chess & large glass dome for stargazing. **££**

Croft Bunkhouse [57 C5] (bunkhouse sleeps 14, self-catering sleeps 16, 3 wigwams sleep 3 max) 7 Portnalong IV47 8SL; m 07591 687489; w skyehostels.com. A variety of friendly hostel accommodation: bunkhouse, self-contained family units, twin rooms & heated wooden wigwams. Situated on peaceful croft beside Loch Harport. Min 2-night stay. **£–££**

Glenbrittle YHA [57 C6] (25 beds) Glenbrittle IV47 8TA; ☎ 01478 640278; w hostellingscotland. org.uk/hostels/glenbrittle; ⊕ Apr–Sep. Basic hostel; great base for walking. Kitchen, USB charging points, bike shed, drying room, laundry, limited shop & alcohol sold. No Wi-Fi. Call ahead out of high season. **£**

Glenbrittle Campsite [57 C6] Glenbrittle IV55 8WF; ☎ 01478 640404; w dunvegancastle. com/glenbrittle/campsite; ⊕ Apr–mid-Oct; ♿. Spectacularly placed campsite right on the beach & surrounded by the Cuillin Hills. **£**

Self-catering

Heatherbell [57 C5] (sleeps 4) Carbost IV47 8SU; w unique-cottages.co.uk/cottages/west-coast/skye-raasay/hb6-heatherbell. Le Creuset pots & pans, heavenly showers & huge brown leather sofas, this is luxurious self-catering. There's an incredible view across Loch Harport & the Cuillin & the house has absolutely everything you need, including an excellent range of Skye- & Hebridean-themed books, some of which are reasonably academic. £696–1,495/week.

✖ WHERE TO EAT AND DRINK

The Old Inn [57 C5] Same contact details as hotel, opposite; ⊕ noon–23.00 daily; ♿. Old-fashioned pub with friendly staff serving decent food (including b/fast), a favourite with locals. Dog-friendly, open fire in winter & traditional live music every Thu all year round & 4 nights a week in summer. **££**

Café Cuil [57 C5] Satran, Carbost IV47 8SU; ☎ 01478 640575; w cafecuil.com; ⊕ 10.00–16.00 Wed–Sun. High quality modern café serving brunch & lunch made with locally sourced, sustainable produce & traditional ingredients. **£–££**

Caora Dhubh Coffee Company [57 C5] Carbost IV47 8SR; w caoradhubh.com; ⊕ 10.00–17.00 daily; ♿. A small take-away café featured in the *Scottish Independent Coffee Guide*, Caora Dhubh roast their own range of coffee & sell a small selection of tasty baked goods, pies & toasties. **£**

Glenbrittle Campsite [57 C6] See above; ⊕ Apr–mid-Oct 08.00–19.00 daily. Cakes, home baking & a specific blend of coffee, for which they visit the growers to choose. **£**

SHOPPING

Carbost Community Shop IV47 8SR; ⊕ 08.30–17.30 Mon–Tue & Thu–Fri, 08.30–13.00 Wed, 09.00–15.00 Sat, 09.00–13.00 Sun. Small community-owned grocery shop.

Cath Waters Gallery & Shop [57 C5] Allt Mòr, Carbostbeg, Carbost IV47 8SH; ☎ 01470 521399; w cathwaters.scot; ⊕ mid-Mar–Oct 10.00–16.30 Mon–Fri (flexible). Small gallery adjoining Cath's

studio, showing artwork – along with cushions, mugs, etc – featuring digital collage, Scottish landscape & textures. Cath used to be a biologist, but found a successful change of direction during maternity leave.

Sconser Scallops Sconser IV48 8TD; ☎ 01478 650304; w sconserscallops.co.uk. Harvested-to-order scallops. Call at least 48hrs in advance. Min £25 spend.

OTHER PRACTICALITIES

Health Carbost Medical Practice, Carbost IV47 8SR; ☎ 01478 640202; w carbostmedicalpractice.gp.scot

Post offices Carbost (IV47 8SR; ⊕ 09.00–noon Mon–Tue & Thu, 09.00–11.45 Fri); Sconser Lodge Hotel (Sconser IV48 8TD; ⊕ 10.00–noon Mon)

WHAT TO SEE AND DO If Minginish has a hub, it is undoubtedly **Carbost** [57 C5]. A loosely arranged string of pretty, white buildings, the small village is nestled on the bank of Loch Harport, surrounded by mountainous scenery in all directions.

Talisker Distillery [57 C5] (Carbost IV47 8SR; ☏ 01478 614308; w malts.com; ⊕ Mar–Oct 10.00–17.00, Nov–Feb 10.00–16.30 daily; tours & tastings £15–150; ☂) Founded in the early 19th century, Skye's oldest distillery hosts various tours where you can learn about the traditional whisky-making process and take a look at their enormous copper pot stills, traditional worm tub and casks.

Talisker Bay [57 C5] A long minor road leads from Carbost to Talisker Bay, a spectacular beach. To get there, it's a 1-mile walk from the end of the road; you can park at the side of the road before the sign that says 'Talisker House, Private Road, No Cars' sign. Follow the arrow that points 'to the beach', along the track to the left. Keep to the right, on the lower ground, when you reach the fork in the track (after a cattle grid). You'll pass Talisker House and shortly afterwards the wonderful rocky and sandy beach, with a slender waterfall on the right-hand side and a towering rock stack on the left; it makes a delightful spot for a picnic.

Fairy Pools and Glenbrittle [57 D6] The main reason most people drive down towards Glenbrittle is to visit the immensely popular **Fairy Pools** (£5 parking). The attractions here are the river-carved rock pools, formed by the Allt Coir' a' Mhadaidh as it flows down from its dramatic Cuillin source. If you're looking for atmospheric solitude, continue down the road to **Glenbrittle**, where there is a wide, grey sandy bay, and take a walk from there.

Rubh' an Dunain [57 C7] The coast path leading southwest from Glenbrittle ends at Rubh' an Dunain, a headland of great archaeological importance. Around Loch na h-Airde, which nearly separates the final lump of land from Skye, there is an incredible example of a **Neolithic chambered cairn** to the north (⊕ 57°09'50"N 6°18'46"W); a **potential Viking port** (⊕ 57°09'40"N 6°18'33"W; page 54), an **Iron Age promontory fort** (⊕ 57°09'38"N 6°18'31"W) and a small **ruined settlement**, which was still home to the MacAskills of Rubh' an Dunain in the 1860s, to the south.

It would be best to use a map (OS Explorer 411 *Skye – Cuillin Hills*) to explore here, or you can use the route described on Walkhighlands (w walkhighlands.co.uk/skye/rubhandunain.shtml).

Walk: Coire Lagan

Distance: 6 miles; time: 4 hours; start/end: Glenbrittle campsite; OS Explorer map: 411 Skye – Cuillin Hills
Taking you right up into the Black Cuillin, this hike has an ascent of 1,935ft, with an element of challenge and spectacular views, though it keeps to a relatively simple and not particularly dangerous route. It is suitable for those who are quite fit and have some hiking experience. Though there is an excellent path for the majority of the route, the final stages require some scrambling; you will need to use your hands at certain points, but only for balance rather than to pull up your own weight. Make sure to check the weather forecast before you set out, and that you are appropriately equipped for a moderate walk (page 37). This description only applies to late spring, summer and early autumn conditions, when winter hiking equipment should not be needed.

A solidly built stone path begins from behind the Glenbrittle campsite toilet block. Take the path east uphill, ignoring the coast path that leads off to the right. Assuming visibility is good, you should be able to guess the location of the corrie from fairly early on in the walk; it is directly below the spikiest summits in view, Sgùrr Mhic Chòinnich (3,111ft).

Ignore a second turning and keep to the left fork heading directly up the hill. Look out for red deer on your way up, and on a clear day you should be able to see Rùm and Canna. Keep on the most obvious path until you reach two large cairns.

From here the path gets smaller and splits at times until you reach an area of solid rock and slight waterfalls. Earlier in the season, when water levels are higher, you should stay to the left of the main stream and take some time finding the easiest route up. You will have to use your hands to help you.

Shortly after the trickiest part, you find yourself in the bowl of Coire Lagan [57 D6] as a small but beautiful loch comes into sight. The Munros Sgùrr Dearg, Sgùrr Mhic Chòinnich and Sgùrr Alasdair surround you from right to left.

Once you've had your fill of the view, descend carefully to the double cairns. From here there's an optional detour of just over a mile: take the turning to the right, which leads you past Loch an Fhir-Bhallaich and close to a slender but towering waterfall. The path is quite easy to follow and eventually leads you down to the road at Glenbrittle. Follow the road back around to the car park. Alternatively, you can retrace your steps down the path.

ELGOL, BROADFORD, SLEAT AND THE SOUTHEAST

ELGOL AND AROUND Elgol is a stunning village with unbeatable views across Loch Scavaig to the Cuillin, although hardly any amenities at all. If you are **driving** down to Elgol, be sure to allow plenty of time as it is a popular place to take boat trips from and even the large car park often doesn't have enough space for the number of visitors. Elgol is also served by a **Stagecoach** service (page 58), but you will have to plan your trip carefully around the times.

Where to stay and eat

Coruisk House [57 E7] (4 rooms inc 2 suites, 1 cottage) IV49 9BL; 01471 866330; w coruiskhouse. com. Simple but elegantly decorated accommodation with a minimal colour scheme. Occasional antiques hint at the building's 300-year history: an original bath in the Upper Steadings suite or a carefully placed antique chair in a bedroom. Accommodation is quiet & intimate, with cocktails on arrival, & evenings are peaceful. Excellent b/fasts including a delicious homemade granola. Separate thatched cottage available for self-catering with the option of B&B Mar–Nov. The **restaurant** (⊕ Mar–Oct 19.00–21.00 Tue–Sun; reservations required; £££) offers carefully crafted dishes made with local, seasonal produce. There are langoustines, lobsters & squat lobsters creel-caught nearby; rope-grown mussels from Sleat; hand-dived scallops from off Sconser; & wild venison from Edinbane. Clare bakes her own bread, they grow & forage some of their produce, & the wine list was compiled after vineyard visits in France & Italy. ££££–£££££

Suilven B&B [57 E7] (1 dbl, 1 pod) IV49 9BL; 01471 866379; w elgolbedandbreakfast. wordpress.com. Run by part-time nurses Donald & Eileen, both originally from the Hebrides. The room has an unattached private bathroom, while the cosy wooden pod has its own small bathroom & kitchenette. Views of Eigg & Rùm from pod & b/fast room. £££

Elgol Bistro [57 E7] IV49 9BL; e elgolbistro@ gmail.com; ; ⊕ Apr–Oct 17.00–21.00 Wed– Sat. Homely, traditional Highland food & drink with a welcoming atmosphere. Book ahead. ££

The Creel [57 E7] IV49 9BL; ; ⊕ Apr–Oct 'when the sun's out'. Very fresh seafood rolls & coffee to take away. £

Other practicalities For a bank, fuel or a post office, you'll need to go to Broadford (page 89).

What to see and do The few loosely sprinkled houses that make up Elgol cling to green fields above the cliffs around Port Na Cullaidh. With a spectacular view across

Loch Scavaig to the Cuillin and the small island of Soay, there's no doubt that this is an extremely picturesque corner of Skye. **Misty Isle Boat Trip** (IV49 9BL; ☏ 01471 866288; w mistyisleboattrips.co.uk) offers trips out to Loch Coruisk, a magical place surrounded by the Cuillin (there's a one-way option for hikers), passing seals and seabirds, with the possibility of seeing dolphins, basking sharks and minke whale.

Most people come and go in one day, simply arriving and leaving for a boat trip straight away, but there is plenty more to explore on foot.

Prince Charlie's Cave [57 E7] Prince Charlie's Cave is actually one of 13 such-named caves in Scotland, according to Tony Oldham's book *The New Caves of Scotland*; the legend goes that Bonnie Prince Charlie spent his last night here before escaping to Mallaig on the mainland. Situated on the coast south of Elgol, it would certainly have been a remote spot to reach overland in those days.

The coast path, which starts as gravel before being reduced to mud and grass, leaves from the upper of Elgol's twin car parks near the pier and heads southwest. Follow the path south around the clifftops for about 1½ miles until you reach Port an Luig Mhòir: a wide, rocky and pebbly beach with an easy route down to it. From here, to reach the cave, you need to turn right and walk west around the small, protruding headland made of wide, flat rocks. There are several caves and tunnels in this area, but Prince Charlie's Cave (⊕ 57°08′06″N 6°06′21″W) is around 200yds from the small headland. About 10ft above the level of the beach, in a dark crack, with some boulders lodged in the base of the entrance and a patch of grass growing on the left, it is not particularly obvious from ground level and requires a short scramble, using your hands, to get inside. The space is deeper than it first appears. You will need a good torch.

Dùn Grugaig [57 E7] The ruins of the prehistoric fort Dùn Grugaig (⊕ 57°08′07″N 6°04′30″W), are thought to date from the 7th or 6th centuries BC. Hidden from view by trees, the ruins can be found towards the southern end of Glasnakille. If you have a car, park it opposite the khaki-green barn and walk 10yds further south down the road before taking a turning to the left, just before the corner of the fence. A faint, thin dirt path then leads downhill through the trees. Before long, you will reach a grassy promontory and the remains of the fort. Be very careful of the cliffs here.

Spar Cave [57 E7] The walk to Spar Cave can only be done at low tide (page 28). Entering into the upper parts of the cave involves a scramble up some easily gripped but very steep rocks, so take care. You should bring at least one strong torch per person and be very aware of the incoming tide.

From the T-junction as you enter Glasnakille, head right and then take a left through the gate into a field, passing some ruins on your left. Follow the faint path that leads towards the sea and down a slope. At the bottom of the slope there is a path to your left, which you should follow for 50yds before taking the path to your right. After 100yds you will come to a steep path that takes you through a crevice down to the shoreline. Walk out towards the sea and clamber over the rocks, following the coastline with the sea on your right. Pass one inlet and then continue until you get to a larger gorge with vertical rock walls, which leads into the cave. The route up the gorge towards the cave is tidal and it is slippery to clamber over the rocks and seaweed.

There is a small dry-stone wall at the entrance to the cave and two possible tunnels: choose the one on the left and follow the passage as it gradually begins to open out. After about 12yds, the walls and floor become covered by white calcium carbonate (spar) and a steep section leads up to a plateau. Standing in this part of the cave, you are surrounded by glistening, cascading formations known as flowstone; water flows down the steeper sections forming clear pools of water at your feet. Popular with visitors since Victorian times, it's an eerie, otherworldly place. Even without the incoming tide, there is a distinct feeling that you should not stay too long.

BROADFORD AND AROUND Down-to-earth Broadford may not be the prettiest place on Skye, but it is a busy little town with a thriving community and a good range of amenities and places to eat. It is easily accessible on a number of **bus** routes (page 58).

Where to stay *Map, page 88*

✳ **Otter Lodge** (5 rooms) Harrapool, Broadford IV49 9AQ; m 07306 667255; w otterlodgeskye. co.uk. Owned & run by outdoor enthusiasts Vanessa & Martin, this relaxed B&B is a perfect choice for hikers, kayakers or climbers who want something more spacious & comfortable than a hostel. Martin used to run the bakery in Bowmore on Islay & bakes 2 or 3 kinds of bread for b/fast. Bedrooms are spacious, with views out towards the sea or the wildflower meadow behind. Private/ en-suite bathrooms. Practical guest lounge with fridge, microwave, fair-trade coffee & plenty of OS maps, plus large drying room for kit. **£££**
Skye Basecamp (34 beds) Lime Park, Broadford IV49 9AE; 01471 820044; w skyebasecamp. co.uk; &. call ahead. Geared towards outdoor types & clients of mountain-guiding company Skye Guides (page 60). Pleasant dorm rooms with good facilities including large kitchen, communal lounge, pool table, drying room for kit & laundry. **££**
Camping Skye Pairc nan Craobh, Broadford IV49 9DF; 01471 550420; w campingskye.com; ⊕ camping Apr–Sep, c/vans & motorhomes Apr– Oct; &. This excellent not-for-profit, community-owned campsite has an unpromising location, with an unappealing entry opposite a builders' merchant on the northern outskirts of Broadford. Once on the site, however, it is quiet & secluded from the rest of town, with a green forest backdrop & extensive grounds. The reception (⊕ 08.00– 20.00 daily) is staffed by knowledgeable locals who can advise motorhome & c/van drivers on which roads might be suitable for them to drive. Modern & comprehensive facilities; free Wi-Fi. Call to check availability. **£**

Where to eat and drink *Map, page 88*

Café Sia Ford Rd, Broadford IV49 9AB; 01471 822616; w cafesia.co.uk; ⊕ summer noon–21.00 daily (flexible), reduced in winter; see website. Wood-fired pizzas, mouth-watering courgette fries, real fruit smoothies, haggis/vegetarian haggis & melted cheese on toasted ciabatta, vegan cheese & gluten-free options. Sit in or take away (from Siaway, round the corner). Gets very busy, but first come first served. **£–££**
Deli Gasta The Old Mill, Harrapool, Broadford IV49 9AQ; 01471 822646; w deligasta.co.uk; ⊕ 09.00–17.00 daily. Fresh salad, baked goods & deli sandwiches, plus proper coffee. Sit inside or take away. **£**
Mrs Mack's Wee Takeaway Torrin IV49 9BA; f; ⊕ check Facebook. B/fast, burger & home-baking van with spectacular view, run by farming family. Pop in on your way down to Elgol. **£**

Shopping

Co-op Main St IV49 9AE; 01471 822649; ⊕ 07.00–22.00 daily; &. Large grocery store with bakery & banking facilities.
The Handspinner Having Fun Old Pier Rd IV49 9AE; 01471 822876; w handspinnerhavingfun. com; ⊕ 09.30–17.30 Mon–Sat. Shop selling yarn, hand-knitted garments & other local crafts. Also runs workshops.
Ragtag Unit 3 Pairc nan Craobh IV49 9AP; 01471 822043; w ragtagskye.org; f Rag Tag n Textile; ⊕ 11.00–15.00 Mon–Fri. Sells secondhand items such as handmade upcycled

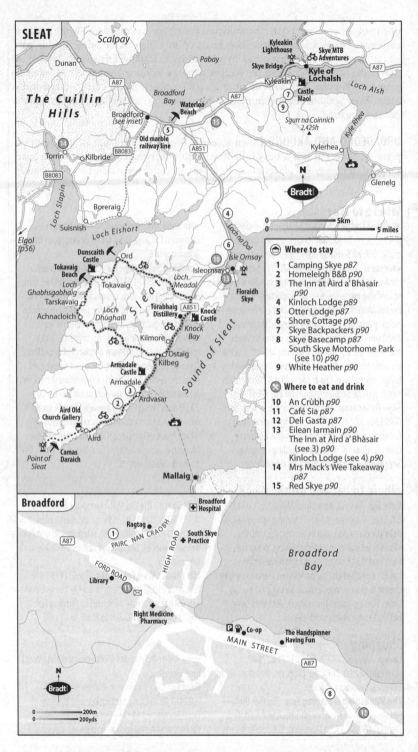

SLEAT

Scalpay

Dunan

The Cuillin Hills

Torrin
Kilbride

Boreraig

Suisnish

Elgol
(p56)

Pabay

Broadford Bay

Broadford
(see inset)

Old marble
railway line

Loch Slapin

Loch Eishort

Dunscaith
Castle
Tokavaig
Beach
Loch
Ghabhsgabhaig
Tarskavaig
Achnacloich

Ord

Tokavaig

Sleat

Loch
Dhùghaill

Kilmore

Àird Old
Church Gallery

Waterloo
Beach

Kyleakin
Lighthouse
Skye Bridge
Kyleakin

Skye MTB
Adventures
**Kyle of
Lochalsh**

Loch Alsh

Castle
Maol

*Sgurr na Coinnich
2,425ft*

Kylerhea

Kyle Rhea

Glenelg

N

Bradt!

0   5km
0   5 miles

Loch
Meadal

Torabhaig
Distillery

Ostaig
Kilbeg

Armadale
Castle
Armadale
Ardvasar

Àird

Point of
Sleat

Camas
Daraich

Isleornsay
Isle Ornsay

Floraidh
Skye

Knock
Castle

Knock
Bay

Sound of Sleat

Mallaig

Loch na Dal

Broadford

Broadford
Hospital

Ragtag

South Skye
Practice

*Broadford
Bay*

PAIRC NAN CRAOBH

HIGH ROAD

FORD ROAD

Library

Right Medicine
Pharmacy

Co-op

The Handspinner
Having Fun

MAIN STREET

N

Bradt!

0   200m
0   200yds

gifts, knitted accessories & toys. Also hosts affordable creative workshops & courses open to all. Local social enterprise focusing on mental health & environment.

Other practicalities

Bank Visit the Co-op (page 87)
Fuel Asda Broadford Express Petrol, A87, IV49 9AE (next to the Co-op); ☎ 01471 581018; ⏰ 24hrs
Health Broadford Hospital (High Rd IV49 9AA; ☎ 01471 822491); South Skye Practice (High Rd IV49 9AA; ☎ 01471 822460); Right Medicine

Pharmacy (Ford Hill IV49 9AB; ☎ 01471 822235; ⏰ 09.00–13.00 & 14.00–17.30 Mon–Sat)
Library Ford Rd IV49 9AB; ☎ 01349 781230; w highlifehighland.com/libraries/broadford-library; ⏰ 10.30–14.00 & 15.00–17.00 Tue–Fri
Post office Ford Rd IV49 9AB; ⏰ 09.00–16.00 Tue–Fri, 09.00–15.00 Mon & Sat, 09.00–17.00 Sun

What to see and do While Broadford makes a good base for exploring further afield, there is little to detain you in the town itself.

About 1 mile east of Broadford, **Waterloo Beach** is a peaceful stretch of sand and seaweed with views out to the tiny uninhabited island of Pabay and the mainland beyond. To get there, follow a side road marked to Waterloo from just east of Broadford.

An easy, waymarked 8-mile walk (&) starts near the filling station in the centre of Broadford and follows the old **marble railway line**, which until 1912 carried marble from the mines to Broadford Pier. It gives good views of the surrounding hills without climbing any elevation. The route is described on Walkhighlands with a map (w walkhighlands.co.uk/skye/marble-line.shtml); it can be extended significantly to visit the coastal villages of **Suisnish** (⊕ 57°10'20"N 5°59'14"W) and **Boreraig** (⊕ 57°10'35"N 5°56'27"W), to the south, which were both cleared in 1853. The extended route will also take you past several waterfalls and give you stunning views over Loch Slapin and to Blà Bheinn. Navigating is simple with a good map and compass, or you can follow the route suggested by Walkhighlands (w walkhighlands.co.uk/skye/boreraigsuisnish.shtml).

SLEAT, KYLEAKIN AND THE SOUTHEAST Sleat Peninsula in the far south and Skye's southeastern elbow are the only entry points from the mainland. While those travelling over the bridge will arrive in the village of Kyleakin, the majority of those coming over on a ferry will arrive in Armadale on Sleat. Often overlooked, Sleat has some beautiful scenery and peaceful beaches. There are no fewer than four substantial castle ruins in the area and several splendidly positioned lighthouses. This is a unique and picturesque part of Skye to visit, easily overlooked on the charge further north.

Stagecoach (page 58) runs services from Armadale to Broadford and Portree. While Sleat's only **bus** routes run along the main A851 road from Armadale, and there are not many pathways for exploring on **foot**, this is a perfect peninsula to discover by **bicycle**.

To **hire a car**, try Drive Skye (Armadale; ☎ 01471 844361; w driveskye.com).

Where to stay *Map, opposite*
An extensive list of **self-catering** properties can be found online at w sleatperfectlyskye.com/places/category/self-catering, or see page 90.

Kinloch Lodge (19 rooms) Kinloch IV43 8QY; ☎ 01471 833333; w kinloch-lodge.co.uk. A 17th-century building in a beautiful lochside location, with manicured lawns & a grove of trees. Ornate antique furnishings, comfortable chairs & open fire in shared spaces. Large, luxuriously decorated bedrooms with great views. **£££££**

Homeleigh B&B (2 rooms) Ardvasar IV45 8RU; m 07736 770943; w homeleigh-skye.co.uk. Comfortable, well-run B&B, with sea views from all rooms. **££££**

The Inn at Àird a' Bhàsair (10 rooms) Ardvasar IV45 8RS; \ 01471 844223; w the-inn-at-aird-a-bhasair.co.uk; ⊕ Mar–Oct. Clean & comfortable inn with friendly staff; rooms have sea or woodland views. Bottom of this price range. **££££**

White Heather Hotel (7 rooms) The Harbour, Kyleakin IV41 8PL; \ 01599 534577; e info@ whiteheatherhotel.co.uk; w whiteheatherhotel. co.uk; ⊕ May–Sep. A large B&B rather than a hotel. Decoration is a bit dated in parts, but friendly place with good facilities & views across harbour to Castle Maol. Small guest study & kitchenette. Phone/email bookings only Oct–Apr. **££–£££**

Skye Backpackers (56 beds) Kyleakin IV41 8PH; \ 01599 534510; w skyebackpackers.com.

Colourful, cheap & cheerful, although quite a lot of beds for the size of the kitchen. Wellie rental available. 2 c/vans in garden have slightly cheaper dorm beds. **£**

South Skye Motorhome Park (5 pitches) An Crùbh, Duisdale Beag IV43 8QU; w ancrubh. com/south-skye-motorhome-park-an-crubh. Community-owned space & facilities for campervans & motorhomes. **£**

Self-catering

❋ **Shore Cottage** (sleeps 5–9) Ord IV44 8RN; \ 01360 622680 (no Sun calls); w independentcottages.co.uk/scottish_islands/ shore-cottage-ref5825. Characterful extended croft house with wonderful games room & large bay window overlooking the loch to the Cuillin beyond. Beautiful, peaceful location. Great for 1 large family or 2 smaller ones. £700–1,200/week.

✗ Where to eat and drink *Map, page 88*

In addition to the options listed here, look out for Skye Bridge Seafoods (m 07766 529907; ▊), a fish and chip van run by friendly local Arnie. Tasty, and you can be assured the fish is fresh and less oily than some other Skye offerings.

Kinloch Lodge Same contact details as hotel, page 89; ⊕ 12.30–16.30 & 18.30–21.00 daily. Gourmet meals created by head chef Jordan Webb. Local ingredients: think Skye roe venison, turnip, leek & a Kinloch-wood foraged bramble jus. **£££**

Eilean Iarmain IV43 8QR; \ 01471 833332; w eileaniarmain.co.uk; ⊕ noon–14.30 & 17.30–20.30 daily. Delicate fine dining & heartier bar meals in a beautiful location looking out over Sound of Sleat & Knoydart. The feeling of a traditional country house. **££–£££**

The Inn at Àird a' Bhàsair Same contact details as hotel, above; ⊕ Mar–Oct noon–23.00 daily. Good pub food served in restaurant, friendly staff & choice of whiskies from local distillery. The bar to one side is a favourite with locals. Pool room behind with 2 tables. **££**

Red Skye The Old Schoolhouse, Breakish IV42 8PY; m 07949 531527; w redskyerestaurant. co.uk; ⊕ noon–14.30 & 17.30–21.30 Mon–Sat. Friendly restaurant serving quality traditional food between Kyleakin & Broadford. The langoustines & sticky toffee pudding are particular favourites. **££**

An Crùbh Duisdale Beag, Sleat IV43 8QU; \ 01471 833417; w ancrubh.com; ⊕ 11.00–16.00 Wed–Sun; ♿. Meaning 'The Hub' in Gaelic, this community enterprise is in a modern building of glass, wood & stone, in an isolated spot. The café is a light, open space with big windows to see the hills. Good coffee, cakes, soup & mains such as burgers. Also hosts exhibitions, concerts, cèilidhs & yoga sessions, & is also the site of the South Skye Motorhome Park (see above). **£**

Entertainment and nightlife Seall (w seall.co.uk) has up-to-date listings for concerts, cèilidhs, performances and other events around Sleat.

Shopping

Arts and crafts

Àird Old Church Gallery Àird of Sleat, Ardvasar IV45 8RN; \ 01471 844362; w airdoldchurchgallery.org; ⊕ Mar–Oct

10.00–17.00 Mon–Fri. Here you'll find atmospheric watercolour landscapes by Peter McDermott & contemporary jewellery by Heather McDermott.

The Blue Studio Tarskavaig, Sleat IV46 8SA; ☏01471 855368; w macartorg.wordpress. com; ⊕ usually 11.00–17.00 Tue & Fri or by appointment. Donald MacKenzie's playful musical, figurative & landscape paintings.

Floraidh Skye Isleornsay, Sleat IV43 8QR; ☏01471 833347; ﬁ; ⊕ check Facebook. Wool, silk, tweed & cashmere clothing & accessories.

Gallery An Talla Dearg Hotel Eilean Iarmain IV43 8QR; ☏01471 833332; w eileaniarmain. co.uk/an-talla-dearg-gallery; ⊕ Apr–Oct, check website for times. Art gallery where local artists exhibit work in exchange for helping to run the gallery.

Food and drink
An Crùbh See opposite; ⊕ 10.00–16.30 Mon– Sat, 10.00–16.00 Sun. Speciality & local foods including fruit, vegetables & fresh bread. Also gifts & alcohol.

Armadale Stores Armadale IV45 8RS; ☏01471 844289; w sleat.org.uk/armadale-stores-shop; ⊕ 08.30–17.30 Mon–Fri, 08.30–15.30 Sat. Community-owned shop with dry food refill station, groceries, meat from Lochalsh Butchers, alcohol & much more. Fuel, too.

Pràban na Linne Eilean Iarmain; ☏01471 833496; w gaelicwhisky.com; ⊕ 10.30–17.00 Mon–Fri. This small company produces 3 Gaelic whiskies & 1 gin (Uisge Lusach) & offers tastings.

Sports and activities South Skye Sea Kayak (w southskyeseakayak.co.uk; £70/105 pp half day/full day) offers a peaceful and exciting way to reach remote stretches of coastline. It's good for wildlife spotting, and suitable for beginners.

Other practicalities
Fuel Armadale Stores (see above)
Health Sleat Medical Centre, Kilmore IV44 8RF; ☏01471 844283
Post offices An Crùbh (see opposite; ⊕ 11.00– 16.00 Mon–Sat); Armadale Stores (see above;

⊕ 09.00–15.30 Mon & Thu–Fri, 09.00–13.00 Wed, 09.00–13.30 Sat); Kyleakin Post Office (Main Street, Kyleakin IV41 8PH; ⊕ 10.00–13.30 Tue & Thu)

What to see and do
Kyleakin Coming over on the Skye Bridge, the first settlement on the island is Kyleakin. There isn't too much to detain you here, but the picturesque **Kyleakin Lighthouse**, designed by the Stevenson family who were responsible for constructing nearly all of Scotland's lighthouses between the late 18th and the mid 20th centuries, is visible across the water on the small island of Eilean Ban. In the east, **Castle Maol** (✪ 57°16'23"N 5°43'14"W) is an atmospheric-looking ruin that was a 15th-century MacKinnon stronghold. You can visit at low tide, when the exposed shoreline means that you can walk around the point anticlockwise and find your way up on the far side; a high-tide land route is possible, but trickier due to thick undergrowth.

Sleat On Sleat, the pretty village of **Isleornsay** sits just across from the tidal island of **Isle Ornsay** and another Stevenson creation, **Isle Ornsay Lighthouse**, which is confusingly built on the nearby islet of **Eilean Sionnach**.

In the village of Teangue, you can join a tour of **Torabhaig whisky distillery** (☏ 01471 833447; w torabhaig.com; ⊕ summer 10.00–17.00 Mon–Fri, 10.00–15.00 Sat & Sun, winter 10.00–16.00 Mon–Fri; ♿; tours & tastings £12–75). Up and running since 2017, this is a small, traditional distillery, and Skye's second, just beginning to release its first expressions now. One of the tour options comes with a chocolate pairing. A couple of hundred yards away is the ruin of **Knock Castle**, built by the MacLeods only to be captured by the MacDonalds; it was passed between the two clans several times before settling as a stronghold of the latter. There are stories of a Green Lady or Gruagach who is said to haunt the castle.

The Skye Trail is a 70-mile hiking route that connects Skye's mighty Cuillin Hills with the spectacular basalt ridge of Trotternish. The 'trail' description may be somewhat misleading, however – unlike the mainland's 'West Highland Way', this route is not waymarked and does not have a consistent path to follow. It is possible to connect with accommodation at the end of each stage, but this will require forward planning; camping is also feasible. Walking south to north, the hike is usually done in seven stages, working around bus routes and times, so you do not necessarily need to carry your stuff all the way. It must be the greatest adventure to be had on Skye, but on no account should you attempt it based on the information provided in this book. A detailed route description, planning, navigation skills, experience and the right kit are all required, as well as some observation and luck with the weather.

For more information, see w skyetrail.org.uk. **Thistle Trekking** (m 07375 789173; w thistletrekking.co.uk/treks/skye-trail), a company based in the lowlands, offer guided group hikes with accommodation and baggage transfer, while Edinburgh-based **Absolute Escapes** (01316 101210; w absoluteescapes.com/holidays/skye-trail) offer self-guided trips with baggage transfer and accommodation.

Armadale Castle (01471 844305; w armadalecastle.com; ⊕ Apr–Oct 09.30–17.00 daily; adult/senior/child 6–18/child under 6 £14/12/8/free;) is said to be the ancestral home of Clan MacDonald. It has extensive gardens with huge, mature trees, perfect for picnics and long afternoons of exploring. The castle, strictly speaking an early 19th-century mansion house, is a ruin that you can only observe from the outside. There is also a well-organised museum, predictably quite heavy on MacDonald-specific history, but including other highlights such as a Gaelic poetry trail, a 100-year-old 18ft skiff and full-scale replicas of Clan MacDonald West Highland grave slabs, which you are encouraged to touch.

A loop around Sleat
Distance: 22 miles, or 31 miles including extension to the Point of Sleat; time: 2–3 hours cycling time, but best as a full day; start/end: Ardvasar; OS Explorer map: 412 Skye – Sleat/Sleite
Excluding the optional extension to the Point of Sleat, this route would be possible to drive, but it makes for an even more excellent day's cycle ride (for bike hire, see page 58). Cyclists should go prepared with food and drink; be especially careful to look where you're going as the road surface can be rough with blind summits; and take the route clockwise for a wind-assisted ride.

Cycle north from Ardvasar as far as **Ostaig/Kilbeg** where there is a post box on the corner and a turning to the left marked to Achnacloich (5 miles), Tarskavaig (6 miles) and Tokavaig (8 miles). Take this road and cycle west, initially through some broad-leaved trees and farmed fields on either side.

Climbing up into the hills, the Cuillin will begin to unfold in front of you as the landscape becomes wilder and rockier. Pause on the banks of **Loch Dhùghaill** to take in the view as the landscape becomes rough with heather, and look out for wading birds.

Descending through the woods, you will shortly be at **Achnacloich**, where there is a shingle bay in front of the white house at Gillean. Following the road to the north, you will shortly come to **Tarskavaig**, where the tiny Communities Hall hosts a pop-up café July and August (⊕ 10.00–16.00 Thu–Fri). Take your time to look out west towards Rùm and Canna. Just after the hall, you can take a turning left down into the village and visit **The Blue Studio** (page 91), or continue on higher ground past **Loch Ghabhsgabhaig** on your left, towards Tokavaig.

Passing two pebbly beaches, you will come to a track leading off to the left marked 'Footpath to Castle'. Leaving your bike off the side of the road, walk down this track to find the remains of **Dunscaith Castle**. Also known as the Fortress of Shadows, the site is named after Sgàthaich, a warrior maiden who, according to tradition, made an earlier fort here her home. Sgàthaich is said to have only trained young warriors who were already brave enough to break through the defences of the fortress. According to folk history, this is where she trained the Irish folk hero Cu Chulainn. The current castle was built around the 13th century and passed between clans MacDonald, MacLeod and MacAskill, before being captured by King James I of Scotland and finally abandoned in the 18th century. It is certainly a ruin, but an impressive one with a striking archway and broken bridge. The pebbly beach just behind it, with views across some tiny islets towards Ben Meabost and the Black Cuillin behind, makes a splendid, sheltered spot to stop for a picnic.

Back on the road, you will bump over lumpy ground before eventually reaching the small sandy bay at **Ord**. This is one of Skye's loveliest beaches, with similar views to those from Elgol, but only a fraction of the visitors. When you have had your fill, continue along the road east and return through birch trees, moorland and past little **Loch Meadal** before reaching the main A851 road.

Take a right at the T-junction with the A851 to return to Armadale, looking out for Knock Castle (page 91) which will appear across **Knock Bay** on your left. Passing Teangue and Kilmore, you will eventually get back to the start.

Those with even more energy should continue down from Ardvasar towards the **Point of Sleat**, where there is a small lighthouse. This headland has spectacular views out to Eigg, Rùm and the Ardnamurchan Peninsula, as well as good chances of seeing marine mammals and seabirds such as gannets. On the return trip, do not miss the opportunity to detour down to **Camas Daraich**, undoubtedly one of the finest beaches on Skye.

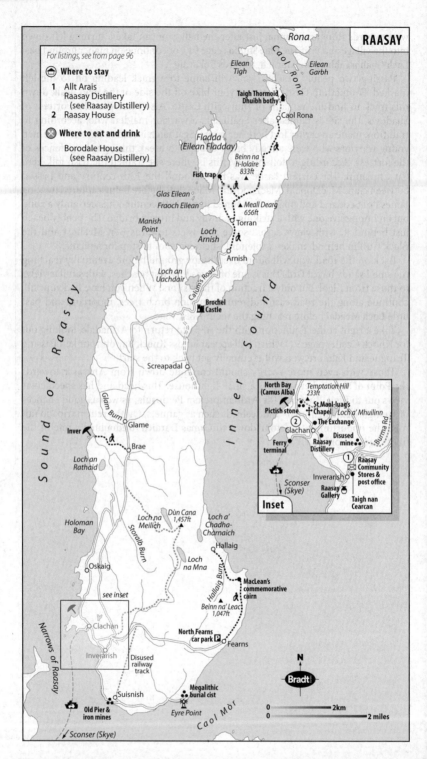

RAASAY

For listings, see from page 96

☐ **Where to stay**

1 Allt Arais
   Raasay Distillery
   (see Raasay Distillery)
2 Raasay House

⊗ **Where to eat and drink**

Borodale House
(see Raasay Distillery)

Rona

Caol Rona

Eilean Tigh

Eilean Garbh

Taigh Thormoid Dhuibh bothy

Caol Rona

Fladda (Eilean Fladday)

Beinn na h-Iolaire 833ft

Fish trap

Glas Eilean Fraoch Eilean

▲ *Meall Dearg 656ft*

Torran

Manish Point

Loch Arnish

Arnish

Loch an Uachdair

Calum's Road

Brochel Castle

Screapadal

Sound of Raasay

Inner Sound

Glam Burn

Inver

Glame

Brae

Loch an Rathaid

Dùn Cana 1,457ft

Storalb Burn

Loch na Meilich

Loch a' Chadha-Charnaich

Hallaig

Loch na Mna

Hallaig Burn

MacLean's commemorative cairn

▲ *Beinn na' Leac 1,047ft*

Holoman Bay

Oskaig

North Fearns car park

Fearns

see inset

Clachan

Inverarish

Disused railway track

Suisnish

Old Pier & iron mines

Megalithic burial cist

Eyre Point

Narrows of Raasay

Caol Mòr

Sconser (Skye)

Inset

North Bay (Camus Alba)

Temptation Hill 233ft

Pictish stone

†St Maol-luag's Chapel *Loch a' Mhuilinn*

② Clachan

The Exchange

Disused mine

Ferry terminal

Raasay Distillery

Burma Rd

① Raasay Community Stores & post office

Inverarish

Raasay Gallery

Taigh nan Cearcan

Sconser (Skye)

N

Bradt

0 — 2km
0 — 2 miles

94

4

Raasay
(Ratharsair)

With turquoise waters that lap into quiet, sheltered coves, plus rocky hills, woodland paths and remarkably fluffy white sheep, Raasay is a breath of fresh air. Measuring just 14 miles long and 4 miles wide, the island is dwarfed by its bigger, busier neighbour Skye and, with regular ferries travelling between the two, is often thought of as an extension of the larger island. This is, of course, a huge injustice – though it might look small in comparison, there is much more to do and see on Raasay than can be accomplished in a couple of days.

The island's highlights include flat-topped Dùn Cana in the centre of the island; a hike to the top gives spectacular views over Raasay, across to Skye and as far as Applecross on the mainland. The far north is wild and uninhabited, providing ample opportunity for adventurers to explore, including the beautiful tidal island of Fladda, once home to a whole community, and a whole host of other fascinating abandoned places including the ruins of pre-Clearance villages and the oppressive, industrial remains of the mining industry.

Much of Raasay's land is run by Forestry and Land Scotland (Inverness; ☏ 03000 676100; w forestry.gov.uk/scotland), which has created intermittent ugly scars on the southern landscape where trees have had to be felled. To their credit, however, Forestry and Land Scotland (formerly the Forestry Commission) has long provided jobs and supported the island's economy, in addition to – and particularly of interest for visitors – maintaining excellent walking paths and producing the best free tourist map of the island.

HISTORY

The history of Raasay is intricately linked with that of the MacLeods, who used both Raasay and Rona, the smaller island to the north, for pirating activities from the 16th century. After supporting Bonnie Prince Charlie in the 1745 rebellion (page 15), the MacLeods went into hiding on the island, which resulted in Raasay House (home to the MacLeod Chief of Raasay) and many other homes being burned down by government troops.

In the 19th century, like many landowners at the time, John MacLeod found himself in debt and finally sold Raasay in 1843 to a George Rainy. After this, life for the island's ordinary inhabitants became increasingly difficult. In a rather bizarre and unusual move, Rainy banned marriages and, echoing the Clearances elsewhere, began to evict villages in order to replace people with sheep. Many people were forced to move to Rona or abroad. By the 1860s, hundreds of people had been forced off the island.

In 1912 William Baird bought the island with the intention of opening an iron mine. He built a small railway, pier, kilns and the two rows of cottages now known

THE RONA RAIDERS

In May 1921, a group of crofters from Rona came to Raasay to reclaim their ancestral land. They were subsequently arrested, tried and sent to prison for 21 days but, in an unusual win for the people, they found public outcry was on their side, with newspapers reporting that Rona had long been overcrowded and that people lived in conditions unfit for human beings. Eventually the Rona Raiders (also sometimes referred to as the Raasay Raiders) were freed and allowed to resettle on Raasay. Today, aside from the island manager and their family, Rona is uninhabited.

as Inverarish Terrace for the workers. Operations had barely begun before World War I broke out, and many of those who would have worked in the mine had to go away to fight. However, the war effort required iron ore and thus in 1916 William Baird signed an agreement to run the mine on behalf of the military. Later that year, the northern part of Inverarish was turned into a prisoner of war camp.

In 1922 the island was bought by the government and the responsibility of managing it was given to the Forestry Commission, providing much-needed employment for islanders. The island's population has risen slightly over the last decade and now stands at around 170. At the time of writing, Raasay Development Trust was in the process of building five new houses on the way to Fearns to help tackle a local accommodation shortage.

GETTING THERE AND AWAY

CalMac (page 30) runs year-round **ferry** services from Sconser on Skye to Clachan on Raasay; the port is on the southern edge of the village. This vehicle and foot passenger ferry takes around 25 minutes (foot passengers/car £2.10/7), with ferries running between three and ten times a day. Tickets cannot be booked in advance; arrive at least 15 minutes in advance.

You can also arrive by **small boat**: Raasay House (see opposite) can arrange pickup/drop-off in Sconser (£20 pp plus £100 standing charge) or Portree by special arrangement.

For moorings, there is a community-owned **pontoon** (w raasay.com/pontoon; ⊕ Easter–Oct), a temporary jetty, next to Raasay's ferry terminal.

GETTING AROUND

While it is a small island compared with Skye, Raasay can seem bigger than you might expect. From the ferry terminal in the south to Arnish in the north is just over 10 miles of **driving**, but the single-track road is slow and winding. With plenty of time and decent weather, a combination of **walking** and **cycling** is the perfect way to enjoy the island at a leisurely pace. Raasay House (see opposite) hires out bikes (£35/20/15 for 7/3.5/2hrs).

 WHERE TO STAY AND EAT *Map, page 94*

Accommodation options on the island are generally centred around the two small townships of Clachan and Inverarish, which are so close together that it is difficult to extract one from the other. Despite being limited in number, accommodation here is of excellent quality, offering everything from dorm rooms to luxury suites. Note, however, that there is no campsite on the island. Self-catering options can be found at w raasay.com/accommodation, and there is a Mountain Bothies Association bothy (Taigh Thormoid Dhuibh; page 44) in the far north.

Raasay Distillery (6 rooms) Borodale Hse, Clachan IV40 8PB; \01478 470178; w raasaydistillery.com; &. The most exclusive & upmarket accommodation option on Raasay, part of the attractive & modern distillery building (page 99). The 2 rooms with Cuillin views are a bit more expensive, but all are of a very high standard. The distillery restaurant, **Borodale House** (check website for opening times; ££), serves an interesting menu focusing on fresh local seafood & Raasay venison. Honesty box bar. **£££££**

✷ **Raasay House** (23 rooms) Clachan IV40 8PB; \01478 660300; w raasay-house.co.uk; &. An enormous sandstone building that's almost 300 years old, Raasay House is situated just 300yds from the ferry port, overlooking its own attractive grounds, with splendid views of the Narrows of Raasay & the Skye Cuillin. Always the island's focal point, it has successfully transitioned from the exclusive home of Clan MacLeod to the community-owned extravaganza it is now. It describes itself as a 'unique island experience' & this is where the vast majority of activity on Raasay happens. With a newly renovated west wing for 2024, accommodation ranges from economy twin rooms with private external bathrooms (from £75) to deluxe super-king rooms with a sea view

(over £250). As well as being the main place to eat on the island, they also organise boat trips & outdoor activities & let out bikes (see opposite). Staff are outstandingly happy & helpful, & there's a historic library for guests to use, with comfortable sofas, wood burner, old books & other objects that give an impression of how it would have once been. There's a games room upstairs with board games, pool table & table football, while interesting projects with local artists aim to inject some more character into the relatively new interior. Dog-friendly. The restaurant (⏰ summer 10.30–23.00 daily, reduced in winter; ££) is open to non-residents as a café late morning, then serving lunches (noon–15.00) & dinners (18.00–20.00), while the bar is also open in the evening. Expect local & seasonal ingredients from the walled garden at the back of the house, plus wild Raasay venison, Raasay Crofters' Association langoustine & Sconser scallops. Lunch is simpler, with soup, toasted flatbreads or haddock & chips. **££–£££££**

Allt Arais (3 rooms) 7 Mill Park, Inverarish IV40 8PA; \01478 660237; w allt-arais.co.uk. Owner Anda is originally from the Outer Hebrides & speaks Gaelic. Spacious en-suite bedrooms & comfortable guest sitting room with impressive, modern wood burner. Excellent b/fast. **£££**

SHOPPING

Raasay's few shops and galleries are clustered in the south of the island (along with the majority of its population). In addition to the options listed, there is a stall selling vegetables, flowers and fruit, with an honesty box for payment, at the entry to the walled garden at Raasay House (see above); The Exchange (next to Raasay Distillery, page 99; ☐) is a tiny building selling local art and coffee; and there's a craft caravan (Taigh nan Cearcan) just downhill from Raasay Community Stores.

Raasay Community Stores 29/30 Inverarish Tce IV40 8NS; \01478 660203; ☐; ⏰ summer 09.00–17.30 Mon–Sat, winter 09.00–17.00 Mon–Sat. Good range of groceries including fruit & vegetables & Raasay Crofters' Association venison, plus local guidebooks & maps.

Raasay Gallery Ferryview, West Suisnish IV40 8NX; m 07765 883591; w raasaygallery.co.uk; ⏰ Apr–Sep 11.00–16.30 Mon–Fri, Oct–Mar noon–16.00 Tue–Fri, though hours can vary. Striking oil paintings in bold colours by owner Gordon J Cheape: portraits, abstracts & landscapes. Also a couple of other local artists.

Raasay House (page 97) runs numerous RIB boat trips ranging from a trip into Raasay Sound to a whole day visiting Rona, all with the chance of seeing seals, seabirds, dolphins, white-tailed eagles and natural rock formations (£65–130 pp). They also offer archery and loch kayaking.

OTHER PRACTICALITIES

The nearest **fuel** stations are in Portree (page 63) and Broadford (page 89) on Skye, so make sure you fill up before you arrive.

The lack of full-time **medical care** on Raasay is a controversial issue. Portree Medical Centre (01478 612013) visits Raasay alternate Wednesday mornings and offers some services.

You can find a **post office** at Raasay Community Stores (page 97; ⊕ 09.30–noon Mon–Sat).

WHAT TO SEE AND DO

SOUTH RAASAY
Around Clachan and Inverarish Two eroded stone mermaids greet everyone who arrives on the island by the Skye ferry; bought by the final MacLeod of Raasay, they were reportedly partly to blame for his bankruptcy in the mid 19th century. The ferry terminal sits in Churchton Bay on the southern edge of Clachan – made up of a scattering of buildings – and from here the village spreads into Inverarish, the island's main settlement, which is around a mile further east.

Around 300yds from the ferry terminal sits Raasay House (page 97); a path leads around its right-hand side to **St Maol-luag's Chapel**. The crumbling remains of this 13th-century church rest on what is thought to have been an earlier religious site from around the 6th century; according to folk history, St Moluag (c510–592) founded the site himself. The surrounding graveyard is a silent and slightly eerie place, sheltered by tall trees. The chapel shows its age through centuries of lichens, well-established moss cushions and a fascinating array of ferns; it has a well-preserved arched window in the east gable and an arched tomb recess on the inner south wall. Slightly to the south is the memorial chapel, which was built much more recently in 1839. The main interest here is a small carved face that peers out from above the east window and is thought to have been saved from an earlier building.

Heading northwest from here, the road passes a rather mysterious and well-preserved **Pictish stone**, standing opposite the pebbly **North Bay (Camus Alba)**. Believed to have been carved around the latter half of the 7th century, the stone has three well-defined carvings, which are a good example of the mixture between early Christian and Pictish culture at the time. The early Christian cross of arcs and chi-rho scroll are at the top; below them are two distinctive Pictish symbols: a sideways tuning-fork symbol halfway down and, at the bottom, a crescent and V-rod. It's notable for being one of only a few Pictish stones discovered in west Scotland (over 200 have been found in eastern Scotland).

To the left of the stone is a small gate and a path marked with occasional red waymarkers, which leads to the top of the small **Temptation Hill**, with splendid views both across Raasay and out to Skye. Heading back downhill, a path leads off to the left (east), reaching a road after a few hundred yards; from here you can turn right, walking south beside the small Loch a' Mhuilinn to reach the distillery (see opposite).

It's worth picking up the free leaflet from Forestry and Land Scotland (page 95), who maintain these marked paths, which has a detailed colour map of this area.

Raasay Distillery (Borodale Hse, Inverarish; ✆ 01478 470178; w raasaydistillery. com; tours & tastings £15–75) On the main road between Clachan and Inverarish, Raasay Distillery released its first single malt in 2020 and now produces both whisky and gin. There's a classic distillery tour with a dram, another that pairs gin and whisky with handmade Highland chocolates, or more exclusive cask tastings to choose from. It's well worth joining the tour that includes a Dunnage Cask Warehouse visit: the towering rows of wooden casks are an impressive sight in themselves, but it's the rich oaky smell of maturing whisky that leaves a lasting impression. The distillery also offers luxurious accommodation and has a restaurant (page 97).

Suisnish Old Pier and the iron-mining industry
By far the most imposing and impressive remains of Raasay's iron-mining history are found down at Suisnish, 1 mile south of Inverarish. Giant funnel-like ore hoppers, abandoned buildings, the concrete pier (built 1913–14) and a huge anchor are reminiscent of brutalist architecture and dominate the scene, but there is also a pebbly beach here that is a good place to spot seals. The remnants of a disused railway lead north-northeast towards another disused mine.

Eyre Point
Following the road east from Suisnish takes you towards Eyre Point, where there is a small, white **lighthouse**; around 80yds north are the remains of a cairn and a **Megalithic burial cist or dolmen** (✥ 57°20'04"N 6°01'19"W). If you are travelling by car, park it at the end of the road (where a sign says 'end of public road') and follow the main track between two fenced fields. Shortly after passing a ruined building in the field on your left, you will see the large stones of the burial chamber protruding high out of the ground some 22yds north of the track. Eyre Point is also one of the best places on Raasay to see otters; go early morning to increase your chances.

Dùn Cana
The most spectacular views on Raasay can be enjoyed by climbing the island's highest peak, Dùn Cana (1,457ft; also called Dùn Caan). This flat-topped peak, which can be seen clearly from Skye, has views across the Narrows of Raasay to the whole of Skye's east coast, as well as to the Cuillin and across the Inner Sound to Applecross and the mainland. There are waymarked routes from Bailemeanach (2 miles) and the Burma Road (just under 3 miles), plus a circular route from Inverarish that is nearly 10 miles long; Walkhighlands describe this last option in detail with a map (w walkhighlands.co.uk/skye/duncaan.shtml).

Walk: Hallaig
Distance: 4 miles; time: 2–3 hours; start/end: North Fearns car park; OS Explorer map: 409 Raasay, Rona & Scalpay
Famous as the eponymous village in Sorley MacLean's 1954 poem, Hallaig was Raasay's largest settlement prior to the Clearances. The village was evicted in 1854 by George Rainy (page 95) who had recently purchased the island; reading Sorley MacLean's poem among the abandoned buildings is a haunting experience.

The road out towards Fearns is dotted with abandoned buildings and, even with just a little knowledge of the area's history, it's hard not to begin to feel a sense of the lost communities before you even reach the beginning of the walk.

From North Fearns car park an obvious track follows higher ground, heading initially northeast and then north along the coastline and beneath the cliffs of Beinn na' Leac, with the sea on your right. The views across to the mountains on the mainland make the first part of the walk well worth doing and you have one of the best chances of seeing eagles on Raasay.

After about 1½ miles, the route passes a commemorative cairn with MacLean's original Gaelic poem and its English translation engraved on to metal plates.

Shortly afterwards, the way begins to get rougher as it passes through some birch woods; you will have to negotiate a route below the ravines in Hallaig Burn before heading uphill towards the remains of over 40 roofless buildings in various states of ruin, with low stone walls that have begun to grow grass on top (⊕ 57°22'20"N 6°00'30"W). To return, retrace your steps.

Walk: Brae to Inver beach

Distance: 2 miles; time: 1–2 hours; start: Brae; end: Inver; OS Explorer map: 409 Raasay, Rona & Scalpay

To reach the starting point, head north of Inverarish for about 4 miles; you'll find a small parking place next to a high fence and metal gate on the left-hand side of the road. The scant remains of the deserted settlement of Brae are beyond the fence and you'll see a small wooden signpost marked 'Inver 1.5km'.

Pass through the gate and continue past the ruined houses on your left. Head downhill towards a wooded area and a lower fence with a metal gate; do not go through the gate but instead bear left and follow a small, often muddy path down through the trees. From this point on the path is narrow but easy to follow.

Most of the route goes alongside what starts as a tumbling stream, but is soon joined by others to become a bigger river that flows into rapids down through a naturally carved rocky canyon. The path weaves through magical birch woods with a carpet of moss and lichens growing from the tree branches, before opening out on to a stretch of heather moorland with a beautiful view towards the Skye Cuillin. Heading back into woodland, there are stepping stones over a small adjoining stream, followed by a ruined building on your right.

Finally, the path leads you out of the trees on to a pebbly beach, divided by the river mouth, where you can picnic while admiring the view out to Skye. Retrace your steps to return to the starting point.

NORTH RAASAY

Brochel Castle With a commanding view across the Inner Sound to Applecross on the mainland, Brochel Castle is a construction of mysterious origins, thought to date from the late 15th or early 16th century. Using a clever combination of strategic positioning and natural rock, combined with masonry, intricate brickwork and lime mortar, the castle is around 49ft high with a commanding position over the northeast coastline. This strategic vantage point was used by the MacLeods to control their wider territory. As the castle remains unrestored, precarious and missing much of the original structure (including its tallest tower), it is dangerous to get too close, but nonetheless the remains still make an imposing sight on the shore.

Calum's Road Heading north from Brochel Castle, the 'main' road becomes Calum's Road. Calum and Charles MacLeod initially constructed a track from Torran to Fladda, further north, between 1949 and 1952, funded by the local council. Residents of the island's far north campaigned for many years for further funding and assistance to connect their homes with the rest of Raasay; eventually the Department of Agriculture's engineering department carried out some initial rock blasting work. However, Calum – also a lighthouse keeper on Rona, not to mention postman, crofter, writer and local historian – ultimately decided to build the road himself. Between the 1960s and 70s, armed with Thomas Aitken's 60-year-old book *Road Making & Maintenance: A Practical Treatise for Engineers, Surveyors and Others*, he almost single-handedly built the 1¾-mile stretch of road between Arnish and Brochel Castle with little more than hand tools. Work on the road, which has steep climbs and descents, traversing boggy moorland and between rocky cliffs and sheer drops, must have been unimaginably hard. Once he had finally finished, the road was surfaced by the local council, but there was nobody left living in the north except Calum and his wife. It makes for a poignant drive or cycle, especially after reading *Calum's Road* (page 267), a well-researched book on the subject by Roger Hutchinson.

Walk: To Fladda at low tide

Distance: 5 miles; time: 1–2 hours; start/end: Arnish; OS Explorer map: 409 Raasay, Rona & Scalpay

The north of Raasay is mostly uninhabited and, with the weather often changing quickly, it would be unwise to attempt much walking in the area without being well prepared for a day hike (page 37). For this route you will need to check tide times in advance (page 28).

One hundred years ago the island of Fladda (Eilean Fladday) hosted a whole community; the population, lacking amenities or even a bridge to connect them to Raasay at high tide, has now dispersed. Only three houses remain and these are not lived in continually throughout the year.

Coming by car, park at Arnish and take the path to the left of the few houses there, which leads along Raasay's west coast. As you wander through twisted birch woods, look out for interesting mushrooms and toadstools in autumn, before the view opens out over the beautiful Sound of Raasay and the tiny islets of Fraoch Eilean and Glas Eilean. Fladda is up ahead; at low tide the beach that connects the island to Raasay shows signs of an old, squared fish trap on the shore.

Assuming you have checked the tide times in advance, it is easy if a little slippery on the seaweed to cross the beach over to Fladda. Do not underestimate this smaller island's size, however; though only around 2 miles long, unless you've come out at the very start of low tide you might struggle to make your way around it in time for the returning tide. That said, it is worth taking the time to look out to sea from the island's west coast as you might catch a glimpse of seals, porpoises or dolphins. With enough time before high tide, it's possible to walk northwest through the old village, which is mostly ruined buildings, towards Loch Mòr, a small lake in the centre of the island.

Back on Raasay, you can return to Arnish the same way you came or take an alternative route southeast, which leads uphill, inland towards the hill, Meall Dearg. This option leads you up into uninhabited hills and eventually to a junction where you can choose to go right, back to Arnish, or left and north in the direction of Rona.

5

The Small Isles

Frequently overlooked, the Small Isles archipelago is made up of Eigg, Rùm, Muck, Canna and Sanday and sits to the south of Skye. Joined by a bridge, Canna and Sanday are generally referred to as a single entity, with 'Canna' often used to describe both islands.

The islands' populations do not relate to their size. Rùm, the biggest at just over 40 square miles, has only around 30 inhabitants, while Canna (just over 5 square miles) is home to about 20 people; smaller Muck, a mere 2.2 square miles, has around 35 people. Eigg's population of roughly 110 is a little over those of Rùm, Canna and Muck combined – unsurprisingly, the island has the most regular ferry connections and receives the most visitors. Note that cars are forbidden on all of the islands unless you have special permission, ferry times are irregular and often cancelled due to bad weather, and mobile phone reception is patchy – in many ways, the Small Isles feel like the Inner Hebrides' final frontier. While travelling around the islands in a hurry is tricky and inconvenient, visitors who can spend more time here, particularly those who love the outdoors and wildlife or are looking for true peace and quiet, will find ample reward. Birdwatching is a particular highlight, with each island offering something special: Rùm and Eigg are both good places to spot birds of prey such as hen harriers and golden and white-tailed eagles; while Rùm is also visited by enormous numbers of Manx shearwaters (page 109); Canna has fantastic seabird colonies including puffins (page 124) and Muck has an abundance of ground-nesting birds.

Distinct in appearance, Eigg, Canna and Muck have some similarity in their volcanic formation. For those of us who aren't geologists, perhaps the most exciting result of this is the basalt columns, similar to the more famous examples at Fingal's Cave on Staffa (page 171) and the Giant's Causeway in Northern Ireland, which are found on all three islands and at their most impressive on Canna. Mountainous Rùm is a conspicuous addition to the group; with a landscape distinct from the other Small Isles – made up primarily of Torridonian sandstone, gabbro, peridotite and granite, which have resulted in a wet heathland, the island is mostly infertile for cultivation and as a result has never been heavily populated.

HISTORY

The Small Isles have a rich and varied archaeological landscape. In the 1980s, evidence of Mesolithic nomad activity on Rùm was thought to be the oldest sign of settlement in Scotland, but this title has now been lost after more recent discoveries elsewhere. There have been findings of 9,000-year-old bloodstone arrow heads on the island, as well as Neolithic axe heads (Eigg) and thumbnail scrapers (Muck). The islands' Bronze Age inhabitants left over 30 round cairns across the archipelago

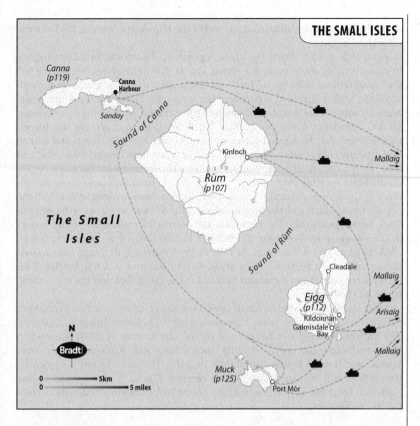

Canna
(p119)

Canna
Harbour

Sanday

Sound of Canna

Kinloch

Rùm
(p107)

Mallaig

The Small
Isles

Sound of Rùm

Cleadale

Mallaig

Eigg
(p112)

Kildonnan

Arisaig

Galmisdale
Bay

Mallaig

N

Bradt

0 ————— 5km
0 ————— 5 miles

Muck
(p125)

Port Mòr

and large numbers of hut circles (page 264) on Canna and Eigg. There are numerous forts (or dùns) dating from the Iron Age (around 800BC to AD100): six on Eigg, four on Canna, three on Rùm and one on Muck (page 126).

Canna and Eigg were both important Christian sites in the early medieval period. The township of A' Chill (which no longer exists thanks to the Clearances; page 104) on Canna is thought to have been the site of a chapel founded by Columba in the late 6th century; Saint Donnán, another priest who attempted to introduce Christianity to the Picts, is the patron saint of Eigg where he was martyred.

Although Norse place names are common, they are more topographical than relating to settlements; some artefacts have been found, mostly on Eigg, including a boat that was uncovered as the sand washed away at Laig Bay, and a sword at Kildonnan.

The more modern history of the Small Isles is as brutal as anywhere in Scotland. In later clan times, the Small Isles were passed between owners including the Clanranald, the MacLeans of Coll and the Earls of Argyll. Situated away from the mainland, the relationships between landowners and ordinary people were particularly unbalanced here, with the lairds rarely living on the islands and deciding the islanders' fates remotely. The 1780s and 90s saw waves of emigration due to high rents and overcrowding; as the kelp industry was thriving at this time, landlords disapproved of the exodus and took measures to ensure the population did not decline. The Clanranalds, for example, built crofting townships to accommodate more workers. The economic and social situation changed entirely when the kelp market collapsed at the end of the Napoleonic Wars in 1815 and the Clearances began.

From 1826 to 1828 nearly the whole population of Rùm was forced to emigrate to make way for more profitable sheep. On 11 July 1826 alone, 300 people left the island on two ships bound for Nova Scotia. This was a traumatic event by all accounts, with a shepherd reporting: 'The wild cries of the men and the heart-breaking wails of the women and children filled the air between the mountainous shores.' Somewhat ironically, Lachlan MacLean (who was renting the island) then realised that he needed someone to look after his 8,000 sheep and had to subsequently collect some other poor souls who had been cleared from Mull and Skye. Only a decade later, the mutton market collapsed and Rùm became a largely uninhabited sporting estate, where wealthy people from mainland Great Britain came to shoot deer. Around the same time, the MacLeans evicted around half the population of Muck and 150 people sailed on the *St Lawrence* from Tobermory to Cape Breton in Canada. The remaining inhabitants were allowed to build houses in the village above Port Mòr and tried to sustain themselves by fishing, but by 1835 they had all left the island. In 1851 all the inhabitants of Canna were moved to Sanday in what became known as the Great Clearance. A' Chill, inhabited for hundreds of years, was cleared and flattened to the extent that now there is nothing left of it to be seen.

Since the Clearances, the Small Isles have struggled to establish permanent populations, but recent years have seen a shift in power towards residents. The entirety of Eigg was bought out by the community in 1997, since when the population has been steadily increasing, and Kinloch, Rùm's only village, was bought by the community in 2010. The rest of Rùm is owned by NatureScot and managed as a nature reserve. Canna is now owned by the National Trust for Scotland and Muck seems to be thriving under its current private ownership.

GETTING THERE AND AWAY

BY FERRY CalMac (page 30) runs services from Mallaig on the mainland (page 260) to the Small Isles, usually stopping at more than one of the islands on each journey. You cannot take your car without special permission, which is usually only granted to residents, people with disabilities or those working on the islands. Blue disability badge holders can arrange for a vehicle permit for Eigg or Muck in advance (☏ 01349 781083; e communityservices.lochaber@highland.gov.uk); it should also be possible for overnight visitors staying on Rùm (e info@isleofrum. com), but Canna doesn't currently have this option. Foot passengers are advised to book in advance; single tickets cost £4.35–5.90.

Timetables change regularly and can be confusing to read; check online (w calmac.co.uk) while planning your trip and just before you travel. Eigg has the most frequent crossings, with six weekly in summer (1hr 20mins if direct); the other islands have around five crossings a week (timings depend on which island is visited first: a direct ferry to Muck takes 1hr 45mins, while sailing to Canna via two other islands takes 4hrs 10mins). Winter services are reduced to three or four weekly sailings. Ferries can be cancelled due to weather at any time, but it happens more frequently between September and March.

Inter-island travel With careful study of the timetables (there is usually one general Small Isles timetable and one with an island by island breakdown – it's worth familiarising yourself with both) you can work out a route visiting multiple islands as part of the same trip (journey times range from 40mins to 2hrs 30mins).

BY SMALL BOAT Arisaig Marine (↘ 01687 450224; w arisaig.co.uk) runs services from the end of April until September on the MV *Sheerwater*, a small passenger boat, between Arisaig and Eigg (2–5 weekly; £12.50 one-way) or Muck (2–3 weekly; £15 one-way). You are advised to book in advance. These trips, which focus on wildlife watching, usually only offer between 2 hours and 5 hours ashore, but single fares are also available. There is a good chance of seeing marine mammals such as seals and maybe minke whales, porpoises or common dolphin, as well as basking sharks and seabirds.

MOORINGS

Canna w theisleofcanna.com/theharbour
Eigg w isleofeigg.org/yachts-wild-camping
Muck w isleofmuck.com (click on 'Getting Here')
Rùm w rumbunkhouse.com/moorings

OTHER PRACTICALITIES

There is no resident **doctor** on any of the islands, but Eigg does have the Small Isles Medical Practice (↘ 01687 482427; ⊕ 09.00–noon Mon–Fri) in Grianan, which is also a dispensary. The islands are served by a visiting doctor, but it's usually more convenient to travel to Mallaig (page 262) for non-emergency medical services or a pharmacy. In an emergency, follow the usual procedure of calling ↘ 999 or 112; coastguards or island-based 'first responders' will initially assist with any emergency care. If necessary, an evacuation can be carried out via ferry, air ambulance, lifeboat, coastguard helicopter or private charter, depending on the circumstances.

Rùm and Eigg have a **post office** integrated into their main grocery shop (pages 107 and 113), Canna has a tiny stand-alone post office (page 120) and Muck does not have any postal or banking facilities at all.

RÙM (RÙM)

The island of Rùm, with a diameter of around 8 miles, is the largest of the Small Isles. Unique among the Inner Hebrides, it appears as a cluster of mountains rising directly out of the sea. The highest point is Askival (2,664ft); the mountains are in fact the eroded roots of an ancient volcano that would have once stood around 6,560ft high. The island's entire small population lives in its sole settlement, the village of Kinloch on the east coast, while the rest of the island is a nature reserve, making it a particularly special place for hikers and birdwatchers. Along with the Manx shearwaters, of which 200,000 arrive each spring, the island also provides the perfect habitat for red-throated divers, golden plovers, white-tailed eagles (there are two or three breeding pairs, depending on whether the third decides to nest on Rùm or Canna) and its three pairs of golden eagles. Look out for white-tailed eagles gliding over the bay, whereas golden eagles are often up above ridges. In late summer, you might be lucky enough to see basking sharks.

GETTING AROUND Visitors are not allowed to bring cars on to the island, but Blue disability badge holders should be able to arrange for a vehicle permit if staying overnight (page 104). Rùm is otherwise best explored under your own steam, either **on foot or by bike**. Kinloch, the island's only village, is just a 10-minute walk from the ferry terminal, on the island's east coast. At the time of writing, Rùm Bunkhouse (see below) was in the process of setting up a bike-hire scheme. Rùm **postcodes** are PH43 4RR.

 WHERE TO STAY AND EAT *Map, opposite*
While Rùm does not have a hotel or anywhere to eat out, the island's accommodation options all provide good value for money. All places to stay are found in Kinloch, excluding two Mountain Bothies Association bothies (page 44), **Guirdil** (northwest Rùm) and **Dibidil** (southeast Rùm). These are free to use, but be sure to adhere to the rules (explained online) and to leave the place clean and tidy. Note that Fliss, who runs both Ivy Cottage and Bramble Bothy, comes to the ferry terminal to collect her guests' luggage (and the guests themselves if needed).

Ivy Cottage (1 dbl, 1 family room) Kinloch; ☎ 01687 462744; w ivycottageisleofrum.co.uk. Having moved to Rùm to work for Scottish Natural Heritage, owner Fliss has lived on the island for more than 20 years & is a great source of local information. The rooms & the conservatory dining room have fantastic views over Loch Scresort. Rooms are spacious, but have sloped ceilings; both en suite. Vegetarian dinner; B&B offered. **££££**

Bramble Bothy (sleeps 2) Kinloch; ☎ 01687 462744; w ivycottageisleofrum.co.uk. Also run by Fliss of Ivy Cottage, this small, but perfectly formed, sustainably built shepherd's hut is off-grid without sacrificing either aesthetics or comfort: it's fully fitted with proper bedding, armchairs, an amazing modern compost loo, wood burner, fridge, hob & sink. Right on the shore of the loch. **£££**

✱ Rùm Bunkhouse (20 beds, 2 cabins & campsite) Kinloch; m 07824 036305; w rumbunkhouse.com; ♿. Community owned & a credit to the Isle of Rùm Community Trust, the bunkhouse is modern & well equipped, with large communal areas, wood-burning stove & a whole wall of windows giving panoramic views of the shoreline – you can eat your meals in a bird hide with a decent chance of seeing otters. Campsite is beautifully situated on the water's edge, with basic facilities including toilets, showers, water taps & a communal shelter with solar USB charging plugs. Cabins are pod-type structures sleeping 1–4 people with mattresses, USB charging, kettles & very basic camping furniture inside. Atmosphere is generally relaxed & guests are an interesting congregation of Hebrides & hiking enthusiasts. Fantastic, warm drying room for kit. Dogs allowed in cabins, but not bunkhouse. **£–££**

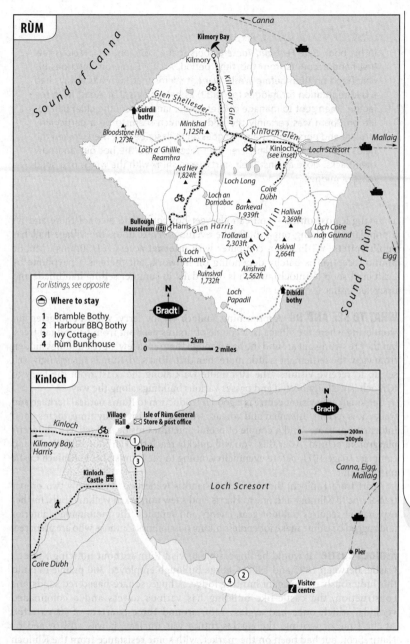

Harbour BBQ Bothy (sleeps 4–6) Kinloch;
m 07906 181029; e harbourhut@gmail.com.
Basic accommodation in a heptagonal wooden
cabin with reindeer-hide rugs, solar lighting,
BBQ grill & chimney in the centre. Book via
email. **£**

OTHER PRACTICALITIES Isle of Rùm General Store (Kinloch; ☎ 01687 460328;
f; ⊕ hours vary) sells groceries, including fresh fruit and vegetables, as well

as having a **post office** – you can also get hot coffee and alcohol there and it's a popular local hang-out spot in the evenings. Next door, the village hall has public **toilets**, Wi-Fi and a computer with **internet** access (£1/30mins). Mobile **phone** reception is patchy depending on network, but there is a payphone by Drift craft shop (Kinloch), which is open daily in summer selling handmade and upcycled crafts.

WHAT TO SEE AND DO Approaching **Kinloch** on the ferry, you'd be forgiven for wondering where the village is; a couple of houses peer out from behind tall trees, but they're strung out around the bay. Though there are a few more buildings hidden from view, the settlement is little more than that. That said, Rùm is surprisingly well set up to receive visitors. The 10-minute walk along the coast from the ferry to Kinloch is well signposted and passes various buildings along the way.

The small, free **visitor centre** is a good introduction to Rùm's natural heritage and walks. It is usually unstaffed and you are welcome to visit at any time; there's good information, games and a couple of useful amenities inside, as well as a **children's playground** behind. After this, you will quickly reach the Harbour BBQ Bothy and campsite (page 107), before eventually coming to the unmistakable **Kinloch Castle** on your left.

Apart from Kinloch, the rest of the island is wilderness. With only two proper tracks, one to Kilmory and one to Harris, and a few unmarked walking trails, further exploration requires outdoor gear, energy and supplies. The mountainous interior and rugged coastline make for endless hiking possibilities for those who are prepared.

Kinloch Castle It would be impossible to visit Rùm without noticing Kinloch Castle. Between 1897 and 1900, George Bullough employed 300 people to build this ludicrously extravagant hunting lodge. A huge, square-based red sandstone construction, the castle-like building has various towers and a colonnaded veranda, which once had a glass roof, around three-quarters of its exterior. At the time of writing, the castle's future was unclear: it was still owned by NatureScot, but had been on the market, with some resistance from the Kinloch community against a sale for what they saw as potentially inappropriate use of the building and land. Neither island residents nor visitors were able to access the castle interior.

Walks and cycle routes The routes to the abandoned coastal settlements of Kilmory and Harris are Rùm's only 'roads' and, while they can also be walked, it is much faster to cycle (page 106). **Wildlife watching** is very accessible on Rùm; exploring beyond Kinloch will improve your chances of seeing species such as golden eagles, as well as lots of red deer.

Walk: Up to Coire Dubh

Distance: 3 miles; time: 2 hours; start/end: Kinloch Castle; OS Explorer map: 397 Rùm, Eigg, Muck, Canna & Sanday

This is a relatively easy hike with an elevation gain of 920ft. Within an hour you are into the wilderness, with great views of the surrounding mountains and down over the coast around Kinloch.

The path leaves from beside the stream that runs just to the south of Kinloch Castle; it's on the left-hand side if you are looking at the castle from the front.

Walk past the castle and then bear away from it to the left, going between two huts to find the start of the path. The route runs southwest, with the burn (Allt Slugan a' Choilich) never far from its left-hand side, through evergreen trees, passing crystal-clear pools and an impressive canyon, all the way up to Coire Dubh (✪ 56°59'53"N 6°18'07"W). After about a mile, take a moment to admire the Manx shearwater sundial, a fitting memorial to biologist Wilf Nelson who died falling from Bloodstone Hill on the west coast in the 1980s.

Coire Dubh is a gentle bowl in the landscape where several small mountain streams meet, surrounded by Barkeval and Hallival mountains with an open view back down over Kinloch, Loch Scresort and the range of An Mullach Mór behind. It is a good place to look out for golden eagles and red deer.

From here you can return along the same path.

MANX SHEARWATERS

Every summer, Rùm becomes home to around a third of the world's entire population of Manx shearwaters. An attractive bird with a white front and black back, they have a curved end to their beak and are just over 30cm long. Manx shearwaters can be seen on Rùm from March until September, but their numbers only become really spectacular in June and July. Breeding around the peaks of Askival (2,664ft), Hallival (2,369ft) and Trollaval (2,303ft), their breeding grounds are not easy to access, something that is made even more complicated by the fact that they only return at night.

The most adventurous and dedicated of birdwatchers can hike up to Coire Dubh (see above) in the early evening and head over to the northeast face of Hallival before dark. Once here, sit down (be careful not to cover a burrow as you do so), turn off your torch and wait for the birds to return; be sure to sit still as they swoop down, squawking and cackling noisily, to their burrows. Trollaval, a peak to the southwest, got its name from Norse settlers, who heard the shearwaters' noises from the mountain and thought they came from trolls. Even if you can't make the hike, you should still be able to hear the birds in the evening and look out for them fishing off the coast during the day.

If you decide to go alone, note any current advice displayed in the visitor centre, take a good torch with plenty of battery life, warm and waterproof clothes, and preferably a GPS device to help with the return trip. The darkness doesn't last long in summer, so another option is to wait on the mountain until it's light enough to see properly. Flasks of hot drinks are a must.

All of the largest animals on Rùm have historically been introduced or reintroduced. The island is supposed have the oldest **Highland pony** stud in the world and the long-haired **goats** are descendants of those brought over for wig making before the Clearances. In 1975, Rùm was the first place in Scotland for **white-tailed eagles** to be reintroduced after they had become extinct in the UK during the 20th century; this turned out to be quite a successful project as there are now estimated to be around 150 pairs spread across the west Highlands' coast and islands.

Red deer are native to the UK and considered by many to be the most majestic and iconic of Scotland's animals. Their history on Rùm is complex. In 1580, during a survey of the area, James VI noted that Rùm had a good population of deer; by 1787, they were extinct on the island, only to be reintroduced for sport by the 2nd Marquis of Salisbury in 1845. At that time the deer were an important economic asset to landowners, as Rùm was used as a hunting retreat.

While some deer stalking still takes place on the island, the population around Kilmory and Mullach Mòr has been protected and studied by the Isle of Rùm Red Deer Project (w rumdeer.biology.ed.ac.uk) since 1972. The Kilmory study area is the easiest place on the island to see red deer. Noticeable by their collars, the studied deer are less nervous of people and unlikely to run away as you walk past them; nevertheless it is important not to approach them directly and to keep dogs under control.

The studied red deer population have helped inform our understanding of red deer and ungulate populations in general; among many less worrying discoveries, the deer have been shown to be affected by climate change, with all their seasonal behaviours getting earlier over the years.

Perhaps the biggest benefit of the project to casual visitors is that these deer are much tamer than those in wild parts elsewhere in Scotland. If you are calm and quiet they are unlikely to run away from you as you walk or cycle past but, as with any large animal you are unsure of, do not attempt to approach them. Be especially careful during calving season (May–June) when, like sheep or cows, mothers will get distressed if you disturb them; and during the rut (September–November) when stags are at their most aggressive and can be dangerous to humans.

Cycle: to Kilmory Bay

Distance: 9 miles; time: 3 hours; start/end: Kinloch; OS Explorer map: 397 Rùm, Eigg, Muck, Canna & Sanday

Begin at the crossroads just north of Kinloch Castle, just before the bridge that heads towards the shop; take the marked track directly inland and head in this direction for around 2 miles. The track is extremely bumpy and rocky for the first section, but soon levels out to a predominantly smooth dirt track. This route takes you through Kinloch Glen and woodland, then across moorland, along the base of Barkeval hill, until you come to a junction near the base of Minishal; take the right fork to go towards Kilmory (left goes to Harris; see opposite) and head north into Kilmory Glen. Soon you will see a notice explaining that you are entering the 'Isle of Rùm Red Deer Project' (see above) and you'll hopefully come across some of the deer themselves.

After about 2 miles, the track reaches Kilmory Bay, a sheltered sweep of sandy beach. There are a couple of glorious sandy beaches and some interesting sea stacks and caves on the west side of Kilmory Bay. Look out for white-tailed eagles, otters and larger marine mammals, as well as birds such as curlews and eider duck.

Just above the mouth of the river is the old settlement of Kilmory and its churchyard. This village was inhabited before the Clearances and is thought to have been a religious site from at least the 7th or 8th centuries. To make the most of Kilmory Bay, bring supplies and make this into a longer day trip.

Cycle: to Harris
Distance: 16 miles; time: 5 hours; start/end: Kinloch; OS Explorer map: 397 Rùm, Eigg, Muck, Canna & Sanday

This is a longer cycle ride that includes quite a steep hill. Starting from the crossroads between Kinloch shop and castle, take the inland route as you would for the walk to Kilmory Bay (see opposite) until you reach a fork. Choose the left-hand track and continue in this direction on the biggest and most obvious route, passing some small waterfalls and a dam, as well as the turning to Bloodstone Hill and Loch a' Ghillie Reamhra leading off to the right, which you should ignore.

Continuing on the same track you will cycle past Ard Nev on your right and the summits of Hallival, Askival, Ainshval and Ruinsival a little further away, walling you in on the left. Of the little lochs that appear in the foreground, Loch an Dornabac is the biggest, with a mountainous backdrop as you begin to descend.

Passing the bulbous volcanic extrusion of An Dornac on the left, the conspicuous columns of Bullough Mausoleum and black, rocky Harris Bay will soon come into view in the distance. The path curves around to the right and lazy beds (page 264) are still visible in fields, showing that this area was once cultivated. Harris was home to a small township before the Clearances and you can still see the low stone wall ruins of their houses on the higher ground around the bay.

The mausoleum, inspired by ancient Greece, is a fittingly ostentatious tribute to the Bulloughs, commissioned by the same Sir George Bullough as Kinloch Castle (page 108) around 1900. Some 80yds northwest and faintly visible from the mausoleum is a partially buried mosaic that marks the original family vault, destroyed on George's instruction after it was likened to a gentlemen's lavatory. Harris Bay itself is a small cove fringed by black rocks; a perfect place to sit quietly and look out for otters, white-tailed eagles or larger marine mammals. It's worth allowing a whole day for the trip to make the most of Harris Bay and its surrounds.

HIKING THE RÙM CUILLIN

Mountainous remnants of a volcano's core, the Rùm Cuillin provide exciting opportunities for serious hill-walking, scrambling and rock climbing. Before setting out, it's essential to be prepared, knowing how to navigate and route find, having proper equipment and spending time doing research in advance. Don't forget to check the weather and let someone know where you are going. There are very few opportunities to fill up water en route, so be sure to take plenty with you. Note that between March and July eagles might nest at Barkeval Ridge; check posters around Kinloch for the latest and be prepared to alter your route to avoid disturbing them. Reliable route descriptions can be found in Peter Edwards's *Walking on Rum and the Small Isles*, the second edition of which (due for publication in 2025) will be co-authored by me.

The second-largest of the Small Isles and by far the most populous, dramatically beautiful Eigg is community owned and runs on sustainable energy. The mighty An Sgùrr (1,289ft), left over from a volcanic eruption 58 million years ago, dominates the skyline: looking north from Galmisdale Bay, on the southeastern coast, it is a huge steep-sided lump of rock rising far above its surroundings, but looking at Eigg from further south it appears as a long, humped ridge – the spine of a sleeping dragon. The island's coastline is mostly rocky, with high cliffs and a couple of wide sandy beaches. Hiking is less dramatic than on Rùm, but nonetheless the views can be spectacular.

In 1695, Martin Martin wrote that 'natives dare not call this isle by its ordinary name of Egg when they are at sea, but island Nim-ban-More' (the isle of big women). We aren't given any further explanation, but stories and references to mythical women circulate the island in the form of place names and folk tales. It

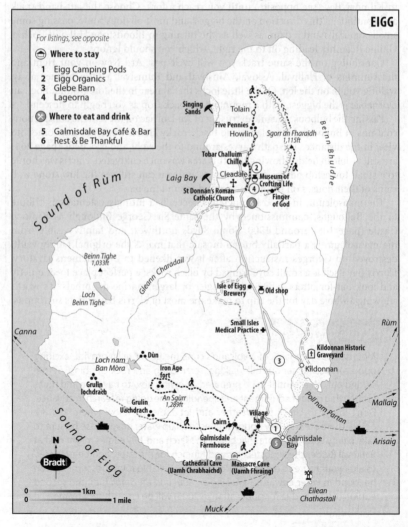

EIGG

For listings, see opposite

⊖ **Where to stay**
1 Eigg Camping Pods
2 Eigg Organics
3 Glebe Barn
4 Lageorna

⊗ **Where to eat and drink**
5 Galmisdale Bay Café & Bar
6 Rest & Be Thankful

is perhaps the richest of the Small Isles for archaeological sites, many of which are accessible by an undemanding bike ride.

GETTING AROUND Cars are only allowed on the island for residents or for Blue Badge holders (page 104), but as its road network is the most extensive in the Small Isles it is particularly convenient for exploring on two wheels. To hire a **bike**, try Eigg Adventures ✳ (Galmisdale Bay; w eiggadventures.co.uk), who offer well-maintained, quality mountain bikes with helmets, friendly service and good local information, as well as sit-on-top **kayak** hire (£20/30 for 1hr/2hrs) around the Galmisdale Bay area. There is also a **taxi** service (Charlie's Taxis; \ 01687 482404). Eigg postcodes are PH42 4RL.

🏠 WHERE TO STAY AND EAT *Map, opposite*

Eigg has excellent accommodation options, ranging from luxury bed and breakfast to simple camping. Self-catering listings can be found on w isleofeigg.org/accommodation. With only a couple of options for eating out, most visitors are likely to end up in Galmisdale Bay Café & Bar (see below), a central gathering place and hive of activity, at some point during their stay.

Lageorna (2 rooms) Cleadale; \ 01687 460081; w lageorna.com. Stunning views over Laig Bay & the Rùm Cuillin. High-quality B&B accommodation with luxurious finishings. Both rooms have great sea views from large windows & are spacious enough to sit in & relax in bad weather. No TVs, but good Wi-Fi connection, & it has good green credentials. Having lived on Eigg for over 40 years, owner Sue is a wealth of information. Packed lunches (£) available. Their small restaurant (⏰ some eves with advance booking; ££) is also open to non-residents, with an exciting 3-course menu (adapted for dietary requirements) & focus on sustainability: organic, local, seasonal where possible. **£££**

Eigg Camping Pods (3 pods, sleeping up to 4) Galmisdale Bay; w eiggcampingpods.com; ⏰ Mar–Dec. Community-owned pods with small heater, fridge, kettle, light & limited electricity. You must bring your own bedding & cooking kit (or eat at Galmisdale Bay Café, a 1min walk away). **££**

Eigg Organics Cleadale; m 07482 622122; w eiggorganics.co.uk. Camping (£7 pp) with basic facilities & an amazing view, plus rudimentary self-catering in Cleadale Bothy (sleeps 4), which is fully equipped with essentials including cooker, wood-burning stove & bedding. Outside compost toilets. **££**

✳ **Glebe Barn** (22 beds); \ 01687 315099; w glebebarn.co.uk. This spacious bunkhouse, 1 mile from the pier, has the comfortable feeling of a large family house. There is plenty of space in the bedrooms, a large communal area for sitting & dining, & sofas in a big conservatory with incredible views over to the mainland. There are local-interest books & maps. Tamsin, who runs the bunkhouse, has lived on Eigg all her life; she can give good tips on walks & the island. **£**

Galmisdale Bay Café & Bar An Laimhrig, Galmisdale Bay; \ 01687 482487; w galmisdale-bay.com; ⏰ hours vary; check online. Good, simple food that's mostly homemade & local. Different lunch & dinner menus. Affordable local seafood, such as Arisaig mussels in creamy white wine & garlic sauce. **£**

Rest & Be Thankful Cleadale; ⏰ summer only, hours vary. Tea, coffee & homemade cake under a gazebo in the garden. Payment by donation in jam jar. **£**

SHOPPING

Isle of Eigg Craft Shop An Laimhrig, Galmisdale Bay; ⏰ May–Sep 11.00–16.30 daily. A nice range of local crafts, plus island maps with marked hiking routes.

Isle of Eigg Shop An Laimhrig, Galmisdale Bay; \ 01687 482432; w isleofeiggshop.com; ⏰ dependent on ferry timetable; check online. Well-stocked grocery shop & bakery with a good range of specialist, sustainable & local products as well as basics, including loose fruit & veg.

OTHER PRACTICALITIES There's a **post office** in Isle of Eigg Shop (page 113; ⊕ 11.00–13.00 Mon & Sat & 10–noon Fri). The An Laimhrig building at the pier (Galmisdale Bay) provides **toilets**, **showers** (£3/5mins), a **drying room** and **laundry** facilities for visitors.

WHAT TO SEE AND DO
The south
Kildonnan Historic Graveyard Situated about 3 miles (by road) from Galmisdale Bay, Kildonnan Historic Graveyard appears to have been used for burials from prehistoric times through to the modern day and is also thought to be the site of Saint Donnán of Eigg's monastery, founded in the 7th century. Donnán, a contemporary of Columba, is said to have been martyred on Eigg in 617, though the circumstances are unclear. The best legend goes that the Pictish queen sent her warrior women to kill Donnán and his monks. After beheading them, the women saw bright lights above the dead and heard enchanting voices. Entranced, they followed the lights up towards An Sgùrr and were led into Loch nam Ban Mòra (Loch of the Great Women), where they drowned.

There is nothing to see of Donnán's monastery today, but there is a ruined church here, built by the 16th-century MacDonald chiefs of Clanranald and which has several interesting carvings. Outside the church there is an elaborate cross shaft dating from the late 14th century in the distinctive type of design associated with the Iona school of sculpture, similar to those on Islay and Oronsay. Inside the church is a stone slab with a double symmetrical cross inside a circle that is thought to be from the 8th or 9th century, a small carving mounted on the wall called Sheela-na-gig (goddess), which is probably pre-Christian, and a number of early grave slabs. A number of carved crosses from Kildonnan can now be found in St Donnán's Roman Catholic Church (page 117). The site overlooks the 19th-century house at Kildonnan Farm, Eilean Chathastail (the island off Galmisdale Bay) and out towards the mountainous mainland.

Walk: Massacre Cave (Uamh Fhraing)
Distance: 2¼ miles; time: 1–2 hours; start/end: Galmisdale Bay; OS Explorer map: 397 Rùm, Eigg, Muck, Canna & Sanday
This walk visits the cave of Uamh Fhraing, with some glorious coastal scenery.

To reach the cave from Galmisdale Bay, walk along the road that climbs up the hill, passing the camping pods on your right, and continue around half a mile through mature sycamore trees. Ignore the first turning and track on the left and the turning on the right towards the village hall, and instead look for a gatepost (⊕ 56°52'41.2"N 6°08'22"W) on your left marked with a small yellow arrow and a pink circle. Go through this gateway on to a substantial track, pass through a second gate marked with a pink circle and keep going for a short time until you see an obvious turning to the left just before you reach a house, where a grassy track heads south. Keep to this grassy track, which dwindles to a path as it veers to the west. About 1 mile from Galmisdale Bay, the path reaches a small metal gate above a clifftop; go through this and along the inside of a fence until you find steep steps descending to the shore, with the entrance to Uamh Fhraing (⊕ 56°52'25.1"N 6°08'43.9"W) in the cliffs on your left.

Commonly referred to as the **Massacre Cave** (see opposite), Uamh Fhraing has been a dark tourist attraction since the 19th century when there were still decomposed bodies in there. Eventually the population of Eigg became so embarrassed by this that they carried out proper Christian burials. There are no

In 1577 around 400 people were massacred in a cave called Uamh Fhraing on the south coast of Eigg. This is part of a grisly running storyline of feuding and revenge between the clan chiefs of the MacDonalds of Clanranald and the MacLeods of Dunvegan on Skye.

It begins on Eilean Chathastail, the small island opposite Galmisdale Bay where the ferry comes into Eigg. A group of women, tending to the cattle there, were abused by passing MacLeod men who were on their way back to Skye from Glasgow. These men were killed by the women's male friends from Eigg, who were an extension of the MacDonald clan; as a result, the MacLeods came back to the island to avenge the deaths. Seeing the MacLeods coming, the inhabitants of Eigg hid in Uamh Fhraing. (If there were really 400 of them then it must have been extremely squashed!) After a while, growing impatient, they sent out a scout. The story goes that the scout was caught and his footprints 'in fresh snow' were followed back to the cave. The MacLeods built a huge fire, blocking the small entrance to the cave, and smoked all the hiding islanders to death.

In retaliation, the MacDonalds sailed to Dunvegan and burned a church full of worshippers alive at Trumpan (page 79). This string of atrocities is one of the most easy-to-follow examples of how dangerous life could be as an ordinary person living in the times of clan warfare. Chiefs had an ultimate power over the lives and deaths of their extended clansmen and communities living on small islands and remote peninsulas were totally at the mercy of their whims.

bones to see now, and the cave is relatively easy to access. You will need a torch if you want to go inside and doing so is very much 'at your own risk' as loose rocks occasionally fall from the roof.

From the cave, at low tide, you can also clamber over the rocks 500yds further west to a second cave called **Cathedral Cave (Uamh Chrabhaichd)**. Head back the way you came to Galmisdale Bay, or return as far as the village hall to continue your walk on to the abandoned village of Grulin Uachdrach (as described below) or climb An Sgùrr (page 116).

Walk: Grulin Uachdrach and Grulin Iochdrach
Distance: 5½ miles; time: 2–4 hours; start/end: Galmisdale Bay; OS Explorer map: 397 Rùm, Eigg, Muck, Canna & Sanday
From Galmisdale pier, follow the road on the left, which climbs gently northwest, soon entering woodland. Keep straight on, bearing left, where the track forks after 500yds (the right fork leads to the village hall). Ignore a left-hand turn, which leads ultimately to the Massacre Cave (see above), and keep straight on, climbing steadily before emerging from the woods through a gate into a grassy field. Follow the track up across the field towards the iconic grey- and red-roofed Galmisdale Farmhouse in the shadow of An Sgùrr, which makes a very striking scene. In the early 19th century this building was a Tacksman's house, improved by the profits of the kelp industry, but it has also been a post office, inn, shooting lodge, factor's house and the proprietor's residence.

Head around to the right-hand side of the house and turn left on to the track; follow this, passing wind turbines on your left. After around 1½ miles you come to a cluster of ruins and one restored building, which mark the remains of **Grulin Uachdrach**, or Upper Grulin (✛ 56°52'45"N 6°10'44"W).

Grulin means 'stony place' and is associated with a mythical battle between two giants; the peculiar boulders scattered around the area are said to have been left as a sign of their struggle. Cleared in 1853, this is the best example of an abandoned village in the Small Isles, with traces of at least 42 ruined buildings, some above and some below the track, in various stages of disintegration, which span several generations of inhabitants through the 18th and mid 19th centuries. All are roofless save one traditional white bothy, which is in the process of renovation, and some others have walls complete to shoulder height. There is also an **Iron Age dùn** (✛ 56°52'44"N 6°10'48"W) on the southwest edge of the township, but it is difficult to identify among the ruins of more recent buildings.

From here, follow a path leading roughly northwest for a further ¾ mile to reach the neighbouring township of Grulin Iochdrach, where there are more ruins.

Retrace your steps to return to Galmisdale Bay; alternatively, you can head up An Sgùrr by following the directions from the grey- and red-roofed house in the description below: this would add another 3 miles and 885ft of elevation to your walk.

Walk: An Sgùrr

Distance: 5 miles; time: 3–4½ hours; start/end: Galmisdale Bay; OS Explorer map: 397 Rùm, Eigg, Muck, Canna & Sanday

An Sgùrr is Eigg's iconic, rocky peak and the island's most popular hike. The panoramic views from the top are spectacular and there is a great feeling of accomplishment from reaching the top of what looks to be an impossible climb from below. This route reaches a summit of 1,289ft, but the route is actually quite simple, with no scrambling on the ascent.

From Galmisdale Bay, walk northwest along the road uphill keeping the camping pods on your right and continue around half a mile through the woodland. Ignore the turning on the right towards the village hall and continue up through the woods until you reach a grassy field.

Follow the track through the field, aiming towards the stone Galmisdale Farmhouse, with its grey and red roof. Pass around to the right of the house and turn left on to the next track; follow this for just over 100yds until you see a stone cairn, which marks the start of a path on your right-hand side which leads uphill, roughly north.

This rough path leads to the base of the towering rock, before heading around and behind it on the right-hand side, north of the rocky cliffs. The climb still looks unfathomable at this point, with the path running along the northern edge of An Sgùrr for just under half a mile. A way becomes apparent as the path cuts up into the side of the hill, through a small crevice in the rock (✛ 56°53'06.7"N 6°10'24.5"W).

Once up on the saddle, take some time to look south, down to the ruins of Grulin Uachdrach (see above) below and across to the northwest to the small island dùn in Loch nam Ban Mòra (Loch of the Great Women; there is a strange folk association that it was once home to some abnormally big women).

Having soaked up the views, turn to the left and make your way around the scant remains of an **Iron Age fort** (✛ 56°53'04"N 6°10'09"W) and along the southern edge of the summit towards the trig point in the east. There are fantastic views out to Rùm, Muck and Ardnamurchan, with the Skye Cuillin behind the northern part of Eigg on a clear day.

Once you've had your fill of the views, return the same way.

The north If you are able, the best way to reach the north end of Eigg is on a bicycle (page 113). Once you have conquered the hills after leaving Kildonnan or Galmisdale Bay, the central stretch is gently undulating with very little traffic. This is a good place to look out for hen harriers who prey on small birds and rodents on the open moorland. Few people live in this part of the island, but there is a small natural history visitor centre and museum inside the **old shop** (⊕ 24hrs; free).

A few hundred yards further north is **Isle of Eigg Brewery** (w eiggbrewery.com; e stu@isleofeiggbrewery.com; ⊕ taproom: summer 13.00–17.00 Mon, Wed & Sat, winter by request). In contrast with most business models, as Scotland's first co-operative brewery its process is intentionally labour intensive, with the main aim to be providing stable jobs on the island. The second aim, aside from making great craft beer, is to be as environmentally positive as possible, with solar panels on the roof and using wild fermentation with local ingredients.

Continuing towards Cleadale you have the option of two lovely beaches: the broad, sandy **Laig Bay** or, further north, the smaller and more secluded **Singing Sands**. The pretty, white **St Donnán's Roman Catholic Church** sits near the northern end of Laig Bay. Apart from during Sunday services, you are welcome to enter the church and have a look at the carved crosses saved from Kildonnan; some are fragments, but there is a wonderfully detailed 9th-century cross in Pictish style.

It's also well worth popping into the **Museum of Crofting Life** (⊕ 24hrs; donation requested), a traditional cottage left largely as it was abandoned, with small collections of other objects such as fishing gear and cobbler's tools.

Walk: Sgorr an Fharaidh

Distance: 3½ miles; time: 3 hours; start/end: just south of Lageorna (page 113); OS Explorer map: 397 Rùm, Eigg, Muck, Canna & Sanday

Like the more famous An Sgùrr (see opposite), this is a climb that looks totally impossible from the bottom but which turns into a relatively easy hike once you know the route. Sgorr an Fharaidh is a dramatic, rocky ridge that sits on the east side of the island's main road.

The route begins just south of Lageorna B&B; walk under the washing line and follow a path up to a wooden stile. Cross the stile and follow the path as it ascends towards a steep gully between two distinct rock stacks attached to the cliff (the one on the right being particularly sharp). Walk up through this gully, crossing a low point in an old stone wall. On emerging from the gully, bear left and continue to follow a path climbing up to a wooden step stile.

Cross the stile and turn left, initially following a well-trodden path northeast along the clifftops; from here you have a bird's-eye view down over Cleadale and the beaches, and out towards the Rùm Cuillin. This tends to be a good place to spot the island's golden eagles.

Follow the path past the **Finger of God** at Bidein an Tighearna, a conspicuous and mostly detached pinnacle of rock, and around the cliff's natural curve, which allows for different angles of the view at each point. Eventually you will pass a few small lochs and then come to a trig point and a fence on the left. Stay on the east side of the fence until you reach a small metal gate.

From here, a path (⊕ 56°56'13.1"N 6°08'38.8"W) leads down to the west in the direction of Singing Sands before you climb up on to the final crown of rock. It would be a shame to miss the panoramic view from this final, small summit; afterwards, return to the path leading downhill. It is a narrow sheep trail, but easy to follow down a series of many hairpin bends to the bottom.

Soon after there's a path to your left that leads southeast towards the few buildings near the bottom of the cliffs that make up Tolain. Look out for light purple heath spotted orchids growing among the grass in spring and summer.

Skirt around the buildings at Tolain to get back on to the 'main road' and head south towards Cleadale. Between Tolain and the farmhouse at Howlin are the turf-covered remains of the settlement of **Five Pennies**. The name refers to 'pennylands', part of a system of valuing land according to fertility, which probably came from the Norse and was taken on by subsequent powers in Scotland. Like Grulin Uachdrach, the history here is complex, with many generations of habitation. The earliest reference is in a charter from 1498, but most of what we can see is much later than that, including some small houses, which would have been lived in by the poorest members of the community, known as 'cottars' at the time as a reference to their small cottages.

Continue on to Cleadale where, opposite Eigg Organics, is **Tobar Chaluim Chille**, a holy well dedicated to St Columba, and slightly further south, on the left-hand side of the road, the Museum of Crofting Life (page 117).

Following this, you pass the war memorial on your right and are soon back at the start of the walk.

CANNA (CANAIGH) AND SANDAY (SANDAIGH)

Arguably the most remote of all the Inner Hebrides, Canna and Sanday feel like a reward for those who take the time to travel there. Joined by a bridge, the two islands share a community and are most often referred to as a single entity, Canna. Unspoilt and impossibly beautiful, Canna is structured like a tiered wedding cake with bands of basalt columns separating plateaus where the sheep and cows graze. These lush, green fields run down to the coastline, where there are towering sea stacks and secluded coves. The only way to get around is on foot or by cycling.

At low tide it is possible to walk across the sand between the two islands, but there has been some form of connecting bridge since the late 19th century. Canna is the larger of the two islands and currently houses more of the population, although this has not always been the case.

Peace, wildlife and scenery are many people's reasons for coming to the Hebrides and it's hard to find anywhere better than Canna for these things. The lime-based basalt columns form many of Canna's towering cliffs and rocky protrusions. Healthy white cheviot and unusually tall, brown zwartble sheep graze on remarkably green grass along with Aberdeen Angus, belted Galloway and the visitors' favourite, Highland cattle. Excluding rabbits, of which there are plenty, wild land mammal species are limited. There are, however, otters and several colonies of grey seals. Between June and September, enormous basking sharks can sometimes be seen from the shore and the very luckiest of people might spot porpoise, dolphin and even occasionally killer whale. More (seasonally) reliable are the seabirds, particularly puffins, kittiwakes, shags, guillemots and razorbills, all of which nest on the islands. There is also a nesting pair of golden eagles and a pair of white-tailed eagles, as well as peregrine, long-eared owls and numerous other species.

⌂ WHERE TO STAY AND EAT *Map, opposite*

Canna has a small handful of accommodation options and one place to eat, all of which have wonderful sea views. For self-catering cottages, see w cannaselfcatering.co.uk.

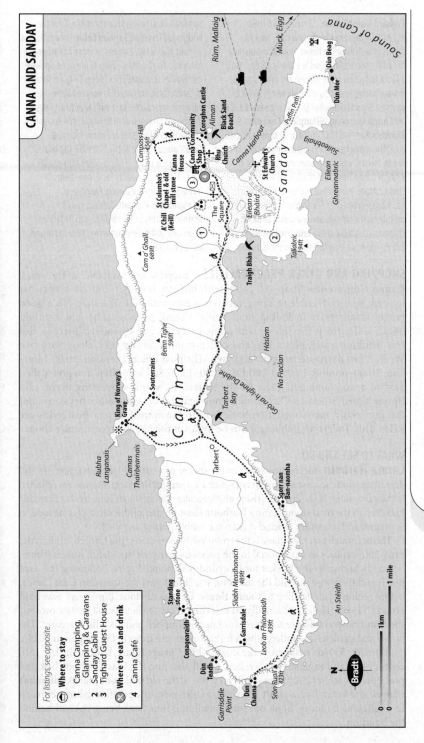

CANNA AND SANDAY

For listings, see opposite

Where to stay
1 Canna Camping, Glamping & Caravans
2 Sanday Cabin
3 Tighard Guest House

Where to eat and drink
4 Canna Café

Sound of Canna

Rùm, Mallaig

Muck, Eigg

Dùn Beag
Dùn Mor
Puffin Path
Suileabhaig
Eilean Ghreannabric
Sanday
St Edward's Church
Canna Harbour
Coroghon Castle
Black Sand Beach
Alman
Rhu Church
Canna Community Shop
Canna House
St Columba's Chapel & old mill stone
A'Chill (Keill)
The Square
Eilean a'Bhàird
Tallabric 194ft
Traigh Bhàn
Háslam
Na Fiaclan
Geo na h-Iighne Duibhe
Compass Hill 458ft
Càrn a'Ghaill 689ft
Beinn Tighe 590ft
Canna
Tarbert Bay
Tarbert
Souterrains
King of Norway's Grave
Rubha Langanais
Camas Thairbearnais
Sgorr nan Bàn-naomha
Sliabh Meadhonach 489ft
Garrisdale 439ft
Leob an Fhionnaidh
An Stéidh
Standing stone
Conagearaidh
Dùn Teadh
Dùn Channa
Sròn Ruail 423ft
Garrisdale Point

N

Bracht

0   1km
0   1 mile

The Small Isles   CANNA AND SANDAY

5

119

Tighard Guest House (3 rooms) ☎01687 462474; w tighard-isleofcanna.com. Spacious rooms in an Edwardian house, positioned up on a hill with spectacular views & a lovely garden. Only 1 room has an en suite, though the other 2 have private bathrooms. Also offers dinner (£20 for 2 courses) & packed lunches (£4) on request. **££££**

✱ **Canna Camping, Glamping, Caravans & Bunkhouse** ☎01687 462963; w cannacampsite. com. The majority of Canna's accommodation is run by Isebail, who also somehow finds time to work at Canna Farm. The traditional whitewashed stone cottage bunkhouse (sleeps 8, £20/night) has a lime-green door & window frames. Sitting prettily on the hillside under a crown of basalt columns, it's simple & old-fashioned inside, but the view out over farmland to the harbour,

Sanday & Rùm beyond is unbeatable. Over the bridge, self-catering **Sanday Cabin** (sleeps 2; min 2-night stay; £260/2 nights) is more luxurious & romantic. The 2 c/vans (sleep 4) are good options for families. 3 simple pods (sleep 2–4) are located in Canna Campsite, which is situated above the village in an isolated spot with beautiful views. Bedding is provided with Sanday Cabin & c/vans & can be rented for other accommodation. **£**

Café Canna West Bothy; ☎01687 482488; w cafecanna.co.uk; ⏱ Apr–Sep 11.00–22.00 Wed–Mon. High-quality local ingredients including foraged seaweed, Canna beef & langoustine. Pre-order lobster, crab & seafood platters so the shellfish can be landed especially, just before you arrive. Booking ahead advised. **£–££**

SHOPPING AND OTHER PRACTICALITIES Groceries are available at the small **Canna Community Shop** (⏱ 24hrs with honesty box; ♿) but are somewhat limited, so it's advisable to bring supplies across with you. The shop has a good range of souvenirs including homemade 'Canna Kitchen' jams and chutney, books and artist prints, along with some groceries and essentials. There is also free drinking water, plus a tea- and coffee-making facility (£1), along with free Wi-Fi. Card payments are now accepted. The **post office** (⏱ noon–16.00 Mon–Thu, 10.00–noon & 14.00–17.00 Fri, 10.00–13.00 Sat) is located in a green shed next to a telephone box, close to The Square; it's worth supporting if you can. **Phone** signal is best on O2 and fairly non-existent on some other networks, but the previously mentioned telephone box is functional. Canna **postcodes** are PH44 4RS. **Toilets** for public use can be found at the pier and community shop.

WHAT TO SEE AND DO

Canna Harbour Sailing boats bob in the shelter of a natural harbour where, on still days, three churches, a scattering of houses and various grazing farm animals are reflected in the calm water. In the distance, rising above Sanday, mountainous Rùm lends a dramatic backdrop to the rural scene. Canna Harbour must be one of the most picturesque in Scotland, and a wander around it is an inevitable part of any visit.

The harbour's first landmark is the rounded, brown-stone **Rhu Church**, built in the early 20th century as a memorial to the previous owner of the island, Robert Thom, and aptly known as the Rocket for its cylindrical, pointed spire. Following the road north and then west around the harbour, you'll first pass the shop and Café Canna, before seeing a gate leading to **Canna House**. Canna's obvious 'Big House' was built around 1863 by Donald Macneill and was later home to Canna's last private owners, the historian and folklore scholar John Lorne Campbell and his wife Margaret. The house and gardens are undergoing refurbishment and expected to reopen in 2025.

A further 550yds past here is the small, white **Change House**, built in the late 18th century and still inhabited today; here you'll also find the island's phone box and post office. Another 220yds west will take you to the **old mill stone** and **St Columba's Chapel**; the latter had a short interlude as the post office before being returned to a religious building. Look out for a small museum that's being opened behind the building.

The Square At the heart of Canna Farm, which loosely encompasses much of the island, The Square is usually a hive of activity, busy with collie dogs, sheep, cows and the people working with them. Opposite the farm is **Eilean a' Bhàird** (Island of the Bard), named after Alasdair mac Mhaighstir Alasdair, a poet who served as factor of the island in the 18th century; he supposedly composed his greatest song while sheltering on the island under an upturned boat.

Walk: A' Chill

Distance: ¾ mile; time: 30mins; start/end: just west of St Columba's Chapel, east of Canna Farm; OS Explorer map: 397 Rùm, Eigg, Muck, Canna & Sanday

Just west of St Columba's Chapel, a gate marked with an orange arrow indicates the beginning of a path that leads to the site of the pre-Clearance village A' Chill (Keill). Leading through a mixture of conifers and broad-leaved trees, the path is lined with wild garlic and bluebells flowering in May.

Although there is nothing to see of A' Chill, it once had 32 houses. These were flattened after residents were evicted in 1851 to make way for sheep, and all that is left in the area now is a graveyard. An impressive **8th- or 9th-century cross** remains here, depicting the Adoration of the Magi, where the 'three kings' gave baby Jesus gifts, and various animals. About 60yds west is the **Punishment Stone**, an ancient form of corporal punishment where the offender's thumb is said to have been jammed into the small hole.

About 100yds further south from the Punishment Stone is the **graveyard**, which itself has some interesting carved slabs.

To return to the harbour follow a path from the graveyard south and then southeast towards the sea until you reach the main road.

Walk: Black Sand Beach and Compass Hill

Whole route – distance: 2½ miles; time: 2 hours. Black Sand Beach only – distance: 1 mile; time: 45 minutes. Start/end: Canna Community Shop; OS Explorer map: 397 Rùm, Eigg, Muck, Canna & Sanday

This easy but rewarding walk takes you through magical woodland and open fields to a pristine sandy beach.

Take the path that starts to the right (east) of Canna Community Shop, which leads past some sheds before beginning to climb through the woodland. Here are broad-leaved sycamores, hawthorn and cherry, the beginnings of a beautiful mature patch of woodland that has been planted for shelter from the wind. Follow the path past a polytunnel, with a high wall on your left; this is the boundary to Canna House gardens.

When you reach a junction there should be a sign with four arrows. Choose the direction that leads towards 'Upper Wood Path to Corigan'; this is the higher of two thin paths leading off to the right.

Wade through the wild garlic, an unmistakable smell even if you can't identify it on sight, and enjoy the **woodland**, purple with bluebells and speckled with yellow primroses in spring. The view soon opens out over an abandoned barn and, further west, two of the islands' three churches.

When you reach a gate on your right, head through it and cross a field towards the barn. Noticing the old water pump on your left, head through the gate down to the **beach** and, if the weather is accommodating, take some time to enjoy a picnic or paddle here.

Across the streaked sand to your left, at the far east of the bay, is the ruin of **Coroghon Castle**, standing on top of sheer basalt cliffs, over 65ft high. The small stone structure consists of two rooms that incorporate the natural rock as partial walls. It is thought to have been a prison, used in the 17th century for the unbalanced Donald MacDonald of Clanranald to hold his wife, Marion MacLeod, hostage.

Once you've had your fill of exploring or paddling, head back through the gate near the barn, where you can choose whether to turn left and walk back along a track to the village or walk up Compass Hill.

To climb **Compass Hill**, look for another gate much higher and off to the right (northeast). Follow the faint, grassy track that leads towards this gate and go through it. Turn right and follow grassy tracks, past a radio mast to the east and the more gently sloped side of Compass Hill. Once you have enjoyed the view at the top, you can either head back to the barn and find the track that leads west to the village, or continue around the coast to the north, where there is a string of spectacular, if precarious, clifftop viewpoints (beware of unpredictable wind gusts channelled through the gullies).

Walk: Souterrains, the King of Norway's Grave and Canna's western coastline

Distance: 13 miles (with several options to turn back sooner); time: 8–10 hours (for the full route); start/end: Canna Farm; OS Explorer map: 397 Rùm, Eigg, Muck, Canna & Sanday

This long walk visits seven archaeological sites around some of the most spectacular coastal scenery in the Inner Hebrides. While some of the route follows tracks or route indicators, other parts cross rough ground where some navigation is required. The western half of Canna is uninhabited, but you are likely to come across some very free-range sheep and cows.

Following the southern coastal road west from Canna Farm, with the sea on your left, you can follow the occasional orange arrows that mark the route as far as the souterrains (page 265).

After passing the majority of the houses, take the right turning through a metal gate, marked towards the campsite.

Passing the campsite on your right, and walking below the huge crowns of basalt columns, notice the biggest rocky promontory sticking out into the sea with a small island off its point; the dangerous rocks around this island are called **Na Fiaclan** or 'the teeth' (✪ 57°02'59"N 6°32'18"W).

Some 550yds further towards Tarbert is a steep-sided sea channel called **Geò na h-Ighne Duibhe** ('the chasm of the black-haired girl'), named after someone who fell into it and drowned. If you're walking along this coastline in the summer months, scan the ocean for basking sharks, which are seen fairly regularly.

Shortly after the channel, the track climbs inland towards a gate followed by a sharp corner, which leads downhill towards a beautiful beach and Tarbet's one building. At the corner, look for the small, orange arrow pointing right (✪ 57°03'35"N 6°32'57"W) and leave the main track here to follow a less distinct path next to a dyke, going roughly north for around 660yds.

After crossing through a hole in an old dry-stone wall, keeping to the left of a small lumpy hill and going over a couple of rudimentary wooden bridges, the faint path splits and another arrow indicates a right-hand turn.

Choose the path following the middle ground, around the side of another small hill, and you should find the entry to the **souterrains** (✪ 57°03'52.5" ✪ 6°32'50.4"W) around 220yds after the last wooden bridge. Set in a lumpy, green, grassy area, characteristic of prehistoric human activity, the souterrains appear as two holes, with some exposed stonework and, on the northern one, a lintel supporting the roof. Look out for golden and white-tailed eagles, of which there is one pair of each on the islands, as well as peregrines and other, smaller birds.

There aren't any further orange arrows to follow from here, but you can find the King of Norway's Grave by continuing northwest for around 330yds into a steep-sided channel that leads towards the sea. Following grassy sheep tracks, head around the left-hand side of a dry-stone wall and you should come down to a flat, grassy promontory, **Rubha Langanais**, with incredible views of the cliffs and coastline in both directions.

The King of Norway's Grave is about 220yds from here at the base of the hill, on the west of the promontory. Regularly placed stones in the vague shape of a boat indicate what has traditionally been thought to be a Viking ship burial; the other explanation is a kelp kiln, which initially seems less exciting until you really think about what that life must have involved. Campbell reported that any interference with the King of Norway's Grave was thought to bring a thunderstorm. There is a similar example of a kelp kiln on Tiree (page 147).

Take some time to enjoy the area. Shags nest on the basalt cliffs at the end of the point and in summer there are decent chances of seeing basking shark, porpoise or dolphin. On clear days, Skye's Cuillin Hills can be seen to the northeast, with the Outer Hebrides' Uists further west, but it still feels like the edge of the world.

From Rubha Langanais you can return the way you came, making the return walk about 6 miles in total from the village, or continue further by climbing the hill behind the King of Norway's Grave and hiking southwest until you reach the low, shallow part of Canna, which bisects the island into two oval lumps.

From here, keep to the east of the wall that runs all the way across the island, walk south beside it until you reach the original, substantial track at Tarbert and a gate going through to the west (✪ 57°03'31"N 6°33'12"W). If you like, you can go down to the lovely sandy beach here or continue around the southwest coast, through a gate and along increasingly dramatic clifftops. Most of the time there is a vague path on this southern route, making it much easier than tramping along the northwest.

Slightly less than a mile after the gate, down below you at the base of the cliffs, is a grassy promontory with some obvious circular ruins (viewed from ✪ 57°02'48"N 6°34'17"W). Named **Rubha Sgorr nan Ban-naomha**, which translates to something along the lines of 'the grassy slope headland of the holy women', this unlikely spot is thought to have been an early Christian establishment of Celtic origins. With no easy access from the sea and at the base of a 295ft cliff, its location is quite remarkable and unique in the Hebrides.

If you have walked all of this in one day, you are already at around 5 miles, with 3 miles left to go back to the village, so there is no shame in turning back now. Those with plenty more energy can continue along the coastline, keeping to the clifftops as you head west. The scenery on this stretch is breathtaking, reminiscent of the Faroe Islands – you're certainly unlikely to see similar to this in the entire region.

Reaching the far west, on the coastline below the trig point (✪ 57°02'49"N 6°36'16"W) is another unlikely ruin. Set on a flat-topped sea stack, inaccessible without rock climbing, are the scant remains of the Iron Age fort of **Dùn Channa**. Unlike at Rubha Sgorr nan Ban-naomha, it is hard to make out traces of the buildings here, but on careful inspection, you can see the remains of a stone wall, half covered with grass.

If you have walked this route as a whole, you have now travelled about 8 miles. Continuing and making the full circle is tempting, but be aware that the ground is quite a lot rougher on the northern coastline, so the easiest route is to head back the way you came.

If you decide to make the full circle, continue to follow the clifftops. There is another fort, **Dùn Teadh** (✪ 57°03'16"N 6°36'17"W), down by the sea in the northwest, which you can also admire from above. The remains of this structure are noticeable by an almost straight wall cutting across the neck of a broad, grassy headland. Compared with Dùn Channa or Rubha Sgorr nan Ban-naomha, it's easier to imagine how Dùn Teadh was accessed along the wide, grassy skirt at the bottom of the cliffs.

A little further northeast, the severely ruined but easy-to-distinguish remains of a settlement at **Conagearaidh** are visible from above. Continuing around the coast, a **standing stone** on a grassy area between two beaches can also be spotted from a bird's eye perspective. There is a colony of seals around here, whose howls you might hear drifting across the bay.

Inland around 300yds from the cliff above Conagearaidh, is the ruined township of **Garrisdale** (✪ 57°03'17"N 6°35'34"W), which was once one of the four farms into which Canna was divided. It was cleared in the 19th century. In fact, there is so much archaeology in this area that you are constantly passing it. John Hunter's book *The Small Isles* (page 267) or careful study of Canmore (w canmore.org.uk) will help you to identify and interpret some of it.

When you finally reach the low area that bisects the two halves of Canna, head south towards the barn at Tarbert and walk back to the village along the main track.

Sanday At just 0.71 square miles, Sanday is only a sixth of the size of Canna, with much of the western end of the island designated as crofting land. Even if you only have time for a flying visit, the beautiful sandy beach, **Traigh Bhàn**, makes a trip across the bridge worthwhile. The beach is hidden behind the sand dunes and rocks just a couple of hundred yards to the west of the bridge. In spring, the hill behind the beach is colourful with wildflowers.

The east side of Sanday is accessed by the coastal road, to your left after you cross the bridge, which runs as far as **St Edward's Church**. This Roman Catholic church was built in 1890, after the Clearances on Canna, when there was a much larger Catholic community on Sanday. It was also used by visiting fishermen from Barra and Eriskay, but has always had problems with damp and has now fallen into disrepair.

From St Edward's you can follow the Puffin Path, marked with orange sticks, to a natural viewpoint for the spectacular grassy, flat-topped sea stacks of **Dùn Mor** and **Dùn Beag** 1 mile away on the south coast. From the end of April to July there are puffins nesting here – it's good to have binoculars as they are often floating in rafts out to sea – and other seabirds such as guillemots, fulmars, kittiwakes, razorbills and shags can be seen on the cliffs.

Returning along the Puffin Path is the easiest way back to the bridge, but you can also romp around the mostly pathless coast in either direction. In Sanday's far east, there's a small lighthouse and a couple of secluded coves, whereas walking west along the quiet south coast, you'll find wonderful places to see seals among the skerries and watch wading birds, such as lapwings with their slow irregular flight and wailing call. Wherever you go, don't forget to look out to sea, as there are good chances of seeing basking sharks during the summer months.

MUCK (MUC)

One of the smallest islands featured in this book, Muck is only 2½ miles from east to west as the crow flies; following the road from the south to the north, it only takes half an hour to walk across the island. However, its craggy coastline of stretching skerries makes walking around it a great deal longer. Inland is green and notably fertile, having been used as a farm for many centuries, which it mostly still is. Residents are particularly welcoming and happy to tell visitors about the island. The small population has a large proportion of children and the island supports a thriving primary school.

Muck's rocky coastline is a haven for wildlife, with huge colonies of both grey and common seals living close to the shore, making the island one of the easiest places to see them in the Inner Hebrides. In spring, game birds such as red grouse, snipe and pheasant fly out as you walk and nesting herons are surprisingly abundant; at any time of year you are likely to see them standing peacefully in small coves around the island.

WHERE TO STAY AND EAT *Map, below*

Muck has a few accommodation options and limited places to eat out; you can find self-catering cottages and further information on w isleofmuck.com.

Gallanach Lodge (8 rooms) Gallanach; \ 01687 462365; w gallanachlodge.co.uk; ♿. Welcoming accommodation with a grand sitting/dining room featuring comfortable leather sofas, a wood-burning stove & panoramic views over the bay. Rooms have solid wooden beds made on Rùm, & shared bathrooms. Non-residents are welcome for evening meals (££) if not fully booked, but must call ahead. Quality food in a grand dining room with a wonderful view. Choice of local shellfish or lamb, & can cater for requirements. £££
The Bunkhouse (4 rooms) Port Mòr; \ 01687 462362; e bunkhouse@isleofmuck.com. Small, modern, purpose-built wooden building with

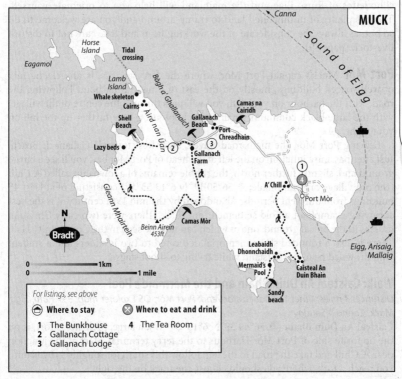

3 bunk rooms & 1 dbl. Well equipped with oven, washing machine, high chair & travel cot; sea view from communal rooms. £24 pp; extra charges for towels (£5) & bedding (£5). Exclusive hire £100/night. **£**

The Tea Room Port Mòr; m 07470 711799; e chocnesschocolates@gmail.com; ⏲ Apr–Sep lunch & some eves, call/email ahead to confirm times. Home baking, sandwiches & soup, as well as shellfish meals. **£**

Self-catering

Gallanach Cottage (sleeps 7) Gallanach; ✆ 01687 462362; w isleofmuck.com. Cosy, simple traditional cottage with spacious bedrooms, garden & amazing sea views. £400–650/week.

SHOPPING AND OTHER PRACTICALITIES Muck does not have a grocery shop, so it is vital to stock up before you arrive. For **local shellfish**, call Vicky and Sandy on m 07444 799787; ∎. The Tea Room (see above) might also be able to help if you run out of something. The **Community Hall** (Port Mòr; ✆ 01687 462362; e info@ isleofmuck.com), a relatively large black building next to the school, has facilities including **Wi-Fi**, **toilets and showers** (honesty-box payments), a **small heritage centre** and a **games room** upstairs. There is also free Wi-Fi in the small pebbledash building next to port.

For **arts and crafts**, pop into the **Green Shed** (Port Mòr; ⏲ 24hrs with honesty box). Muck **postcodes** are PH41 2RP.

WHAT TO SEE AND DO Even if you are only on Muck for a short time it is well worth walking across the island to **Gallanach**, which has the island's best sandy beach. Exploring the island further, Beinn Airein is Muck's highest hill and gives the best views across the Small Isles; familiarising yourself with the distinctive silhouettes of Rùm, Eigg and the mainland will help you to orientate yourself. There is plenty of uninhabited land to tramp around and you are welcome to do so but, as always, be considerate of the working farm and take care not to disturb livestock (page 49).

Port Mòr
Muck's capital Port Mòr, where the ferry arrives, is an eclectic mix of well-spaced buildings, mostly on the east of a natural harbour. Following the road, with the harbour on your left, you will pass through the centre of the village, with the large black community hall and school just a little further up the hill on your right.

Leaving Port Mòr, the main road travels northwest towards Gallanach Beach. Just after passing a junction on the left at the head of Port Mòr bay, you'll see a burial ground and, slightly further north, the rubble remains of a township called **A' Chill** (the old village or Sean Bhaile; ✛ 56°50'11"N 6°13'53"W) consisting of at least 48 buildings from different periods. Abandoned by the mid 19th century, it is the best surviving example of an old settlement on Muck. There were two early Christian crosses in the burial ground, one of which can now be seen in the Community Hall. There is also a rounded stone memorial dedicated to two islanders and a student who drowned near Horse Island while trying to shoot stags.

Walk: Caisteal An Duin Bhain and the Mermaid's Pool
Distance: 3 miles; time: 1–2 hours; start/end: Port Mòr; OS Explorer map: 397 Rùm, Eigg, Muck, Canna & Sanday

Caisteal An Duin Bhain (✛ 56°49'39"N 6°13' 39"W), a large, prehistoric fort, is on the opposite side of Port Mòr Harbour to the ferry terminal. Start at the junction near A' Chill and take the road to the left; follow this south for roughly 110yds until you reach a fork, where you should choose the track on the right.

Just after the stone house with swings outside, you will come to a sharp corner, just after which you should leave the track to continue in the same direction south. Walk around half a mile over the higher ground of Dùn Bàn until you reach the fort. It is an obvious round lump, covered in grass on top, but with some visible remains of the walls above the natural rock. Climbing on top is not difficult and proves to be an excellent viewpoint across the sea to Ardnamurchan.

From here, continue around the coast for about 660yds, with the sea on your left. You will then reach a ruined farmstead (⊕ 56°49'40.7"N 6°13'55.5"W) and the vague remains of a slipway at **Leabaidh Dhonnchaidh**, as well as a restored building.

Some 220yds further south from the restored building is the deep **Mermaid's Pool** and a series of other rock pools that are only exposed at low tide; also at low tide, a walk a little further around the coast will lead you to a tiny, beautiful **sandy beach**.

To return to Port Mòr, retrace your steps to the restored building and Leabaidh Dhonnchaidh, then head northeast across fields and the raised, rocky moorland of Dùn Bàn back towards the village.

Gallanach and around
From Port Mòr it takes around half an hour to reach the north coast on foot. Once you've traversed the island, if you turn off right at a sharp corner to the left (just past a barn) and follow the grassy track down to the gate in a dry-stone wall, you will come to the little beach of **Camas na Cairidh**. Here, a dragon spine tail of rocks divides sand from a rocky beach and acts as a natural pier so you can walk out into the sea when the tide is right. This stretch of coast is frequented by otters and a good place to sit quietly and look out to sea for large mammals and birds.

A quarter of a mile further west is the old **Port Chreadhain** (⊕ 56°50'32"N 6°14'53"W), which consists of two slipways and a quay used up until the 19th century; part of a large common seal colony rest on the rocks here, so be careful not to startle them. A little further is **Gallanach Beach**, by far Muck's most glorious stretch of sand. At low tide, you can see the remains of an old, rocky **fish trap** in the sand directly below the farm. There are flocks of oystercatchers and a variety of curiosities in the area such as an anchor and various old farm implements.

Northwest from Gallanach
The headland of **Àird nan Uan** can be reached by taking a gated turning to the left (away from the sea) just after Gallanach Farm and then turning right and walking north after about 100yds. There are two cairns here from the Neolithic or Bronze Age, the more northern of which has also been used as the MacEwen family grave.

Near the end of the headland, on the Gallanach side, you can climb down to the shore, where there is a whale skeleton. The piece of land to the north, which nearly gets cut off at high tide, is **Lamb Island**. From here it is just about possible to walk out to the larger **Horse Island** on a low spring tide. It's advisable to check your tide calculations with a local in advance, and to wear tough-soled water shoes and take sticks as the crossing requires negotiating seaweed-covered rocks. Hundreds of birds nest on Horse Island, with the cliffs at the north end supporting a small population of difficult-to-spot puffins. Allow yourself at least half an hour to get back across to Lamb Island.

Following the coastline from Àird nan Uan, with the sea on your right, will bring you to a restored croft house with a turf roof. Around 220yds further on is **Shell Beach**, a secluded little cove whose name is explained on closer inspection.

Walk: Beinn Airein and Camas Mòr

Distance: 3 miles; time: 2 hours; start/end: Gallanach; OS Explorer map: 397 Rùm, Eigg, Muck, Canna & Sanday

This walk covers terrain that can be boggy, with an ascent and descent of 453ft. To reach Shell Beach from Gallanach, take the small gate on the left just after the farm buildings and go directly west across the base of Àird nan Uan peninsula.

From Shell Beach head inland, passing over a small section of dry-stone wall and continuing south for a couple of hundred yards. Notice the regular ridges in the ground that create a striped pattern; these are **lazy beds** (page 264).

From here, join a track that leads roughly southwest around the base of some crags. Follow it for about 300yds, with the sea on your right, before bearing off left and heading up into the valley, Gleann Mhairtein.

From the valley you can climb up **Beinn Airein** (453ft) by first climbing up to the saddle with Beinn Airein on your right and then choosing one of the small paths that climbs up to the top (✪ 56°49'52"N 6°15'32"W).

Heading out to the summit, near the edge of the cliffs overlooking the coast, there are wonderful views out to Ardnamurchan, Mull and Coll. You can see the beach **Camas Mòr** (Big Bay) below on the left. There is a route down to the bay firstly heading northeast through the steep fields below, then passing through a metal gate and then head down towards the bay.

Camas Mòr is a designated area of Special Scientific Interest due to its incredible array of fossils that date from between 60 million and 3 billion years ago, particularly gryphaea, a type of oyster known as 'devil's toenails', which are obvious even to the casual observer.

To return to Gallanach Farm and the main road from the bay, head directly north (inland) around the left-hand side of the trees and out to the back of the farm. Aim for the far left of the farm buildings, on the left-hand side of a fence that climbs a small hillock, and you will soon reach the gate (✪ 56°50'24"N 6°15'22"W) back on to the main road.

6

Coll (Cola) and Tiree (Tiriodh)

Jutting out into the Atlantic, with nothing to protect them from thousands of miles of wind and swell, Coll and Tiree are the most westerly islands in the archipelago. With sweeping stretches of fine sand and secluded coves of coloured pebbles, both islands have spectacular beaches, and the machair here (crushed shells blown ashore to form a calcium-rich base) supports a unique ecosystem of delicate plants, insects and birds. Coll and Tiree are well known for their croaking corncrakes, but in springtime the sky is a cacophony of whooping lapwings, honking geese and the melodies of hundreds of tiny songbirds.

Geologically, both islands are made from ancient crystalline rocks, some of the oldest in Europe; formed during the Lewisian period, they underwent a lengthy and complicated process of folding and high temperature metamorphism deep within the earth's crust. Particularly on Coll, but also on Tiree, this process has left veins of black and sparkling pink and grey quartz. The marginally warmer waters of the Gulf Stream provide good feeding grounds for gigantic basking sharks and marine mammals – and even the occasional coconut from the other side of the Atlantic. In winter, the islands' isolated positions make them incredible places for stargazing.

Like most siblings, Coll and Tiree are bound together by circumstance; they have as many distinguishing features as the qualities they share. Although there are only 2 miles of sea separating them and both islands are low lying (at 463ft Ben Hynish on Tiree is the highest hill between them), their landscapes are visibly different. Central Tiree is a vast, flat plain with its only hills in the corners; in contrast, Coll is made up of lumpy hillocks – rock erupts from the heather inland and coastal sand dunes form miniature landscapes that rival Skye's Fairy Glen (page 74) without a hint of the accompanying Instagram fanatics. Despite both islands being a similar size geographically, Tiree's population of over 700 people is the fourth largest in the Inner Hebrides and several times bigger than Coll's 170. Particularly well known for its watersports, Tiree also gets many more visitors.

HISTORY

Despite their seemingly remote locations, Coll and Tiree have been inhabited since prehistoric times, with remnants left from every era. Peculiar Megalithic cup-markings on Tiree's Ringing Stone and sporadically placed Bronze Age monoliths give us little insight into the people, but there are many fortresses from the Iron Age, including a couple of brochs; the excavated Dùn Mòr on Tiree is a splendid example.

Columba, usually associated with Iona and much celebrated for his role in having brought Christianity to Scotland, founded a daughter monastery, Magh Luinge, on Tiree, though it is uncertain where. His feelings on the island are unclear, as he is reported to have banished Iona's unwanted demons to Tiree, as well as sending

Of the houses built on Coll and Tiree in the 19th–20th centuries, there is an interesting distinction in architectural style. On Tiree the main dwelling type was the Hebridean blackhouse, with double walls and a streamlined, hipped roof that did not overhang the walls. On Coll, single walls and overhanging roofs were the norm. This is thought to be a result of either the slightly more sheltered conditions on Coll or maybe just a difference in the landowner's ideas. There is now a mixture of buildings on both islands, but Tiree still has a much higher density of blackhouses than any other Inner Hebridean island.

monks there for penance. Around this time, under Dál Riata in the 6th century, Coll was controlled by the Cenél Loairn family whose descendants would later resurface under the name MacLean and, if all the claimed connections are to be trusted, popped up again to buy Breachacha Castle in 1965.

The Norse followed at the end of the 8th century, leaving several forts on Coll and many place names across both islands; Tiree's capital Scarinish, for example, derives from a translation of 'cormorant point' – a name that rings true to this day.

The 12th to 17th centuries – the reign of Somerled and his descendants the 'Lords of the Isles', and then subsequent clan rulers – was a turbulent period for both islands, with residents held hostage to the whims of feuding leaders who sought revenge and power. Tiree passed from the MacDougalls to the MacDonalds and finally to the MacLeans, who eventually went bankrupt and sold the island to the Campbells in 1674. The Campbells, Dukes of Argyll, still own the majority of Tiree to this day. A branch of Clan MacLean were granted Coll by Alexander of Islay, Lord of the Isles from 1423 to 1449, and managed to hold on to the island for nearly 500 years.

By 1800, Coll had around 1,000 inhabitants, while the population of Tiree, swelled by the landscape's remarkable fertility, built up to almost 4,500 in the 1830s. Money from the kelp industry and the relative efficiency of growing potatoes supported ever-growing numbers until potato blight and the crashing kelp market led to a starving, destitute population on Coll in the 1830s, and a similar fate befell Tiree following the potato famine of 1846. Large numbers from both islands emigrated by choice, and the Clearances here were not as savage as in some parts of the highlands and islands – though the stories about them are nuanced, including that of an 1886 rebellion on Tiree that led to two warships being anchored and the conflict finishing with a sports day where the local team famously beat the marines.

Tiree has a proud history as a pivotal RAF base during World War II and remnants of this time are easy to spot as you travel around the island. Crossapol (on Tiree) was also the site of an Italian prisoner of war camp, but apparently the men were often free to walk around the island as they pleased.

Today, Tiree has the strongest Scottish Gaelic presence in the Inner Hebrides – around a third of the population are still able to speak the language, whereas the figure on Coll, and across Argyll generally, is closer to 4%. Tiree also has a higher concentration of crofting land; contrastingly, most of the land on Coll is now privately owned, following the death of the last laird in 2012.

GETTING THERE AND AWAY

Note that campervans, caravans and those camping with a car are not allowed to arrive on Tiree without first booking a pitch (page 141).

BY FERRY CalMac (page 30) runs most days from Oban to Coll in around 2 hours 40 minutes, or it's 3 hours 50 minutes to Tiree (Coll: foot passengers/car £9.50/50.65; Tiree: foot passengers/car £11.45/62.50). The journey between Coll and Tiree on the same ferry takes 55 minutes (foot passengers/car £3.75/17.15). Once a week in summer a ferry also goes from Coll and Tiree to Castlebay on Barra (marked with 'A' on the same timetable; foot passengers/car £9.80/51.25), which takes 2 hours 45 minutes. Note that crossings are cancelled on a fairly regular basis during winter and rough weather.

Ferries arrive in Arinagour on Coll (half a mile south of the village) and Scarinish on Tiree (half a mile northeast of the main village); on Coll, the Coll Hotel (page 134) and Kip Poulson (\ 01879 230479) can provide pre-arranged pickup (for a fee).

THE FERRY JOURNEY FROM OBAN TO COLL AND TIREE

No matter how tired you might feel from the previous stages of your journey, falling asleep on the ferry to Coll and Tiree would be a mistake. Remember to take your coat on board whatever the weather, so you can sit out on deck and scan the ocean for wildlife. Calm seas improve your chances of spotting harbour porpoises, common and bottle-nosed dolphins, minke whales and basking sharks. On the other hand, rough weather and strong winds are a good time to search the skies for seabirds; during summer there are large numbers of gannets, razorbills, guillemots, kittiwakes, shags, fulmars and Manx shearwaters, and there's a slim possibility of seeing puffins.

Leaving Oban, look back to McCaig's Tower, the impressive round folly that dominates Oban's skyline, and the ruins of Dunoile Castle before the ship passes between tiny Maiden Island on the starboard side and Kerrera's obelisk to the port side (appropriately, a memorial to David Hutcheson, one of the founders of the ferry company that later became Caledonian MacBrayne or CalMac).

Shortly afterwards, you will pass between Lismore Lighthouse, one of the most spectacular in the region, and Duart Castle on Mull, narrowly avoiding the notorious Lady's Rock. This is the entry point into the Sound of Mull. For the next 25 miles you will travel between the east coast of Mull and the wild, mainland Morvern Peninsula. Taking occasional glances at one of the wonderful nautical route maps to be found in the ferry's corridors, you should be able to identify the ruined castle on Ardtornish Point (Morvern side) followed by the colourful houses of Tobermory's harbour opposite the mouth of Loch Sunart, which divides Morvern from the Ardnamurchan Peninsula on its northern bank. A little later, the imposing Mingary Castle, now encasing a luxury hotel, stands overlooking the Sound of Mull's northern entry, with Glengorm Castle, an impressive 19th-century country house on the other side, southwest.

The ferry sails onwards into open water. On a clear day, the dramatic outline of Rùm appears behind Ardnamurchan Lighthouse and, with the low shape of Coll growing larger to the west, you might be able to spot the tiny Treshnish Isles to the south. Those going on to Tiree will pass by this string of unique islands quite closely, getting the best possible view of the Dutchman's Cap (page 171) without going on a special boat trip.

MOORINGS

Coll Caledonian Maritime Assets Ltd, Arinagour PA34 4DB; \01879 230347 (choose option 2); w cmassets.co.uk

Tiree Gott Bay Moorings PA77 6UH; \01879 220074; w isleoftiree.com/gott-bay-moorings

BY AIR Coll Airport is located in the southwest of Coll; Hebridean Air (w hebrideanair.co.uk) fly here from Oban. There is no onward public transport, but both the Coll Hotel (page 134) and Kip Poulson (page 131) can provide pickups when possible (arrange in advance).

Tiree Airport is in the centre of the island and served by flights from Glasgow with Loganair (w loganair.co.uk) and from Oban with Hebridean Air (page 32). Pickup can be arranged with John Kennedy Transport (page 139). Car hire is also available (page 139).

COLL

Coll, the more northerly of the two islands, is often described by visitors and residents alike as 'what the Hebrides used to be like'. Far from almost everything except Tiree, the island has a close-knit community, with several inhabitants happily insisting that 'you have to be mad' to live there. Visiting in sunny spring, when the machair is sprinkled in rare carpet flowers and turquoise water laps at two dozen spotless, fine sandy beaches, you begin to wonder if they are trying to foster that impression in order to keep the island a secret. Life is centred around the main village, **Arinagour**, a planned settlement built around 1800 in the hope of establishing a new linen industry, where strings of small, white cottages look out across a quiet single-track road to their harbourfront gardens; a row of whitewashed, round trawler weights forms a picturesque notice not to drive on the grass and everybody seems to have at least one boat waiting for their sunny days off. Arinagour boasts a couple of shops, two excellent places to eat and all of the island's amenities.

Low lying but lumpy inland, Samuel Johnson's description from 1773 still applies today:

FESTIVALS AND EVENTS

Check w visitcoll.co.uk for yearly dates and information.

MARCH AND OCTOBER/NOVEMBER

Coll & the Cosmos
w collbunkhouse.com/dark-skies-coll-cosmos. A weekend-long course in astronomy to celebrate Coll's special dark skies (adult/child 12–17yrs £175/125).

JULY

Isle of Coll Fishing Competition
Arinagour; ☐. One of the competition rules is that locals must bring a

visitor along with them in their boat. Organisation is a little haphazard, so either ask someone in advance (in person or on the Facebook page) or just turn up on the day & see if anyone can fit you in.

AUGUST

Coll Half Marathon
w collhalfmarathon.org.uk. Running races including half marathon, 10k, 5k & children's 1k.

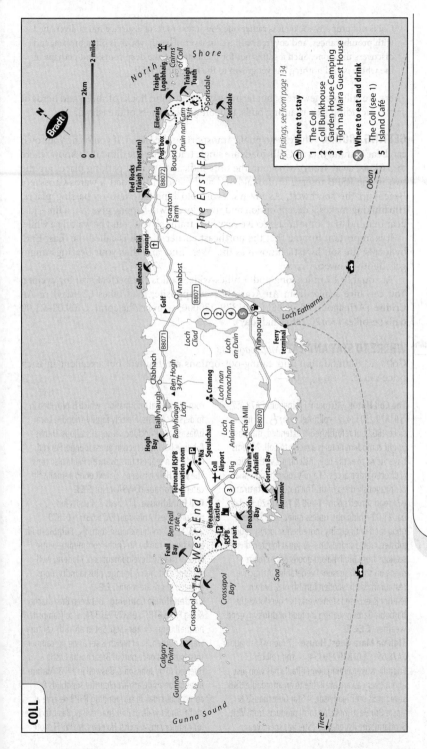

COLL

Gunna Sound

Gunna

Calgary Point

Crossapol Point

Crossapol Bay

Feall Bay

▲ Ben Feall 216ft

The West End

Breachacha castles

Breachacha Bay

RSPB car park

Totronald RSPB information room

Hogh Bay

Ballyhaugh

Ballyhaugh Loch

▲ Ben Hogh 347ft

Clàbhach

Ná Sgeulachan

Coll Airport

Uig

Loch Anlaimh

Dùn an Achaidh

Gortan Bay

Harmonie

Acha Mill

Loch nan Cinneachan

Crannog

Loch Cliad

Loch an Duin

B8070

B8071

Arinagour

Loch Eatharna

Ferry terminal

Arnabost

Gallenach

Burial ground

Toraston Farm

Red Rocks (Tràigh Thorastain)

Post box

Bousdo

Druim nan Carn 151ft

Eileraig

B8072

The East End

North Shore

Tràigh Logabhaig

Tràigh Tuath

Cairns of Coll

Sorisdale

Soa

Oban

Tiree

For listings, see from page 134

Where to stay
1 The Coll
3 Coll Bunkhouse
2 Garden House Camping
4 Tigh na Mara Guest House

Where to eat and drink
The Coll (see 1)
5 Island Café

Bradt

0 2km
0 2 miles

N

Coll and Tiree   COLL

6

Col is not properly rocky; it is rather one continued rock, of a surface much diversified with protuberances, and covered with a thin layer of earth, which is often broken, and discovers the stone. Such a soil is not for plants that strike deep roots; and perhaps in the whole island nothing has yet grown to the height of a table.

There are still very few trees, but farming continues and flocks of sheep and herds of cattle, including free-roaming bulls, inhabit most corners of the island.

GETTING AROUND There is no public transport on the island. If you bring your own **car**, bear in mind that all Coll's roads are single track. It can be difficult to know where to park as, away from Arinagour, the only indicated, official parking places are the two in the RSPB reserve (Totronald and at the end of the road towards Crossapol Beach) in the southwest. As always, avoid blocking gateways or passing places. **Hitchhiking** makes a decent option and most locals will happily give you a lift – just bear in mind that some areas receive very little traffic so you could be waiting a while.

It is important to note that the northeast corner of Coll is called the 'East End' by locals; the southwest is known as the 'West End' and thus your bearings might get slightly skewed.

At roughly 13 miles long and 3 miles wide, Coll is the perfect size for **cycling**. You can hire a bike from **An Acarsaid** (see opposite; road bikes £20/day) or **An Cridhe** (Arinagour PA78 6SY; 01879 230000; w ancridhe.com; ⊕ 09.00–21.00 daily; e-bikes £35/20 24hrs/half day).

WHERE TO STAY AND EAT *Map, page 133*
Coll's accommodation and eating-out options are limited, but excellent in each price range.

The Coll Hotel (10 rooms) Arinagour PA78 6SZ; 01879 230334; w collhotel.com; &. An inn since 1802 but refurbished & extended, this busy, bright & modern hotel is a credit to Coll. 7 rooms have views over the bay, including 2 with patios & direct garden access. Family room has original & ridiculously deep bath. The hotel's **restaurant** (⊕ food served noon–14.00 & 18.00–20.30 daily, bar 11.00–midnight, unless quiet; ££) serves good food with quality ingredients: locally caught lobster, crab, langoustines & squat lobster; dived scallops from Mull; baked goods & ice cream made on site; & seasonal vegetables. Attractive restaurant with wooden furnishings, brown leather & exposed stonework; bar overlooks the harbour. Garden seating for food or drinks in good weather. ££££

Tigh na Mara Guest House (7 rooms) Arinagour PA78 6SY; 01879 230354; w tnmcoll.com. Friendly & welcoming owner Paula has won just about every award available to an affordable B&B: straight 5s on Tripadvisor, '4 Star Guesthouse' & 'Taste Our Best' for using local products from Visit Scotland; the list goes on. She has spent years compiling local information, which is provided in folders for guests. Fiercely family-friendly. Local b/fast specials include seasonal scallops. Drinks & home baking served in guest lounge. Packed lunches on request (in advance). Paula also runs The Wee House (sleeps 2) next door, a small self-catering cottage (£455/week). £££

Coll Bunkhouse (14 beds & 4 spots for motorhomes) Arinagour PA78 6SY; 01879 230217; w collbunkhouse.com; &. Purpose-built bunkhouse run by An Cridhe community centre & local charity Development Coll. Modern, well-equipped kitchen & lounge, plus laundry. Dogs allowed in private rooms. ££

Garden House Camping Between Breachacha & Uig PA78 6TB; 01879 230374; e collcampsite@hotmail.com; ⊕ Apr–Sep. Set in an 18th-century walled garden, ¼ of which is set aside for campers, this spot was once part of Breachacha Castle & was referred to by Johnson & Boswell in 1773. Mature trees on one side attract plentiful songbirds & corncrakes croak in surrounding RSPB reserve at night. Short walk to Breachacha Bay. Basic facilities for campervans & tents. No dogs. No Wi-Fi. Note

that the turning is easily missed (⊕ 56°35'49.3"N 6°36'46.5"W). **£**
Island Café Shore St, Arinagour PA78 6SY; ☎ 01879 230022; w islandcafecoll.co.uk; ⏰ 09.00–11.00 & noon–14.00 Wed–Sat, 18.00– 20.30 Wed–Fri. Not just a café but also a restaurant serving tasty, hearty meals including local seafood. Good range for vegetarians/vegans. Friendly family business in relaxed setting. **£–££**

SHOPPING
An Acarsaid Arinagour PA78 6SY; ☎ 01879 230329; ⏰ summer 09.00–13.00 Mon–Sat, winter 09.00–noon Mon–Sat. Gift shop with Katie Morag children's books (set on Coll) & wool, rugs, knitted jumpers, etc, from own Hebridean sheep. Take the left after Island Café.
Coll Stores Arinagour PA78 6SY; w collstores. com; ⏰ 10.00–13.00 Mon & Sat, 10.00–13.00 & 16.00–17.00 Tue & Thu, 16.00–17.00 Wed & Fri; ♿. Small, but well-stocked grocery store. Possible to call in advance to pre-order.
✻ **Lighthouse Gallery** Arinagour PA78 6SY; ☎ 01879 230479; w kippoulson.com; ⏰ hours vary. This shed hosts a tiny gallery selling beautiful watercolours. To get here, follow the road & signs up the hill past the post office for around 500yds; it's well worth the walk.

SPORTS AND ACTIVITIES Summer, particularly July and August, is the best time to see basking sharks; while boat trips offer better chances, they can also be seen off the coast, so don't forget to look out for fins and tails poking out of the water while you're at the beach. There's also a golf course (Coll Golf Course; Cliad Farm PA78 6TE; w visitcoll.co.uk/golf; ⏰ Jun–Aug; 9 hole course; day adult/child/family £10/3/20; week adult/child/family £15/5/30; payment taken in the Coll Hotel, opposite).

OTHER PRACTICALITIES Coll's excellent community centre **An Cridhe** (see opposite; ♿) has a gym, toilets, showers, paid internet, tea and coffee. Check their noticeboard for events.

Fuel Coll Fuel, Arinagour PA78 6SY; ☎ 01897 230388; ⏰ 10.00–noon Tue & Sat, 15.00–17.00 Thu

Health Coll Medical Practice, Arinagour PA78 6SY; ☎ 01879 230326; ⏰ 09.00–13.00 Mon–Tue & Thu–Fri, 16.00–21.00 Wed
Post office An Acarsaid, Arinagour PA78 6SY; ☎ 01879 230329; ⏰ 09.00–13.00 Mon–Sat

WHAT TO SEE AND DO Coll's main attractions are its beaches, birds and basking sharks. There's plenty on the island to explore, but rushing around to try and see everything would be severely missing the point. The island's main village, Arinagour, is pretty but very small, so it's likely you'll spend most of your time exploring the rest of the island.

The East End Beautiful, secluded, sandy beaches are strung along the north coast of this side of Coll, for over 6 miles between the North Shore beaches and Gallenach.

Walk: Beaches between Sorisdale and Eileraig
Distance: 2½ miles; time: 2 hours; start: Sorisdale; end: Eileraig; OS Explorer map: 372 Coll and Tiree
This walk starts at Sorisdale, once a thriving community and still a working croft, which has a pleasant beach, but it's well worth pressing on north around the coast to the wild North Shore. It finishes in Eileraig, but there isn't much in the way of paths and you can walk as much or as little of the coastline as you like before rejoining the road, which is never more than a mile away.

At **Sorisdale**, parking is permitted in an unlikely spot to the left of the sign that reads 'keep clear turning only' but take care not to block the turning area, exit or gate. Look for the wooden sign next to a gate that directs you towards 'the bay 150m' and 'North Shore 650m'; follow this footpath east to the coast. The beach at Sorisdale is pleasant but not as picturesque as the wild North Shore.

Keep the sea on your right and walk north for around a mile along the coast; the route passes a small bay lined with colourful pebbles and on clear days you should be able to make out the curious outline of Eigg and mountainous Rùm on the northern horizon. Descend through the dunes to **North Shore**: try to follow paths where you can to avoid harming the fragile habitat, and look out for orchids among the marram grass.

The scattering of tiny islands laid out before you are known as the **Cairns of Coll** and were bought in 2014 by the author Alexander McCall Smith for £300,000, in an attempt to preserve them. He intends to do 'absolutely nothing' with them and donate them back to the Isle of Coll as a nature reserve when he dies. They are home to large colonies of common and grey seals, which you might see bobbing inquisitively in the water around North Shore or basking on rocks.

The first of the North Shore beaches you reach is **Tràigh Tuath**, followed by smaller **Tràigh Logabhaig** around 500yds to the west.

At the far western side of Tràigh Logabhaig you can climb up to **Druin nan Carn** (151ft) for a better view over the coast, before descending towards the small pebble and sand bay at **Eileraig**, where a long-ruined farmstead overlooks the coast.

Continuing further from here requires cutting inland and negotiating around fences, so it makes a sensible point to head to the road and form a circular walk back to Sorisdale.

From Bousd to Gallenach Fantastic beaches are the East End's main attraction, but take a moment to notice a couple of historical sites and other points of interest. On the **post box** (✪ 56°40'57.8"N 6°29'12.1"W) at Bousd, 'GR' indicates a date between 1910 and 1936, the reign of King George V. A mile west of Bousd, **Red Rocks (Tràigh Thorastain)** is a beautiful sandy beach with tidal islands opposite Cloiche Farm and only about 100yds off the road. Though it isn't wheelchair accessible, it might be a good option for people who can't walk great distances due to its proximity to the road. The **burial ground** beside the road at Toraston has some interesting grave slabs that might be from the 17th or 18th centuries and the sand dunes west from here are among the most impressive on the island. These sandy hillocks are similar in appearance to Skye's Fairy Glen, but you are infinitely more likely to have them to yourself.

Central Coll
The north coast Continuing along the north coast, the T-junction of the road from Arinagour north to Sorisdale and south to Ballyhaugh, at **Arnabost**, is marked by many colourful buoys hanging on the fence. At **Ballyhaugh** you can park a car carefully in the reserved spaces on the sides of the road before the cattle grid and gate of the Hebridean Centre in order to climb **Ben Hogh**, which, at 347ft, is Coll's highest hill; the short climb affords a spectacular view across the Inner Hebrides.

Starting at Ballyhaugh, walk through the gate marked to 'Hogh Bay', but then bear left around the lake towards a second gate, a good place to see barnacle, Greenland white-fronted and greylag geese, as well as tufted ducks and other species.

There are also an unusually high number of ancient **crannogs** (page 263) in Coll's interior, but you will need to navigate to them across boggy ground. For enthusiasts, the following are particularly worth the effort of visiting: **Dùn Anlaimh** (✥ 56°37′08″N 6°35′06″W) in **Loch nan Cinneachan** with the remains of a causeway that, according to tradition, was later defended by a Norse chief; one (✥ 56°36′34″N 6°35′01″W) in **Loch Anlaimh** slightly further south; the remains of two crannogs (✥ 56°38′17″N 6°33′22″W) in **Loch Cliad**; and another one (✥ 56°37′44″N 6°32′49″W) in **Loch An Duin**.

Head along the southeast bank of the lake on an intermittent path that sticks to higher, dry ground. Cross two broken dry-stone walls and walk about 100yds past the east end of the lake before heading uphill to the saddle between three vague peaks. The peak to the southeast is a few feet higher, but the ground is very boggy between them so, unless you are really intent on reaching the top, it is better to head up left just before you reach the highest part of the saddle and find a small stile (✥ 56°37′43.5″N 6°35′55.2″W) over the fence there. From the OS marker, on a good day, you can see as far as Jura and the Treshnish Isles, including the distinctive Dutchman's Cap or Bac Mòr, a wide, flat rim around a single round lump, to the south; the Outer Hebrides northwest; and Rùm directly north. Some 50yds north is the **Rocking Stone**, a boulder left by a glacier or thrown by a giant depending on who you ask. It is balanced on three stones; I did not try rocking it and would not advise it either.

From the top, find a sensible route down towards a large rock in a dry-stone wall (✥ 56°37′51.7″N 6°35′57.9″W), 200yds northwest of the Rocking Stone, where the wall can be crossed without damaging it. Head in the general direction of two blackhouses on the other side of the road, but take the diversion to a small ruined settlement that is still relatively intact with some windows and doors. From here, bearing slightly right and going over the hill, you will see the collection of houses that form Clabhach and a couple of gates to the road. Turning left on the road, it is less than a mile back to your starting point of Ballyhaugh.

Hogh Bay, backed by dunes, might win the prize of the most spectacular beach on Coll. There are rip currents here, making it an inadvisable place to swim, but the waves can be perfect for experienced surfers. It can be reached from Ballyhaugh or by following the track north from the RSPB car park at Totronald.

The south coast There are a couple of hidden beaches and archaeological sites that can be found by following the airport road from Arinagour, although not all have sensible parking nearby. Arriving by bike (page 134) will give you easier access to the crannogs in particular, otherwise you can drive to the RSPB parking and explore the West End from there.

Just after Acha Mill, south of the B8070, is a ridge of pink and white quartz. This once provided a natural defensive position for the Norse fort **Dùn an Achaidh** (✥ 56°35′53″N 6°35′27″W), of which a few courses of stone wall remain.

Another mile west along the road, there is walking access to **Gortan Bay**: a lovely sandy beach with the remains of a shipwreck. You can just about find somewhere to park off the road without blocking the passing place or gate, opposite a large wooden shed and pretty white house with a slate roof and small glass conservatory on the front. Follow the track beyond this gate for just under a mile to its end, where you need to bear slightly left to get to the beach. The *Harmonie*, a wooden barque from Norway, was stranded in the bay in 1890, an accident which, thankfully, nine of her ten crew survived. The shipwreck (✪ 56°35'12.3"N 6°36'03.8"W), only accessible at low tide, is a gnarled spine of planks and metal, slimy with green seaweed and providing solid anchorage for a limp forest of bladderwrack. Take off your shoes and socks as the sand can be soft and waterlogged here when the tide has just receded.

Breachacha Bay and its castles Wide, sandy Breachacha Bay, home to many ringed plovers, is dominated by three enormous (privately owned) buildings: the imposing grey fortress close to the shore, a likely home for a Disney villain, is the reconstructed **(Old) Breachacha Castle**; behind it, if looking from the beach, is the ostentatious mansion house known as **(New) Breachacha Castle**; and the third, a flamboyantly crenellated construction, lower than the others on the shoreline further south, is still a working farm.

Totronald The two standing stones at Totronald are known as **Na Sgeulachan** (Teller of Tales; ✪ 56°36'35.3"N 6°37'09.6"W). James Boswell, writing about his Hebridean explorations in 1773, recounts a traditional practical joke associated with these 'triangular flagstones':

> Of latter times they are used for putting a trick on any stranger who is passing that way. He is desired to lie down behind the easternmost one (or westernmost, according to the route he is on) and told that he will hear everything that is said by the company, who stand at the other stone; and while he is lying in patient attention, the company get off and leave him; and when he at last gets up, he finds himself all alone.

The **RSPB information room** at Totronald gives some good information about the birds and wildlife living in the area and allows you to record your sightings, along with checking those of others. There is a special corncrake-viewing platform here, plus an official car park (but no toilet facilities). Along with Balranald in North Uist, Coll is one of the best places to see corncrakes in the UK. They are still notoriously difficult to spot, but their 'crex-crex' croaks come from all directions in summer and particularly towards the end of April and beginning of May. From spring to September, the RSPB reserve is filled with all manner of birds including swooping lapwings, redshanks and burbling snipe with their elongated beaks. Winter is dominated by honking Greenland white-fronted, barnacle and greylag geese, but you might see hen harriers, merlins or tiny, fat snow buntings.

The West End The West End of Coll is wild, surrounded by fine sandy beaches and only possible to explore on foot after parking at the RSPB car park at the road end, slightly east of Crossapol and Feall Bay. An 8-mile walking route to remote **Calgary Point** is described by Walkhighlands (w walkhighlands.co.uk/islands/calgary-point.shtml).

Feall A track from the RSPB car park leads about a mile northwest to Ben Feall. At only 216ft, this hill manages to give a commanding view out to Rùm in the north, the Treshnish Isles in front of the Ross of Mull and Ben More (page 164) to the southeast, and even the Paps of Jura in the far distance; Tiree barely rises above Gunna, the uninhabited island beyond Coll's West End. There is a strange arrangement of large stones here thought to be an ancient burial cist (⊕ 56°35'54.9"N 6°39'10.5"W) and a more obvious memorial seat dedicated to the last Laird of Coll, who died in 2012.

The smaller hill just to the southwest of Ben Feall was once the site of a fort; there is little to see of it now, but its strategic position affords a spectacular view over sandy **Feall Bay**. Heading down to the beach, listen out for seals singing mournfully on the rocks. There is rubbish disposal for beach plastic at the RSPB car park if you feel like doing a good deed.

TIREE

Known to some in Gaelic as 'Tìr bàrr fo thuinn' (the land below the waves), Tiree is remarkably difficult to distinguish from a distance. Only nearly upon arrival do you begin to see the expanse of carefully placed, unassuming houses spreading into the distance on patchwork green croft land. Walking along the miles of spotless sand or taking a dip in the crystal-clear waters that surround it is enough for most holidaymakers, though the island is also famous for its watersports. Whether you take the plunge or not, there is nowhere quite comparable in the Inner Hebrides.

GETTING AROUND At 12 miles long and 3 miles wide, with attractions and settlements spread evenly across the island, Tiree is too big for most people to get around on foot, but with some unusually good alternatives on offer you do not necessarily need to bring a vehicle.

By car/taxi Tiree has a good range of indicated car parks. It is important not to drive on the machair or sand dunes as this destroys the unique and fragile habitat that makes Tiree so special. You can hire a car from **Tiree Car Hire** (Scarinish; m 07393 501940; w tireecarhire.com). To hire a taxi, try **John Kennedy Transport** (m 07789 551959; e info@johnkennedytransport.co.uk).

FESTIVALS AND EVENTS

MAY

Tiree 10K & Half Marathon
w tireefitness.co.uk/events/10k. Hugely successful running races; entry opens in Oct & fills up immediately.

JULY

Fèis Thiriodh 🔲. Festival of music, language & culture.
Tiree Agricultural Show 🔲. Highland dancing, farm-animal showing & after-show cèilidh.
Tiree Music Festival
w tireemusicfestival.co.uk. Camping music festival with 2,000 tickets; always sold out.

SEPTEMBER

Tiree Ultramarathon
w tireefitness.co.uk/events/tiree-ultramarathon. A spectacular 35-mile run around the whole island. Entry opens the previous Oct & fills up immediately.

OCTOBER

Tiree Wave Classic
w tireewaveclassic.co.uk. The longest-running professional windsurfing event in the world, founded in 1986. Fleets range from Juniors to World Cup Professional Windsurfers.

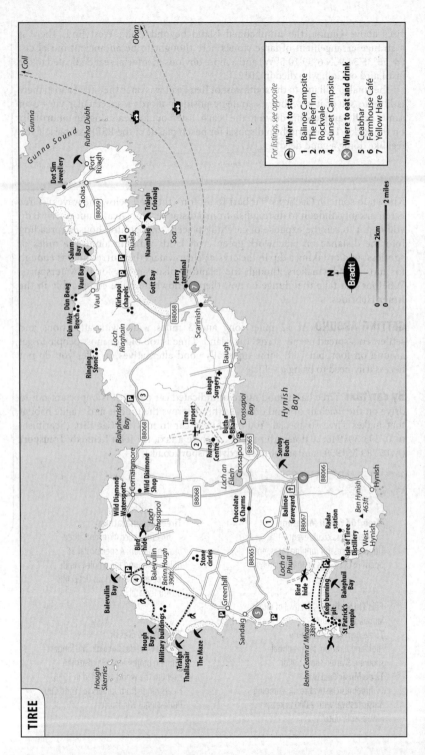

TIREE

For listings, see opposite

Where to stay
1 Balinoe Campsite
2 The Reef Inn
3 Rockvale
4 Sunset Campsite

Where to eat and drink
5 Ceabhar
6 Farmhouse Café
7 Yellow Hare

Bradt

0   2km
0   2 miles

N

↑ Coll

Oban →

Gunna
Gunna Sound
Rubha Dubh
Port Ruadh
Dot Sim Jewellery
Caolas
B8069
Traigh Crionaig
Naomhaig
Soa
Ruaig
Salum Bay
Vaul Bay
P
Kirkapol chapels
Gott Bay
P
Ferry terminal
Dùn Mòr
Dùn Beag
Bràgh
Vaul
Loch Riaghain
Ringing Stone
Scarinish
B8068
Balephetrish Bay
B8068
Baugh Surgery
Baugh
Hynish Bay
Tiree Airport
Rural Centre
Bith a' Bhaile
Crossapol Bay
Crossapol
Cornaigmore
Wild Diamond Watersports
Wild Diamond Shop
B8068
Soroby Beach
Loch an Eilein
B8065
Chocolate & Charms
Balinoe Graveyard
B8066
Loch Bhasapol
Bird hide
Balevullin
Beinn Hough 390ft
Stone circles
Greenhill
B8065
Radar station
Ben Hynish 463ft
West Hynish
Hynish
Isle of Tiree Distillery
Loch a' Phuill
Bird hide
Kelp burning pit
Balephuil Bay
St Patrick's Temple
Beinn Ceann a' Mhara 338ft
Sandaig
Balevullin Bay
P
Hough Bay
Military buildings
Tràigh Thallasgair
The Maze
Hough Skerries
B8067

By bike As most of the island is very flat, cycling can be an excellent option, but strong winds might make you appreciate the extra power injection from an e-bike. At **Tiree Fitness** (Tir a Chladaich, Sandaig PA77 6XQ; m 07867 304640; w tireefitness.co.uk/bike-hire), fitness enthusiasts Will and Becky offer high-quality bike hire, including lightweight hybrids (£20/15/85 day/additional days/week), e-bikes (£35/25/170 day/additional day/week) and kids' bikes (£15/10/65 day/additional day/week), with tag-alongs and child seats available. They also do bike servicing, repair and spares. Book in advance and collect from Sandaig, or they can deliver to your accommodation, the pier or airport (£25 inc collection).

Off-road wheelchairs The **Tiree Trust** (The Island Centre, Crossapol PA77 6UP; m 07391 239502; e ranger@tireetrust.org.uk; &) offers two different types of wheelchair for using on beaches and grass. They are free to borrow, although donations are appreciated; phone ahead.

WHERE TO STAY *Map, opposite*
In addition to the accommodation listed here, there is a huge number of self-catering options on Tiree – they are great for longer stays, but you must book well in advance. Some properties are traditional blackhouses or croft houses and can even be right on the beachfront; w isleoftiree.com/accommodation provides uncommonly comprehensive listings with photos. Note that campervans, caravans and motorhomes are not allowed on Tiree without first booking a pitch. Drinking water, toilets and chemical waste disposal are available opposite An Iodhlann Museum in Scarinish, while there is a shower at Pier Laundry (Pier, Scarinish PA77 6UH; ✆ 01879 220440; w pierlaundry.co.uk; ⏰ 24hrs), which also offers self-service laundry, as well as linen hire (1 week notice needed for the latter).

The Reef Inn (8 rooms) Crossapol PA77 6UP; m 07990 633953; w reef-tiree.com. In the centre of the island, this airy, modern guesthouse is decorated in a luxurious Nordic style with underfloor heating. Dogs welcome with a cleaning charge. **££££**

Balinoe Campsite Near Balinoe & Heylipol PA77 6TZ; m 07712 159205; w tireecampsite.co.uk; ⏰ Apr–Oct. Lovely, old-fashioned campsite with basic bathroom facilities, surrounded by working croft land. Inside seating & kitchen for campers in modernised World War II Nissen hut. Barn for storage of bikes, watersports equipment, etc. 2 cute & very basic pods & 1 bothy (sleeps 3) have mattress & electricity, but you'll need to bring your own bedding. Bookings via website only. **£**

Croft Camping [not mapped] ✆ 01879 220074; e camping@tireetrust.org.uk; w isleoftiree.com/croft-camping. This scheme was set up to protect Tiree's delicate machair habitats & contribute something towards the traditional crofting communities that are the mainstay of island life. A series of around 10 participating crofts are spread around the island, with a livestock-free piece of land set aside in each for up to 3 camping pitches. If you are visiting Nov–Mar, call or email rather than trying to book online. **£**

Sunset Campsite Sunset Croft, Balevullin PA77 6XD; m 07748 286784; w sunsetcampsitetiree. com; ⏰ Apr–Sep. Close to Balevullin Bay, this spot has grass pitches for motorhomes, campervans & tents. There are also 2 pods (sleep 2 or 4 using pull-out sofa bed; can only rent by the week in Jul–Aug) with basic self-catering facilities & linen provided. **£**

Self-catering
Rockvale 35 Balephetrish PA77 6UY; m 07900 102856; w rockvaletiree.co.uk; &. With 5 en-suite bedrooms & a bright lounge, this spacious property sleeps 10 (or more by prior arrangement). Bed linen is Egyptian cotton, there is a guest lounge with book exchange & good information on walks/ Tiree in general. Peaceful location surrounded by green fields & a short walk from Balephetrish Bay. Dogs welcome if arranged in advance. Drying space for wetsuits, bikes, etc. £1,000–2,300/week.

✗ WHERE TO EAT AND DRINK   *Map, page 140*

Opening times on Tiree seem to be particularly sporadic and there is not a huge variety of options, so it is best to plan ahead if you want to eat out.

Ceabhar Restaurant Sandaig PA77 6XQ; 📞01879 220684; f; ⏰ Apr–Oct 18.30–20.30 Wed–Sat. This is the best place to eat on Tiree, but extremely popular & difficult to get a table without reserving well in advance. Ever-changing menu with local produce, 'if not Tiree, then Scottish'. Always meat, fish & vegetarian/vegan options, plus pizza. Brew their own beer. ££

Farmhouse Café Balemartine PA77 6UA; 📞01879 220107; f; ⏰ Apr–Oct; ♿. With chickens queueing at the front door & a sunny conservatory overlooking farmland with Highland cows & ponies, this spot offers good coffee, cakes & light lunches. Small shop attached sells own Highland beef, as well as Tiree-made candles, fudge, woodturning, T-shirts, etc. £

Yellow Hare Pier, Scarinish PA77 6TN; 📞01879 220440; w yellowhare.co.uk; ⏰ check online; ♿. Good coffee & home baking including bagels & pancakes, plus a tasteful gift shop. £

SHOPPING

Bùth a' Bhaile Crossapol PA77 6UP; 📞01879 220581; f; ⏰ 08.00–18.00 Mon–Sat; ♿. Large, friendly, independent shop selling groceries, baked goods, alcohol, newspapers, secondhand books & just about everything else.

Chocolate & Charms Tràigh a Chiobair, Heylipol PA77 6TY; 📞01879 220037; w chocolatesandcharms.co.uk; ⏰ Apr–Christmas noon–16.00 Mon, Wed & Fri–Sat. Jeweller Becky runs this excellent little shop/café. Her jewellery is lovely & relatively affordable, taking inspiration from the natural colours & shapes of Tiree, including using moulds from shells found on the beach. Also sells delicious chocolate made on Tiree by her friend Jo, & local-interest books, while the café sells homemade cakes.

Co-op Scarinish PA77 6UH; 📞01879 220326; ⏰ 07.00–22.00 daily. Small supermarket.

Dot Sim Jewellery Greasamull, Miodar Rd, Caolas PA77 6TS; m 07906 002896; w dotdotsim. com; ⏰ Apr–Oct noon–17.00 daily (flexible). Elegant high-end jewellery.

Tiree Crab Company Scarinish PA77 6UH; m 07765 422831; f; ⏰ 10.00–16.00 Mon–Fri, reduced hours in winter; check Facebook. Small shop selling fresh, local seafood & sandwiches.

SPORTS AND ACTIVITIES

Tiree's conditions for wind- and kitesurfing are among the best in the world, making it Scotland's most famous **watersports** location. Tiree born and bred William Maclean established **Wild Diamond** (w wilddiamond.co.uk) in 1998, when the sports first started to take off; he and his professional staff offer lessons, courses and equipment hire for abilities ranging from 'beginner to super-hero level' for windsurfing, bodyboarding, kitesurfing, surfing, kayaking and stand-up-paddleboarding. Their windsurfing school for beginners and intermediates (page 145) is based on Loch Bhasapol, and for kit visit their shop (Cornaigmore PA77 6XA; m 07712 159205; ⏰ changeable, check online).

Tiree Equestrian (m 07833 031764; w tireeequestrian.org; 45min beginner rides £40–45 pp) offers **pony trekking** along Soroby Beach. Tiree Fitness (Tir a Chladaich, Sandaig PA77 6AQ; m 07867 304640; w tireefitness.co.uk) hosts beach **yoga sessions** through the summer.

Tiree Sea Tours (m 07788 810623; w tireeseatours.co.uk; £40–125pp) offer **boat trips** to Skerryvore Lighthouse, the Treshnish Isles to see puffins, and Staffa, Iona and Coll for lunch, as well as wildlife watching and fishing trips. You have a good chance of seeing marine mammals and basking sharks during the summer months.

OTHER PRACTICALITIES

Bank RBS, Scarinish PA77 6UH; ⏰ 09.30–14.30 Tue & Thu, 10.00–14.30 Wed. UK RBS & NatWest customers can withdraw cash inside the branch; foreign-bank customers might be able to get a cash advance with a debit/credit card & photo ID. No ATM.

Fuel Crossapol Filling Station, Tiree Community Development Trust Office, The Island Centre, Crossapol; ⊕ 09.00–17.00 Mon–Wed & Fri, 09.00–18.00 Thu, 09.00–13.00 Sat

Health Baugh Surgery, Baugh PA77 6UN; ✆ 01879 220323; ⊕ reception 09.00–noon

Mon–Fri, 14.00–17.00 Mon & Wed–Fri (outside these hours, calls are diverted to on-call doctor's phone)

Post office Scarinish (PA77 6UH; ⊕ 09.00–13.00 & 14.00–17.30 Mon–Wed & Fri, 09.00–13.00 Thu, 09.00–12.30 Sat); Bùth a' Bhaile (see opposite; ⊕ 08.00–17.00 Mon–Sat)

WHAT TO SEE AND DO

Scarinish Distinctive white-walled blackhouses with Tiree's characteristic tarred black roofs, along with the sandy beach and skeletal remains of the large schooner *Mary Stewart* make Scarinish Harbour both picturesque and interesting. The *Mary Stewart*'s final sailing was in 1937, after which she was left to rest on the beach for some time before eventually being blown up for firewood.

In a red corrugated metal building, at the west end of Scarinish, **An Iodhlann Museum** (PA77 6UH; ✆ 01879 220793; w aniodhlann.org.uk; ⊕ Jul & Aug 10.00–16.00 Mon–Fri; Sep–Jun 10.00–13.00 Mon & Wed–Thu; donations welcome; ♿) is Tiree's small, but excellent heritage centre. Information is well presented, interesting and easy to understand. There is not a huge amount in the way of physical exhibits, but highlights include Tiree-related military remnants like a homemade cigarette lighter made in the 1930s using parts of a brass grease gun, a Neolithic or Bronze Age saddle quern, and a full female outfit from the 1800s. An online genealogy service is also available (£5/hr).

An Turas, winner of 'Scottish Building of the Year' in 2003 is a Marmite attraction. A long, partially roofless modern structure, built by two young architects and a group of artists who aimed to celebrate Tiree's natural and architectural heritage, it has also been referred to as an 'elongated bus shelter'. The small structure is just on the left of CalMac's office at the ferry terminal, so you can decide for yourself.

The east

Beaches The vast, smooth expanse of **Gott Bay** (Tràigh Mhòr) stretches 2 miles east from Scarinish. Patterned sand slips into turquoise water, the intensity of blue increasing incrementally with the depth of the water. Sunny days glimmer on ripples further out or, in high seas, the horizon is broken by white horses. When you can see it, the horizon is lined by the Treshnish Isles with Ben More behind. To the west of the beach is Mallachaig, 'the cursed rock', which was condemned never to grow seaweed after Columba tried to tie his boat there and it got washed away. For drivers, there are several marked car parks at the eastern end of the beach. On the shore near the settlement of Ruaig is **Naomhaig** (⊕ 56°31'23"N 6°46'25"W), 'the blessed one', another rock that Columba managed to secure his boat to – successfully this time, meaning it was allowed to continue hosting seaweed. In this direction you will also find the **tidal island of Soa**. A visit just before low tide (page 28) might allow you to walk across. Surrounded by water and sand, this horseshoe of grass and rocky shoreline supports flocks of birds – Arctic terns soar above black-headed gulls, swooping lapwings, dunlin and passing families of shelduck – during nesting season the raucous chorus will remind you to tread carefully and stay on the grassy track where possible to avoid accidentally stepping on eggs. Do not linger too long as the tide rises quickly across the flat sand that separates Soa from 'mainland' Tiree. Just past the headland at Ruaig, Gott Bay turns into **Tràigh Crionaig**. Depending on the wind, this can be a more sheltered sandy beach, with rows of rocks and seaweed leading out into the sea and the few buildings off to one side.

At the far eastern end of the island is **Port Ruadh**. To find parking for this lovely beach, go past the house with the phone box outside in Caolas and cross the cattle grid. Keep straight on (northeast) for 50yds until you can't drive any further ahead, but instead turn right over another cattle grid. Immediately on your left is a parking area marked with cones and posts.

From here, walk down a grassy track that veers downhill to the left and you will pass a few picturesque whitewashed blackhouses with black felted roofs. Port Ruadh is a beautiful and secluded bay, with views across Gunna Sound to Coll; look out for basking sharks. At low tide, the stretch of barnacle-encrusted rock on the southern edge has fascinating rock pools. Some are deep enough for kelp to grow in, whereas others are shallow and coated pale pink; a perfect place for children and interested adults to discover sea anemones, small blennies, crabs, sea urchins and maybe even starfish.

There are more sandy beaches around the northeast, though they are generally better left for exploring on foot or by bicycle, as finding places to park is difficult.

Kirkapol chapels These two ruined chapels of religious and historical importance can be found behind Tiree Lodge Hotel on Gott Bay. The Norse origins of the name 'Kirkapol' – with 'kirk' meaning church – imply the religious significance of this settlement pre-dates both chapels. The nearer of the two ruined buildings, set within its own walled graveyard, is a 14th-century parish church. In front of the church's largest entry archway, there are a set of horizontal grave slabs, one of which, though overgrown, has what is thought to be the oldest representation of a claymore in Scotland. In a similar design, but smaller and set on a hill overlooking the area, is the ruin of an older 13th-century chapel. There is a good interpretation board at the entrance, which might help you identify several small Latin crosses that have been incised into rocks around the area; these are also thought to imply an earlier origin of Christian worship. More examples can be found at St Patrick's Temple in the southwest (page 147).

The north coast
Ringing Stone From the east end of Balephetrish Bay, a long stretch of yellow-grey sand in the centre of the island's north coast, you can walk 1½ miles along the coast to the Ringing Stone (⊕ 56°32'09.3"N 6°50'16.1"W). This large and obvious boulder was brought to this spot by the last Ice Age, 10,000 years ago. The circular cup markings are thought to be Megalithic in origin, and a small interpretation sign nearby suggests a theory behind them; you may as well guess your own interpretation as evidence from this time period is totally inconclusive. Local folklore has it that the rock was thrown over from Mull by a giant and that Tiree will sink into the Atlantic if it is ever removed. If you hit it with another stone, it emits a strange ringing tone, hence the name.

This stretch of coastline is home to Arctic terns, sanderlings, ringed plovers, oystercatchers, eider and many other species.

Dùn Mòr Broch, Vaul ✴ Occupying the summit of a rocky knoll, only 5 minutes' walk from the hamlet of Vaul, are the exceptionally well-preserved remains of an Iron Age broch and its outworks. Thought to be around 2,000 years old, the characteristic round building was partly excavated in the late 1800s, before the remainder of the soil was removed to achieve its current state in the 1960s.

During the broch's habitable existence, its walls are thought to have been about 26ft high and it would have been used as a stronghold. Though the remaining wall is only around 6ft high, much of the building's original features can be gleaned from its remains. The central space is over 29ft in diameter and enclosed within a characteristic double dry-stone wall and gallery construction, which adds another 14ft of width in all directions. Shards of pottery found during excavation imply it was built by an invading force, but there were also bronze and silver rings, rotary querns, glass ring beads, tools, and weaving and metalwork tools, among other things. A later addition was a 'disarticulated skeleton', buried after an apparently violent death, potentially relating to the Vikings.

Some 500yds east of the broch, just past a miniature blackhouse, is a second grass-covered fort, **Dùn Beag**. Thought to be an oval dùn rather than another broch, this one is also worth a visit.

Loch Bhasapol The **bird hide** at Loch Bhasapol affords good chances of seeing ducks such as pochards, as well as sedge warblers, reed buntings and the hen harriers coming to eat them, among the reeds and still water. To reach it, take the turning towards Kilmoluaig, just after you pass Wild Diamond Windsurfing School, and park off the road in front of the ruins of a cottage. The bird hide is 100yds southeast; there are some ID charts and benches inside. According to folk history, the 'Battle of the Sheaves' might have been fought between Loch Bhasapol and Cornaigmore Beach: the islanders apparently drove off an invading force of Vikings using bundles of plants as weapons.

The west
Balevullin In the northwest corner of the island are the sprinkling of traditional houses, farm buildings and wandering livestock that make up **Balevullin** and, at the end of the road, stunning **Balevullin Bay**. This attractive sandy beach, busy in summer, is a favourite with surfers.

Walk: Hough Bay, Beinn Hough and the remains of a World War II RAF station
Distance: 5 miles; time: 3 hours; start/end: Balevullin Bay car park; OS Explorer map: 372 Coll & Tiree

This meandering walk takes in open farmland, sand dunes and a long stretch of beach, before climbing 390ft Beinn Hough; potentially a little muddy underfoot, it is otherwise relatively unchallenging.

From Balevullin Bay car park, follow the single-track road back through the village; the thatched cottage with red doors on your right is one of the finest examples of a traditional blackhouse in all of the Inner Hebrides.

At the T-junction, turn right and follow the tarmacked track up the hill, past an ugly concrete building on your left, the first and least interesting of the World War II remnants en route. Heading west, towards the sea, this track will lead you all the way down to Hough Bay, but there are several intriguing **military buildings** along the way (⊕ 56°30'42.9"N 6°58'37"W). More recently some of these buildings have been used as sheep barns. The floor is unsafe, so just peer inside from the doorway.

Continue to the lengthy stretch of sand and colourful pebbles that forms **Hough Bay**. There are grey seal colonies on the rocks far offshore; you might see one bobbing in the water, but also listen for their plaintive howling drifting across the bay. On a clear day you can see the Outer Hebrides from here.

As you follow the sheep tracks through the dunes, look out for orchids, which flower from May into the summer, and notice the small, yellow, slipper-like flowers: bird's-foot trefoil (*Lotus corniculatus*), sometimes known as 'eggs and bacon', which also bloom in warmer months. Modestly pretty, these flowers are a good source of food for the caterpillars of several butterflies and moths, which you should also look out for around your feet.

Reaching the end of Hough Bay, you should meet a track running up towards the hill, Beinn Hough.

If you are not in a rush, take some time to explore the area before taking the track. Only 200yds south, invisible from the end of Hough Bay, are a couple of small, sheltered pebbly beaches called **Tràigh Thallasgair**. These are home to eider duck and curlew and make a pleasant place to stop for a picnic.

Take the track towards **Beinn Hough**. In spring, your walk along this track will be accompanied by noisy oystercatchers, lapwings and geese as you pass more military remains towards the base of the hill.

Beginning to climb the hill on a small path, you will soon reach a broken tarmac road, which will take you uphill, off to the left and around a hairpin bend before reaching a mast. Look out for dark purple marsh orchids here. The loud humming at the mast informs you that it is still in use, so keep a sensible distance and find the small sheep trail leading off to the left, just before you reach the fence.

You can follow this path up to the top, where there is a 360° view of the whole of Tiree, patchwork croft land and unassuming houses scattered across the central plains and, on a clear day, Skye to the north and the Outer Hebrides northwest. Beside the trig point is another ruined RAF building; though the concrete is undeniably ugly, the stunning views through broken windows give these buildings an uncertain appeal, similar to that of Brutalist architecture.

Follow the intermittent and broken series of small concrete steps and posts down to a small lower military building before heading slightly left towards the lowest part of a saddle in the hill and down towards the north coast on a grassy path.

From here, aim for the rusty posts of a long-lost gate and continue north for about 200yds more until you reach the same track you began the walk on. Turn right on to this track and head back into Balevullin village.

South from Balevullin Travelling south from Balevullin, the main road forks at the few houses that make up Hough. If you take the left fork, southeast, and continue for about half a mile you will notice a blue sign on your right marking '**stone circles**'. Do not expect Stonehenge or even the atmospheric circle at Lochbuie on Mull (page 167), as all but one of the stones across these two massive circles have either fallen over or been robbed. Despite the unspectacular positioning and surrounding sheep dung, the space seems to hold a heavy silence and, since the stones are thought to date from the Neolithic or Bronze Age, we should perhaps not be too critical of the damage they have endured over the several thousand years since their positioning.

The Maze (Tràigh Thodhrasdail/Ghrianal on the OS map), a long sandy bay, backed by dunes and interrupted only by occasional beautifully smooth, sculpted, stripy rocks, might just be the most spectacular beach on Tiree. On calm days, tiny ringed plovers pace up and down at the edge of each lapping wave, picking out titbits to eat. There is parking at Greenhill, 200yds away, although the sandy track down to Greenhill was quite severely eroded at the time of my visit and not easy to negotiate in a small car.

In early autumn, the bird hide overlooking **Loch a' Phuill** is an excellent place to watch dunlins, more ringed plovers and redshank, along with black-tailed godwits, greenshanks and whimbrels. Other birds such as gulls and kittiwakes visit to wash in the fresh water and speedy swallows swoop up midges in the summer. There is parking at Balephuil Bay.

The south coast
Walk: Balephuil Bay, St Patrick's Temple and Kenavara seabird cliffs
Distance: 3 miles; time: 2 hours; start/end: Balephuil Bay; OS Explorer map: 372 Coll & Tiree
This varied circular walk visits a spectacular beach, several archaeological sites and cliffs that are home to large populations of seabirds. The route covers sand and grassy paths, climbing to a grand height of 338ft.

Balephuil Bay, another of Tiree's lovely sandy beaches, is slightly dominated by the 'golf ball' radar station to the east; a useful navigation tool from almost anywhere on the island. With the sea on your left, walk west along the beach until you reach its end and follow the low grassy tracks along the shore. There is an obvious **kelp burning pit** or kiln (✧ 55°27'21.3"N 6°58'10.7"W), rare evidence of an industry that was once the backbone of Tiree's economy.

Follow this grassy track until it leads you up through the yellow irises to **St Patrick's Temple** (✧ 56°27'12.7"N 6°58'19.6"W). All that remains standing of this medieval chapel is part of the east gable end, but there are two cross-incised stones and the grass-covered remains of several other buildings, possibly huts, on platforms in the vicinity. There is no evidence that St Patrick ever visited Tiree.

The path begins to climb around the coast from here and soon brings you to some spectacular seabird cliffs, where swooping fulmars guard their nesting sites in the cliffs below during the summer months.

Follow sheep tracks to the southwest corner, where the fence starts. There is nothing but the Atlantic Ocean between this point and America. Take the time to search for Skerryvore Lighthouse (see below) on the southwest horizon.

Keep the fence between yourself and the sea on your left and follow it north until you reach a large cairn with a wooden cross embedded. Head down into the saddle and up to the higher peak of **Beinn Ceann a' Mhara**.

From here you can follow the fence down towards the ruins of a sheep pen, before heading towards the giant 'golf ball' on small paths through the machair and strange sand-dune hillocks. Eventually you will reach a fence and have to skirt around it via the beach before getting back to the car park.

The far south The southernmost peninsula of Tiree ends in two unconnected roads. West Hynish, where common seals can often be seen basking on rocks, is home to **Isle of Tiree Distillery** (1A West Hynish PA77 6UF; m 07591 005871; w tyreegin.com; tours & tastings £18–70) – the island's first legal distillery since the 19th century. Here you can try their classic and pink gins, as well as learning about Tiree's distilling heritage and the whisky-making process they have recently embarked upon. They also run longer sessions where you can choose botanicals and make your own gin to take away.

Over on the east coast, Hynish was the base for building the magnificent **Skerryvore Lighthouse** and was later used as the shore station, housing the lighthouse keepers and their families. What is left now is a strange assortment of buildings, with a round signal tower used between 1844 and 1937 to provide semaphore communication with the lighthouse. Other points of interest at Hynish include the pier and harbour, now filled with sand, and two excellent exhibitions put on by the Hebridean Trust (w hebrideantrust.org): **The Story of Skerryvore Lighthouse** (Morton Boyd Hall, Hynish; ⊕ May–Sep open access; £3 suggested donation; ♿)

and **The Treshnish Isles** (Old Cowsheds, Hynish; ⊕ May–Sep open access; £3 suggested donation; ♿). In the summer, you can also book a 90-minute guided tour of the shore station through the Hebridean Trust's website (w hebrideantrust. org; adult/child £15/5).

The central south coast At the junction of the roads to Hynish and Balephuil is **Balinoe Graveyard**, also known as Soroby. It is thought, without any proof I'm aware of, that this is the site of a monastery founded by Columba and presided over by St Baithane, his cousin. There is nothing to see of a monastery, but the graveyard was used by the MacLean chiefs between 1390 and 1680 and the strange and rather squat Maclean's Cross (⊕ 56°28'12.2"N 6°53'57.2"W) may be of interest. Carved into a Latin cross on one side and Celtic on the other, it is conspicuous in the graveyard and thought to be early medieval.

Heading north, the road passes **Loch an Eilein** and **Island House**, now a holiday home, which stands on the remains of the island's only castle. A MacLean garrison tried to hold this castle after their bankrupt chief sold Tiree to the 8th Earl of Argyll, Archibald Campbell, in 1674. Campbell successfully besieged the castle on at least one occasion around the years 1678–9 and by the time John Fraser was minister on Tiree (1678–97) he described the castle as 'ane ruinous tour surrounded with ane trintch of stone and earth'. The stone walls here were built during the potato famine around 1846 by the starving, but able-bodied, proportion of the population in exchange for famine relief aid.

The road to the airport will also lead you to the **Rural Centre** (PA77 6UP; w isleoftiree.com/attractions/146238-rural-centre; ⊕ 10.00–16.00 Mon–Fri; ♿; free), Tiree's cattle mart, which also has some interesting information about crofting on Tiree throughout the year, and Aisling's Kitchen, a café serving lunches (m 07557 510330; ◼; ⊕ Apr–Oct 11.00–16.00 Mon–Fri, Nov–Mar 11.00–15.00 Tue–Thu; £).

Crossapol Bay (Tràigh Bhagh) is a beautiful sandy bay alongside the road that returns to Scarinish. There was an Italian prisoner of war camp here during World War II and you can still see the remains of various military buildings along this stretch of road.

7

Mull (Muile), Iona (Ì Chaluim Chille), Ulva (Ulbha) and Gometra (Gòmastra)

Wild and mountainous, Mull is synonymous with soaring eagles; there are thriving populations of both white-tailed and golden species, and you have better chances of seeing them here than anywhere else in the UK. Golden eagles are particularly at home around lofty peaks; at 3,169ft, Beinn Mhòr (meaning 'large mountain') is Mull's highest, and also its only Munro. Despite the climb, on a clear day the effort to reward ratio is probably the most favourable of all the Inner Hebridean hikes, providing a viewpoint over the whole region: you can see the Skye Cuillin in the north, Jura's Paps in the south and just about everything between. Curiously, Mull is not known for its beautiful beaches, although the island's stretches of sand are also superlative, if mostly hidden away at the end of boggy romps or delicate cliff paths.

Mull is deceptively large and, with a population hovering somewhere just over 3,000 (a third of whom live in the thriving capital Tobermory), is totally uninhabited for large swathes of its south and west coastline. The majority of the interior is also inaccessible by road and, outside of its few main villages, the honesty box shop is still going strong. With fertile land and an abundance of seafood, some of Mull's most surprising delights can be found in tiny farm shops and producers' markets, as well as in the thriving restaurant scene. Be aware that shops and restaurants can close earlier than you might expect elsewhere, there are very few ATMs, and some small businesses will only accept cash. Pre-booking accommodation is essential, especially in summer.

Off the far west of the Ross of Mull, the tiny island of Iona is well known for its association with the 6th-century monk St Columba and his role in spreading Christianity into Scotland. Though half the islands in the Inner Hebrides claim to have some association with the saint, the evidence on Iona is indisputable. This idyllic speck of land is where he grew his monastic community, building a much earlier incarnation of Iona Abbey, which for centuries was the dominant religious and sometimes even political institution in the region. Top of the list for both pilgrims and history enthusiasts, Iona Abbey is popular with day visitors, but those who stay a little longer, taking the time to discover the island's secluded coves and flower meadows, will be rewarded with the peace and tranquillity that we can only assume attracted Columba to settle there in the first place.

With one of the smallest populations in this book, community-owned Ulva is a different island altogether. Only the most intrepid Inner Hebridean visitors will think to make this trip, and for that they'll be richly rewarded.

For listings, see from page 160, unless otherwise stated

🛏 Where to stay

1 Achnadrish House
2 Calgary Bay
3 Craignure Bunkhouse *p165*
4 Crannich
5 Dervaig Bunkrooms
  Glengorm Castle
  (see Glengorm Castle)
6 Killiechronan Camping
7 Pennygate Lodge *p165*
8 Pennygown Holiday Park
9 Sheiling Campsite *p165*
10 Tiroran Motorhome Stopover
11 Treshnish

✴ Where to eat and drink

12 Am Birlinn
13 ar bòrd
14 Calgary Café
15 Croft 3
16 The Hen House
17 The Old Post Office &
  Lochbuie Larder *p165*
  Pennygate Lodge
  p165 (see 7)

Tobermory (p156)

Aros Park & Lochan a Ghurrabain waterfalls
Mull Theatre

Bunavullin

Aros

Ardnacross Farm Shop

A848

Killundine

S o u n d   o f   M u l l

B849

MORVERN

Ardtornish

A884

Loch Teàrnait

Aros Castle

Salen Bay

Salen

Pennygown Chapel

Lochaline

Fishnish

Mull Pony Trekking

B8035

K e a l

B8073

Gruline

Macquarie's Mausoleum

Knock

Loch Ba

Garmony

A849

Scallastle

3
7
9

L o c h   n a   K e a l

MULL

Dùn da Ghaoithe 2,513ft

Craignure
Torosay Castle

Eilean Bàn

Duart Castle

Oban

Ben More 3,169ft

Lochdon

A849

B8035

L u s s a   G l e n   M o r e

Inverlussa Mussels

Loch Sguabain

Loch Airdeglais

A849

Loch Spelve

Ben Buie 2,352ft

Croggan

Loch Fuaran

Pennyghael

Moy Castle
Stone circle

Lochbuie

17

Laggan Bay

Kinlochspelve

Loch Uisg

F i r t h   o f   L o r n

Loch Buie

Carsaig

Carsaig Bay

N

Bradt

Ellenabeich/ Easdale

Seil

Easdale Island

Balvicar

0 — 5km
0 — 5 miles

Mull, Iona, Ulva and Gometra

7

HISTORY Continually inhabited since the last Ice Age, there is evidence of Mesolithic people living in coastal caves on Mull and, later, Neolithic farmers. The Bronze Age Beaker People left some of their corded pottery, as well as burial cairns, cists and potentially some of the great many standing stones, such as the atmospheric circle near Lochbuie (page 167). Iron Age remnants are mostly defensive, including various forts and brochs. This is a theme that continued right into clan times; guarding both the Sound of Mull and Firth of Lorn, Mull was strategically placed to control the waterways of western Scotland.

From around the 5th century AD, Cenél Loairn – a powerful family group who were descendants of Loarn mac Eirc, a legendary king of Dál Riata – are thought to have controlled Mull, along with their stronghold in northern Argyll. This is of particular interest to members of Clan MacLean who, despite 1,000 years of strife interrupting their reign of power, retained their identity as descendants of Loarn mac Eirc and have now regained their seat at Duart Castle (page 166). The name Loarn or Loairn also persists to this day, covering the predominantly mainland region of Lorne, the Firth of Lorn waterway and Scotland's favourite Lorne sausage (a flat square as opposed to the widespread 'link' variety).

In the meantime Dál Riata was destroyed by the Norse who, in keeping with the rest of the region, left little more than place names in the archaeological record. The appropriately named Dervaig, for example, originates from Old Norse ('dervig' meaning 'good inlet'). After Somerled's (page 15) rise to power, his son Dougall (ancestor of the MacDougalls) inherited the former territory of Cenél Loairn, including Mull. After Somerled's brother-in-law's heirs, the Crovan dynasty who held the title of 'Kings of the Isles', claimed loyalty to the English crown, the MacDougalls complained to King Haakon of Norway, who preceded to split their kingdom and bestow the MacDougalls with the title of 'Kings of the Hebrides'. Aros Castle (page 161) and Ardtonish on Morvern were then built to help maintain control over the Sound of Mull.

In the late 13th century, the MacDougalls backed the wrong side of a violent dispute over Scottish kingship and their land was confiscated by the victorious Rovert de Bruys. The power of Norway having slipped away, a new 'Lordship of the Isles' emerged in their shadow. Beginning on Islay, by 1437 the Lords of the Isles had moved their power base to the twin castles of Aros and Ardtonish, holding on to it until their treachery resulted in King James IV of Scotland forfeiting their lands.

The MacLeans then rose again under the approval of King James, basing their power at Duart Castle and building the Moy tower house at the bay of Loch Buie (page 167). The MacLeans held control until the mid 17th century when they chose the wrong side of religious politics and, after a two-year struggle with Campbell, Earl of Argyll, they were eventually suppressed, retreating to Cairnburgh Castle on the Treshnish Isles (page 171) in 1680. Campbell, in turn, ruled over Mull for over half a century until the Heritable Jurisdictions Act diminished his power to that of a mere landlord.

In the 18th and 19th centuries, farming and the kelp industry (page 15) were mainstays of the economy. Tobermory was the brainchild of the British Society for Extending the Fisheries and Improving the Sea Coasts of the Kingdom: work started on the 'New Village' in September 1789, a regrettable time of year to start a building project in the Hebrides, and was significantly slowed down by heavy rainfall and mud slides. In time the village was completed, but hopes of a thriving fishing industry were never fulfilled; herring shoals had swum away and during the

Dùn Hallin, an Iron Age broch on Skye's Waternish Peninsula PAGE 78
above
(KF)

The prehistoric Bodach and Cailleach standing stones on Gigha are thought to represent a man and woman PAGE 254
right
(KF)

West Highland grave slabs depict warriors, swords and crosses, each stone telling the story of the person it commemorates. This example lies at Finlaggan PAGE 223
below right
(KS/S)

There are mysterious standing stones across the region. Pictured: Fingal's Limpet Hammers on Colonsay PAGE 210
below left
(PT/VS)

top
(C/S)
Medieval fortress Duart Castle on Mull is home to an excellent museum PAGE 166

above left
(PT/VS)
Tiree has the Inner Hebrides' highest concentration of traditional blackhouses
PAGE 130

above right
(KL/VS)
The Museum of Islay Life has interesting exhibits from the island's dramatic history
PAGE 232

below
(KF)
In the 18th and 19th centuries, the Slate Islands were at the centre of the Scottish
slate mining industry; here the weathered slates cover the beach in Cullipool, Luing
PAGE 202

The unique circular Kilarrow Church in Bowmore PAGE 219   above left
(KF)

The impressive ruins of the Augustinian priory on Oronsay PAGE 211   top right
(PT/VS)

In 1598 on Islay, the MacLeans were burnt to death in Kilnave Chapel PAGE 233   above right
(4/S)

St Edward's Church, Sanday, with Rùm's dramatic cliffs behind PAGE 124   below left
(NN/S)

On Seil, Kilbrandon Church is famous for its dramatic stained-glass windows
designed by Dr Douglas Strachan PAGE 199   below right
(KF)

above left
(IBM/S)
Sheltered bays are perfect for kayaking PAGE 48

top right
(PT/VS)
Tiree is world famous for its watersports PAGE 142

above right
(4/S)
The majority of Rùm is a mountainous wilderness, but adventurous hikers can spend the night in bothies such as Dibidil in the remote southeast PAGE 106

left
(KF)
Thrift (also known as sea pink) along the coast of Islay

below
(KF)
The old Tor Mòr quarry and beach on Mull PAGE 172

The incredible basalt columns around Staffa's Fingal's Cave have inspired centuries of art and music PAGE 171
above
(R/S)

Climb Mull's highest peak, Ben More PAGE 164
below left
(m/S)

Calum's Road was constructed by hand to connect the far north of Raasay PAGE 100
below right
(AL/VS)

above left (E/S) On Coll, Tiree, Iona and Islay, listen out for the rare corncrake's distinctive 'crex crex' call from April into the summer PAGE 11

above middle (MF) Shags stand proudly on coastal rocks and nest among cliffs across the islands PAGE 10

above right (MC/S) Look out for short-eared owls in moorland glens across the archipelago PAGE 10

below (MF) Grey seals are a common sight along the islands' coastlines PAGE 8

bottom left (SD/S) One quarter of the world's whale and dolphin species visit Inner Hebridean waters; pictured here is a common dolphin PAGE 8

bottom right (MF) Otters are relatively common, but elusive PAGE 7

Introduced to the Inner Hebrides, goats now roam the islands in feral herds PAGE 8

top left
(KS/S)

Elusive pine martins live on Skye, Seil and Mull PAGE 8

above left
(MM/S)

Jura's 6,000 red deer outnumber humans 30 to one PAGE 241

above right
(KF)

The waters here are one of the best places in the world to see basking sharks PAGE 8

below
(MP/S)

Napoleonic Wars there was more money to be made from kelp. When the fighting was over in 1815, the collapse of the market brought many desperate families to Tobermory. Decades of poverty, overcrowding and disease followed in the capital.

Just as things seemed to be improving on Mull, the potato blight around 1845 brought famine and forced many families to seek better fortunes elsewhere. The Clearances were as complicated here as anywhere in the Highlands, with some tenants receiving a voluntary 'assisted passage' abroad and others being forcibly removed. Often people simply couldn't afford to pay for an onward journey and were evicted into extreme poverty and survival in an urban environment that they did not know. Francis Clark's evictions on the nearby island of Ulva were particularly notorious, with a population decline from 500 to 150 over the course of a decade. A story in Tobermory's Mull Museum recounts how one bed-ridden woman had the thatch removed from her roof, excluding a small portion just over her bed. The population of Mull declined from 10,000 to 3,000; meanwhile, the Campbells could still afford to build turreted manor houses such as Torosay 'Castle', completed in 1858. By the turn of the 20th century, Mull was home to more sheep than people.

Tobermory became a naval base in World War II with Commodore Sir Gilbert Stephenson, known as 'The Tobermory Terror', given the task of setting up a training station there. In 1964, the construction of a new pier in Craignure allowed regular motor vehicle transport to Mull for the first time which, along with improving mainland access for inhabitants of the island, enabled the growth of the island's tourist industry. While the more traditional industries of agriculture, fishing and forestry continue, tourism provides seasonal income for much of Mull's population throughout the summer months.

GETTING THERE AND AWAY Unless you're sailing your own boat, the only way to reach Mull is by **ferry**. CalMac (page 30) runs three services to Mull. Vehicles must be booked in advance. From Oban (page 257) to Craignure takes around 50 minutes, sailing as often as ten times a day in summer or as little as five times a day in winter (foot passengers/car £3.90/14.70).

Less common routes run between Tobermory and Kilchoan on the mainland Ardnamurchan Peninsula (35mins, up to 7 times daily in summer & infrequently Mon–Sat in winter; foot passengers/car £3.05/9.55); and Fishnish on the east coast of Mull to Lochaline on mainland Morvern (18mins; max of 14 daily in summer; min 4 daily in winter; foot passengers/car £2.70/7.90).

There are **moorings** at Tobermory Harbour (℡ 01688 302876; m 07917 832497; w tobermoryharbour.co.uk) and Ulva Ferry Pontoon (m 07557 378953; w ulvaferrypontoon.co.uk).

GETTING AROUND Holidaying on Mull without a **car** is perfectly feasible if you stay close to the main road between Tobermory, Craignure and Fionnphort. To reach some of the island's more remote locations, however, you will most likely want your own wheels, or have plenty of time and patience for hitchhiking. Excluding the A roads, which run up the island's east coast and along the south, the majority of driving on Mull is remarkably slow and tricky; even the A roads are mostly single track and on others you will have to negotiate around few passing places, hairpin bends and, surprise, monstrous pot-holes. Driving times should not be underestimated; it can easily take 3 hours to get from Calgary to Fionnphort if there are many cars coming the other way.

Car hire is available in Tobermory from Harbour Garage (℡ 01688 302103; e enquiries@harbourgarage-tobermory.co.uk; f).

Bus travel is quite feasible on Mull, but you'll need to check times and stops online or in a bus stop before travelling. Many services do not run on Sundays and are drastically reduced in winter. West Coast Motors (page 30; &) runs the 95/495 (Craignure–Salen–Tobermory), the 96/496 (Craignure–Bunessan–Fionnphort) and the 494 (Tobermory–Dervaig–Calgary).

Ulva Ferry Community Transport (m 07775 531301; w ufct.co.uk; &) run a **minibus** service from Calgary via Ulva Ferry to Salen from Friday to Sunday on request. The minibus or their electric car can also be booked for other journeys when available.

Mull is undeniably hilly, but the scenic western coastal route is a proper expedition to try by **bike** for fit cyclists. The long track out to Burg Estate (page 164) and the forestry trails in north Mull are good for less serious cyclists or those who are keen to avoid cars. Bikes can be hired from Cycle Mull (Ardmore Road, Salen PA72 6JJ; m 07484 330047; w cycle-mull.co.uk; e-bikes/mountain bikes/children's bikes £30/20/10).

TOURIST INFORMATION AND TOUR OPERATORS For **tourist information**, visit the Craignure iCentre (The Pier PA65 6AY; ☏ 01680 812377; w visitscotland. com; ⏰ Apr–Dec 09.30–17.00 daily; &). Check out **Mull and Iona Food Trail** (w mullandionafood.co.uk) for producers, farm shops and places to eat; and **Mull and Iona Arts Trail** (w mullandiona.art) for local galleries, events and craft fairs. Many of the island's guided tours listed here are also wildlife orientated, where local knowledge really comes into play.

Mull Magic ☏ 01688 301213; w mullmagic.com. Guided walks ranging from easy to challenging, covering different areas of Mull, Iona & Ulva. Pick-up/drop-off in Tobermory or Salen.

Mull Wildlife Tours ☏ 01680 812440; w mullwildlifetours.co.uk. Wildlife- & nature-orientated day tours with a max of 4 guests, starting in Craignure.

Nature Scotland m 07743 956380; w naturescotland.com. Tours, usually starting from Tobermory, include small-group nature-orientated day tours with walks, & multi-day trips with renowned wildlife photographers.

Walk Mull The Power House, Carsaig PA70 6HD; ☏ 01681 704025; w walkmull.co.uk. Guided walks, wild swimming, navigation training & wild camping expeditions with mountain leader Tony Mclean.

TOBERMORY AND AROUND A decade or two ago this colourful fishing port town was mostly known to a certain generation and their parents as the setting of the BBC children's TV programme *Balamory*. My first visit in 2004 was accompanied by a constant background hum of the cheery theme tune; the show finished in 2005 and although it's still possible to find related souvenirs, sanity seems to have returned. Less pricey than Skye's Portree (page 60) and with quite a bit more going on than Islay's Bowmore (page 219), Tobermory is my personal favourite of the islands' capitals and makes a good base for both solo travellers and those without their own transport. Although the colourful houses appear to have a hint of irony in a downpour, there are a good range of short indoor activities to entertain children and adults alike.

 Where to stay *Map, page 156*

Tobermory is a lively place to stay, with plenty of good accommodation options.

Tobermory Hotel (15 rooms) 53 Main St PA75 6NT; ☏ 01688 302091; w thetobermoryhotel. com; &. Stretches across several refurbished historical fishermen's cottages. Cosy, well-managed hotel with a bar & restaurant. **££££–£££££**

APRIL
Mull Music Festival Tobermory;
m 07765 244396; f. Small, free
music festival.

MAY
Mull Sevens w mullrugby.co.uk.
Rugby sevens tournament.

JUNE
Isle of Mull Sportive
w mullsportive.co.uk. Cycling races of
44/87 miles around Mull.

JUNE/JULY
Round Mull Race
w obansailingclub.org/round-mull-
race. Sailing competition.

JULY
Highland Games Erray Park,
Tobermory; w mullhighlandgames.
com. Traditional Highland dancing,
tossing the caber & hammer throwing,
as well as piping & track events.

JULY/AUGUST
**Mull Half Marathon, 10k &
Junior Road Races** Tobermory;
w mullrunners.com

AUGUST
Bunessan Show Bunessan; f.
Lively agricultural show, which
regularly hosts performances from the
Mull & Iona Pipe Band.

SEPTEMBER
Mendelssohn on Mull Festival
w soundwavesscio.org.uk. A week of
musical performances directed by the
Doric String Quartet.
Mull Fiddler's Rally Aros Hall,
Tobermory; look out for notices in
shops. Fiddlers (violin players) from
all over Scotland gather together for
1 evening.

OCTOBER
Mull Rally w mullrally.org. Closed-
road car rally.

HOGMANAY
Tobermory fireworks Locals &
visitors gather on the harbourfront
to watch a public display
around midnight.

Fairways Lodge (5 rooms) Erray Rd PA75 6PS;
\01688 302001; w fairways-lodge.co.uk. Andrew
has been running this spotless B&B for over a
decade. It is in an elevated position, a little way
out of the main town & perfect for golfers as it's
right next to an excellent 9-hole course (page 158).
Lovely balcony with amazing views over Calve
Island. **££££**
Tobermory Youth Hostel (27 beds) Main St
PA75 6NU; \01688 302481; w hostellingscotland.
org.uk/hostels/tobermory; ⊕ Apr–Sep. Light pink
building run by Hostelling Scotland. Moderately

sized kitchen & common room. Choice of private &
shared rooms. **£**
Tobermory Campsite & Caravan Holidays
Dervaig Rd PA75 6QF; \01688 302615;
w tobermory-campsite.co.uk; ⊕ Mar–Oct,
sometimes on request in winter. Friendly, green
campsite just over a mile out of Tobermory (about
30mins' walk); also inexpensive shepherd's huts.
Must bring own bedding, but it has kettle, toaster,
microwave & fridge. Motorhomes must book
ahead. Free Wi-Fi. **£**

✕ **Where to eat and drink** *Map, page 156*
Right on the harbour's edge, there's no distance from fishing boat to plate in
Tobermory, making it an excellent place to try seafood. Eating establishments are
proud to source their ingredients locally.

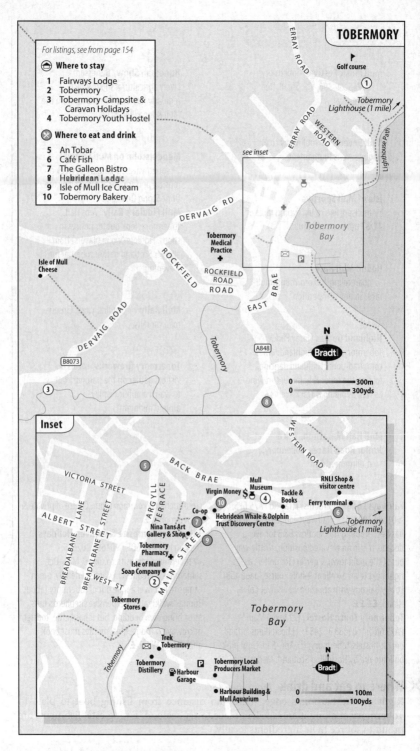

Golf course

ERRAY ROAD

WESTERN ROAD

ERRAY ROAD

Tobermory
Lighthouse (1 mile)

Lighthouse Path

see inset

For listings, see from page 154

Where to stay
1 Fairways Lodge
2 Tobermory
3 Tobermory Campsite & Caravan Holidays
4 Tobermory Youth Hostel

Where to eat and drink
5 An Tobar
6 Café Fish
7 The Galleon Bistro
8 Hebridean Lodge
9 Isle of Mull Ice Cream
10 Tobermory Bakery

DERVAIG RD

Tobermory
Medical
Practice

ROCKFIELD ROAD

ROCKFIELD
ROAD

Tobermory
Bay

Isle of Mull
Cheese

DERVAIG ROAD

EAST BRAE

B8073

Tobermory

A848

Bradt

N

3

8

0 ————— 300m
0 ————— 300yds

Inset

WESTERN ROAD

BACK BRAE

VICTORIA STREET

ARGYLL TERRACE

5

ALBERT STREET

BREADALBANE LANE

BREADALBANE STREET

WEST ST

Virgin Money

10

Mull
Museum

4

Tackle &
Books

RNLI Shop &
visitor centre

Ferry terminal

6

Tobermory
Lighthouse (1 mile)

Co-op

7

Hebridean Whale & Dolphin
Trust Discovery Centre

Nina Tans Art
Gallery & Shop

Tobermory
Pharmacy

Isle of Mull
Soap Company

2

9

MAIN STREET

Tobermory
Stores

Tobermory
Bay

Trek
Tobermory

Tobermory

Tobermory
Distillery

Harbour
Garage

P

Tobermory Local
Producers Market

Harbour Building &
Mull Aquarium

N

Bradt

0 ————— 100m
0 ————— 100yds

The Galleon Bistro Post Office Brae PA75 6NT; e info@thegalleontobermory.co.uk; w thegalleontobermory.co.uk; ⏰ noon–14.00 & 18.00–21.00 Tue–Sat (reduced in winter). Owners Martin & Elaine bought this small restaurant during the coronavirus pandemic, setting it up as a family business & providing the best produce from Argyll on a seasonally changing menu. Think the day's catch of langoustine fettuccine with butter-poached tails, dill cream & citrus essence, followed by a dark chocolate mousse with Ledaig whisky foam. £££

Café Fish The Pier PA75 6NU; 📞 01688 301253; w thecafefish.com; ⏰ Mar–Oct 16.30–22.00 Tue–Sat. Good, reliable, local seafood. ££

Hebridean Lodge 1 Baliscate PA75 6QA; 📞 01688 301207; 📘; w hebrideanlodge.co.uk; ⏰ 12.30–15.00 Thu–Sat but vary; check Facebook. High-quality lunches with a strong focus on local produce; menu dependent on season & that day's catch. Reservations only. Evening take-away sometimes available & advertised on Facebook. ££

An Tobar Argyll Tce PA75 6QB; 📞 01688 302211; w antobarandmulltheatre.co.uk; ⏰ 10.00–18.00 daily; ♿. Set in an old church overlooking the harbour; it is a steep climb up there, but worth it for inexpensive vegetarian food, pastries, coffee & cocktails. £

Isle of Mull Ice Cream Main St PA75 6NT; 📘; ⏰ flexible. Little pink building on the seafront. Ice cream made on site from local milk. Bench behind possibly has the best view of any eatery in Tobermory. £

✳️ **Tobermory Bakery** 26 Main St PA75 6NU; 📞 01688 302225; w tobermorybakery.com; ⏰ 09.00–16.00 Mon–Sat. Light-blue building on harbourfront. Big cups of proper coffee, home-baked cakes, soup, filled rolls & pastries & excellent vegan sausage rolls. Also bread, exciting flavours of jam & small deli with local produce: venison, highland beef, cheese, etc. Table service or take-away. £

Nightlife and entertainment An Tobar (see above) is a centre that hosts art exhibitions, concerts and other events. South of Tobermory by 1½ miles, the 100-seat Mull Theatre (Druimfin PA75 6QB; 📞 01688 302211; w antobarandmulltheatre. co.uk) is a venue for both local dramatic performances and visiting plays from further afield.

Shopping Nearly all Tobermory's shops are located on Main Street in the colourful buildings overlooking the harbour. While there are not many options for clothes shopping, there are a good variety of small independent shops selling both essentials and gifts.

Arts and crafts

Isle of Mull Soap Co 50 Main St PA75 6NT; w isleofmullsoap.scot; ⏰ summer 09.00–22.00 Mon–Sat, 10.00–16.00 Sun, reduced hours in winter; check online. Handmade soap & eco-toiletries such as bamboo toothbrushes.

Nina Tans Art Gallery & Shop The Gallery Loft, 37 Main Street PA75 6NT; w ninatans.com; ⏰ Apr–Sep, hours vary. Upstairs in The Gallery, a Gothic revival-style church built in 1878, Finnish artist Nina Tans runs this contemporary art gallery & shop, with her own vibrant watercolour seaweed paintings on display, as well as a selection of tasteful Scottish homeware including woollen blankets. While you're in the building, take a moment to admire the fabulous stained-glass rose window, which is an original feature.

Food and drink

Co-op 33 Main St PA75 6NT; 📞 01688 302004; w coop.co.uk; ⏰ 07.00–22.00 Mon–Sat, 10.00–22.00 Sun. Small supermarket with bakery.

Isle of Mull Cheese Sgriob-ruadh Farm PA75 6QD; 📞 01688 302627; w isleofmullcheese. co.uk; ⏰ Apr–Oct shop 10.00–17.00 daily, café 10.00–16.00 Sun–Thu. Beautiful farm (the only dairy farm on the island), making excellent cheese sold from The Glass Barn farm shop & café.

Tobermory Local Producers Market Next to the Tobermory Harbour Building, PA75 6NU; ⏰ 11.00–14.00 Mon. All the best of local produce: scallops, seasonal vegetables, honey, venison, bread, pies…

Tobermory Stores 60 Main St; 📞 01688 302808; 📘; ⏰ Apr–Oct 07.00–18.00 daily,

Nov–Mar 07.00–18.00 Mon–Sat (flexible), 10.00–16.00 Sun. Meat & veg from Glengorm, Isle of Mull Cheese, homemade pies & other local products.

Other supplies

Tackle & Books 7 Main St PA75 6NU; ☎ 01688 302336; w tackleandbooks.co.uk; ⊕ Apr–Oct

09.00–17.30 Mon–Fri, 11.00–16.00 Sun, Nov–Mar 10.00–13.00 & 14.00–17.00 Mon–Sat. Bookshop selling guidebooks, stationery & art supplies, plus fishing tackle.

Trek Tobermory Main St PA75 6NR; ⊕ Apr–Oct 09.00–21.00 daily, Nov–Mar 10.00–16.00 daily. Reasonably priced outdoor gear & friendly service.

Sports and activities Tackle & Books (see above) is the best place to get information and a map about **fishing** on Mull. They also issue permits for certain lochs and rivers listed online. There's also a nine-hole **golf course** (Tobermory Golf Club; Erray Rd PA75 6PS; m 07727 067063; w tobermorygolfclub.com) overlooking Tobermory Bay. For **wildlife and boat trips**, try:

Sea Life Mull w sealifemull.co.uk; adult/child £70/35 for 4hr trips. Wildlife-watching boat trips with the hope of finding seals & maybe even minke whales, basking sharks, dolphins, harbour porpoise & white-tailed eagles. Work alongside HWDT (see opposite) & the aquarium (see below).

Tobermory Bay Tours m 07873 756286; w tobermoryboattrips.co.uk. Owner & skipper Lyndsey set up & ran Mull Aquarium before embarking on this newest venture. She runs inexpensive small-boat trips with a focus on wildlife around Tobermory Bay. Tours range between 1 & 1½ hours with a sunset option: adult/child £15–40/6–20.

Other practicalities

Bank Virgin Money; 20 Main St PA75 6NU; ⊕ 09.30–16.00 Mon–Tue & Thu–Fri, 10.00–16.00 Wed

Fuel Harbour Garage, Ledaig car park PA75 6NR; ☎ 01688 302103; ⊕ 08.00–18.00 Mon–Fri. There's also a mechanic.

Health Tobermory Medical Practice (Rockfield Rd PA75 6PN; ☎ 01688 302013); accident &

emergency in Craignure (page 166); Tobermory Pharmacy (46 Main St PA75 6NT; ☎ 01688 302431; ◻; ⊕ 09.00–17.00 Mon–Tue & Thu–Fri, 09.00–13.00 Wed & Sat)

Post office Tobermory Post Office, Hus Gate, Ledaig PA75 6NR; ⊕ 09.00–13.00 & 14.00–17.30 Mon–Tue & Thu–Fri, 09.00–13.00 Wed, 09.00–12.30 Sat

What to see and do Tobermory has a whole string of fantastic little attractions, with more indoor diversions for children than most small Scottish towns. Mull's cultural and natural heritage is presented in a varied and engaging manner, with something for visitors of all ages and a whole range of interests.

Mull Aquarium (Ledaig PA75 6NR; ☎ 01688 302876; w mullaquarium.co.uk; ⊕ Easter–Oct 09.30–17.00 Sun–Thu (flexible); adult/concession/child £6.50/6/5.50) Keeping animals for a maximum of four weeks, this fascinating attraction is Europe's first 'catch and release' aquarium. Local fishermen and children bring in interesting species, and staff at the aquarium use them to educate visitors. Octopus, probably the most exciting marine guest, are only kept for two weeks and released due to their high intelligence. Popular touch-pool demonstrations are hosted every 20 minutes in summer months, where visitors have a chance to hold species such as starfish, squirting scallops, hermit crabs and urchins.

Tobermory Distillery (Ledaig PA75 6NR; ☎ 01688 302647; w tobermorydistillery. com; ⊕ Apr–Oct 10.00–17.00 daily, Nov–Mar 11.00–16.00 daily) Originally established as Ledaig Distillery in 1798, Tobermory is Mull's only distillery and one of the oldest in Scotland. It produces two contrasting single malts: the non-peated Tobermory and the heavily peated Ledaig; plus a newer Hebridean Tobermory gin. Tours cost £18.50 per person, including two drams (one 12-year-old Tobermory and a ten-year-old Ledaig) and last 45 minutes. There's also an option for 'Warehouse 1 Tastings', which cost £50 and take 1 hour 15 minutes, with tutored tastings of four warehouse and premium drams.

Hebridean Whale and Dolphin Trust (HWDT) Discovery Centre (28 Main St PA75 6NQ; ✆ 01688 302620; w hwdt.org; ⊕ Apr & May 09.00–17.00 Mon–Fri, Jun 09.00–17.00 daily, Oct 09.00–17.00 Mon–Thu, Nov 09.00–17.00 Mon & Thu) This modern exhibition centre has an inspiring and informative film playing, touch-screen information about species and distribution, and a couple of whale bones. Check in advance on their website for scheduled talks and activities, including guided coastal walks to Tobermory Lighthouse and Glengorm.

Mull Museum (Columba Bldgs, Main St PA75 6NY; ✆ 01688 301100; w mullmuseum.org.uk; ⊕ Easter–Oct 10.00–16.00 Mon–Sat; other times library & archives by arrangement; donations welcome) An endearingly old-fashioned museum crammed with invaluable, well-researched information and interesting exhibits, including delicate jewellery thought to have been lost by medieval pilgrims on their way to or from Iona. It's worth visiting towards the beginning of your time on the island if you're a history or archaeology enthusiast; as well as providing vital background information, it can help you locate and interpret the most interesting archaeological sites on the island.

RNLI shop and visitor centre (Ferry port PA75 6NU; free) A small exhibition about the Royal National Lifeboat Institution with a little information and history, as well as fun outfits for children to try on.

Tobermory Lighthouse The 'Lighthouse Path' is signposted just past the RNLI centre on the left-hand side of the pier. This 2-mile return walk is easily followed along the coast, running through mature, broad-leaved woodland, with bluebells in May and the scent of wild garlic. Eventually the view opens up across to Ardnamurchan with fishing boats bobbing in the Sound. Look out for cetaceans, which are regularly seen on this stretch of water. You will soon reach the lighthouse, which you cannot go inside. Keep a close eye on small children and dogs as there are steep drops in places.

Aros Park (w forestryandland.gov.scot/visit/aros-park) Roughly 1½ miles south of Tobermory centre, near the Mull Theatre (page 157), a series of short, marked woodland trails visit the peaceful Lochan a Ghurrabain, two majestic waterfalls in the Aros River and the shoreline, where there is a lovely view across to Tobermory Harbour. Following the green trail, with Tobermory Bay on your right, you can walk to Tobermory (1 mile).

NORTHERN AND CENTRAL MULL
With settlements small and spaced out, northern and central Mull are fantastic for wildlife, discovering unknown archaeological sites and generally exploring wild places.

The only **public transport** serving this part of Mull is a request service run by Ulva Ferry Community Transport (page 154).

⌂ Where to stay *Map, page 150*

Townships are few and far between in this wild part of Mull and accommodation options are sporadically placed. For self-catering, as well as those listed below, options can be found at w visitmullandiona.co.uk/listing-type/self-catering.

Dervaig Bunkrooms (6 beds) Dervaig village hall PA75 6QN; m 07919 870664; w dervaigbunkrooms.co.uk; ☐. Modern bunkhouse with 2- & 4-bed private rooms. **£**

Crannich Aros PA72 6JP; ☏ 01680 300495; w crannich.co.uk. Campsite in a secluded, inland glen with electric hook-up for campervans, motorhomes & c/vans. **£**

Killiechronan Camping Killiechronan Estate PA72 5JU; ☏ 01680 300403; ⊕ Mar–Oct. Very basic & cheap camping in lovely spot on the shore of Loch Na Keal. Sinks & toilets at farm. **£**

Pennygown Holiday Park Glenforsa, Aros PA72 6JN; m 07799 711125; w pennygownholidaypark.com; ⊕ Apr–Oct; ☐. Camping & pods on the banks of the Sound of Mull, with lovely view of Morvern; but next to the A849, which makes it a little less peaceful. Pods (**£££**) sleep up to 4 & have bedding, kettle, toaster, microwave & fridge. **£**

Tiroran Motorhome Stopover Tiroran Community Forest PA69 6ET; e admin@swmid. co.uk; w swmid.co.uk/our-projects/tiroran-community-forest-and-sawmill/tiroran-aires. A peaceful spot for self-contained motorhomes & campervans. 2-night max stay. **£**

Calgary Bay To the south of Calgary Bay is a council-owned space allocated for small campervans & tents, with public-access toilets. Free.

Self-catering

Achnadrish House ('The Cabin' sleeps 2, 'The Wing' sleeps 6) Dervaig PA75 6QF; ☏ 01688 400388; w achnadrish.co.uk. A 200-year-old self-catering shooting lodge is divided into 3 parts (the owners' house, The Cabin & The Wing), with pigs & chickens. Ideal location for walking, cycling & wildlife. Min 1-week stay in Jul–Aug; The Cabin £400/week, The Wing £825/week.

Glengorm Castle 5 miles northwest of Tobermory PA75 6QE; ☏ 01688 302321; w glengormcastle. co.uk. Built in 1860, Glengorm Castle is an imposing, turreted manor house that offers a range of short-stay apartments & self-catering properties within the castle & on the estate (see opposite). Visit the website for prices and options.

Treshnish Calgary PA75 6QX; m 07342 015431; w treshnish.co.uk. 8 dog-friendly cottages & 1 shepherd's hut on Treshnish Farm, in a quiet location in the far northwest of Mull. £400–860/week.

✗ Where to eat and drink *Map, page 150*

Despite the low population density, northwest Mull has a superb selection of small, locally owned restaurants; foodies would do well to spend a few days in the area just to take advantage of this.

ar bòrd Dervaig PA75 6QN; ☏ 01688 400647; w dervaigrestaurant.com; ⊕ summer 18.30–21.00 Wed–Sat. Small restaurant with seasonal set menu (£47.50), featuring highlights such as creel-caught shellfish landed in Croig & wild venison smoked in-house. Pre-booking essential. **£££**

Croft 3 Fanmore PA73 6LX; m 07973 448284; w croft3mull.co.uk; ⊕ Apr–Sep 18.00–late Tue–Sat, 13.00–16.00 Sun, Oct–Mar 13.00–16.00 Sun. Seasonal 3-course set menu served in simple, high-ceilinged building on working croft with aims towards self-sufficiency. Sunday roasts & occasional evening meals in winter (check online for dates). **£££**

Am Birlinn Penmore Mill, Dervaig PA75 6QS; ☏ 01688 400619; w ambirlinn.com; ⊕ 16.00–21.00 Wed–Thu, noon–14.00 & 17.00–21.00 Fri–Sun; ☐. Beautifully presented, high-quality local food in an impressive modern wooden building. Book in advance. **££**

Calgary Café Calgary PA75 6QQ; ☏ 01688 400256; w calgary.co.uk; ⊕ Easter–Oct 10.30–16.00 Wed–Sun. Coffee, b/fast rolls, home-baked cakes & lunches in attractive café with outside eating area. Also small selection of local meat & cheese. **£**

✳ The Hen House Fanmore, Ulva Ferry PA73 6LX; ⊕ closed at the time of writing, but well worth double-checking on your way past. Small wooden shed with picnic tables outside & incredible view of Ulva. Delicious

quiche. Tries to avoid single-use plastic & provides wooden forks, paper plates & discount for own cup. £

Shopping

Ardnacross Farm Shop Aros PA72 6JS; w ardnacross.com/farm-shop; ⊕ hours vary. Lamb, beef & venison straight from the farm.
Dervaig Post Office & Stores Dervaig PA75 6QJ; ☏ 01688 400208; w dervaigshop.co.uk; ⊕ 09.00–18.00 Mon–Sat, noon–14.00 Sun; ♿. Incredibly large & well-stocked grocery shop considering

location. Fresh fruit & veg, meat & dairy, coffee machine, alcohol & snacks.
Salen SPAR, Malcolm Elliot Post Office & Stores Ltd Salen PA72 6JB; ☏ 01680 300472; ⊕ 08.00–19.00 Mon–Sat, 10.00–17.00 Sun. Relatively large grocery shop; also sells local-interest books.

Sports and activities

Mull Charters Ulva Ferry PA73 6LY; ☏ 01680 300444; w mullcharters.com. Wildlife-watching trips with the specific aim of seeing/photographing white-tailed eagles.
Mull Pony Trekking Killiechronan Estate (near Gruline) PA72 6JU; m 07748 807447; ⓕ. Riding over hills or along the beach.

✳ **Turus Mara** Ulva Ferry PA73 6LY; ☏ 01688 400242; w turusmara.com. Boat trips out to the Treshnish Isles & Staffa from Ulva Ferry. Puffins (May–Jul) & other great wildlife opportunities. Plenty of time ashore on both Lunga & Staffa, & friendly, knowledgeable crew.

Other practicalities

Fuel MacDonald's Filling Station, Salen PA72 6JF; ⊕ 07.30–18.00 Mon–Sat, closed Christmas & New Year

Health Salen Medical Practice, Ardmor Rd, Salen PA72 6JL; ☏ 01680 300327
Post offices Dervaig Post Office & Stores (see above); Salen SPAR (see above)

What to see and do

The central east coast The ruins of **Pennygown Chapel** stand just to the east of the A849 in central Mull, with views across the Sound of Mull to Morvern. Thought to be from the 13th century, the site is shrouded in myth; people used to leave small requests for the fairies until one day a chancer left a small stick and asked for it to be turned into a ship's mast; the fairies responded by moving out, never to be heard of since. Look out for the figures of a man and woman carved in relief on two 17th-century grave slabs. Inside the chapel is the intricately carved base of a 16th-century cross.

Heading north from the small village of Salen, also the easiest place to cut across to the west coast, there are a couple of gently rotting old boats on the muddy shore; the skerries and islets around **Salen Bay** are frequented by common seals. On the other side of the bay is **Aros Castle** (⊕ 56°32'01"N 5°57'54"W); already in ruins by Martin Martin's visit in 1695, it was initially built by Clan MacDougall who held it for a while before losing it to the MacDonalds; they later lost it to the MacLeans. If you have a car, take the turning towards 'Aros Mains' and park in the small indicated car park; you can explore on foot from there.

The northern coast A windy road leads out to **Glengorm Castle**, an extensive 19th-century manor house now run as holiday accommodation (see opposite). Although the interior is reserved for guests, the surrounding estate is a rewarding area to visit. Now quiet and secluded, Glengorm had an unpleasant beginning; James Forsyth, who bought the estate in 1850, removed around 70 tenants over the following few years before he built his new 'castle'. There's a story that he asked an old woman what his new residence should be called, not understanding that her suggestion, 'Glengorm' (meaning 'the blue glen'), referred to the smoke from the burning roofs of the houses of those he evicted. The current owners are much more hospitable and there is a café where visitors are welcome to park in the car park and explore the estate on foot; there are several interesting archaeological sites to be found – including a trio of standing stones – and good chances of spotting cetaceans, particularly bottlenose dolphins, as well as the five resident mating pairs of hen harriers.

Walk: Two secluded sandy beaches

For both beaches – distance: 4 miles return; time: 2 hours. For Port na Beach only – distance: 2 miles; time: 1 hour. Start/end: Croig; OS Explorer map: 374 Isle of Mull North & Tobermory

Calgary (see below) has a well-deserved reputation as Mull's finest beach, but Port na Beach and Langamull are two hidden gems with only a fraction of its visitors. The route out to them is easy-going, initially following tracks that become grassy or sandy in places; the section between Port na Beach and Langamull crosses open fields and gentle coastline.

From the B8073, take the turning for Croig and park in a small place opposite the harbour and sea wall (⊕ 56°36'19"N 6°14'05"W). You can walk out to the tiny island beyond the sea wall for an interesting perspective, before walking along the track marked 'Croig Farm'; it's just over a mile north to beautiful **Port na Beach** (⊕ 56° 36'43"N 6°15'16"W). This idyllic pocket of sand is only beaten in peacefulness by **Langamull Beach**, a further mile southwest across grassy, unpathed coastline. Higher ground gives you a view out to Rùm and Coll and you might see seals bobbing in the sea. At Langamull, green grass runs down to the sea, where sheep graze quietly on small islands and the water is tropically turquoise. To return, retrace your steps to Croig.

Towards Dervaig The road to Dervaig from Tobermory (the B8073) passes some peaceful lochs before heading down a couple of sets of sharp hairpin bends. The second set of hairpins are surrounded by clusters of standing stones; there is a small car park at the top of the hill, and another smaller place to park at the sharp corner below. Just southwest of the graveyard at this second parking place, you will notice a quite broken set of **four standing stones** (⊕ 56°35'12"N 6°10'24"W), one of which has been set into a dry-stone wall with a casual nonchalance to its history.

The attractive settlement of **Dervaig** is most memorable for **Kilmore Church**. Built around 1904 by the architect Peter Macgregor Chalmers (who also built Rhu Church on Canna; page 120), it has a tall white spire and colourful stained-glass windows. The Kilmore Cross, part of which is now protected inside the church, is also said to have been the grave of John Campbell, the 'grisly lad', and was made in the 14th or 15th century, Iona School style. The sheltered waters of **Loch a' Chumhainn**, on which Dervaig sits, have made Dervaig a popular settlement throughout history and are also a favourite haunt of otters. For the best chance of spotting one, spend some time quietly observing the grassy banks of the loch around dawn or dusk.

Calgary The tiny township of Calgary packs a punch in terms of nearby visitor attractions. Most visitors come here for **Calgary Bay**, an idyllic stretch of sand that has the reputation of being Mull's best beach; it's also one of the most accessible on the island.

Opposite Calgary Bay is the walled **Calgary Burial Ground** with an early Christian stone carved with crosses on both sides, one of which is upside down. The cross stone stands on a raised area, just in front and to the left of three modern gravestones and next to another well-weathered grave slab. The stone itself is simple and weathered, but shows that this site has had a religious significance for over 1,000 years.

Just north of Calgary Bay, **Calgary Gallery** (☏ 01688 400256; w calgary.co.uk; ⊕ 10.30–16.30 Tue–Sun) is an excellent art gallery with local pieces in clay, wood, mosaic, watercolour, oils, tapestry and mixed media. More famous is their open garden and woodland walk, **Calgary Art in Nature** (£2 including map), with hidden sculptures, a zip line, rope swing, willow tunnels and plenty of artistic detail. There is also a great view over Calgary Bay.

The wild west coast The coastline from Calgary all the way down to the Ross of Mull is either a delight or a horror depending on how much of a hurry you're in. The scenery is sublime, with views out to the Treshnish Isles and then looking across Loch Tuath to Gometra and Ulva. Driving conditions are tricky, with deep potholes in parts, sharp turns and very few passing places along certain stretches. Near Kilninian is a deserted black beach, **Traigh na Cille**, which makes a beautiful spot for a picnic if you can find somewhere to park without blocking either gateways or passing places.

In Ballygown, a hamlet just northwest of Ulva Ferry, is **Lip na Cloiche** ✳ (☏ 01688 500257; w lipnacloiche.co.uk; ⊕ dawn–dusk all year; £2.50, cash-only). This densely planted, layered garden winds around several levels. Flowers, specifically chosen to help the bees, and delicate scents of lemon balm follow you around the intricate paths and gardener Lucy's artistic touches are everywhere. Outdated farming implements frame the way and a wonderful circle of glass fishing floats reflects the sunshine (if you are lucky enough to have some). Lucy also has a small craft shop in her porch.

Opposite Ballygown, between Lip na Cloiche and the small headland called Rubha Leadaig, is a well-preserved broch called **Dùn nan Gall** (⊕ 56°30'36"N 6°10'26"W), although there isn't anywhere sensible to park very nearby. Shortly further south is a parking place for **Eas Fos Waterfall**; this pretty cascade is only 20yds away and much more impressive after rain. Further south, at the tiny township of **Ulva Ferry**, you can catch the passenger boat to Ulva (page 179).

As the road turns east, skirting around **Loch na Keal**, the scenery becomes even more spectacular. Those driving all the way along the western coast will quickly become familiar with the outline of tiny, uninhabited Eorsa in the middle of the loch; there is also a good selection of places to pull over in order to stop and admire the view. Those who are searching for eagles with binoculars should spend some time scouring the hilltops and coast here; both species live around this area.

Just after the small settlement of Gruline is **Macquarie's Mausoleum**. A small, stone structure of particular interest to Australians, Lachlan Macquarie was born on the Isle of Ulva in the mid 18th century. Because of his work as the Governor of New South Wales, he became a prominent figure in colonial times and is now nicknamed 'The Father of Australia'. The tomb is shared by the National Trust of Scotland and the National Trust of Australia, but it is important to note that you must walk the final section in order not to drive over private land.

Skirting the base of Beinn Bheag and Beinn a' Ghraig, the way becomes even more dramatic as it approaches Ben More (page 164).

In 1811 John MacCulloch, a geological cartographer, discovered an impressive phenomenon. When the volcanic rock of Ardmeanach was forming, a huge conifer was engulfed in molten lava and left behind its 39ft-tall shape, imprinted in a wall of basalt sculptures that now form the cliff.

In the far west of the Burg Estate, the imprint of this fossilised tree (✛ 56°22'16.1"N 6°12'28.7"W) can be reached on a rough 10-mile return walking route (w walkhighlands.co.uk/mull/fossil-tree.shtml). Though not a great idea for anyone with a fear of heights, the walk takes you along the clifftops, where you will notice the basalt formations below that were created by a series of lava flows. Eventual access to the shore is also tidal and via a long, rickety ladder. This coastal path is also prone to landslides, which might block the route; updates can be found on the National Trust for Scotland's website (w nts.org.uk/visit/places/burg).

The Burg Estate and the Ardmeanach Peninsula The Burg Estate occupies 2 square miles at the most westerly tip of Ardmeanach, one of Mull's most untouched peninsulas. It is owned by the National Trust for Scotland (w nts.org.uk/visit/places/burg) and forms part of Ardmeanach's 'Special Area of Conservation', recognised for its exceptional plant life. Unusual species such as grass of Parnassus and delicate Iceland purslane thrive in the rich volcanic soil here, a habitat that supports notably colourful and interesting species of insect such as tiger beetles and the rare Scotch burnet moth, as well as larger animals: ravens, eagles and feral goats.

To reach the Burg Estate, take the side road that heads west at Killinichen Bay; you can park at Tiroran car park to continue on foot, following the main track that leads further west. The initial stages are good and would be manageable for pushchairs or wheelchairs with some assistance on steeper parts, but it gets much rougher after a couple of miles.

Several cleared townships lie near the track along Ardmeanach Peninsula's south coast, including the ruined houses at **Salachry** (✛ 56°22'13"N 6°07'51"W) and **Culliemore** (✛ 56°22'18"N 6°08'30"W), which were both evicted in the mid 19th century. While the coastline is a glorious setting for an afternoon walk, life in these remote settlements would have been a struggle against the elements through the winter months.

Walk: Ben More

Distance: 5¾ miles; time: 6 hours; start/end: Dhiseig; OS Explorer map: 375 Isle of Mull East
Though this route is less than 6 miles, it ascends and descends 3,100ft, so hikers should prepare for a whole-day walk (page 37). While the views are incredible on clear days, in bad weather hiking without reliable offline navigation could be dangerous and, considering there will be nothing to see, for most people there is probably little point in attempting it.

If you have a car, park in the small car park (✛ 56°26'57"N 6°04'04"W) between the few buildings at Dhiseig and the shore at Traigh Doire Dhubhaig. There is a sign to read from Benmore Estate (☎ 01680 300229) with important information about deer stalking, which usually occurs between August and October. From here a side road leads up to Dhiseig; follow it for about 400yds before bearing right around the buildings and going through a small gate to find the path. Splitting occasionally, the correct path follows close-by the river, Abhainn Dhiseig, as it tumbles down small waterfalls and through gorges. An Gearna, a smaller hill on the flanks of Ben More, is above you and to the left, though this route aims directly for Ben More. Being the biggest mountain in the area, with the direct route also being the most sensible from here, it is quite easy to navigate to the top in clear weather. Around 2 miles into the walk, you will find that the path crosses Abhainn Dhiseig. As you begin to ascend more steeply, take some time to look back and admire the view of Ulva and northern Mull, and do not forget to keep checking the sky for eagles. Sometimes you might be lucky enough to see both white-tailed and golden eagles flying together.

Nearer the top of the Munro, there is some scree to navigate. Though this will slow you down, it should not be a problem for intermediate to experienced hill-walkers. Following the ridge southeast, there is a substantial and much-appreciated rock shelter at the summit, as even in calm weather this can be a windy spot. Looking down to A' Chioch in the northeast, with a backdrop of Beinn Fhada, Beinn Talaidh and other hills across central Mull behind, the view is truly spectacular. To the south are Islay and the Paps of Jura (page 242); the Treshnish Isles, Coll and Tiree are to the northwest; and Ireland is visible on a very clear day. Rùm and the Skye Cuillin are to the north, majestic as ever from every angle. There is no other place in the Inner Hebrides from which you can see the whole region so clearly. Retrace your steps to return to more sheltered ground and head back the way you came.

CRAIGNURE AND THE SOUTHEAST Receiving nearly all of Mull's visitors, but mostly only as they speed to and from the ferry, Craignure is a small, leafy village, down-to-earth and welcoming. Though the ferry is not particularly obtrusive, the port's mere presence seems to hurry people through. Ignoring the ferry terminal, Craignure has a pleasant shoreline, great for wading birds, and lovely views up Loch Linnhe.

Where to stay *Map, page 150*

Pennygate Lodge (6 rooms) PA65 6AY; 01680 812333; w pennygatelodge.scot; ⊕ Mar–Oct. Luxury accommodation in a 1831 old manse. House stands proudly at the end of a striped lawn with patches left wild for the bluebells, looking out over the bay. **££££–£££££**

Shieling Campsite (18 permanent tents, 5 glamping tents, 2 cottages sleeping 4) PA65 6AY; 01680 812496; w shielingholidays.co.uk. Large waterfront campsite on secluded peninsula. There is space for c/vans, campervans (book ahead) & tents, plus several accommodation options including the 'Shielings' (spacious, permanently erected, uninsulated tents with basic self-catering facilities inside), fully equipped & insulated glamping tents, & the cottages. Free Wi-Fi, & effective covered drying tents for clothes. **£–££££**

Craignure Bunkhouse (4 rooms) PA65 6AY; 01680 812043; w craignure-bunkhouse.co.uk; &. Modern, small but well-equipped bunkhouse. Underfloor heating fuelled by biomass. Bookings for entire rooms only. Closed in daytime for cleaning. **£**

Where to eat and drink *Map, page 150*

Pennygate Lodge See above; m 07885 563751; ⊕ Feb–Oct 11.30–14.00 & 18.00–20.30 Mon & Wed–Sat, noon–15.00 Sun; book evening meals in advance. Elegant meals cooked with local ingredients & served in an attractive Georgian dining room. **£££**

The Old Post Office & Lochbuie Larder Lochbuie PA69 6ER; 01680 814153; w oldpostofficelochbuie.co.uk; ⊕ mid-Apr–Oct 10.00–15.30 daily. Teas, coffees, lunches & cake beside peaceful Loch Buie. You can also pre-order quality ready-meals with local ingredients. **£**

Shopping

The Craignure Stores & Post Office (SPAR) PA65 6AY; 01680 812301; w craignurestores.co.uk; ⊕ 07.30–18.00 Mon, 08.00–18.00 Tue–Sat, 10.00–17.00 Sun. Relatively well-stocked local grocery shop with some fruit & veg, alcohol & essentials, as well as a bakery & sandwiches.

Inverlussa Mussels Near Loch Spelve PA65 6BD; ◷ when available. Self-service mussels in ice box:
☏ 01680 812109; w inverlussa.com/mussel-farm; £2.50/2kg or £6/5kg.

Other practicalities

Fuel The Craignure Stores & Post Office
(page 165). Ask inside before filling.
Health Mull & Iona Community Hospital,
Craignure PA65 6BG; ☏ 01680 300392

Post office The Craignure Stores & Post Office
(page 165)

What to see and do
Walk: A woodland walk from Craignure
Distance: 3 miles; time: 2 hours; start/end: Craignure; OS Explorer map: 375 Isle of Mull East
The woodland walk from Craignure to **Torosay Castle** is beautiful, with a great view
across to Duart Castle, though note that Torosay is a private residence and cannot
be visited. The return journey is via the coast.

Start on the road going south from Craignure; pass the garage on your left
and continue until you see a track leading off to the left with white gate posts, a
small house and a sign that says 'Private Road no unauthorised vehicular access'
(✪ 56°27'59"N 5°41'53"W). You can follow this track through the woodland, with
sunshine dappling through huge broad-leaved trees, the smell of wild garlic and
startled red deer.

The track leads all the way to Torosay where, before you reach the 'castle' itself
(more a large house), you can take the hairpin bend down to the left and head down
to take a look at the old jetty (✪ 56°27'29"N 5°40'41"W), where thrift is growing
and there is a spectacular view of Duart Castle across the bay.

From the jetty, you can continue along a path that leads around the coastline. It is
a rougher walk than the woodland track, but you cannot get lost if you keep the sea
on your right. You'll initially pass an outrageously sized memorial cross, followed by
a strange structure thought to be an old explosives store; look out too for otters and
wading birds such as curlews around the tiny tidal island of Eilean Bàn. The faint
path eventually leads to the grassy and rocky shoreline below Sheilings Campsite
on the west side of Craignure; it's then a short stroll back to the village.

Duart Castle (3 miles southeast of Craignure PA64 6AP; ☏ 01680 812309;
w duartcastle.com; ◷ Apr & early–mid-Oct 11.00–16.00 Fri–Wed, May–Sep
10.30–17.00 daily; grounds open access; adult/child/family £9.50/4.50/23.50) Of all
the castle museums covered by this book, Duart is the most rewarding. A fortress
rather than a turreted affair, it stands in a dramatic position between the Firth of
Lorn and Sound of Mull.

An early MacDougall stronghold, Duart started its existence as a simple fortified
dwelling. More complex additions were built later by the MacLeans who erected a
tower house on four levels, incorporating one existing wall and utilising others to
form a courtyard. They lost the castle in the 1670s, and it fell into disrepair over
many generations until Sir Fitzroy MacLean finally bought it back in 1911.

The museum is spread across several of the (now restored) castle's floors,
beginning in the courtyard with information on the restoration, before heading
inside to the kitchens, original well and dungeons, with an atmospheric recording
of seagulls and a prisoner vomiting. Upstairs, past the pantry, are a collection of
fascinating Ordnance Survey diagrams from 1748, followed by the spectacular
Sea Room and its unbeatable view. From here you can look out to 'Lady's Rock'
where, in the early 16th century, one particular Lachlan MacLean, wishing to marry

another woman, dropped off his wife and left her to drown: she was then rescued and the MacLean was murdered by her brother.

Next you will enter the banquet hall, with many generations of MacLean chief portraits observing your progress around the collection of historical swords and guns. Everything is labelled, sometimes with extensive anecdotes and often, endearingly, written out by hand in fountain pen. Despite the new stove, the wind howls through the castle's rock walls and you are unlikely to want to take off your coat.

Upstairs again is the state bedroom and dressing room, an outrageously tall, floral, four-poster bed, and a small, but wonderful collection of 18th- and 19th-century outfits. There is a portrait of Sir Charles MacLean, painted during World War II 'in exchange for a packet of cigarettes' and a huge number of family photos, which may be of interest to those with a hereditary connection.

Up a tight final staircase is a rather dated timeline of objects, including cannonballs that were found in the mortar during restoration and a key from the captain's chest of the Spanish galley that blew up in Tobermory Bay. From this level, you can access the battlements for a view of the dozens of chimneys, the Lismore Lighthouse and the mountainous mainland beyond. Once you have finished exploring the castle, take some time to visit Duart Point and look out for porpoises and dolphins, which are known to pass by. **The Tearoom** café serves sandwiches and soup at lunchtimes (⏲ noon–15.00 daily; £).

Lochbuie One of Mull's many beautiful, hidden corners, **Lochbuie** is at the end of a long single-track road. A small car park is indicated just before a bridge, from which white painted stones lead for around half a mile through several fields to the **stone circle** (✦ 56°21'30"N 5°51'29"W). Though not quite comparable with Lewis's famous Callanish Stones, this site is the most impressive and atmospheric of its type in the Inner Hebrides. From here you can rejoin the track going south and follow it bearing right at the first building, before choosing to go either left or right at the fork around the farm buildings. Down at the shore is the imposing **Moy Castle**, another defensive post of the MacLeans, much of which was built in the 15th century. Hikers have infinite further possibilities from here. There are fallow deer living in this area and don't forget to check the sky for eagles.

Returning to the main road and heading west, you will travel along the Lussa River and through Glen More; this stunning stretch of road weaves through the mountains, passing a glorious view of Loch Airdeglais and Loch Sguabain and approaching Ben More (page 164) to the north.

FIONNPHORT AND THE ROSS OF MULL Samuel Johnson describes the journey to Iona on horseback across Mull as a great inconvenience, 'traversing this gloom of desolation', but today there's no doubting that the Ross is absolutely stunning. Like Johnson, most rush through on their way to Iona but, with great hill-walking and beautiful beaches, the Ross of Mull is a perfect place for outdoors people and nature lovers. In the far west, the village of Fionnphort is small but bustling; it has a lovely beach of its own, and many of the Ross's amenities.

West Coast Motors (page 30) run a **bus** route from Craignure to Bunessan and Fionnphort.

Where to stay   *Map, page 168*

Considering its small size, Fionnphort has a reasonably large collection of quality B&Bs. Self-catering properties are more widely distributed, tucked away in beautiful

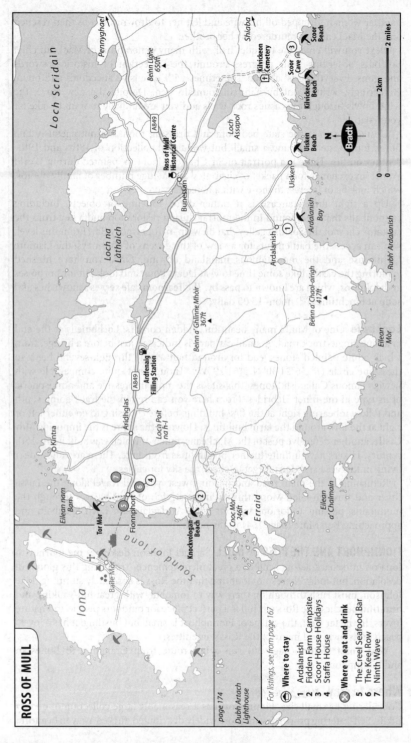

ROSS OF MULL

page 174

Dubh Artach Lighthouse

Iona

Baile Mòr

Sound of Iona

Eilean nam Bàn

Tòr Mòr

Fionnphort

Knockvologan Beach

Eilean a' Chalmain

Eilean Mòr

Erraid

Croc Mòr 246ft

Loch Poit na h-I

Àridhglas

Kintra

Ardfenaig Filling Station

A849

Benn a' Chaol-ainigh 417ft

Benn a' Ghlinne Mhòir 367ft

Ardalanish

Ardalanish Bay

Rubh' Ardalanish

Uisken

Uisken Beach

Loch Assapol

Bunessan

Ross of Mull Historical Centre

A849

Loch na Làthaich

Loch Scridain

Pennyghael

Benn Lighe 650ft

Shiaba

Kilvickeon Cemetery

Scoor Cave

Kilvickeon Beach

Scoor Beach

N

Bradt

0   2km

0   2 miles

For listings, see from page 167

Where to stay
1 Ardalanish
2 Fidden Farm Campsite
3 Scoor House Holidays
4 Staffa House

Where to eat and drink
5 The Creel Seafood Bar
6 The Keel Row
7 Ninth Wave

corners of the Ross; Visit Mull and Iona (w visitmullandiona.co.uk/listing-group/accommodation) have an extensive list of options.

Staffa House (4 rooms) Fionnphort PA66 6BL; 01681 700677; w staffahouse.co.uk; ⏰ Apr–mid-Oct. High-quality, comfortable B&B. Janice is welcoming & takes pride in looking after guests. Guest lounge with local info & maps, plus good environmental principles, with solar-panel hot water. Chris used to be a chef & often puts on evening meals, which are of exquisite quality, using the best, sustainable produce available. They grow their own vegetables & make their own jam. Packed lunches can be provided. Min 2-night stay. **££££**

Ardalanish South of Bunessan PA67 6DR; 01681 700265; w ardalanish.com. Overnight motorhome parking without facilities in spectacular coastal location. Open all year; pre-booking not required. **£**

Fidden Farm Campsite Knockvologan Rd PA66 6BN; 01681 700427; w fiddenfarm.co.uk; ⏰ Apr–Sep; &. Beautifully situated, popular campsite on the beach near Erraid, part of a farming family business now in its 3rd generation. Dogs must be kept on leads. Wi-Fi available in some areas. Cannot be booked in advance, but might be full on bank hol w/ends. **£**

Self-catering

Scoor House Holidays (6 properties sleeping 4–8) Scoor, Bunessan PA67 6DW; m 07729 414615; w scoorhouse.co.uk; ⏰ Mar–Dec. Range of simple, affordable self-catering properties in a great, secluded location. £375–650/week.

✕ Where to eat and drink *Map, opposite*

With fishing boats bringing in their catch on a daily basis, Fionnphort is the perfect place to try some of Mull's excellent seafood. Bear in mind that most eating establishments are seasonal.

Ninth Wave Bruach Mhòr, Fionnphort PA66 6BL; 01681 700757; w ninthwaverestaurant.co.uk; ⏰ May–Sep 13.00–16.00 Wed–Sun; &. Award-winning restaurant serving 4-course set-menu lunches. Fresh produce from own croft garden, local seafood. Perfectly presented. Children over 12 only. **£££**

The Keel Row Fionnphort PA66 6BL; 01681 700458; w thekeelrowmull.co.uk; ⏰ Apr–Oct noon–late daily, Nov–Mar noon–late Thu–Sun. Community-owned pub & restaurant serving hearty meals with regular live music nights. For meals, book a table online. Take-away also available. **££**

The Creel Seafood Bar Fionnphort pier PA66 6BL; 🖪; ⏰ 10.00–19.00 daily. Small shed with picnic tables, selling fish & chips, scallop & black pudding rolls, fresh sandwiches & salads. **£**

Shopping

Arts and crafts

Ardalanish Isle of Mull Weavers South of Bunessan PA67 6DR; 01681 700265; w ardalanish.com; ⏰ Easter–mid-Oct 10.00–17.00 Mon–Sat, 11.00–16.00 Sun, mid-Oct–Easter 10.00–16.00 Mon–Fri. Working farm & weaving mill with shop selling high-quality woven clothing & blankets, as well as its own Highland beef & Hebridean lamb. Warm drinks & homemade pasties in summer.

Fingal Arts & Crafts Fionnphort PA66 6BL; 01681 700470; w ferryshopmull.co.uk; ⏰ 09.30–18.00 Mon–Sat. Sells souvenirs & postcards; there's a bookshop attached, with a good collection of local guides & maps.

South West Mull Makers Columba Centre, Fionnphort PA66 6BL; w southwestmullmakers.co.uk; ⏰ Apr–Oct, hours vary. A collective of artists & artisans from the south of Mull who have not quite decided what their group is, but run this shop together. The wide selection of goods includes paintings, hand-decorated shoes, clay-work, postcards & adorable knitwear.

Food and drink

Grocery stores here are limited to corner shops & honesty box stalls. Consequently, it is probably a good idea to bring some essentials with you, especially if you are planning on self-catering.

The Ferry Shop Fionnphort PA66 6BL; \01681 700470; w ferryshopmull.co.uk; ⊕ 09.00–18.30 Mon–Sat. Basic grocery supplies & ATM.
Pennyghael Stores & Post Office Pennyghael PA70 6HB; \01681 704229; w pennyghaelstores.

co.uk; ⊕ 09.00–17.00 Mon–Sat. Small shop with groceries & gifts.
SPAR Bunessan Post Office Stores, Bunessan PA67 6DB; \01681 700395; ⊕ 09.00–18.00 Mon–Sat, 10.00–16.00 Sun. Groceries, alcohol & coffee.

Sports and activities Staffa Trips (\01681 700755; w staffatrips.co.uk; ⊕ Apr–Oct) offer visits to Staffa and Fingal's Cave, with puffins present May–July.

Other practicalities

Bank There's an ATM at The Ferry Shop (see above)
Fuel Ardfenaig Filling Station, Coach Hse, Ardfenaig PA67 6DX; ⊕09.00–18.00 Mon–Sat. Also sells delicious local tablet.
Health Mull & Iona Medical Group, The Surgery, Bunessan PA67 6DG; \01680 342000

Post offices Bunessan (PA67 6DR; ⊕ 09.00–13.00 & 14.00–17.00 Mon–Fri); The Ferry Shop, Fionnphort (see above; ⊕ 09.00–17.30 Mon–Tue & Thu–Fri, 09.00–13.00 Wed & Sat); Pennyghael Stores & Post Office (see above; ⊕ 09.00–13.00 Mon–Thu, 09.00–14.00 Fri)

What to see and do Though there is plenty of alternative hiking and exploration, the Ross of Mull is most spectacular for its beaches. The main road runs along the northern coast, with fantastic views across gentle Loch Scridain, with Ardmeanach and Ben More behind. However, most of the region's sandy shores are down long and difficult minor roads to the south, often with some amount of walking needed to reach them.

Pennyghael Pennyghael is a peaceful village that looks over the muddy head of Loch Scridain. It was most likely named from 'Pennyland of the Gael', referring to a system where land was valued against the penny.

Bunessan From Pennyghael, the coastline continues quietly, eventually revealing views of the Treshnish Isles and Staffa. Shortly afterwards, you will reach the village of **Bunessan**, a small crofting and fishing community.

Ross of Mull Historical Centre (Ionad Eachdraidh an Rois Mhuilich; Millbrae Cottage, Bunessan PA67 6DG; \ 01681 700659; w romhc.org.uk; ⊕ Easter–Oct 10.00–13.00 Mon–Fri) This small, locally run heritage centre, set in an old mill building, has an archive, genealogy information and cultural exhibitions. The community volunteers who run it also provide visitor information, including a range of local information publications, internet access, hot drinks and a picnic area.

Kilvickeon and Scoor A junction between Bunessan Primary School and the village centre leads southeast towards the farm and beaches at Scoor. These 3 miles of badly surfaced road pass Loch Assapol and lead to several options for shorter walks to amazing beaches and interesting archaeological sites. The OS Explorer Map 373 (*Iona, Staffa & Ross of Mull*) and a compass will help you to navigate in this remote area of Mull. You can park at the junction near **Kilvickeon Cemetery** and the ruined 13th-century church for both Kilvickeon or Scoor (⊕ 56°17'53"N 6°11'05"W).

The cemetery and ruined church are well worth exploring in themselves, with several interesting grave slabs in the burial ground. Additionally, on the left of the church entrance at the west end of the north wall, about a foot above you, is a severely weathered carving believed to be a 'sheela na gig' (a figurative carving of a

The tiny islands between Mull and Coll are part of the **Loch na Keal conservation area**. Staffa, from the Old Norse for 'stave' or 'pillar', for obvious reasons, is best known for Fingal's Cave and its dramatic basalt columns. The small island is unique and has been admired by visitors since the 18th century.

The Treshnish Isles consist of: Lunga, known for its colonies of around 6,000 nesting puffins; Fladda (flat island); Am Baca Mòr (Bac Mòr), also known as the Dutchman's Cap owing to its distinctive shape; Bac Beag; Sgeir an Eirionnaich; Sgeir a' Chaisteil; Cairn na Burgh Mòr and neighbouring Cairn na Burgh Beag. Aside from the puffins, there are also colonies of guillemots, kittiwakes, razorbills and shags living across the islands and the waters are among the best in Scotland for seeing minke whale, porpoises, dolphins and basking sharks, along with the enormous colonies of grey seals that bob in the water or lollop on rocks.

While they are now uninhabited, this was not always the case. The remaining parts of Cairnburgh Castle, an important fortress for over 500 years, occupies the adjacent islands of Cairn na Burgh Mòr and Cairn na Burgh Beg, at the northeast of the Treshnish string. The site was first mentioned in the 13th-century *Hákonar saga Hákonarsonar* (an Icelandic saga written about the Old Norse kings) as the property of an island king related to Somerled, before later being held by MacLeans and then Campbells. Other signs of habitation are strung along the chain; even the Dutchman's Cap, which has no obvious way up on to it, has the ruined remains of shielings.

There is an excellent exhibit about the islands in Hynish on Tiree (page 147), or you can arrange boat trips through Alternative Boat Hire (page 176), Turus Mara (page 161), Staffa Trips (see opposite), Tiree Sea Tours (page 142) and various other operators based mostly on Mull or in Oban.

naked woman with an exaggerated vulva). They are found all over Europe, but their purpose or meaning is a matter of much debate.

Kilvickeon Beach This double beach with a tidal island, slightly to the west of Scoor can be reached by following the arrow pointing along a track directly opposite the parking area; it runs in a generally southeasterly direction all the way down to the excellent, sandy beach. It is around 1½ miles return and suitable for families.

Scoor To reach Scoor, walk down the left-hand track from the junction by the cemetery, which leads generally southwest for half a mile to the cluster of buildings at Scoor Farm. There are three possible options from Scoor Farm: you can walk down to the beach; visit a cave with markings over 1,000 years old; or take an inland route to the abandoned village of Shiaba. The first two options are short but rough return routes of a mile or less (a total of 2 miles from Kilvickeon Cemetery car park), while to reach Shiaba is about 3 miles return (4 miles from the car park). Do watch where you are putting your feet as there are adders (page 11) in summer.

From Scoor Farm, the beach is accessed by walking about half a mile over fields, followed by a short, but steep section traversing down a muddy pathway to the sand. The view from the cliffs is spectacular. With lovely sand, and surrounded by cliffs, with skerries leading out into the water, **Scoor Beach** is completely worth the effort to get there. In summer months, you should look out to sea for basking sharks. The water is magically clear; if you have a wetsuit or are brave enough to stand the cold, you could bring a snorkel to make the most of it.

To reach the **cave** (⊕ 56°17'23"N 6°10'27"W), bear right from the farm and walk towards Ploughman's Cottage, the furthest south of the buildings at Scoor. There is a rough path to the southeast side of the cottage, which then bears south over grassland before following a stream down the gully to the shore. The cave is tucked into the east side of the gully. It has many carvings of crosses and other markings, probably dating from the 6th to 9th centuries. You will need a torch to explore it properly.

The abandoned settlement of **Shiaba** (⊕ 56°17'48"N 6°08'28"W; route & map: w walkhighlands.co.uk/mull/shiaba.shtml) can be reached from Scoor Farm by heading around the left-hand side of the largest building, Scoor House. The route, which heads about 1½ miles away to the northwest, is best navigated with an OS map and compass or GPS. It was here, in the mid 19th century, that more than 100 people were removed from their homes by the Duke of Argyll; around a dozen roofless houses are all that remains of their existence. With lush green grass leading down to a bay, and the cliffs of Carsaig to the east, Shiaba was once a thriving township, with a school, sheep and cows. Although some people were evicted to other areas of Mull, where they tried to scrape a living on less fertile land, many others went overseas. By the 1861 census there were only 18 people living at Shiaba, and by 1871 there was just one shepherd left. Lonely shepherds continued to live in Shiaba Cottage until the 1930s, when a storm finally blew the roof off.

Uisken Beach and Ardalanish Bay

Opposite the car park in Bunessan, a side road leads towards the secluded beaches at Uisken and Ardalanish. With a place to park just yards from the sand, **Uisken** is one of the few beaches on Mull that doesn't require much of a walk to access. A gentle cove made of pale sand and sheltered by rocky, offshore islets, on a good day you can see as far as Jura.

Ardalanish, a small settlement and home to Ardalanish Isle of Mull Weavers (page 169), has its own beautiful bay, which is only 600yds from the car park. Stretching across the best part of a mile, smooth sand leads down to gloriously clear water with a few protruding strips of rock. Looking past the wilderness peninsula of Rubh Ardalanish, there's a view of Colonsay on the horizon.

Fionnphort

In Fionnphort, the pretty port village where ferries arrive and leave for Iona (see opposite), it's impossible to miss 'Fingal's Rock' in the middle of the beach. The story goes that it was thrown there in a temper by Fingal the giant on his way between Staffa and Ireland, which caused the crack that can be seen today. Numerous other stories and names for the rock abound but, regardless, it is almost certainly a glacial erratic.

From Fionnphort you can walk north along sheep tracks, keeping the sea on your left, for around half a mile to **Tor Mòr**. Best known as a quarry for the Ross of Mull's characteristic pink granite, signs of its history are only visible from the presence of a small pier. This beautiful sandy beach is sheltered by the tidal island of Eilean Eòin and it appears to be unknown to almost all of Fionnphort's visitors.

From here, you can continue along the coast for a pleasant 1½-mile walk to the hamlet of **Kintra**, where cows often roam the beach. You'll notice Iona is mostly hidden from view by the small, uninhabited Eilean nam Ban just off the coast.

Erraid

The inhabited tidal island of Erraid was a signal station for the Dubh Artach and Skerryvore lighthouses. It has a row of cottages built for the keepers and

Dubh Artach is the name of a remote rocky islet at the end of a long and dangerous scattering of skerries, 15 miles southwest of Mull. This area was responsible for 30 shipwrecks between 1800 and 1854, and in 1863 the steamer *Bussorah* was wrecked on her maiden voyage; all 33 people aboard were lost. Finally, a huge storm in 1865 destroyed 24 boats within 48 hours.

Although a lighthouse here had previously been thought impossible, work began on one in 1867. An iron barracks was erected to house the workers during construction. This sturdy structure turned out to be a well-chosen upgrade from previous wooden versions, when it saved the lives of engineer Alan Brebner and 13 other men trapped inside it for the course of a five-day storm in August. With 75ft waves crashing down above them, blocking out all light for several seconds at a time, water came in through the trap door and swept away all of their food. They managed to survive.

Standing at 144ft, Dubh Artach Lighthouse was completed in 1872. One hundred years later it was automated, ending an era and a romantic, lonely profession that had certainly saved hundreds of lives. It remains one of only four Scottish lighthouses situated more than 10 nautical miles from the shore.

was also used as the land base for building Dubh Artach Lighthouse (see above), 15 miles southwest of Mull, which was designed by David and Thomas Stevenson.

In the novel *Shipwrecked*, by Thomas's son Robert Louis Stevenson, the main character is marooned on Erraid and believes he is stuck there, before passing fishermen point out that he can just walk across at low tide. With forward planning, you can also reach the island at low tide and climb the highest point Cnoc Mòr (246ft) for wonderful views over many tiny islets and to the abbey on Iona.

IONA

A small and magical place, at around 4 miles long and 1 mile wide, Iona has wonderful beaches, fields of wildflowers and makes a fascinating excursion for geologists owing to its Lewisian and Torridonian rocks. The island is, however, far better known for its history as a centre for the spread of Christianity, of learning and as the base of one of the most important monastic systems in Great Britain.

Although Iona receives a great many visitors, the small island somehow manages to absorb them without losing the best of its character. The abbey is by far its main attraction, but a respectful silence is usually maintained inside, and the religious, spiritual and historical sites are large and well enough spread out that you need not fear the dense crowds of pilgrims found in the Vatican or more accessible sites elsewhere. To leave other people behind, simply walk out of the village in any direction.

HISTORY After founding the religious centres of Kells and Durrow in Ireland, Columba, a scholar and warrior priest, was forced to flee from Ireland after the Battle of Cul Dreimhne in AD563. Along with his 12 companions, he is supposed to have sailed and landed at the southern end of Iona on a beach now named Port a' Curaic'. Once settled, they built their cells at Tor Abb, just west of the present-day abbey.

Over the following 200 years, Iona became an important centre of learning, producing carvings of a particular style, such as the Kildalton Cross on Islay

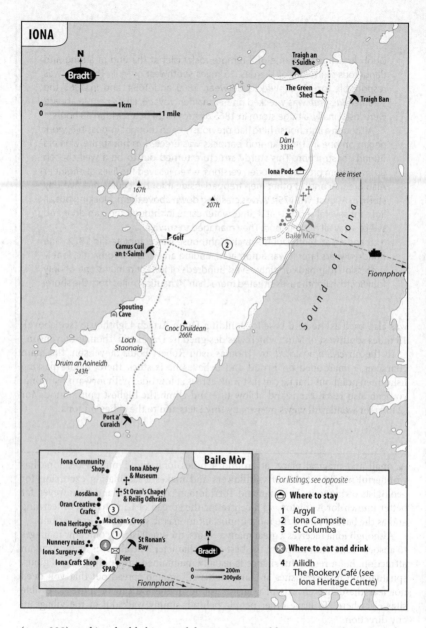

IONA

N

Bradt

0 ——— 1km
0 ——— 1 mile

Traigh an t-Suidhe

The Green Shed

Traigh Ban

Dùn I
333ft

Iona Pods

see inset

167ft

207ft

Baile Mòr

Golf

Camus Cuil
an t-Saimh

②

Sound of Iona

Fionnphort

Spouting
Cave

Cnoc Druidean
266ft

Loch
Staonaig

Druim an Aoineidh
243ft

Port a'
Curaich

Baile Mòr

Iona Community
Shop

Iona Abbey
& Museum

St Oran's Chapel
& Reilig Odhràin

Aosdàna

Oran Creative
Crafts ③

Iona Heritage
Centre

MacLean's Cross

①

St Ronan's
Bay

N

Bradt

Nunnery ruins

④

Iona Surgery

Iona Craft Shop

SPAR

Pier

0 ——— 200m
0 ——— 200yds

Fionnphort

For listings, see opposite

⊟ **Where to stay**
1 Argyll
2 Iona Campsite
3 St Columba

⊗ **Where to eat and drink**
4 Ailidh
   The Rookery Café (see
   Iona Heritage Centre)

(page 228), and invaluable historical documents, in addition to providing a base for converting the Picts to Christianity. It is probable that the beautiful Book of Kells was created on Iona in the 8th century. It wasn't long after that Iona's new Christian Celtic culture came under attack from the Norse. The community was raided by Vikings in 795, 802 and 806; in the wake of the 806 raid, where 68 inhabitants were killed, the Abbot of Iona fled across to Kells. From then on, a very small community of devout monks struggled on in Iona, ready to die for their cause. One, Blathmac, who deliberately came to the island with the hope of being martyred, succeeded in being so by hiding the shrine of St Columba and refusing to give up its location under interrogation. The small island was raided again in 845, 878 and 986, but a small group of monks survived until the 11th century when life was finally settled enough to build monastic buildings for the remaining few.

As a spiritual centre, many early kings of Scotland were buried on Iona and in 1203 a new Benedictine-style abbey was built, with the nunnery added five years later. Both were active until the Reformation when, in 1561, Iona was seen to be too close to Rome; it is thought that a reforming mob destroyed the buildings and crosses. Despite the destruction, the nunnery ruins are still the most complete example of a medieval nunnery in Scotland.

In 1609, a meeting was held on Iona to establish the authority of the reformed church. 'The Statutes of Iona' were agreed and it was decided that Scottish clan chiefs should send their heirs away to be educated in English-speaking Protestant schools. This was one of the roots of the disconnection between landowners and the people who worked for them, and ultimately could be blamed for some of the casual disregard of tenants when it came to the Clearances 200 years later. Gaelic was being lost.

Though work had already begun through the Duke of Argyll and Iona Cathedral Trust, much of the lengthy process of the abbey restoration was steered by a Reverend George MacLeod from 1938. Convinced that 'work is worship', he employed members of his newly founded 'Iona Community' to work on the project, which continued for many decades. Most of the members came from either Mull or Iona, speaking Gaelic and forming a new community on the island, which still survives in some form today.

GETTING THERE AND AROUND CalMac (page 30) run frequent **ferry** sailings between Fionnphort and Iona, a route that takes around 10 minutes and is only open to foot passengers (unless you have a disability badge). Keep a lookout for porpoises as you sail.

Although most people can't bring a car, Iona is small and centred around the only village, Baile Mòr. For many people, **walking** is completely feasible, but a **bicycle** would allow you to reach the north end or western beaches more quickly; you can hire one from Iona Craft Shop (page 176; £15/20/30 for 3/12/24hrs). There is also a local **taxi** service (Iona Taxi; m 07810 325990; w ionataxi.co.uk), which can also pick up from Mull if required.

TOURIST INFORMATION National Trust for Scotland (w nts.org.uk/visit/places/iona; ⊕ open access) offers an unstaffed shelter on the main road leading away from the pier, providing illustrated maps and local information.

WHERE TO STAY AND EAT *Map, opposite*
Staying on Iona overnight or longer will give you an entirely different impression of the island; once the last of the day-trippers have left, you can absorb the same silence and sanctity appreciated by generations of monks. While St Columba Hotel collects your luggage and the Argyll Hotel is only a couple of minutes' walk from the ferry terminal, you will have to walk, cycle or hire a taxi (see above) to reach the campsite and other accommodation. A range of versatile self-catering options are offered by **The Green Shed** (Lagandorain PA76 6SW; ☏ 01681 700642; w greenshediona.co.uk) and **Iona Pods** (PA76 6SW; m 07935 219079; w ionapods.com). There are a few good places to eat, with a great range of locally caught and grown produce, but eating establishments are mostly seasonal and close for a few months in winter.

St Columba Hotel (27 rooms) On the road from Baile Mòr to Iona Abbey PA76 6SL; 01681 700304; w stcolumba-hotel.co.uk; ⏰ end Mar–Oct; ♿. Peaceful location about ½ a mile north of the ferry terminal, from where your luggage will be collected. Shared sitting room with fireplace & wonderful sunny lounge with huge windows & sea view. Substantial price difference between rooms with/without sea view. The large restaurant (⏰ Mar–Oct 11.00–20.30 daily; ♿; ££–£££) serves quality local food, with much grown on the island. There's a great view & extensive outdoor seating. ££££–£££££
Argyll Hotel (17 rooms) Baile Mòr waterfront PA76 6SJ; 01681 700334; w argyllhoteliona. co.uk; ⏰ late Mar–Oct. Historical hotel made of Ross of Mull pink granite, with oldest parts dating from the 1860s, situated in the centre of the village, only 100yds north of the ferry terminal. Each room is different & sea/courtyard view is reflected significantly in price. In the restaurant

(⏰ Mar–Oct 10.00–20.00 daily; ££), much of the freshly prepared food is grown in their 1-acre grounds, including strawberries, herbs & seasonal vegetables. Good vegan & gluten-free options. Best to book, for dinner especially. £££
Iona Campsite Cnoc Oran PA76 6SP; m 07747 721275; w ionacampsite.co.uk. Basic campsite in beautiful location with sea view, southwest of Baile Mòr. £
Ailidh Baile Mor PA76 6SJ; m 07846 172931; f; ⏰ flexible hours, mostly in summer & occasionally other times of year. Fish tachos, Neapolitan-style pizza & delicious doughnuts – it might not be the sort of food you expect to find on Iona, but this small take-away has been a welcome addition to the foodie scene. £
The Rookery Café Iona Heritage Centre (see opposite) PA76 6SJ; w ionaheritage.co.uk; ⏰ Apr–mid-Oct 10.30–15.00 Mon–Sat. Lunches, baked goods & hot drinks. Lovely leafy garden seating, with indoor seating too. £

SHOPPING Iona has a small **SPAR** grocery shop (Baile Mòr PA76 6SJ; 01681 700321; ⏰ 10.00–16.00 Mon–Sat). It also has a range of small gift shops selling locally sourced crafts, artwork and other souvenirs:

Aosdàna St Columba Steadings PA76 6SJ; 01681 700121; w aosdanaiona.com; ⏰ mid-Mar–Oct 10.00–17.00 daily. ♿. Elegant, Iona-themed jewellery.
Iona Community Shop Opposite the abbey PA76 6SN; f ionacommunity; w ionabooks.com; ⏰ mid–late Mar 10.00–17.00 Mon–Fri, late Mar–Oct 10.00–17.00 Mon–Sat, noon–17.00 Sun; ♿. Although the Iona community is a religious one, their large shop sells a good range of books, crafts & knitting to interest anyone, regardless of faith.

Iona Craft Shop Baile Mòr PA76 6SJ; 01681 700001; w ionacraftshop.com; ⏰ Apr–Oct 10.00–17.00 daily, Nov–Mar 10.00–15.00 Tue–Sat. A good selection of high-quality knitwear, some of which is made from Iona wool.
Oran Creative Crafts St Columba Steadings PA76 6SJ; w orancrafts.co.uk; ⏰ Easter–Oct 10.00–17.00 daily. ♿. A craftworkers' co-operative of 7 members making/selling different art forms & crafts.

SPORTS AND ACTIVITIES The Iona **golf** course (⏰ open access; free; scorecard £1 from post office), towards the south of the island, has 18 holes and dates back to 1886. To go **sailing**, try Alternative Boat Hire ✳ (01681 700537; w boattripsiona. com). Mark Jardine, originally a sea kayaker, takes people on sailing trips in the *Birthe Marie*, a renovated traditional fishing boat with a gaff ketch rig. He runs trips to the Treshnish Isles, as well as less commonly visited islands such as Gometra, Inch Kenneth, Soa and Eilean a' Chalmain (Island of the Dove), among other places such as Traigh Geal on the south coast of Mull and even Dubh Artach Lighthouse (page 173). Possibly even more exciting than the destinations themselves is the sailing; you are welcome to join in as much or as little as you feel comfortable doing. Your chances of seeing some of these waters' most exciting species are increased by the silent passage of the boat. Trips to see puffins on Lunga during nesting season cannot fail to impress, but there are also chances of spotting basking sharks, porpoises, dolphins and even minke whale, along with unusual seabird species such as shearwaters, razorbills, guillemots, skua and kittiwakes.

OTHER PRACTICALITIES

Health Iona Surgery, Baile Mòr PA76 6SJ; ☏01680 342000

Post office 50yds northwest of ferry terminal, Baile Mòr PA76 6SJ; ⊕ 09.00–13.00 & 14.00–17.30 Mon–Tue & Thu–Fri, 09.00–13.00 Wed, 09.00–12.30 Sat

WHAT TO SEE AND DO With so much to see within easy walking distance of the ferry terminal, even just a day trip to Iona is very worthwhile. As you land on the island you will notice lovely **St Ronan's Bay**, which sits directly in front of the main village of Baile Mòr and makes an admirable spot for a picnic.

The Nunnery ruins (⊕ open access) Around 200yds northwest of the ferry terminal are the remains of an Augustinian priory. Founded in the early 13th century, it consisted of a church, chapter house and living quarters and is thought to have been in use until the nunnery was dissolved in 1574. Now largely roofless, it is an extensive and peaceful ruin that retains some of its pink-stone walls with archways, rounded windows and a section of vaulted ceiling, surrounded by grassy areas and plant borders with benches allowing you to stop and sit for a while.

MacLean's Cross Passing the medieval St Ronan's Church, just north of the nunnery, and continuing 160yds further along the main street, you will come to MacLean's Cross. This elaborate 15th-century, free-standing cross is carved with intricate entwined foliage and a crucifix on its western face.

Iona Heritage Centre (PA76 6SJ; w ionaheritage.co.uk; ⊕ Easter–Oct 10.15–16.30 Mon–Sat; donation requested) Once the manse for the church next door, both of which were designed by Thomas Telford. As the island's heritage centre, it now houses collections of photographs, which may be of interest to those with ancestral links to Iona, as well as local information about island life and geology.

St Oran's Chapel and Reilig Odhráin (⊕ open access) Between St Columba Hotel and Iona Abbey sits the modest St Oran's Chapel and its burial ground, Reilig Odhráin. Some of the chapel is thought to be from as early as the 9th century, but other parts date from the 12th and the roof has been restored much more recently. It is the oldest relatively intact building on Iona. Kenneth MacAlpin, King of the Picts and, according to legend, the first King of Scotland, was buried here in the mid 9th century, along with the proceeding Scottish kings until Macbeth, who died in the mid 11th century. According to folk history, it was also the final resting place of many Irish, Norwegian and French kings, but nothing remains to tell us of these early burials. There is a good collection of West Highland grave slabs, impressive within the region, but somewhat diminished by the huge number kept in Iona Abbey.

Iona Abbey (PA76 6SQ; w historicenvironment.scot/visit-a-place/places/iona-abbey-and-nunnery; ⊕ Apr–Sep 09.30–17.30 daily, Oct–Mar 10.00–16.00 Mon–Sat; adult/ concession/child £10/8/6) Iona Abbey is the impressive modern restoration of a grand Benedictine abbey, the original of which was begun in the 13th century. A large stone building with slate roofs, the abbey was once home to a community of monks and is now a focal point for pilgrims who visit Iona for its connection with St Columba and the centre of Christianity he founded. Along with the abbey building itself and the historical artefacts it contains, the ticket also allows you entrance to the Abbey Museum and grounds, which encompass a number of additional interesting archaeological sites. The whole site is well maintained and explained through a comprehensive array of plaques, labels and signs, as well as the free audio guide.

In the grounds, **Tòrr an Aba**, a small hill to the left of the path just after the entry gate, is all that remains of what is thought to have been St Columba's cell, which was mentioned in writing by his contemporary Adamnan. The short climb also gives a rewarding view over the abbey and the large crosses standing in its grounds, with an ocean backdrop. Also within the grounds, the excavated **Sraid nam Marbh** (Street of the Dead) leads from the abbey to Reilig Odhráin burial ground, and is thought to have been part of a 1,000-year-old processional route for bodies to be carried from the landing place at Martyr's Bay (south of the modern pier) to their final resting place. It was 7ft wide and cobbled with Ross of Mull granite, but all that remains now is an indented track with some stones exposed between overgrown grass.

The abbey interior is usually silent apart from the echoes from visitors' careful footsteps. For pilgrims and other interested visitors, the Iona Community welcomes all to its **church services** (see: w iona.org.uk/our-resources/worship-at-iona-abbey). Otherwise, you are free to wander and discover its hidden corners for yourself. **The Great Church** is the grandest of the abbey's interior spaces, with high, stone archways and mighty carved pillars.

Those with a greater interest in history than religion may find the huge collection of **West Highland grave slabs** in the **Cloister** of most interest; even the large collection on Oronsay (page 210) is diminished in comparison. In the Cloister, a covered walkway around a square, grass-covered courtyard, light streams through the pillars on to the swords, ships and intricate foliage carved into the stones. There is an engraving dedicated to Aonghus Óg, one-time 'King of the Isles' on Islay.

Around the back of the abbey is the small **Abbey Museum,** which holds delicate and invaluable artefacts, including the remains of the three mighty crosses of St Matthew, St John and St Oran. There is also a tiny bronze head which, as the label suggests, has a striking similarity to the faces depicted in the Book of Kells.

North from the abbey Allowing at least a couple of hours, you can discover some of Iona's peaceful northern end. Continuing north along the road from the abbey, houses become scarce and the fields are sprinkled with wildflowers in spring and summer; soon you will be alone with the sound of corncrakes (in May), and views across to the tiny island of Eilean nam Ban and the west coast of the Ross of Mull. A mile northwest of the abbey, an indicated path leads up the 333ft hill **Dùn I**. A cairn at the top marks the end of a pilgrimage route, which is piled high with stones carried across Iona from a beach in the south. The vantage point gives you a good view across the whole island. Continuing north along the main track for another mile, you will reach the idyllic beaches of **Traigh an t-Suidhe** and **Traigh Ban**.

The south end Following the roads initially south from the ferry port and then west across the island for about a mile, you can walk past the campsite (page 176) to the machair and **Camus Cuil an t-Saimh** ('the bay at the back of the ocean') with thousands of colourful pebbles, corncrakes and the possibility of seeing basking sharks in summer months. To the south, the rocks around **Spouting Cave**, which shoots water into the air, are a good place to see rock-loving seabirds such as shags.

Finding a path running south more centrally through the island will bring you to tiny **Loch Staonaig** and, within another mile and a half, down towards **Port a' Curaich** or Columba Bay, where the man himself is thought to have initially landed. Regardless of your interest, it is a lovely place for a picnic with views across rocky skerries and islets to tiny Soa further south. OS Explorer map 373 (*Iona, Staffa & Ross of Mull*) is helpful for navigating the south end of Iona.

ULVA AND GOMETRA

A few minutes' sailing on a tiny passenger ferry is all it takes to reach Ulva from Mull, but this comparatively small island has a distinct identity of its own. Ancient broad-leafed woodland, carpeted in spongy moss and bony lichen, spreads over the eastern interior, with craggy moorland and heathered hills occupying the west; the varied coastline is comprised of dramatic basalt formations, salt marsh and rocky beach, all of which provide valuable habitat for a diverse assortment of wildlife, including raptors, otters and the rare slender Scotch burnet moth.

At just 7½ miles long and 2½ miles wide, the island currently supports a population of 16, but the echo of its dramatically more populous history is inescapable as you walk around the coast, with countless stone ruins sheltered in the valleys. In 1846, 500 people were cleared from Ulva in one of the largest forced Clearances in Argyll. Purchased with a population of 604 by Francis William Clark in 1835, the population had fallen to 53 by 1889. It's reported some of those people were evicted without warning, the thatch of their roofs set on fire and the remaining population despatched to 'Starvation Point' on Aird Glass, where Clark left the elderly to survive on shellfish and seaweed until they died.

The 20th century brought little reassurance to the community of Ulva and the population continued to decline; by 2018, it was down to single figures, when the island was bought by its population and a group from northwest Mull through the 'Right to Buy' scheme. This community ownership is still in its infancy, with a population increase back into double digits and various projects in the pipeline, but a question mark remains over some of the island's buildings, including Ulva House, which need a substantial investment of both time and money if they are to be retained.

Despite its close proximity – separated only by a tidal channel and bridge at Ulva's far west end – even smaller island Gometra is a different kettle of fish again. Owned by wealthy environmental campaigner Roc Sandford since 1991, it's home to a few people and a lot more sheep, and is worth the 12-mile return walk from the Ulva ferry if only to visit the tiny but remarkable Gometra Gallery (page 181).

GETTING THERE AND AROUND A small passenger **ferry** runs from Ulva Ferry (on Mull) to Ulva (Jun–Aug 09.00–17.30 Sun–Fri, Sep–Oct & Apr–May 09.00–17.30 Mon–Fri). Slide the panel left to reveal a red sign beneath to summon the ferry, but don't forget to replace it once the boat is on its way. There's a small ticket office with the facility to accept card payments beside the Boathouse restaurant (page 181) on the Ulva side.

Considering you can't take a car to Ulva, **walking (or cycling)** is the only way to get around.

WHERE TO STAY AND EAT *Map, page 180*

✳ **Ulva Hostel & Campsite** (14 beds inc 3 private dbls) Ardalum House PA73 6NA; m 07538 969697; w ulvahostel.co.uk. Ardalum House was originally built as a hunting lodge

7

ULVA AND GOMETRA

Mull

Laggan Bay

Loch Tuath

Ulva Ferry

Pier

Ulva House & Walled Garden

Ulva Church

Starvation Point

A'Chrannag 387ft

Livingstone's Cave

Dùn Bhioramuill

Ormaig

Ruined watermill

Cragaig Bothy

Kilvekewan Graveyard

Benn Chreagach 1,027ft

Ulva

Bridge

Gometra Gallery

590ft

Gometra

Little Colonsay

For listings, see from page 179

Where to stay
1 Ulva Hostel & Campsite

Where to eat and drink
2 The Boathouse

KEY
—— Farm Circuit
—— Livingstone Walk
- - - 'Main road' to Gometra
—·—·— Ormaig and South Side
········ Woodland Walk

N

0   1km
0   1mile

Bradt

by the Clark family around 1860, but has taken a multitude of forms in the last few decades, serving as accommodation for most of the current population at some point or another. Current owners Andy & Yvette have recently transformed the grand old building into a hostel with a tasteful refurbishment, now offering inexpensive dorm beds & comfortable private rooms, as well as a couple of cosy yurts in the garden & the option to camp with your own tent. Campers have access to indoor kitchen, bathroom & laundry facilities. **£**

The Boathouse PA73 6LZ; e theboathouseonulva@gmail.com; ⊕ Apr–Sep 09.00–17.00 Mon–Fri, Jun–Aug also 11.00–17.00 Sun. Just a few steps from the ferry, this small restaurant serves excellent seafood including Ulva prawns. Indoor & outdoor seating. **£–££**

WHAT TO SEE AND DO There are signposted walks ranging from 2 to 12 miles, but it's a good idea to carry *OS Explorer map: 374 Isle of Mull North & Tobermory* as the paths are occasionally unclear.

The 2-mile **Farm Circuit** (followed clockwise) keeps to good track suitable for mountain bikes. It begins by passing **Ulva House Walled Garden**, which is being maintained and improved by a group of volunteers – visitors are welcome to roam around, enjoying the mown pathways and admiring the recently restored greenhouse. The route continues by passing the majority of the island's currently inhabited buildings, before taking a short detour to the whitewashed T-plan **Ulva Church**, designed by Thomas Telford and completed in 1828.

The varied 4-mile **Woodland Walk** (page 182) encompasses part of the Farm Circuit, along with exploring more of the coastline and woods following narrow trodden paths, while 5-mile **Livingstone's Walk** extends the circuit further, indicated by white marker sticks for the least obvious part of its course in Ulva's far south. Though he only visited the island once himself (in 1864), David Livingstone – the famous missionary and explorer – had family connections to Ulva, with his paternal grandparents living in one of the now-ruined stone houses. A short detour leads up to **Livingstone's Cave** (⊕ 56°28'04"N 6°10'19"W), on the southwestern flank of A' Chrannag – with a great view down over the coast, the dank cavern is most remarkable for being the discovery site of a midden deposit relating to both the Mesolithic and Neolithic eras, with the oldest components dated to at least 7,800 years ago.

If you have a day to spend on Ulva, following the track and signs for '**Ormaig and South Side**' comes highly recommended, with a route suitable for more capable mountain bikers. From the ferry to the ruined village of **Ormaig** is 5 miles return; here stand around 18 roofless stone buildings with spectacular views along the cliffs and coastline of south Ulva, as well as out to Inch Kenneth and Mull's Ardmeanach Peninsula (page 164) in the south, a scattering of skerries and islets on to Little Colonsay and Iona beyond to the southwest, and the distinctive Dutchman's Cap in the Treshnish Isles on the far west horizon. From Ormaig, you can continue to follow a path a further 700yds west to the remains of a cruck-framed **watermill**. A further mile beyond the mill, passing Cragaig Bothy (which is rented out as very basic self-catering), is the 15th- or 16th-century **Kilvekewan Graveyard** (Cille Mhic Eoghainn).

The longest of Ulva's signposted walks, starting again from the ferry and Boathouse, leads just over 5½ miles (11 miles return) to the bridge connecting **Gometra**. Following the 'main road' (a track) and signs for Gometra through Ulva's central west and around the north coast, this route is suitable for both walkers and mountain bikers. On the Gometra side, following the only track available southwest for a further mile brings you to **Gometra Gallery** (⊕ open access), a stone building with a corrugated metal roof, which has work from local artists and craftspeople, as well as (at the time of my visit) a phenomenally well-stocked honesty box grocery shop with fresh fruit and vegetables, canned food and snacks. A further mile from the gallery is the row of four houses that accommodates the majority of the population.

Walk: Woodland Walk

Distance: 4 miles circular; time: 2 hours; start/end: the ferry pier; OS Explorer map: 374 Isle of Mull North & Tobermory

Although it can be very wet in parts, this route is suitable for most walkers, following tracks and paths across varied, but unchallenging terrain in Ulva's far west.

Start at the ferry pier, facing The Boathouse, turn right and follow the track, passing the turning for the thatched Sheila's Cottage on your right. Continue uphill for 130yds until you reach a junction; turn left, following a signpost for 'Farm Circuit, Woodland Walk, Ulva House and Walled Garden'.

Follow this track for 500yds – passing through a gateway, past an old John Deere tractor and across a field with a seaweed-strewn, salt marsh shoreline on your left – until the track splits just north of Ulva House Walled Garden. Here, turn left on to a track and follow it for 280yds, passing a long blue shed, until you reach a concrete platform and junction, where a sign for 'Woodland Walk' points left. Go along this track for 200yds until you reach another signpost and a row of upright stones indicating where you should leave the track and join a narrow path through blackthorn bushes.

This path rises through mixed woodland, with moss-covered boulders, tree roots and a dry-stone wall. As you reach the edge of a patch of evergreen trees, go through a gate on your left into a grassy field. Follow a trodden path southwest, then south, across two joined fields, with the sea on your left. As you reach the south coast, bear right and head down a set of rock steps, then follow a path as it descends to the shore, crossing a stile over a dry-stone wall. Dùn Bhioramuill, a prominent rock on which is a circular enclosure, the burial place of the Clark family, comes into view up ahead.

Follow the shoreline west for 800yds until you reach a gate on your right and a signpost. Going through the gate is the quickest way back to the ferry (1 mile north), but if you want to continue, follow a sign for 'Woodland Walk' to join a track that heads southwest uphill, passing through a gate after a short distance. Enter a field and contour around the rocky knolls on your right until you reach another signpost after 200yds. Ignoring the white stick markers, which show the way to Livingstone's Cave (page 181), follow the 'Woodland Walk' sign pointing right, past some rusty farm machinery, and follow the most obvious path as it heads northwest, directly inland.

Occasional wooden arrows point out the best path around overgrown crowns of basalt, and a wooden platform assists the crossing of a particularly swampy area. Continue to climb, with Dùn Bhioramuill now on your left, and stay on the more obvious path bearing left when it splits, going around a rocky knoll. After 750yds, keep on the path as it begins to descend through woodland and, upon reaching its lowest point (350yds further), step over a burn, cross a track and climb up over a stile, still following signs for 'Woodland Walk' (if you're in a hurry, turning right on to the track here would take you back to the ferry).

Follow this path for 800yds as it rises across heathered ground and through woodland, passing through a gate and continuing northwest (bearing left) – look out for huge bracket fungus growing on the ancient, moss-covered trees. Cross a bridge over a stream and ignore a right turn, continuing until you reach a junction with a signpost.

Walk straight ahead as indicated by the 'Woodland Walk' arrow and follow a path up over a rise. As you reach a high point after a couple of hundred yards, Ulva Ferry comes into view; descend the same distance again through the trees, ignoring a right turn, until you see the impressive white building of Ulva Church. On reaching the church, turn right and join the track heading southeast. Follow the track for ¾ mile back to The Boathouse, ignoring three right turns.

8

Lismore (Lios Mòr) and Kerrera (Cearara)

Those with a fascination for castles should head directly to Lismore and Kerrera: these two small islands in the Firth of Lorn have three substantial ruins, one excellent broch and countless dùns between them. Both islands are green and fertile, with plenty of sheep, interesting rocky coastlines and unusual hilly landscapes. Of the two, Lismore has a substantially bigger population and thus a lot more going on.

LISMORE

Curiously positioned halfway up the Firth of Lorn, Lismore is separated from the mainland Highlands and Mull by just a few miles of water in every direction. Although the island itself is low-lying, it is surrounded by mountainous scenery: Loch Linnhe cuts into the Great Glen in the northeast with the mighty Ben Nevis and Glen Coe in the distance; Ben Cruachan is on the skyline to the southeast; Mull lies to the southwest; and the wild coast of the Morvern Peninsula runs parallel to Lismore's coast, only 3 miles to the northeast. The surrounding higher ground, particularly the hills on Mull, means that Lismore lies in a rain shadow, enjoying significantly better weather than much of its surroundings. The island is around 9 miles long and 1½ miles wide, with a limestone base that is unusual in the Inner Hebrides; thankfully this means that midges are not an issue.

Green fields, interrupted by rocky protrusions, are separated by undulating dry-stone walls, and houses are scattered in a rather haphazard manner – the biggest settlement, Achnacroish, is only a few buildings. The island's shop, church and heritage centre are somewhat sporadically dotted along the central main road with little else around them. In the north, Port Ramsay is picturesque but has no amenities whatsoever, while the far south of the island is totally uninhabited. Despite its proximity to the mainland, Lismore hasn't lost its island feel.

HISTORY The earliest evidence of humans on Lismore came in the form of a Neolithic polished stone axe head that has been dated to 3500BC. In addition, there are a number of Bronze Age burial cairns, including the large and well-preserved Cnoc Aingeal (Fire Hill), where the later kings of the Picts are also said to have been cremated. Then there's Tirefour Castle (page 189), an imposing Iron Age broch on the east coast, plus several less impressive remains from the same period.

From the 6th century AD, Lismore was an important centre of Celtic Christianity thanks to St Moluag. A contemporary of Columba (page 14), Moluag's legacy has been substantially less well documented, but he may have been even more consequential in the process of evangelising the Picts.

Moluag's arrival on Lismore is a subject of much speculation: a folk tale describes St Moluag and Columba racing across the Lynn of Lorn to be the first to land on Lismore and found a monastery. The story goes that Moluag only won by cutting off his finger and throwing it ashore. An alternative version suggests that as he stood on a rock on the Irish coast it detached itself so he could drift across the ocean.

What is certain is that in 562 he founded a community on Lismore and went on to found two other important centres of Christianity in Scotland at Rosemarkie near Inverness and Mortlach (now known as Dufftown) in Moray. These three communities became the Roman Catholic diocese of the Isles, Ross and Aberdeen. A millennium later, Moluag was still stated to be the patron saint of Argyll. The island's Gaelic name, Lios Mòr, is ancient Gaelic for 'great courtyard' or 'garden' and is thought to be in reference to his monastery.

During the medieval period, the castles of Coeffin and Achadun were built on the island and the MacDougalls, who still own much of nearby Kerrera (page 191), were a powerful force in the region. Lismore was also the seat of the Bishop of Argyll until 1507 when it was moved to Kintyre on the mainland. The Duke of Argyll still owns most of Lismore today.

Following similar patterns to the rest of the region, Lismore's population fell dramatically in the mid 19th century. Cheaper imported food from the colonies undercut Lismore's once-thriving grain industry, fisheries failed and the kelp market crashed; there was a lack of employment and food, coupled with long harsh

SPRING

Lismore Spring Fair A chance to buy the best of local produce; check local noticeboards.

JULY

Lismore Agricultural Show f lismoreshow1

Lismore Sports & Raft Race f. A day of entertaining contests, with a barbecue.

DECEMBER

Lismore Christmas Craft Fair Check local noticeboards.

WINTER

Taproot Music & Literature Festival f isleoflismore. 4 days of word, film & sound, with a diverse line-up of visiting & local artists.

winters and bad summers between 1836 and 1838. The famine was felt severely and in around 1839 a public appeal was held to raise funds to prevent starvation; £50,000 was raised for food in the area. The 1840s held more severe winters and the cattle market subsequently collapsed. By 1880, the population had dropped from a peak of 1,500 to 621. Today Lismore's population stands at around 170.

GETTING THERE AND AROUND CalMac (page 30) run **ferries** from Oban to Achnacroish (1hr; foot passenger/car £3.05/13.00) up to five times a day. Argyll and Bute Council (01631 730383; w argyll-bute.gov.uk/port-appin-point-lismore-ferry-timetable) operate a foot passenger ferry regularly throughout the day from Port Appin (on the mainland) to Point at the far north end of the island; it takes 10 minutes and costs £2.30.

If you bring a **car**, note that, with very few allocated car parks, Lismore is hands-down the worst place to find a parking spot in the Inner Hebrides. There is also no filling station on the island, so make sure you fill up on the mainland. All but the smallest of campervans will struggle to fit in the infrequent passing places. Don't be alarmed if you see someone driving along missing a door – an interesting law states that an island without a mechanic should not require inhabitants' vehicles to have the standard yearly MOT check.

Given the small size of the island, a **bike** is significantly more convenient for exploring; you can hire one from Lismore Bike Hire (m 07376 425996; w lismorebikehire.co.uk).

Explore Lismore (page 189) also offer a **taxi** and shuttle service.

WHERE TO STAY AND EAT *Map, page 188*

The majority of Lismore's accommodation is self-catering; full listings are available at w isleoflismore.com/accommodation/self-catering. Options for eating out are very limited. When ferry times are favourable, you could opt to take the short ferry to Port Appin (see above) for evening meals. At the ferry terminal you can also find for sale excellent cakes from the Dutch Bakery (PA34 5UN; f dutchbakerylismore; ⊕ Easter–Oct daily & occasional w/ends year-round; £) with an honesty-box payment system.

Lismore Bunkhouse & Camping (12 beds) Baleveolan Croft PA34 5UG; m 07720 975433; f; &. Good green credentials, well-equipped

kitchen, comfortable communal areas & plenty of books. There are resident Highland cows & chickens. With the help of volunteers, they

LISMORE

For listings, see from page 187

Where to stay
1. Lismore Bunkhouse & Camping
2. The Sailean Bothy

Where to eat and drink
Isle of Lismore Café (see Ionad Naomh Moluag)

Bradt

N

0   2km
0   2 miles

Lynn of Morven

Lynn of Lorn

Point

Airds Bay

Port Appin

North Shian

South Shian

Eriska

Port Ramsay

B8045

St Moluag's Chair

St Moluag's Cathedral

269m

Castle Coeffin

Ionad Naomh Moluag (Lismore Gaelic Heritage Centre)

Lismore Stores & post office

Tirefour Castle

Loch Baile a' Ghobhainn

Eilean Dubh

Achnacroish

Sailean

Ballygrundle

B8045

Kilcheran Loch

Eilean na Cloiche

Kilcheran

Eilean nan Gamhna

Camas Nathais

Oban

Bernera

Achadun Bay

Achadun Castle

Achinduin

Bernera Bay

Barr Mòr 417ft

An Dùn

Loch Fiart

Fiart Farm

Dalnarrow

Dùn Chruban

Lismore Lighthouse

Eilean Musdile

188

have planted thousands of broad-leaved trees. Private & bunk rooms. Tent camping & space for 2 campervans. A purple letter box marks the entry. **£**

The Sailean Bothy (sleeps 4) Sailean PA34 5UG; 📞 01631 760282; w airbnb.com; ⊕ Mar–Dec. Beautifully basic self-catering accommodation in a remote location on Sailean Bay. Similar facilities to camping: compost toilet outside & no shower. Mattresses provided, but bring your own bedding. **£**

Isle of Lismore Café Ionad Naomh Moluag (Lismore Gaelic Heritage Centre) PA34 5UL; m 07745 536902; w isleoflismorecafe.jimdofree. com; ⊕ Apr–Oct 11.00–16.00 daily; ♿. Hot drinks, sandwiches & burgers. Inside & outside seating with wonderful views. Dinner/take-away available some Fri eves: check website for dates & book in advance. **£**

SPORTS AND ACTIVITIES Children are welcome to use the play park near the school in Achnacroish. Other activities offered on Lismore are somewhat unusual. The following options happen sporadically when the organisers have both time and participants. **Mairi Campbell** (w mairicampbell.scot) hosts various musical retreats and workshops, or you can go on seaweed foraging walks (w lismoreislandhome.com). **Explore Lismore** (📞 01631 760291; m 07490 416255, 07578 646689; w explorelismore.co.uk) offer bespoke Land Rover island tours and shepherding adventures.

OTHER PRACTICALITIES Lismore only really has one shop, **Lismore Stores & Post Office** (PA34 5UG; 📞 01631 760272; ⊕ 09.00–17.00 Mon–Tue & Thu–Fri, 09.00–13.00 Wed & Sat; ♿), a small but well-stocked community-owned shop selling hot drinks and groceries, plus free Wi-Fi (donations welcome). There's also **The Sailean Project** (Sailean PA34 5UG; 📞 01631 760170; w saileanproject.co.uk), a small-scale farm with ethical credentials offering same-day deliveries of beef, lamb, poultry and eggs on the island, which can be ordered online.

The nearest **doctors' surgery** is in Port Appin (page 262) and the nearest **hospital** in Oban (page 259). Note that you can't get **fuel** on the island.

WHAT TO SEE AND DO The useful website **Walk Lismore** (w walklismore.co.uk) details many routes all over the island, and is well worth delving into.

The north At the north end of Lismore, Point is the location of the foot passenger ferry to the mainland. From here, it's possible to walk about a mile around the coast (with the sea on your right) to **Port Ramsay** (also reachable by road). This idyllic row of white workers' cottages overlooks tidal islands and out towards Morvern on the mainland; the muddy flats support a rich ecosystem and are a favourite with herons and other wading birds.

Tirefour Castle (⊕ open access; free) On the east side of the island, a turning marked to 'Balure' leads to ruined Tirefour Castle. Despite its name, this substantial ruin is not in fact a castle but the best example of an Iron Age broch (page 263) in the whole of Argyll. The grass-topped walls are almost 16ft tall in places and 13ft wide, enclosing a courtyard 39ft across. Complete, it may have been 49ft tall. One thing's for certain: it commanded a magnificent position over the Lynn of Lorn, tiny Eilean Dubh island and out towards the mainland.

Relics of St Moluag (page 185) Indicated by a wooden sign and visible from the road, **St Moluag's Chair** (⊕ 56°32'24"N 5°28'00"W) is a natural seat in a rock, which sits in a field beside the road. The chair's arms were broken off by a roadman towards the end of the 19th century. It is said that St Moluag used to sit here and meditate; sitting on it used to be considered a cure for rheumatism.

A little further south is the pretty, whitewashed local church, also known as **St Moluag's Cathedral** (w isleoflismore.com/island-groups/parish-church). Visitors are welcome to join services and the door is always open at other times. This was the cathedral church of the medieval diocese of Argyll, built some time between the 12th and 14th centuries. Although it is dedicated to St Moluag, there are no remains here from the early Christian period, though it is likely that the building occupied the site of an earlier church dedicated to the saint. Despite its name, don't expect a cathedral – the church is rather modest in size – although there are some wonderful carved grave slabs from the 14th and 15th centuries outside.

Ionad Naomh Moluag (Lismore Gaelic Heritage Centre) (PA34 5UL; 01631 760030; w lismoregaelicheritagecentre.org; ⊕ Apr–Oct 11.00–16.00 daily; ⅁; free) This modern building has a well-presented museum with interesting information, archives and artefacts such as the 'Port Appin Head' (a pagan Celtic carving), a Norse-era link plate made of gold, and coins from the 13th and 14th centuries. Outside is a replica 'cottar's house', Taigh Iseabail Dhàidh, set out as it would have been in the late 19th century. There's also a shop selling local arts and crafts, as well as a café here (page 189).

✳ Walk: Castle Coeffin
Distance: 2 miles; time: 1–2 hours; start/end: St Moluag's Cathedral; OS Explorer map: 376 Oban & North Lorn
The moss- and grass-covered remains of Castle Coeffin (⊕ 56°32'16"N 5°29'25"W) are some of the most atmospheric in the Inner Hebrides.

Around 220yds south of St Moluag's Cathedral you will see a minor crossroads; take the track on the right. Follow this track southwest for about 200yds before taking the left route when it forks. After another 380yds or so the track curves around to the right and begins to head north. Continue in this direction for just under a mile until you see Portcastle Farm and the castle on your left; a magnificent fish trap is visible on the shore at low tide, just a few yards to the south of the castle.

When you reach a junction, join the track leading left, downhill towards the sea and the castle, though be aware that horses are kept in these fields and try not to disturb them.

Positioned on a small promontory jutting out into the sea, the castle ruins are small, but atmospheric, next to a peaceful rocky bay. Castle Coeffin is named after Caifen, the son of a Norse king. Caifen's sister Beothail ('of the golden hair') is said to have lost her lover in a battle in Norway. Distraught, she died of a broken heart and they buried her at the castle. Beothail then haunted the castle until they dug up her body, washed her bones in the well and took them across to Norway. One finger bone was forgotten, however, and her spirit refused to rest until they found it, so Caifen and his men searched and were eventually able to take it across. It is said that you can still hear Beothail's sighs in the wind. What exists today of Castle Coeffin is not the Norse stronghold, but the severely ruined remains of a 13th-century hall-house and bailey, with some later additions, probably built by the MacDougalls of Lorn. Unsurprisingly, the naturally strategic position was popular throughout the ages.

To return to the cathedral, retrace your steps the way you came.

The south
Sailein and Achadun Castle Taking the minor road towards Achinduin on the west coast, you can turn off right to reach the farm and shoreline at **Sailean**, also known as Salen. Here you can see the remains of an impressive 19th-century lime quarry and kilns (✪ 56°30'54"N 5°31'06"W). The Sailean Project (page 189) is based here and you might have a chance to see their Highland cows. Further down the west coast is the 13th-century **Achadun Castle** (⊕open access), probably built by the MacDougalls. It fell out of use in the 16th century, but the ruined walls are substantial, giving you some concept of its original scale.

From here, look out for the small tidal island of **Bernera**; it's possible to walk out there with careful planning – you'll need to check tide times (page 28) in advance. Bernera is said to have been settled by St Moluag and his monks in the 6th century. St Columba is also supposed to have used the island as a retreat and is said to have preached under a huge yew tree there. The tree was felled and the trunk turned into a staircase in Lochnell Castle near Oban; it is said that the staircase survived despite the rest of the building being burned twice.

Exploring the far southwest Back on the island's main road, if you take the road that leads off to the right at **Baligrundle** it's possible to follow the coast to the south. Note, however, that the road deteriorates dramatically around **Loch Fiart** and it is easy to get a car stuck in the mud. Around 300yds southwest of the head of Loch Fiart are the grass-covered remains of **An Dùn** (✪ 56°28'49"N 5°33'22"W). Probably once a broch, the spot is possibly more interesting to most people for its glorious views over the loch and across the green surrounding landscape. From here there is a 6-mile return walk out to Rubha Fiart, at the far southwest point of Lismore.

Continuing along the track you will pass Fiart Farm, followed by a small pond in a pretty, green valley, before reaching the buildings at Dalnarrow. Choosing the track following nearest to the sea, you will soon come to the ruins of **Dùn Chruban** (✪ 56°27'51"N 5°35'06"W), the scant remains of a fortress set on top of a natural rocky outcrop. From here, it's only possible to continue for another mile further southwest; climb up the hill at the end for a vantage point with views out to the lovely 19th-century **Lismore Lighthouse** on the island Eilean Musdile, as well as across to Duart on Mull, the Morvern Peninsula and to Kerrera in the south. The dramatic coastline, rocky crags and sheltered hollows were once used to hide a small-scale illegal distilling industry in the 18th and 19th centuries.

KERRERA

Just across the water from Oban, Kerrera's decision not to allow visiting cars makes it a totally different world from the mainland. Peaceful and green, it is a hilly island with a substantial 16th-century tower house, Gylen Castle, and lovely views of Mull and the mainland across the Sound of Kerrera. It is about 5 miles long and 2 miles wide. Aside from the sheep grazing quietly above the rocky shoreline, there are about 70 residents.

GETTING THERE AND AWAY CalMac (page 30) run a foot-passenger **ferry** from Gallanach Road (southwest of Oban) to Kerrera regularly from 08.30 to 18.00; it takes only a few minutes to cross and costs £1.70. Day visitors should check the last returning ferry time carefully at the port or ask the ferry crew. Parking at Gallanach Road is quite limited, but the 417 **bus** service run by West Coast Motors (page 30)

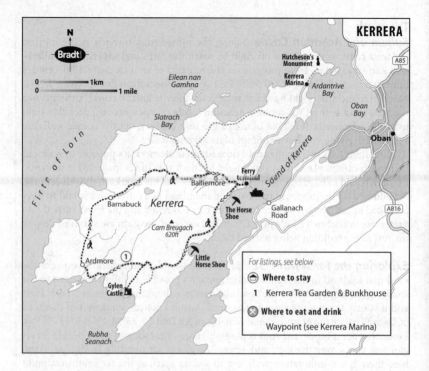

goes from Oban to Kerrera Ferry/Gallanach Road twice a day on school days. Times revolve around children getting to Oban for school and are thus not very convenient for organising a day trip.

There are **moorings** at Kerrera Marina (Ardantrive Bay, Kerrera; 01631 565333; w kerreramarina.com).

 WHERE TO STAY AND EAT *Map, above*

Kerrera Tea Garden & Bunkhouse (sleeps 7) PA34 4SX; m 07951 964231; w kerrerabunkhouse. co.uk; Easter–Sep 11.00–16.00 Thu–Mon. The bunkhouse is only booked exclusively (min 2-night stay), so perfect for groups of friends or family. Inexpensive café serving hot drinks & cakes, as well as international soups & stews in the colder months & fresh salads in the height of summer. **£**

Waypoint Restaurant Kerrera Marina, Ardantrive Bay PA34 4SX; 01631 565333; w kerreramarina. com/waypoint; Apr–Sep 13.00–20.00 Thu–Sat, 13.00–15.00 Sun. Sit-down meals with ingredients from owners' farm & local fishing boats. Water taxi can be arranged from Oban. **££**

WHAT TO SEE AND DO Unsurprisingly, given that it's a car-free island, the best way to see the island is on **foot**. The walk described below is ideal for day visitors; if you're staying longer, you can take the time to explore more widely and at a slower pace.

Walk: Gylen Castle and southern Kerrera

Distance: 7 miles; time: 4 hours, but a whole day is recommended; start/end: Kerrera ferry terminal; OS Explorer map: 359 Oban, Kerrera & Loch Melfort

From the port, turn left (you can check the telephone box here for local postcards, which you can buy on an honesty box system) before taking a lower track along the coast that passes the **Horse Shoe**, a gently curved bay. Ignore the minor turning up to the right here and the first white house. Some time later you will come to the **Little Horse Shoe**, a picturesque circular bay. At the next fork, follow the signs to the castle and Tea Garden, taking the turning bearing right inland and up the hill.

Once you reach the bottom of the hill, just before you get to the Tea Garden (see opposite), take the turning towards the left, past a small compost toilet, and follow signs to the castle.

The imposing remains of **Gylen Castle** ('castle of fountains') have been preserved rather than restored, maintaining its venerable atmosphere without the danger of it collapsing on anyone's head. Free to enter and accessible up steps, you can actually (and unusually for the Inner Hebrides) climb inside and get a great sense of the original vantage point. An L-plan tower house, it consists of a square main block and stair tower, originally commissioned by Duncan MacDougall and completed in 1582. It is set strategically on a naturally high, rocky peninsula, situated to command the southern approach to Oban. The castle was besieged and burned by a Covenanter army led by General David Leslie in 1647 and subsequently left unoccupied.

If you are short on time, returning along the same route is the quickest and easiest way back to the ferry, but continuing to make a circular route is more rewarding. Return to the main track, which leads behind the Tea Garden and roughly west, then northwest to the couple of buildings at **Ardmore**. At the white house with the grey extension, you need to bear right up through the gorse. Accompanied by its coconut scent, a rocky path will lead you up to a large pond on a plateau. The path becomes faint and grassy as it heads on to open land, with views out to sea on your left. After some time, the grassy path returns to a more substantial track and you descend to the farmhouse at **Barnabuck**, which was once a larger settlement.

There are occasional signs indicating the way back to the ferry, which help you along the way. Passing the ruined buildings around Barnabuck, the path soon begins to climb up the hill again and over to the east side of the island. The views over the coast and small islets around Eilean nan Gamhna are spectacular, but it is not a pleasant climb if you are rushing for the last ferry.

Passing above a farm on your left, head straight on through the gate to return to the ferry or turn left to head up towards the north end of the island. You can find a description of this route (which is to the **Hutcheson's Monument** obelisk – a memorial to one of the founders of CalMac) on Walkhighlands (w walkhighlands.co.uk/argyll/kerrera-hutcheson.shtml); the route is around 3 to 4 hours return.

9

The Slate Islands

Although the name of this group of four islands summons images of grey mining towns and industrial scenery, this could not be further from reality. Centre of the Scottish slate industry in the 18th and 19th centuries, only Seil, Luing and tiny Easdale still have permanent communities, while Belnahua, now abandoned, makes a ghostly silhouette opposite Luing's biggest village Cullipool. Glasgow Cathedral, Lorn's Armaddy Castle, Appin's Castle Stalker and many other important buildings in Scotland are still roofed in Easdale slate. The abandoned quarries have weathered gently over time to form a unique landscape: their walls, caved in by winter storms, have left squared-off pools of glowing turquoise water, separated by thin bulwarks of rock. Owing to its small size, Easdale is the most defined by these features – aerial photos show a large percentage of the island's surface to be water rather than earth or rock. By contrast Luing, pronounced 'Ling', seems startlingly green, an emerald in the clear, clean waters rushing past it. The further you get away from Clachan Bridge (known as 'The Bridge Over The Atlantic'), which connects Seil to the mainland, the more wild and peaceful the islands become.

The Firth of Lorn Marine Special Area of Conservation includes the Slate Islands, the north end of Jura and other, uninhabited islands such as the Garvellachs and Scarba. The area has been chosen for protection because of its rocky reef habitats; exposed or underwater depending on the depth and tide, they support colonies of sponges, brittlestars, sea ferns and cup coral, making the habitat among the most biodiverse in Europe. On a larger scale, these waters are one of the best areas in Europe to see porpoises, bottlenose dolphins (there's a resident pod of 30) and occasionally even minke whales. Otters also appear to be unusually common here, with locals reporting that they now see more of these elusive creatures than they did over a decade ago. The area is also one of the only places in the UK where seal numbers are still increasing, with colonies of around 20,000 common seals and 110,000 grey seals. Additionally, these waters are covered by the Loch Sunart to the Sound of Jura Marine Protected Area as the last stronghold of the flapper skate. The largest of all the European skates and rays, capable of reaching over 8ft long and over 6ft wide (across the wings), this curious-looking fish will never rival the fluffy panda as an appealing conservation poster child, but it is critically endangered.

Between the publication of the first and second editions of this book, a huge nature restoration project was launched on Luing and Scarba, seeing the planting of 250,000 native broadleaf trees and the creation of 4 acres of wetland – some of the ponds and young trees line the walk from Ballycastle Fort to Kilchattan (page 202).

Aside from history and natural heritage, possibly the most striking attribute of the Slate Islands is the notably friendly and welcoming attitude of local people.

The **Atlantic Island Centre** on Luing (w isleofluing.org/what-do/events-calendar) hosts art exhibitions, talks and events through the year. In September is the **World Stone Skimming Championships** (Easdale Island; w stoneskimming.com), by far the biggest event on the Slate Islands, with more than 300 people entering every year, sometimes coming from as far away as Japan and Australia.

GETTING THERE AND AWAY

Seil is attached to the mainland by a bridge (page 198), which makes it simple to get on to the island. From Seil there is a small passenger boat to Easdale (page 199) and a vehicle ferry across to Luing (page 201); neither of these crossings take much more than 5 minutes.

TOURIST INFORMATION

There is no official tourist information centre on the Slate Islands, but Luing's Atlantic Islands Centre (page 201), The Slate Islands Heritage Trust Centre (page 199) on Seil and the Easdale Island Folk Museum (page 200) on Easdale are informative on the islands' history, sights and natural heritage. Online information is available about Luing (w isleofluing.org), Seil (w seil.oban.ws) and Easdale (w easdale.org), as well as from the more history-focused w slateislands.org.uk.

OTHER PRACTICALITIES

Despite being only a stone's throw from the mainland, the Slate Islands are lacking in some basic amenities: there is nowhere to fill up with **fuel** and network coverage is patchy, so do not rely on online maps.

Health Easdale Medical Practice, Seil PA34 4TL; ☎ 01852 300223; w easdalemedicalpractice.scot.nhs.uk

Post offices Balvicar Stores (page 198; ⊕ 08.30–17.00 Mon–Tue & Thu–Fri, 08.30–12.30 Wed, 09.00–13.00 Sat); Luing Stores (page 202; ⊕ 11.00–13.00 Mon–Fri, 11.00–14.00 Sat)

SEIL (SAOIL)

A curious crossover between mainland and island, Seil is accessibly close to Oban and day trips from here down to Ellenabeich or Easdale village are a popular choice for those short on time. Away from the main settlements much of Seil is wild and uninhabited with plentiful walking opportunities – but you'll need a decent map.

GETTING THERE AND AROUND Only half an hour's **drive** south of Oban and without the need to catch a ferry, Seil is arguably the easiest of the Inner Hebridean islands to access. There is no fee for crossing the Clachan Bridge and it can be walked, cycled or driven over.

West Coast Motors (☎ page 30; ♿) runs the 418/18 Oban–Clachan–Balvicar–Noth Cuan–Ellenabeich **bus** service several times a day from Monday to Saturday, making it easy to reach most of the island.

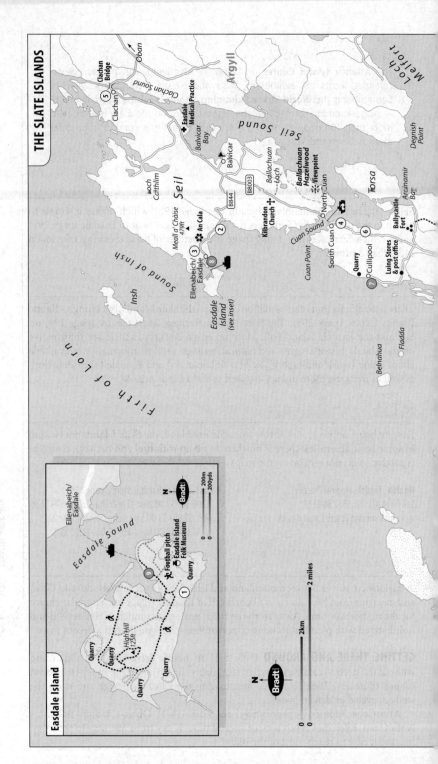

THE SLATE ISLANDS

Easdale Island

Ellenabeich/Easdale

Easdale Sound

Quarry
Quarry
Quarry
High Hill 125ft
Quarry
Quarry
Football pitch
Easdale Island Folk Museum
Quarry (1)

Bradt

0 — 200m
0 — 200yds

Oban

Clachan Bridge
Clachan
(5)
Clachan Sound
Easdale Medical Practice
Balvicar Bay
loch Cèithlim
Balvicar

Argyll

Seil Sound

Seil

Meall a' Chàise 479ft
An Cala (3)
(2)
Ellenabeich/Easdale

B844
B8003
Kilbrandon Church
Ballachuan loch
Ballachuan Hazelwood Viewpoint
North Cuan
Cuan Sound
(4)
Cuan Point
South Cuan

Torsa

Loch Melfort

Degnish Point

Ardanamir Bay

Sound of Insh

Insh

Easdale Island (see inset)

Firth of Lorn

Fladda

Belnahua

Quarry
Cullipool
Luing Stores & post office
(6)
(7)
Ballycastle Fort

Bradt

0 — 2km
0 — 2 miles

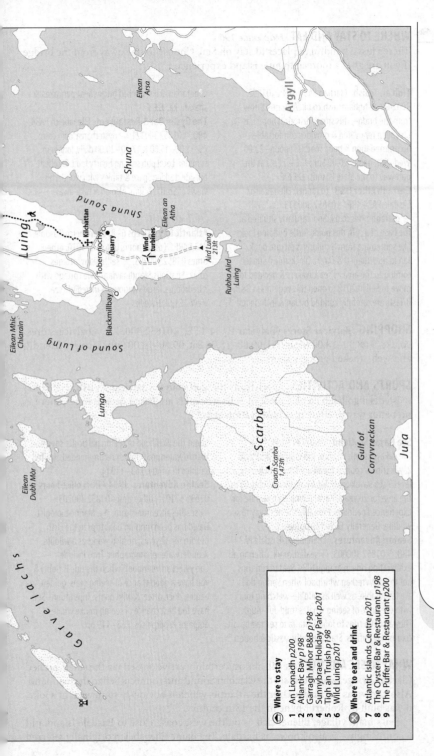

Where to stay

1 An Lionadh *p200*
2 Atlantic Bay *p198*
3 Garragh Mhor B&B *p198*
4 Sunnybrae Holiday Park *p201*
5 Tigh an Truish *p198*
6 Wild Luing *p201*

Where to eat and drink

7 Atlantic Islands Centre *p201*
8 The Oyster Bar & Restaurant *p198*
9 The Puffer Bar & Restaurant *p200*

WHERE TO STAY AND EAT *Map, page 196*

There's just a handful of places to stay on Seil. Choose to stay away from the bridge if you are after a more authentic island experience.

Tigh an Truish Clachan PA34 4TN; 01852 300242; w tighantruish.co.uk. A stone's throw from the bridge, this small, historical hotel has just been renovated & provides comfortable accommodation & good food (noon–22.00 Wed–Sat, noon–20.00 Sun; ££–£££) at the gateway to the Slate Islands. ££££

Garragh Mhor B&B (4 rooms) Ellenabeich/Easdale PA34 4RF; 01852 300513; w garraghmhor.co.uk. Spectacularly situated at the base of a cliff, this quirky little building looks like something from a children's picture book. Jan (a nutritionist) & Daz (a blacksmith) started coming to the area as sea kayakers & decided to move to Seil in 2018 to open this vegetarian B&B. B/fasts are carefully curated by Jan & include full

vegetarian, fruit-stacked buckwheat pancakes & shakshuka. £££

The Oyster Bar & Restaurant Ellenabeich PA34 4RQ; 01852 300121; w oysterbareasdale.com; 11.00–15.00 & 17.30–20.00 daily, longer in summer. Local pub serving hearty food. Excellent outside decking space & tables with wonderful views of Scarba & Jura. Also offer take-away. £–££

Self-catering

Atlantic Bay (sleeps 6–8) Ellenabeich/Easdale PA34 4RF; office hours 01631 571010, other times 01852 300203; w seilholidaycottages. co.uk. Spacious Scandinavian-style cottage with 3 bedrooms, large windows & incredible sea views. £1,500/week.

SHOPPING **Balvicar Stores** (Balvicar PA34 4TE; 01852 300373; w balvicarstores. co.uk; 08.30–18.00 Mon–Fri, 09.00–18.00 Sat, 09.30–14.00 Sun) is a very friendly and well-stocked grocery shop.

SPORTS AND ACTIVITIES Apart from the **golf course** (Balvicar; 01852 300087; w isleofseilgolfclub.co.uk), most of Seil's activities are based on the water; there is no better way to enjoy the conservation area.

Sea Kayak Scotland m 07771 918431; w seakayakscotland.com. Individually designed kayak trips & courses for all abilities with Kenny, a level 5 sea kayak coach who has been operating in the area for 20 years. Kayak/camping gear hire for experienced paddlers. Probably the best way to see wildlife. Generally £65–130 pp/day.

Seafari Adventures Ellenabeich/Easdale PA34 4RQ; 01852 300003; w seafari.co.uk. Offering an exhilarating ride in orange RIBs, Seafari run trips out to Corryvreckan whirlpool when spring tides are favourable, as well as wildlife-watching tours with the hope of seeing whales (mid-Jul–Aug). They also run trips to Iona & Staffa to see the basalt columns & puffins. Staff are enthusiastic & honest

about the likelihood of seeing particular species. Warm/waterproof clothes recommended; limited sailings in winter. £53–110 pp.

Sealife Adventures PA34 4TR; office hours 01631 571010, other times 01852 300203; w sealife-adventures.com; . Marine biologist David has been running boat trips in the Firth of Lorn for 32 years; he also works as a wildlife & underwater photographer. Trips include Corryvreckan whirlpool (when the tide is right) & you have a good chance of seeing seals, golden/sea eagles, deer, otters & wild goats. Trips in Jun–Sep have the best chance of seeing minke whales, dolphins & porpoises. £68–119 pp.

WHAT TO SEE AND DO You will almost certainly arrive on Seil via the small, arched **Clachan Bridge**, which crosses the Clachan Sound and connects Seil to the mainland. Also known as the **Bridge Over the Atlantic**, which is obviously somewhat of a joke, it was built by Robert Mylne in the 18th century.

Seil's main village, **Ellenabeich**, is on the west coast, close to Easdale Island and – confusingly – is also known as Easdale. The name Ellenabeich originally referred

Assuming that a service is not taking place, you can park at **Kilbrandon Church** and walk down the private road leading east that starts on the opposite side of the road. Less than a mile down this road a marked turning to the right will take you towards the small Ballachuan Loch and Ballachuan Hazelwood Nature Reserve (w scottishwildlifetrust.org.uk/reserve/ballachuan-hazel-wood).

The woodland is an important habitat for elusive pine martens and in autumn and winter you should come across interesting lichens and fungi, while butterflies live on the grasslands around the loch between May and July.

The area is maintained by the Scottish Wildlife Trust and there is a map and information near the beginning of the trail. Paths are quite overgrown, but the woodland is relatively small, so it should be easy enough to explore.

to a small island that lay in the channel between Seil and Easdale Island and was quarried away to just the rim. The space between Ellenabeich Island and Easdale on Seil was filled with waste material from the quarry until enough ground was created to build the rows of houses that still stand there today. Soil from Ireland, previously used as ships' ballast, was then added to make a little more land for the houses' gardens; these houses, built on Ellenabeich, became a small part of the village of Easdale. In 1881, a great storm filled the rest of the quarry with water, closing down its operations, and today's landscape is a confusing combination of land that was once part of the sea and water where there used to be land. To add a further layer of complication, the name Ellenabeich has recently evolved to mean the whole village (of Easdale), presumably because of the confusion between Easdale on Seil and Easdale Island, but you will still find the village on Seil referred to as Easdale by certain locals and on the front of some buses.

To get a sense of local history, or for further information on the area, it's worth making your first stop **The Slate Islands Heritage Trust Centre** (13a Ellenabeich PA34 4RQ; w slateislands.org.uk; ⊕ 11.30–16.00 Sun–Fri mid-Apr–Oct; donation requested). This small but fascinating museum is almost as great a wealth of information as the volunteers who work there, with written notices mirroring their humour and all levels of society represented in their exhibits. There is a particularly interesting model of a working slate quarry.

Near the primary school are the beautiful 90-year-old gardens of **An Cala** (PA34 4RF; ☎ 01852 300237; ⊕ Apr–Oct 10.00–18.00; donation requested), full of quirky sculptures and water features. Ellenabeich is also where you can catch the small passenger ferry across to Easdale Island (see below).

Further south, on the western side of the road, is **Kilbrandon Church**, most famous for its striking stained-glass windows designed by Dr Douglas Strachan. These show scenes from the Bible and particularly the Sea of Galilee. In the central window on the east wall, Jesus is shown quelling a great storm from a boat; the colours and sense of movement are very dramatic.

EASDALE ISLAND (EILEAN ÈISDEAL)

The smallest permanently inhabited Inner Hebridean island, Easdale is totally unique. Without any cars and accessed by a short passenger ferry journey from Ellenabeich on Seil (journey takes a couple of mins; ⊕ 07.45–12.45 & 14.15–21.00 Mon–Sat, 09.15–12.45 & 14.15–18.15 Sun, additional sailings at 07.15 &

23.00 Mon–Sat or 19.00 Sun can be booked before noon the day before by calling ☏01852 300794; £250 return; pay on the boat), it is one of the few islands in this book that I can recommend visiting as a day trip, but you could stay for longer. There are community-owned **moorings** in Easdale Sound (w easdale.org/harbour/index.htm).

WHERE TO STAY AND EAT *Map, page 196*

Self-catering is the only option on Easdale. See w easdale-experiences.com for a couple of traditional cottages.

An Lionadh   (sleeps 8–10) PA34 4TB; ☏01688 400388; w anlionadh.co.uk. This is a truly spectacular 4-bed self-catering house, right on the beach with the feeling of an enormous beach hut. It has quite a few interesting nautical curiosities such as a huge model boat, telescope & old-fashioned diving helmet. Quiet location & unfenced lawn down to the sea. £1,250/week.

The Puffer Bar & Restaurant ☏01852 300022; w pufferbarandrestaurant.co.uk; ⊕ café 11.00–16.00 Thu–Sun, restaurant 18.00–20.30 Sat, pub 18.00–late Thu–Fri, 16.00–late Sat. Easdale's only place to eat & drink serves sandwiches & soup from the café, while the restaurant serves great seafood including haddock battered with Fyne Ales jarl; scampi; & local langoustines. £

WHAT TO SEE AND DO   In the east of the island, southeast of the football pitch, **Easdale Island Folk Museum** (PA34 4TB; ☏ 01852 300173; w easdalemuseum.org; ⊕ Apr–Oct noon–15.00 daily) has displays on the slate industry, army volunteers, geology, boats and other aspects of Easdale Island life.

Walk: Around Easdale Island
Distance: 1½ miles; time: 1 hour; start/end: Easdale village; OS Explorer map: 359 Oban, Kerrera & Loch Melfort

This walk covers easy, flat terrain unless you decide to go up High Hill, which makes it marginally more difficult.

Disembark from the ferry and turn right just before the large collection of wheelbarrows; these are used for transporting heavy items around the island.

Follow the road into the village, passing the modern-looking community hall and Puffer Restaurant & Bar on your left, and the play park on your right. When you reach the square football field, surrounded by small white cottages that were once lived in by quarry workers (now homes for islanders), turn right down towards the harbour.

Follow the waterfront until you reach a sign with an arrow pointing left for 'Quarries' and 'High Hill'. From here, take the indicated rocky path that leads through piles of slate splinterings, ruined buildings and out on to the rim between two large **quarries** filled with aquamarine-coloured water. They are a bizarre clash of industry and nature, more picturesque than you would imagine. Keep an eye out to sea for marine mammals such as porpoises and stay on the path as it turns left and climbs some steps.

To reach **High Hill**, Easdale's highest point, take an unmarked but obvious left-hand turning after a ruined building on your left, just before the L-shaped, water-filled quarry on your right. This path will take you to a small, green bench where you must bear right up to a grassy area with a picnic bench and trig point on top of the hill. Be careful to watch small children and dogs as there are sheer drops off the plateau. On a clear day, you can identify the surrounding islands and landmarks by reading the directions off the top of the trig point: Mull, Kerrera, Seil, Luing, Belnahua and parts of the mainland can all (potentially) be seen. Return the same way to the small, green bench and back down the steps to the main path.

From here, follow the path past the L-shaped quarry, then another larger quarry that's also full of water and some more dry and increasingly overgrown pits. The path soon passes a pretty pond on the left and through blackthorn bushes that are covered in white flowers in spring; this area is home to large hosts of sparrows that flock between perches as you pass.

Eventually you will come to a short alley between two walls and into the back of the village. Follow the sign for 'Ferry, Hall, Pub & Museum' and keep the sea to your right. Bear left to join with the main path through the village, and back to the football pitch.

LUING (LUINN)

Of the three substantially inhabited Slate Islands, Luing is the least visited. It is the biggest of the three and you can take a car there, making it less of a novelty than Easdale, but don't let that put you off: Luing is a beautiful island with its own pretty rows of white miners' cottages, aquamarine water-filled mines and slate scrap beaches. The main road leads along its raised spine: open grassy fields, rich with wildflowers in spring, end in rocky shores and glorious views of the sea, Torsa and mainland Argyll. It's a peaceful island with excellent walking routes and plenty of space for wildlife. Look out for glossy red-brown Luing cattle; originally bred in 1947 from beef cattle shorthorns and Highlanders for their hardiness, but now recognised as a separate breed.

GETTING THERE AND AROUND Argyll and Bute Council (℡ 01852 300252; w argyll-bute.gov.uk/isle-luing-isle-seil-ferry-timetable) runs a regular and inexpensive **car ferry** between North Cuan on Seil and South Cuan on Luing (another example of settlements spanning across a stretch of water). The journey takes only a few minutes (foot passengers/car £2.50/9.70 return).

All of Luing's roads are single track, but at less than 6 square miles it does not take long to get around the island by car. Travelling by **bicycle** can be even more enjoyable, allowing you to stop and admire the views more easily. You can hire a bike from Sunnybrae Holiday Park (see below; w oban-holiday.co.uk/things-do/bike-hire; ⊕ Apr–early Oct; adult/child £20/15).

WHERE TO STAY AND EAT *Map, page 196*

Wild Luing (8 cabins) South Cuan PA34 4TU; m 07765 870111; w wildluing.com. Designed & built on Luing in 2022 by owners Emily & Jack – with help from Jack's family – these remarkably spacious, luxury self-catering cabins each sleep 2. The peaceful setting has uninterrupted views across a beautiful, sheltered bay scattered with rocky islets to neighbouring island Torsa & out towards Seil Sound. There are rolltop baths, outdoor firepits & full kitchen facilities (with complimentary Scottish tablet); choose between super-king or twin beds. Look out for otters & seals along the shore, & throw the doors open first thing in the morning to enjoy the dawn chorus. Owners & staff are knowledgeable about the island & can help suggest places to explore. **££££**

Sunnybrae Holiday Park (6 static homes, 2 lodges) South Cuan PA34 4TU; m 07432 622211; w oban-holiday.co.uk. Forget your preconceived notions of holiday parks – Sunnybrae is a breath of fresh air. Pale green c/vans & grey roofs are absorbed into the shoreline, while interiors are well equipped, with ovens & full-size bathroom suites. Ask for one on the water's edge & it's like having a personal bird hide. Seabirds float past in the current & otters live along the shoreline. The owners are environmentally conscious, let wildflowers grow for the insects, provide compost bins & sell local produce on site. Orchid Lodge (sleeps 4; &) is the most luxurious option. £620–1,170/week.

Atlantic Islands Centre 23, Cullipool PA34 4TX; ℡ 01852 314096; w isleofluing.org/atlantic-islands-centre; ⊕ Apr–Oct 11.00–15.00

Wed–Sun, Nov–Mar reduced hours (check online); selling coffees, goods from Luing Bakery, soup,
also take-away/bar some eves; &. Modern café salads & lunch specials. £

SHOPPING Decorated in blue-and-white stripes like a beach hut, **Luing Stores and Post Office** (Fladda, nr Cullipool PA34 4TX; \ 01852 314276; f; ⏲ 11.00–16.00 Mon–Fri, 11.00–14.00 Sat) is a great little store selling bread from Luing Bakery and some groceries, as well as slate-themed gifts, knitted accessories and coffee.

WHAT TO SEE AND DO Luing's main settlement, **Cullipool**, is a quiet, seaside village, dwarfed by a huge quarry in the north. It has pretty, white miners' cottages, similar to those in Easdale, and a jagged beach made of half-cut pieces of slate, some of which are studded with fool's gold. The prettier, water-filled quarries are said to be home to huge numbers of toads.

While in Cullipool, do not miss the **Atlantic Islands Centre** (page 201). The café is downstairs, while upstairs are changing exhibitions of local interest and information about Luing's history. There's also an excellent view across to Fladda Lighthouse and Belnahua.

Walk: Ballycastle Fort to Kilchattan

Distance: 2½ miles; time: 1½ hours; start: Ballycastle Fort, near Ardinamir; end: Kilchattan; OS Explorer map: 359 Oban, Kerrera & Loch Melfort

This is an easy walk, though it can get muddy in places. The route takes in two interesting archaeological sites and wonderful views along the coastline. To make it a 5-mile circular route, return from Kilchattan to Ardinamir along the road.

To reach **Ballycastle Fort** (⊕ 56°14′51″N 5°37′47″W), now little more than rubble remains of an imposing dùn, take the main road that runs south from the ferry terminal, then follow the left turn marked towards 'Ardinamir'.

The fort is half a mile down the road, up on a hill to the left, standing in a strategic position with a clear view across Ardinamir Bay to the island of Torsa and Seil Sound beyond. The easiest access is provided by a left turn; follow the track through a gate and climb the small hill below the dùn on its southeast side.

On the opposite side of the road is a turning on to a farm track leading south; take this and choose the higher track at the fork you come to shortly afterwards. Ignoring several right turns, this track is easy to follow and leads above the coastline for about 2½ miles, taking in glorious views of Loch Melfort and Shuna. The landscape is green and gently undulating, with newly planted native trees and ponds providing good habitat for wildlife; you might spot smaller birds of prey such as kestrels, beautiful white and black male hen harriers, short-eared owls and buzzards.

When the track eventually meets the main road, turn left and walk a short distance to the ruins of the **old parish church of Kilchattan** and its **burial ground**. Although this building dates from the 12th century, the site is thought to have had religious significance for substantially longer. Careful inspection of the outer faces of the ruined building should reveal rudimentary carvings or graffiti of boats. They are thought to depict medieval galleys or birlinns, which are consistent with a style used in the 12th or 13th century. Contradictory arguments suggest that they refer to either a failed military expedition in 1249 by King Alexander II or King Haakon's fleet coming from Norway in 1263. There were of course many other boats passing Luing and thus there are a number of other suggestions as to the carvings' meaning.

Toberonochy Luing's second-largest settlement, Toberonochy mostly consists of a couple of rows of pretty whitewashed cottages, built in the late 18th and early 19th centuries for people working in the quarry. Walking down through the village, past the village hall, you will come to a large pier with lovely views across to the island of Shuna and along the coastline of Luing. Further south, there is a gently rotting boat and a couple of beaches. If you want to have a look at the mine, which is water-filled and curiously picturesque with sheer diagonally striped slate walls and twisted trees growing on top, go through a metal gate on the opposite side of the road from the pier and follow a path around past a few sheds for around 100yds.

Àird Luing The south of Luing is only really inhabited by birds and Ardlarach Farm's cattle. The farm is managed with biodiversity in mind and is home to flocks of Canada and greylag geese, swooping lapwings and long-beaked snipe.

OTHER SMALL ISLANDS IN THIS AREA

Invaluable havens for wildlife, none of the other, somewhat mysterious, Slate Islands has more than a handful of inhabitants or a regular ferry connection. Looking out to sea, you will get to know their silhouettes on the horizon; some of the organised boat trips allow you a closer look as you pass them, while both Seafari and Sealife Adventures (page 198) can organise private landing tours.

BELNAHUA Northwest of Luing, Belnahua was the fourth of the main Slate Islands, but is now uninhabited. It was once home to 200 people who worked in the quarries, but now all that remains is the ruins of their cottages and a huge water-filled mine that takes up most of the interior.

FLADDA Fladda is dominated by its lighthouse and the lighthouse keepers' cottages, which were built in 1860 by the Stevenson brothers. It is also known to host a large colony of terns.

LUNGA Situated west of Luing, Lunga is privately owned and used to host an activity centre for schoolchildren, though it has now closed down – not to be confused with Lunga in the Treshnish Isles further northwest.

SCARBA Relatively large and round, Scarba is now uninhabited and separated from Luing by the 'Grey Dogs' tidal race and from Jura by the Gulf of Corryvreckan with its famous whirlpool (page 245). You can sometimes see the wild boar that live here on boat trips.

SHUNA Shuna is privately owned with a working farm, several holiday cottages (☎ 01852 314244; w islandofshuna.co.uk) and lots of deer. On the northwest shore lies the wreck of an old ferry; it has a turntable for cars and was later used for transporting cows, before being beached here when it was no longer needed. Visitors that stay are picked up as foot passengers and given a small motorboat for the duration of their holiday.

TORSA Lying between Seil Sound and Cuan Sound, Torsa is very close to the shore of Luing's Ardinamir Bay. It has one house and the ruins of a 16th-century hunting lodge. At the time of writing, the whole island was on the market: offers over £1,500,000, should you be tempted.

Coming from the north, about 220yds after the turning to Toberonochy there are some large barns and farm buildings. Taking a right turn (on foot) just after the biggest barn should bring you to a cattle grid and the beginnings of a track that leads around 2 miles all the way down to Àird Luing – the southernmost point of the island. As the track sticks to higher ground, you have consistently great views of Scarba, Shuna, the mainland, as well as out to sea. The small islet in the wide bay at Eilean an Atha on your left is thought to have been an ancient dùn.

At the end of the track, you should be able to see a trig point up on your right. The Garvellachs, Belnahua and Mull are off to the west; Scarba and the north end of Jura are south. Take some time to scan the water for porpoises and dolphins if it is a calm day.

The coastline in this part of the island is wild and unpathed, lending itself to a more adventurous romp, with plenty of birds, such as little ringed plovers and herons, and chances of spotting otters.

10

Colonsay (Colbhasa) and Oronsay (Orasaigh)

At 10 miles long and 2 miles wide, Colonsay is a relatively small island, with a varied landscape that's dramatic in places, plus beautiful sandy beaches and some interesting pockets of archaeology. With a population of 133, there are plenty of wide-open spaces and its isolated location makes the island a rewarding place to watch the night sky. To the south, neighbouring Oronsay (Oransay to some locals) is attached by a tidal sand bank and would be nothing more than a footnote if it were not for its wonderful Augustinian priory. With a large collection of carved grave slabs and two Celtic crosses, as well as the ruins of the buildings themselves, the priory is comparable to Iona Abbey in many ways, but with only a fraction of the visitors. Both islands are also notable for their birdlife, with Oronsay being an RSPB reserve and Colonsay's teeming seabird cliffs among the richest in birdlife of anywhere in the region.

COLONSAY

GETTING THERE AND AWAY CalMac (page 30) offers two **ferry** options for getting to Colonsay: the service from Oban takes 2 hours and 15 minutes and runs five times a week in summer or three times a week in winter (foot passengers/car £8/41.15); Islay to Colonsay takes 1 hour and runs twice a week in summer and sometimes once a week in winter (foot passengers/car £4.50/19). Ferries arrive at the main settlement of Scalasaig; Colonsay Holidays (w colonsayholidays.co.uk) offer a pickup service for £25.

Hebridean Air Services (08458 057465; w hebrideanair.co.uk) **fly** from Oban to Colonsay return and from Colonsay to Tiree; the airfield is on the west coast; pickup is available from Colonsay Holidays (w colonsayholidays.co.uk; £25).

There are also **moorings** at Queen's Bay (w colonsay.org.uk/projects/yacht-moorings).

GETTING AROUND All of Colonsay's roads are single track and several sharp corners and blind summits mean that extra care is needed when **driving**. The central 'ring road' is 8 miles long and many of the island's main highlights are long detours off this; the island is therefore too big for most people to get around on foot, but a **bicycle** could do the job nicely. To hire a bike or **paddleboard**, visit Colonsay Bike and Board Hire (m 07970 673942; w colonsaybikesandboards. co.uk; bikes £20/90 day/week, paddleboards £40/150 day/week, plus a £5 delivery charge).

WHERE TO STAY AND EAT *Map, below*

The Colonsay Estate owns the majority of the island and runs most of its accommodation. You can find extensive self-catering listings and information on **w** colonsay.org.uk/accommodation and **w** colonsayholidays.co.uk/cottages. There are only three places to eat out, two of which are open seasonally.

The Colonsay Hotel (9 rooms) West Scalasaig PA61 7YP; \ 01951 200316; **w** colonsay-hotel. com; ⏰ Feb–mid-Dec. Friendly & well run,

the Colonsay Hotel occupies a proud, historical building with stylish, modern interiors in a delicate colour scheme. Just 500yds west of

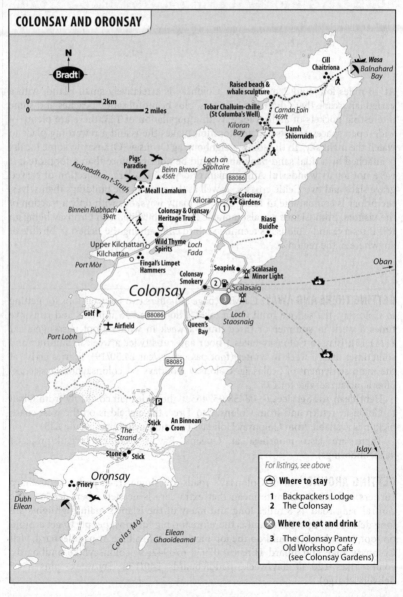

COLONSAY AND ORONSAY

Bradt

N

0 ——— 2km
0 ——— 2 miles

Cill Chaitriona
Wasa
Balnahard Bay

Raised beach & whale sculpture

Tobar Challuim-chille (St Columba's Well)

Carnan Eoin 469ft

Kiloran Bay

Uamh Shiorruidh

Pigs' Paradise

Beinn Bhreac ▲ 456ft

Loch an Sgoltaire

Aoineadh an t-Sruth

Meall Lamalum

B8086

Kiloran

Colonsay Gardens

①

Binnein Riabhach ▲ 394ft

Colonsay & Oronsay Heritage Trust

Riasg Buidhe

Oban

Upper Kilchattan
Kilchattan

Wild Thyme Spirits

Loch Fada

Port Mòr

Fingal's Limpet Hammers

Colonsay Smokery

Seapink

Scalasaig Minor Light

②

Scalasaig

③

Colonsay

Golf

B8086

Airfield

Queen's Bay

Loch Staosnaig

Port Lobh

B8085

P

Stick
An Binnean
Crom

The Strand

Islay

Stone
Stick

Oronsay

Priory

Dubh Eilean

Caolas Mòr

Eilean Ghaoideamal

For listings, see above

⊖ **Where to stay**
1 Backpackers Lodge
2 The Colonsay

⊗ **Where to eat and drink**
3 The Colonsay Pantry
  Old Workshop Café
  (see Colonsay Gardens)

206

APRIL/MAY

Colonsay Book Festival
w colonsaybookfestival.com
A celebration for lovers of literature
& books, this festival has a different
line-up of visiting authors each year.

Colonsay Spring Festival
w colonsayspringfest.com.
A fortnight's celebration of nature, art,
foraging, craft & heritage.

AUGUST

Colonsay International Open
w visitcolonsay.co.uk/about/golf. A
relaxed golf championship open to all.

SEPTEMBER

Ceòl Cholasa w ceolcholasa.co.uk.
Traditional music festival.

OCTOBER

Food & Drink Festival
w visitcolonsay.co.uk/events

the ferry terminal, with sea views out towards Jura. The hotel's restaurant (⏲ mid-Mar–Oct 08.00–21.00 daily, bar until late, reduced hours Feb–mid-Mar & Nov–mid-Dec, closed mid-Dec–Jan; ♿; ££) serves hearty, locally sourced dishes such as Balnahard beef burgers & Colonsay ale-battered haddock. Drinks include 2 local gins & beer from the Colonsay Brewery. Choose between comfortable leather sofas & log fire in the bar or the more formal restaurant with stunning views. ££££
Backpackers Lodge (16 beds) PA61 7YU; ☎ 01951 200312; w colonsayholidays.co.uk/backpackers. An old-fashioned cottage in a very secluded location, 500yds southeast of Kiloran. ££

The Colonsay Pantry Scalasaig PA61 7YW; ☎ 01951 200325; w thecolonsaypantry.co.uk; ⏲ 11.00–15.00 & 18.00–21.00 Mon, Wed & Fri–Sat, extended hours in summer (check online); ♿. Family business open since 1988, serving good food. Clean & attractive interior, though it appears rather uninspiring from the outside. Has small gift shop, serves alcohol & also does take-away. Booking required for evening meals. £–££
Old Workshop Café Colonsay Gardens PA61 7YU; w colonsayholidays.co.uk/gardens-cafe; ⏲ Apr–Sep noon–17.00 Tue & Thu, Oct noon–16.30 Tue & Thu. Friendly service, filled rolls & hot drinks. £

SHOPPING Colonsay has one place to buy groceries (The Island Shop) and a small, but varied selection of other shops.

Arts and crafts

House of Lochar Scalasaig PA61 7YR; ☎ 01951 200232; w colonsay.eu/CSA Bookshop.htm; ⏲ Easter–mid-Oct 10.30–12.30 Mon–Sat. Specialist Scottish publisher & bookshop with a great selection of local titles & wildlife identification books & charts.
Old Waiting Room Gallery Scalasaig PA61 7YT; w theoldwaitingroomgallery.com; ⏲ May–Oct, hours vary; check online. Local arts, crafts & gifts.
Seapink Scalasaig PA61 7YW (400yds north of The Island Shop); m 07850 230000; w seapink.co.uk; ⏲ Apr–Oct 11.00–14.00 Mon, Wed & Fri–Sat (flexible). Hats, yarns, knitting kits & garden twine from The Colonsay Wool Growers, along with other local crafts.

Food and drink

Colonsay Smokery Scalasaig Steading PA61 7YW; m 07493 939876; w colonsaysmokery.com; ⏲ summer 10.30–12.30 Tue–Sat. Traditionally filleted, cured & smoked Atlantic salmon.
The Island Shop Scalasaig PA61 7YW; ☎ 01951 200265; w theislandshop.co.uk; ⏲ summer 09.30–17.30 Mon–Fri, 09.00–13.30 Sat, winter 09.00–12.30 Mon, Wed & Fri–Sat, 12.30–16.00 Tue & Thu. Well-stocked shop with good assortment of loose veg. Pre-order & delivery service available, including fresh fish delivered Sat.
Wild Island Distillery Dunoran, Scalasaig PA61 7YZ; ☎ 01951 200190; w wildislandgin.com; ⏲ 15.00–17.00 Mon, Wed & Fri–Sat. Gin infused with native botanicals.

Wild Thyme Spirits Tigh na Uruisg, Upper Kilchattan PA61 7YR; 01951 200082; w wildthymespirits.com; ⊕ 09.00–23.00

Mon–Sat, 11.00–17.00 Sun. Distillery with a range of 4 gins, 1 liqueur, vodka & a ready-to-drink cocktail.

SPORTS AND ACTIVITIES

Once you arrive on Colonsay, look out for posters around Scalasaig as local events and activities are often advertised this way. There's an 18-hole **golf** course (Colonsay Golf Course, Traigh an Tobair Fhuair/Port Lobh PA61 7YW; w visitcolonsay.co.uk/about/golf; sgl round/membership £10/60; pay fees at the Estate Office, Colonsay House) on the machair, 'golf as it was first played'.

Colonsay might look like a small island on the map, but there's some good **hill-walking** (w visitcolonsay.co.uk/about/walking); while here you can conquer all of the island's 22 'MacPhies', hills over 300ft (91.46m); the whole route is around 20 miles and involves lots of hill-walking over rough ground.

OTHER PRACTICALITIES

Fuel The Island Shop (page 207); community owned; card only.

Health Scalasaig PA61 7YW; 01951 200328. For appointments call 09.00–10.30 ideally, or any time if urgent.

Post office Scalasaig PA61 7YW; ⊕ 09.00–13.00 & 14.00–17.00 Mon & Fri, 09.00–13.00 Tue, Wed & Sat, 10.00–17.00 Thu, 16.00–17.00 Sun. This is also where you should check tides for the crossing to Oronsay.

WHAT TO SEE AND DO

The north Colonsay's main settlement is **Scalasaig**, roughly halfway down the east coast. A small village of around 20 loosely scattered houses and shops, nestled at the base of low hills, this is where the ferry arrives and is home to most of the island's amenities. From here, a ring road of sorts traverses the middle of the island, with a road heading off north to Kiloran Bay, and another south towards Oronsay. North of Scalasaig is **Scalasaig Minor Light** (⊕ 56°04'16.3"N 6°11'02.1"W), a tiny white and red lighthouse that looks a lot like a baby's bottle. Originally built by David Stevenson in 1903, it has recently been moved from nearby Rudha Dubh and restored.

Around 1 mile further north, it's possible to do a 2-mile return walk out to the abandoned village of **Riasg Buidhe**. To start this, look for the track opposite a lay-by, which leads to a recycling centre and a small car park just before it (⊕ 56°04'47.3"N 6°11'15.7"W); walk around the left-hand side of the recycling centre fence, following a faint path and join a track that leads east towards the sea. Pass two ruined buildings on your left and follow the track, which is a little unclear in places, until you come to an abandoned village. The village was deserted in 1922, when the estate provided occupants with new houses nearer Scalasaig. The ruins are a desolate place and a reminder of harder times gone by. There is a terrace of houses that you would assume had been built as a block, but oral history reports that they were built one by one by the inhabitants themselves. Slightly elevated to the south are the remains of an early chapel, although little can now be distinguished. A wonderful 8th-century cross was found here, with Celtic decorations and a face, suggesting a longstanding religious significance to the site. It has now been moved to the gardens of Colonsay House, while a small slab engraved with a cross is now in the National Museum in Edinburgh; unfortunately, nothing is left to indicate its existence.

Surrounded by woodland, just east of the road that heads towards Kiloran Bay, is the centre of Colonsay Estate. Belonging to Colonsay House, a private residence, **Colonsay Gardens** (⊕ Apr–Sep noon–17.00 Tue & Thu, Oct noon–14.30 Tue & Thu; adult/child £3/1) has several historical gems among its lawns, mature trees and rose gardens; the previously mentioned **Riasg Buidhe Cross**, the lens from Rubh a Mhail Lighthouse on Islay (built in 1874), an old millstone and other objects of interest are hidden around the grounds.

Walk: Kiloran Bay to Balnahard Bay

Distance: 7 miles; time: 4–5 hours; start/end: Kiloran Bay; OS Explorer map: 354 Colonsay & Oronsay

This is a very rewarding walk with two stunning beaches, interesting archaeological sites and a varied coastline.

Begin by either walking north along the yellow sands of Kiloran Bay or following sheep tracks through the dunes. At the end of the beach there are the remains of a dead whale, likely to be there in some state for the next few years at least. It's possible to explore the caves at the northern end of the bay with a torch; **Uamh Shiorruidh** (✪ 56°06'33"N 6°10'38"W) is deep and L-shaped.

From here, head back to the beach and up on to the grass, heading inland at the base of the cliffs until you reach a solid track; turn left on to it and begin to climb the hill.

About 200yds up this track you might notice a tooth-shaped rock (which has been placed here) on your right. On the opposite side of the track, around 40yds west and 5yds south, is **Tobar Chaluim Chille** or St Columba's Well (✪ 56°06'34"N 6°10'33"W). Covered with a slab of rock, this stone-walled spring is initially difficult to spot as you walk down towards it, but quite unmistakable once found. Ferns grow from the cracks between rocks and layers of moss and lichen give a little indication to its age. The well is said to have been blessed with healing properties by St Columba himself.

Continue along the track for around another mile, passing a raised beach with pebbles that have been moved into the shape of an enormous whale – an art installation started by Julian Meredith – as the track bends around to the right, heading east past the impressive buildings at Balnahard Farm. This end of the island is a good place to spot wild goats (not to be confused with the Hebridean black sheep that are farmed here).

Eventually you will come to a small barn on your left and the end of the proper track. Bearing slightly left, head down through the dunes to **Balnahard Bay**. The severely rotten and rusted shipwreck here is what remains of the steamship *Wasa*, which caught fire off Colonsay in May 1920. It is now in two parts and only partially visible, poking out from the sand.

Once you have enjoyed the beach, head back to the barn; on its far side, follow a fence across to the right. In an enclosed field, where there is a small gate for access, are the remains of **Cill Chaitriona**, a chapel standing within its burial ground (✪ 56°07'19.0"N 6°09'00.1"W), with a hollowed stone font and much-weathered early cross in the opposite corner to the gate.

From the ruined chapel, the easiest way back to Kiloran Bay is to return to the track; that said, now you will have your bearings, it is much more exciting to follow the high ground above the coast. There are wonderful views of the craggy coastline and, on a clear day, across to Mull in the north.

The west coast On the western side of the 'ring road', just before Kilchattan Primary School, is a white building with a grey slate roof that used to be the Baptist church and is now the **Colonsay and Oransay Heritage Trust** (w spanglefish. com/colonsayandoransayheritagetrust; ⊕ daily; donation requested). This small museum has an eclectic mix of locally relevant exhibits and information, including the old telephone exchange, useful maps of archaeological sites, photos of what life was once like, and a few whale bones.

Walk: Pigs' Paradise and the seabird cliffs ☀

Distance: 5 miles; time: 3 hours; start/end: Upper Kilchattan; OS Explorer map: 354 Colonsay & Oronsay

This walk visits the most spectacular stretch of coastline on Colonsay – in fact, it's among the most impressive in the entire Inner Hebrides. Note, though, that it is very exposed and can be treacherous in bad weather.

In Upper Kilchattan, take the turning marked towards 'Alister Annie's' and go up the track, passing a white house, a stone house and a green barn on your left.

Continue straight on, passing through a gate, until you are nearly at Gortean House (a white house with a red roof). Go around the house to the left and then carry on straight along grassy paths. After crossing over a stile, continue in the same direction until you reach the cliffs over the sea. There is already a spectacular view, but it is only a taste of what's to come.

Turn right and walk along the clifftops with the sea on your left. You can go along narrow grassy paths until you reach a channel, at Aoineadh an t-Sruth, down to a wide platform of grass on a lower level. The route runs underneath one wall of cliffs with another set of cliffs below, bringing you closer to guillemot nesting sites above the sea.

You can walk northeast at this lower level for about 400yds before an easy way back to the top presents itself; you will need to clamber back up to the higher clifftops when the way runs out.

Shortly afterwards it's possible to get down closer to the sea again, past a memorial cairn and on to a large, grassy promontory called **Meall Lamalum** that is thought to have been a fort (✪ 56°05'34"N 6°14'01"W). This naturally defensive position has tremendous views, allowing you to look back along the coastline to see layer upon layer of towering cliffs disappearing into the distance. Waves crash against the exposed rocks below and razorbills, shags, guillemots, gulls and fulmars fish in the surrounding waters.

Retracing your steps but up to the clifftops again you can walk about 500yds further to **Pigs' Paradise**, between the hill Beinn Bhreac and the small cove at Port Bán (✪ 56°05'36"N 6°13'40"W); a sheltered area of grass surrounded by high cliffs, this is where pigs are rumoured to have been kept. The easiest way to return is along the higher coast path.

Back on the main road in Kilchattan, the standing stones known as **Fingal's Limpet Hammers** are on the left-hand side in a field beneath a grey house. Presumably this is yet another reference to the famous giant.

ORONSAY

GETTING THERE AND AWAY The crossing to Oronsay (also known as Oransay, or Orasaigh in Gaelic) can only be attempted when tide times are favourable; these are displayed with an explanation in the post office (page 208) and Colonsay Hotel (page 206), where you should also ask for advice before crossing. As the natural causeway is only exposed for a limited amount of time, which changes every day, it is sometimes not possible to cross at all. The best times to visit Oronsay are the two days following full moon and new moon; it's worth checking tide times in advance online (w tides.willyweather.co.uk: search for 'Colonsay – Eilean Olmsa' and then deduct 10 minutes for local conditions).

As the Strand, the section of muddy sand between both islands, is covered in broken shells in some places, you might prefer to take wellies or water shoes, rather than cross in bare feet. In order to make the most of the time available, cross as the tide is still receding, while the water is ankle deep; some standing water usually remains over the way, even at low tide.

If you have a car, park at the Strand car park, at the end of the road that leads south; from the car park it is a 5-mile return walk to the priory.

Be sure to allow plenty of time to return back to Colonsay, rather than risk being stranded.

WHAT TO SEE AND DO Visible to the southeast from the car park is a curiously jutting rock called **An Binnean Crom** (the crooked pinnacle), which is also known as Hangman's Rock. Walking along the shoreline with the sea and Oronsay on your right-hand side, you will begin to see the hole in An Binnean Crom, which was supposedly used to loop a rope through for executions in the 17th century.

An Binnean Crom is directly inland from a stick on the shoreline that lines up with another stick and an upright stone (✪ 56°01'42.4"N 6°13'42.1"W) on Oronsay, marking the route across to the smaller island. **The Strand** is a good place to see twite, lesser redpoll, meadow pipit, linnet, stonechat and many other exciting species of bird. As you walk across, scan the seabed for crabs, anemones, cockles and other sea creatures.

Once you reach Oronsay, an obvious track leads southwest and then south for about 1½ miles to the ruined **priory**. According to tradition, the site was originally a Celtic monastery founded by St Columba in 563 and the current Augustinian building was later refounded by John, Lord of the Isles in the 14th century. The priory first appears on record in 1353 and in the early 16th century it was home to an important school of monumental sculpture. There are two Celtic crosses outside: the Great Oronsay Cross from around 1510 with a crucifix and interlacing foliage, and a second, smaller cross that is more weathered, with a carving in relief of the Virgin Mary. Inside the prior's house, a building to the northwest of the priory, is a wonderful collection of carved grave slabs: swords, priests, stags, knights, ships and intricate patterns are all well preserved.

From the priory, if the tide times allow, linger to enjoy the island's status as an **RSPB reserve**: you can return briefly along the track you came in on, before heading south through a field full of geese, lapwings or (usually invisible) corncrakes depending on the season, towards what appears at a distance to be a standing stone, but is actually a modern memorial. From here you can head down to a beautiful **sandy beach**. Look out for golden and ringed plovers, dunlin and oystercatchers.

11

Islay (Ìle)

With a gentle landscape and a magical quality felt by many, Islay holds a special place in the hearts of locals, known as Ìleachs, and repeat visitors alike. Aside from the whisky (see opposite), which is world-renowned, most visitors come to Islay for its beautiful, empty beaches and the wildlife. The island has plentiful grey and common seals; red, roe and fallow deer; ten pairs of golden eagles; an otter for every mile of coastline; and incredible numbers of wintering geese (over 30,000 barnacle and 4,000 Greenland white-fronted). With 41 of Scotland's 46 pairs, Islay is also one of the only places you have a chance of seeing red-legged choughs.

Rich in archaeology, Islay also has probably the most attractive collection of lighthouses in the region, some of which are truly remote, but with others easily viewed from the main roads. Although Islay's population of around 3,200 is one of the Inner Hebrides' largest, drivers still wave to each other in passing and it's not unusual to come across two cars stopped in the middle of the road with their windows open for a chat.

HISTORY

At Port Na Seilich, on Islay's east coast, radiocarbon dating puts evidence of human activity as among the earliest known in western Scotland: sometime between 9000BC and 7700BC. This evidence would have been left by Ice Age hunter-gatherers and, as the temperature began to rise and conditions became a little more favourable, people began to settle here; there are Mesolithic kitchen middens dating on the island from around 7000BC. From Neolithic times there were more permanent settlements. At least eight roundhouses from the late 2nd millennium BC have been found at An Sithean (page 233), and there are various other burial cairns and standing stones from the Neolithic and Bronze ages including an excavated Neolithic chambered cairn between the Port Mòr Centre building (page 231) and the sea. There is a wealth of forts, dùns and crannogs dating from the Iron Age.

From the time we have written records, about halfway through the 1st millennium AD, up until the turn of the 18th century, Islay is portrayed as both prominent and bloody. Written history gives us the names of lairds and leaders, but not much detail about the ordinary inhabitants. Luckily, on Islay, there are strong folk traditions and, in the past few decades, these have begun to be recorded.

From the 6th century, during the time of Dál Riata, Islay was ruled by the family group of Cenél nÓengusa. According to the *Senchus fer n-Alban* (*The History of the Men of Scotland*), the island saw various battles including one in 627 between Uí Chóelbad (a branch of the Ulster kingdom Dál nAraidi) and an army of Dál Riata, which resulted in the death of the Irish king's son.

Dál Riata's dominion was eventually demolished by the Vikings, who began their raids as early as the end of the 8th century. From the island's Norse place names

Irish monks are probably responsible for first introducing the distilling process to Islay. The island is very rich in peat, ancient layers of partially decayed vegetation that forms in bogs and contains a lot of energy. Peatland is naturally a very efficient carbon sink, locking carbon dioxide out of the air in the same manner as a fossil fuel, and has been burned on Islay for many generations. In remote locations you will notice that the water runs an orangey brown; this is also due to the peat. During whisky making, peat fires are used to dry malted barley, leaving a distinctive flavour. The peaty taste of whisky is calculated in ppm of phenol: Scottish whiskies generally have up to 30ppm; the Islay whiskies are often more than 50ppm.

In 1644, when the new Excise Act levied a tax on whisky, the operation went underground and illicit stills were hidden in remote corners of the island, in hidden coves and secret caves. The first official, recorded distillery was Bowmore, founded in 1779.

DISTILLERIES AND TOURS Today there are ten working distilleries on Islay, most of which are grand, whitewashed buildings with slate roofs, distinctive pointed pagoda chimneys and their names painted neatly in enormous black letters, allowing them to be identified from out at sea.

On the northeast are **Bunnahabhain** (page 224), **Ardnahoe** (page 223) and **Caol Ila** (page 223); **Bowmore** is central (page 222); **Bruichladdich** (page 232) and **Kilchoman** (page 234) are in the western Rhinns; and **Laphroaig**, **Lagavulin** and **Ardbeg** (all page 227) are along the southeast coast. All of these distilleries run tours and tastings ranging from £10 for a quick look around (followed by a dram, of course) to a couple of hundred pounds, where tutored tasting of some of the older and rarer expressions is the focal point. Closed since 1983, **Port Ellen** (w malts.com/en-row/brands/port-ellen) has been restored and extended by Diageo, one of the world's largest alcoholic drink producers – and the same company responsible for closing it in the 1980s – who finally opened the site in April 2024. At the time of writing, visits were restricted to irregularly scheduled, free open days and high-end tours starting at £200. Additionally, several new distilleries are beginning to spring up around the island, causing local debate about sustainability from both environmental and social perspectives.

In addition to whisky, there is also **Islay Rum** (page 226), **Islay Gin** (page 222) and **The Botanist** Islay dry gin (page 232).

You can also stock up on Islay whisky and other local spirits from Bowmore's Islay Whisky Shop (page 221).

– such as Nerabus (meaning 'nether' or 'lower farm') and Port Askaig ('ash tree harbour') – it's evident that, after the initial period of conquest, many of the Norse who settled here were not Vikings, but farmers happy to be left in peace. One of the most significant leaders of the Norse Kingdom of the Isles, Godred Crovan, is associated with Islay and is thought to have died of pestilence (the plague) on the island in 1095. According to folklore, the standing stone at Carragh Bhan near Kintra Farm marks his grave.

In 1156, there was a battle off the coast of Islay between Godred Olafsson, the unpopular grandson of Godred Crovan, and Somerled. Though this 'Battle of

ISLAY

N

0   5km
0   5 miles

Bradt!

Colonsay, Oban

Jura

Loch an Aircill

Beinn an Oir 2,575ft ▲
Beinn a' Chaolais 2,405ft ▲

Loch a' Chnuic Bhric

Camas An Staca

Claig Castle

Cabrach

A846

Feolin

Sound of Islay

An Cladach

Rhuvaal Lighthouse

Port Askaig

Bunnahabhain Distillery

Ardnahoe Distillery

Caol Ila Distillery

Persabus Pottery

Kells

Finlaggan

Loch Ballygrant

Loch Smigeadail

Standing stone

Loch Finlaggan

Ballygrant

Gortantaoid

Loch Cam

Esknish

A846

Islay Woollen Mill

Killinallan

Islay House Square

Bridgend

(2)   (11)

(12)

Ardnave Point

Nave Island

Ardnave Loch

Loch Gruinart

Craigens Farm

(13)

Blackrock

B8017

Uiskentuie

A847

Inndaal

Kilnave Chapel

(6)

Loch Gruinart RSPB Reserve

Loch Gruinart RSPB visitor centre

B8017

Culbuie

An Sithean

Conisby

Bruichladdich

Sanaigmore

B8018

Loch Gorm

Rhinns

Ballinaby

Kilchoman Distillery

Kilchoman

Saligo Bay

Machir Bay

Kilchiaran Chapel

214

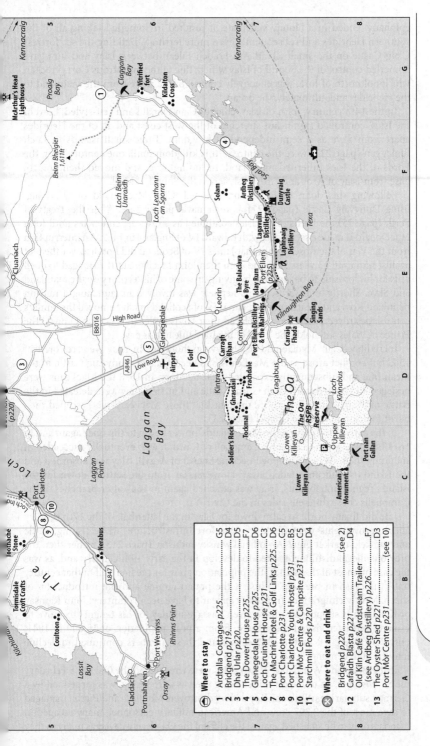

Where to stay

1	Ardtalla Cottages p225	G5
2	Bridgend p219	D4
3	Dha Urlar p220	D5
4	The Dower House p225	F7
5	Glenegedale House p225	D6
6	Loch Gruinart House p231	C3
7	The Machrie Hotel & Golf Links p225	D6
8	Port Charlotte p231	C5
9	Port Charlotte Youth Hostel p231	B5
10	Port Mòr Centre & Campsite p231	C5
11	Starchmill Pods p220	D4

Where to eat and drink

	Bridgend p220	(see 2)
12	Cafaidh Blasta p221	D4
	Old Kiln Café & Ardstream Trailer	
	(see Ardbeg Distillery) p226	F7
13	The Oyster Shed p221	D3
	Port Mòr Centre p231	(see 10)

215

epiphany' ended in a bloody stalemate, it resulted in Somerled taking all of the southern Hebrides and subsequently even more territory. Building the sea fortress Claig Castle on the small island Am Fraoch Eilean between Islay and Jura gave Somerled control of the Sound of Islay which, due to the monstrous Corryvreckan whirlpool north of Jura, was effectively control of the route from the mainland to the Hebrides and, ultimately, the ocean.

In the 14th century, John of Islay, chief of Clan Donald and self-styled 'Lord of the Isles', controlled significant stretches of the west coast and all of the Hebrides apart from Skye as a semi-independent kingdom. Three small islands in Loch Finlaggan (page 223) were the centre of this kingdom until, one century later, the Lords of the Isles inherited more land, including Skye, and moved their control base from Islay of Aros and Ardtonish across the Sound of Mull.

Following this, John of Islay's son founded 'Clan MacDonald of Dunyvaig', using Dunyvaig Castle (page 227) as their naval power base. After the Treaty of Perth (page 15) the Lords of the Isles continued as crown dependencies until John MacDonald II made a secret deal with Edward IV of England in 1462. An interruption from the War of the Roses meant that James IV of Scotland did not discover the plot against him until 13 years later and even then John MacDonald II managed to quell calls for his lordship to be forfeited by giving up some of his territory on the mainland and Skye. Shortly afterwards, John's nephew was involved in launching a raid on mainland Ross and the exasperated James IV of Scotland finally removed the family's control, destroyed Finlaggan and placed their lands under the Scottish Crown. The Prince of Wales still holds the 'Lord of the Isles' title to this day.

Incredibly, Clan MacDonald of Dunyvaig's holdings in Islay were restored in 1545 but conflict arose as the MacLeans had been granted Dunyvaig Castle in the meantime and subsequently expanded their territory. In 1578 the MacLeans were besieged and ousted from Loch Gorm Castle and in 1598 they were defeated in the Battle of Traigh Ghruinneart; it's thought that those MacLeans who escaped then burnt to death in Kilnave Chapel (page 233).

In the early 17th century, the MacDonalds' power began to slip once again and in 1614 Islay was given to Sir John Campbell of Cawdor, who eventually succeeded in subduing them. When Campbell became Sheriff of Argyll, Islay was absorbed and the island's significance faded away. However, far from life settling down for the island's regular inhabitants, Islay was attached again in 1647 after branches of the Campbells chose different sides in the Civil War.

Life did finally begin to calm down for Islay in the latter half of the 17th century and improvements were made in transport infrastructure, while fishing, cattle and the kelp market grew. An official whisky industry (page 213), rather than the previous illegal distilling, started to develop in the early 19th century and, as was the case on most of the islands, the population grew for the first half of that century until the crash in the kelp industry, the potato famine and the introduction of sheep. Mostly emigrations from Islay appear to have been voluntary; John Ramsay of Kildalton is supposed to have given passage money for his tenants to move to Canada and later visited them there. From a peak population of 15,000 in 1841, only 7,375 were left by the 1891 census and these numbers continued to decline into the 20th century.

In 1918, during World War I, two ships were wrecked off the Oa. On 5 February the SS *Tuscania*, an old luxury liner being used as a troopship, was torpedoed by a German submarine. While the Royal Navy destroyers *Mosquito* and *Pigeon* managed to save most of the 2,397 crew and American military personnel, many escaped in lifeboats only to be smashed against the cliffs of the Oa. Ìleachs saved as many as they

MAY
Fèis Ìle/Islay Festival of Music & Malt w feisile.co.uk. Now intrinsically linked to whisky, Islay's fèis is the biggest in the Inner Hebrides. As well as the traditional cultural events, each distillery hosts an open day & visitors come from across the world to join the festivities. The island's accommodation gets booked-up well in advance.

JULY
Cantilena Festival w cantilenafestival.co.uk. A week of chamber music in various venues across Islay.

JULY/AUGUST
Islay Half Marathon w islayhalfmarathon.co.uk

AUGUST
Islay Show Bridgend; w islayshow. co.uk. Agricultural Show.

SEPTEMBER
Islay Book Festival w islaybookfestival.co.uk. Author talks, poetry, performances & workshops.

Islay Jazz Festival w islayjazzfestival.co.uk. Hosted by Lagavulin Distillery (page 227), this small festival sells out quickly, with visitors coming to Islay especially to attend performances from a mix of creative jazz & blues musicians.

NOVEMBER
Islay Sessions w frasershawtrust. com. Small folk festival.

could, but still 126 bodies washed up on Islay's beaches and around 40 more were lost at sea. The people of Islay did their best to gather and identify the bodies, sewing an American flag from a picture in an encyclopaedia to honour the dead.

On 6 October, disaster struck again. The troopship HMS *Otranto* collided with HMS *Kashmir* in a storm off the Oa and, despite another rescue attempt and hundreds of American soldiers being saved, 431 lives were still lost and, again, washed up on the shore. Sergeant Malcolm MacNeill recorded the details of the dead bodies and his notebook is preserved in the Museum of Islay Life (page 232). The huge monument on the Oa was erected by the American Red Cross to remember these lives lost.

During World War II, the RAF built an airfield that is now used for civilian planes, as well as using Bowmore and Loch Indaal as a base for its flying boats. Since the war ended, agriculture, fishing and whisky have remained Islay's largest industries, with tourism growing over recent years. Once the political centre of the region, life now continues on a quieter level. If present-day Islay is the centre of anything, it is whisky distilling. Alongside other industries, the seemingly ever-growing number of Islay distilleries keeps unemployment to a bare minimum, but a shortage of accommodation is problematic for young people wanting to establish themselves independently, as well as for anyone looking to move within or to the island.

GETTING THERE AND AWAY

BY FERRY CalMac (page 30; foot passengers/car £7.25/36.70) sails from Kennacraig on the mainland to Port Askaig [214 F3] in the northeast or Port Ellen [215 E7] in the south around five times daily in summer and one to five times daily in winter. The journey takes 2 to 3 hours and can be cancelled/redirected in high wind. In summer you can travel between Islay and Colonsay or Oban once or twice a week or just to Colonsay once a week in winter. Argyll and Bute Council (page 237) also run a car and passenger ferry from Port Askaig on Islay to Feolin on Jura.

MOORINGS There are moorings at Port Askaig Pier (Argyll & Bute Council; 01586 552552; w argyll-bute.gov.uk/roads-and-travel/marine-services/port-askaig-pier) and Port Ellen Harbour Association [map, page 225] (44 Frederick Cres, Port Ellen; m 07464 151200; w portellenmarina.co.uk).

BY AIR Loganair (w loganair.co.uk) fly twice daily between Glasgow and Islay Airport [215 D6] (PA42 7AS; 01496 302361; w hial.co.uk/islay-airport). The flight takes about 40 minutes and can be cancelled due to poor visibility.

GETTING AROUND

Islay is the third biggest island in the Inner Hebrides but, as the island's main roads take a more direct route and its main settlements are closer together, travelling around is significantly quicker than on either Skye or Mull. Taking a car is not essential as the **bus** network connects all of Islay's larger villages and ports: Argyll and Bute Council/Islay Coaches (01496 840273; w argyll-bute.gov.uk/isle-islay-portnahavenport-askaig-bowmore-port-ellen-ardbeg) runs the 450/451 service from Portnahaven/Port Askaig to Bowmore, Port Ellen and Ardbeg several times a day. Or you can **hire a car** locally: Islay Car Hire (01496 810544; w islaycarhire.com) supplies cars to the airport and ferry terminals.

Two different types of **beach wheelchairs** are available to borrow for free (donations welcome) from Sidekick (e hello@sidekickcharity.org; f).

TAXIS

Bodach Islay Taxis m 07513 066029; w bodachtaxis.com
Bruichladdich Taxis m 07899 942673; w bruichladdichtaxis.weebly.com
Carol's Cabs m 07775 782155; w carols-cabs.co.uk
Islay Taxis 01496 850170; w islaytaxis.com

Jim's Islay Taxi m 07967 505991; w jims-islay-taxi.co.uk
Lamb Taxi m 07846 055399; w lambtaxi-islay.co.uk
McIntyre Private Hire m 07359 489038; w mcintyreprivatehireislay.co.uk

BY BIKE While the island is gently hilly, cycling is an unhurried way to see Islay, giving you access to more remote attractions and, unless you hit the ferry traffic, roads remain quiet enough to make it enjoyable. You can hire a bike from:

Islay Bike Hire [map, page 220] 51A Jamieson Street, Bowmore PA43 7HL; m 07376 351438; w islay-bikehire.co.uk; bikes/e-bikes £25/35 a day; delivery & collection available

Islay E-Wheels [map, page 225] Rear car park of No 1 Charlotte Street Hotel, Port Ellen PA42 7DF; m 07497 090716; w islayewheels.co.uk; bikes/e-bikes/premium e-bikes (with larger motor) £25/30/40 a day; delivery & collection available

SPORTS AND ACTIVITIES

The Machrie **golf** course [215 D6] (PA42 7AN; 01496 302310; w themachrie.com) is an 18-hole links course; originally designed in 1891, it has had a £40 million renovation and now has every facility you might desire. For other **outdoor activities and wildlife watching**, try:

Fatbike Tours m 07973 725456;
w kayakwildislay.co.uk/fatbike-page. Variety of
fatbike routes to choose from for cyclists of all
abilities, including riding along the beach.
Islay Outdoors Bruichladdich PA49 7UN;
℡ 01496 850643; w islayoutdoors.com. Donald
James (DJ) MacPhee, previously a gamekeeper on
the island, offers a range of guided wildlife walks,

fishing & foraging trips, bookable for 1–4 people &
adapted to suit the group's interests & abilities.
Islay Sea Adventures Lagavulin PA42 7DX;
℡ 01496 300129; w islay-sea-adventures.co.uk. Gus
Newman has several small motorboats & offers tours
for coastal sightseeing, wildlife watching, fishing
& visits to Corryvreckan. Weather permitting, trips
leave from Port Ellen Harbour every day in summer.

BOWMORE, BRIDGEND AND THE NORTHEAST

Bowmore, Islay's capital, is surprisingly small. Its most striking features are the
harbour and Kilarrow Church, which surveys the village from the top of the hill.
Built in 1767, the building is circular – so the devil couldn't find corners to lurk in
– and unique within the region. There are small villages at Bridgend, the junction
between west, northeast and south; Ballygrant; Keills and at the ferry terminal
at Port Askaig. The far north is wild, with plentiful hiking and wildlife, but most
people go to this part of Islay to visit Finlaggan, the ruined centre of the Lordship
of the Isles, or one of the distilleries.

For **tourist information**, visit Bowmore iCentre (The Square, Bowmore PA43 7JP;
℡ 01496 305165; ⊕ Apr–Oct 09.30–17.00). Staff are friendly and helpful; there's also
a small on-site shop.

WHERE TO STAY Though there are plenty of rather luxurious places to stay, this
part of Islay is generally lacking in budget accommodation; look to the Rhinns
(page 230) for more affordable options.

The Lochside Hotel [map, page 220] (12
rooms) 20 Shore Street, Bowmore PA43 7LB;
℡ 01496 810244; w lochsidehotel.co.uk.
Traditional Scottish interiors & great harbour
views. **£££££**
The Bowmore House [map, page 220] (5
rooms) Shore St, Bowmore; ℡ 01496 810324;
w thebowmorehouse.co.uk. Set in an old bank

building from 1898, this friendly B&B has large,
comfortable rooms, 4 of which have sea views.
Complimentary dram on arrival or with b/fast if
you're game. **££££**
Bridgend Hotel [214 D4] (11 rooms) Bridgend
PA44 7PQ; ℡ 01496 810212; w bridgend-
hotel.com. Located in the centre of the island,
Bridgend Hotel has bright, airy bedrooms, some

ESTATES AND DEER STALKING

On the east side of Islay, the majority of the interior is split into several
large estates. For the purposes of visitors, the estates offer self-catering
accommodation, fishing permits and deer stalking on their lands. Deer
stalking is traditional on Islay and remains part of the economy, with people
visiting the island especially to take part.

Stalking generally takes place between July and February, during which
time walkers should follow signs giving specific instructions and phone
numbers, which should be attached to boundary gates on shooting days.

Some of the larger estates on Islay are: Ardtalla (w ardtallacottages.co.uk),
Callumkill (w callumkill.com), Dunlossit (℡ 01496 840232; w dunlossitestate.
com), Islay Estates (℡ 01496 810221; w islayestates.com) and Laggan (℡ 01496
810235; w lagganestate.com).

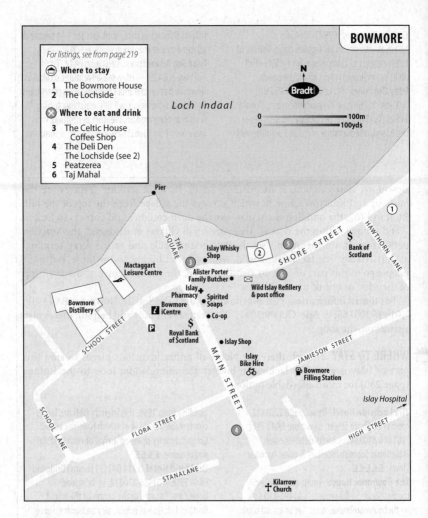

For listings, see from page 219

Where to stay
1 The Bowmore House
2 The Lochside

Where to eat and drink
3 The Celtic House
   Coffee Shop
4 The Deli Den
   The Lochside (see 2)
5 Peatzerea
6 Taj Mahal

with garden views, others overlooking the tiny village of Bridgend itself, which is surrounded by woodland. **££££**

Dha Urlar [215 D5] (4 rooms) Cruach PA43 7JQ; 01496 810531; w dha-urlar-bed-&-b/fast. co.uk. In a peaceful location, 1 mile southwest of Bowmore, this welcoming B&B is surrounded by moorland with views of the Paps of Jura. Cosy guest lounge with wood burner. **£££**

Starchmill Pods [214 D4] (2 pods) High Rd, near Bridgend PA43 7LW; m 07494 173966; w starchmillpods.co.uk. An affordable self-catering option in a peaceful location off the 'High Rd' (B8016), which you'll need a car or bicycle to reach. 1 pod sleeps 4 & the other 6. Min 2-night stay. **££**

WHERE TO EAT AND DRINK

Bridgend Hotel [214 D4] Same contact details as the hotel (page 219); ⏰ daily, b/fast 07.00–10.00, lunch 11.00–14.00, dinner/take-away 17.00–21.00; ♿. An Ìleach favourite for special occasions. Good food with a focus on local produce,

much of which comes from Islay Estates, who own the hotel. **££**

The Lochside Hotel [map, above] Same contact details as the hotel (page 219); ⏰ 12.30–15.00 & 17.00–20.30 daily. Dine in the conservatory with views over Bowmore Pier, fishing boats & Loch Indaal. Seafood caught by local fishermen including langoustine & scallops. ££

Peatzerea [map, opposite] 22 Shore St, Bowmore PA43 7LB; 01496 810810; w peatzeria.com; noon–22.00 daily; . Smart, modern pizza restaurant with consistently friendly staff. £–££

Cafaidh Blasta [214 D4] Islay Gaelic Centre, PA43 7LN; 01496 810818; w islaygaeliccentre. co.uk/cafe; Apr–Dec 10.00–16.00 daily; . Simple, good-value sandwiches & baked potatoes (11.30–15.00), fresh cakes & coffee. Friendly service. £

The Celtic House Coffee Shop [map, opposite] Shore St PA43 7LD; 01496 810304; w theceltichouse.co.uk; 10.00–16.30 Mon– Sat. Quiet, friendly café, upstairs from the book & gift shop (see below). £

The Deli Den [map, opposite] Top of Main Street, Bowmore PA43 7JH; 01496 305442; 08.15–16.00 Mon–Fri, 08.15–20.00 Sat. Little yellow take-away selling choose-your-own-filling sandwiches & hot food with chips. £

✳ **The Oyster Shed** [214 D3] Bunanuilt, Gruinart PA44 7PW; 01496 850256; Islay Oysters; 10.00–16.00 Thu–Sat (last orders 15.00). The long drive out to this eatery is well worth the effort. It's spectacularly situated on the eastern shore of Loch Gruinart, where the oysters themselves have been grown as a farm diversification by the Archibald family since 1987. If you like them natural, that's an option with lemon, but deep-fried they're less of an acquired taste. Also on the menu are focaccia sandwiches, with fillings such as hand-picked Islay crab with seaweed butter, saffron mayo, lettuce & capers, & options for vegetarians/vegans. £

Taj Mahal [map, opposite] Shore Street, Bowmore PA43 7LB; 01496 810033; ; noon–14.00 & 16.30–22.00 daily. Bangladeshi & Indian food: the take-away my husband & I get when we've had a particularly long week. I usually have the chef's special Badami, but spicier options are available. £

SHOPPING There are a few great independent options for stocking up on either groceries or high-quality ingredients for special occasions. In addition to the shops listed, look out for fresh free-range eggs along the High Road between Port Ellen and Bowmore, and other small pop-up stalls selling local produce.

Arts and crafts

The Celtic House See above; 09.30–17.00. Bookshop, quality gifts & clothing.

Islay Shop [map, opposite] 47 Main St, Bowmore PA43 7JJ; 01496 810424; w theislayshop. com; 09.30–17.00 Mon–Sat. An 'everything else' shop with stock ranging from make-up to lunch boxes.

Islay Woollen Mill [214 E4] Bridgend; 01496 810563; w islaywoollenmill.co.uk; 09.00– 16.30 Mon–Fri, 10.00–16.00 Sat. Tweed designed & woven in-house. Their cloth designs have been used in films such as *Braveheart* & *Forrest Gump*.

Persabus Pottery [214 F3] PA46 7RB; 01496 840243; w persabuspottery.com; noon–16.00 Tue–Fri, noon–15.00 Sat. Landscape, seascapes & floral design pottery.

Spirited Soaps [map, opposite] Main St, Bowmore PA43 7HZ; 01496 810938; w spiritedsoaps.com; 10.00–16.00 Mon–Sat. Handmade transparent whisky soaps & toiletries using natural ingredients.

Food and drink

Alister Porter Family Butcher [map, opposite] Shore St, Bowmore PA43 7LB; 01496 810365; A.S. Porter Family Butcher; 08.00–13.30 & 14.15–17.00 Tue–Sat. Quality meat.

Bridgend Shop Bridgend PA44 7PQ; 01496 810335; ; 09.00–18.00 Mon–Fri, 09.00– 17.00 Sat. Grocery shop, much bigger than you might expect. Loose fruit & veg.

Co-op [map, opposite] Main St, Bowmore PA43 7JJ; 01496 810201; 07.00–22.00 daily; . Biggest grocery store on the island.

Islay Whisky Shop [map, opposite] Shore St, Bowmore PA43 7LB; 01496 810684; w islaywhiskyshop.com; 09.00–17.30 Mon– Sat. Groceries & whisky.

Jean's Fresh Fish Jamieson St, Bowmore PA43 7HL; m 07715 036041; 08.30–14.30 Fri. Mobile fish van that visits Bowmore.

Wild Islay Refillery [map, opposite] Shore St, Bowmore PA43 7LB; 09.00–17.00 Mon–Fri, 09.00–12.30 Sat. Post office that doubles as a zero-waste refill food shop.

OTHER PRACTICALITIES

Banks Bank of Scotland (Shore St, Bowmore PA43 7LB; 03457 213141; ⊕ 09.30–12.30 & 13.00–15.00 Mon–Fri); Royal Bank of Scotland (Main St, Bowmore PA43 7JJ; 01496 810555; ⊕ 09.30–14.30 Mon–Tue & Thu–Fri, 10.00–14.30 Wed)

Fuel Bowmore Filling Station, Jamieson St, Bowmore PA43 7HP (01496 810348; ⊕ 08.00–17.00 Mon–Fri, 08.30–16.00 Sat, 11.40–15.30 Sun); Port Askaig Pump Stores, Port Askaig PA46 7RD (ask at hotel if unattended)

Health Islay Hospital (Gortonvogie Rd, Bowmore PA43 7JD; 01496 301000; includes minor injuries

unit); Islay Pharmacy (42 Main St, Bowmore PA43 7JJ; 01496 301591; w islaypharmacy.co.uk; ⊕ 09.00–18.00 Mon & Wed–Fri, 09.00–13.00 Tue & Sat)

Laundry Mactaggart Leisure Centre (see opposite); Islay Laundry Services (Islay House Square, Bridgend; m 07919 417258; ⊕ 09.30–12.30 Mon–Tue & Thu–Fri)

Post offices Wild Islay Refillery, Shore St, Bowmore PA43 7JH (⊕ 09.00–17.00 Mon–Fri, 09.00–12.30 Sat); Bridgend PA44 7PQ (⊕ 09.00–noon 13.00–15.00 Mon–Tue, 10.00–noon 13.00–15.00 Wed & Fri, 09.00–13.00 Thu)

WHAT TO SEE AND DO

Bowmore A simple Bowmore pleasure is strolling down to the end of the **pier**. This gives you an unusual perspective of the village and across Loch Indaal; there is occasionally a seal in the water and usually some small fishing boats.

You can also visit **Bowmore Distillery** (School St PA43 7JS; 01496 810441; w bowmore.com; ⊕ 10.00–17.00 Mon & Fri, 09.30–17.00 Tue–Thu & Sat; tours & tastings £22–80;), the oldest distillery on Islay, established in 1779 and home to the world's oldest whisky maturation warehouse. The distillery's bar, **Bowmore Whisky Tasting Bar** (⊕11.00–16.30 Tue–Sat) is the perfect place to enjoy a special dram, with its fantastic view across Loch Indaal.

Bridgend and around Heading along the coast northeast, you have lovely views over **Loch Indaal** and, in winter, many geese, before shortly reaching **Bridgend** [214 D4]. While the village is easily bypassed completely, there is a short, circular walk around pretty **Bridgend Woods** from the shop. It goes alongside the road via Nancy's Path in the direction of Bowmore for about 500yds, before turning off right into the mature woodland. You can follow the grassy track through tall trees down to the River Sorn, where you can either go left towards the loch or walk upstream back to

ISLAY HOUSE SQUARE

An indicated turning off the A846, just 100yds north of Bridgend, leads to Islay House Square [214 D4]. First established by Walter Campbell in the 1790s, this large, open square is surrounded by the buildings that once housed servants working at nearby Islay House and provided space for their workshops. Today it has an interesting collection of local businesses, including **Islay Studios Gallery** (01496 810010; w islaystudios.co.uk; ⊕ Mar–Jan 10.00–17.00 Mon–Sat), the photography gallery of Mark Unsworth, which doubles as a café £; **Islay Quilters** (w islayquilters.org.uk; ⊕ 14.00–16.30 Mon–Fri, 11.00–16.30 Sat;); **Islay Whisky Vault** (01496 810357; ; ⊕ 11.00–18.00 Mon–Sat), a shop full of rare and unique bottles; **Isle of Islay Gin Ltd Visitor Centre** (w isleofislaygin.co.uk; ⊕ 11.00–16.00 Tue–Sat), selling Islay-made Nerabus gin infused with Islay heather; and **MA MacKinnons Marmalade Shop** (01496 810695; ⊕ 10.30–16.00 Tue–Sat), a gift shop offering more than marmalade.

the north end of the village. The woodland floor is carpeted with vibrant bluebells
in the spring months.

You'll also find Islay House Square (see opposite) less than half a mile north of
the village.

Finlaggan
[214 E3] ☏ 01496 840644; w finlaggan.org; ⊕ open access; adult/
concession/child under 16 £4/3/free) Just past Ballygrant, Finlaggan is the
archaeological jewel in Islay's crown and one of the most important sites in western
Scotland. Once the central power base for the Lords of the Isles (page 15), the small
collection of ruined buildings here have a surreal location on the tiny islands of a
loch. After crossing a wooden walkway over the water, visitors can wander around
the ruins on **Eilean Mòr** (which means large island). The ruined buildings include
the Lords' residence, the Great Hall and 14th-century chapel, as well as the remains
of a stone jetty, food preparation area and grave slabs. Unusually for the Inner
Hebrides, sites are well indicated and easily identifiable. There are no fences or
cordoned-off areas, apart from the grave slabs which are protected with transparent
perspex, and out of high season you are likely to have the place to yourself. There
is an excellent, modern visitor centre (⊕ Apr–Oct 11.00–17.00 Mon–Sat), which is
also where you pay for your admission; if the centre is closed – put the money in
the honesty box before the bridge.

This site seems to have been of high importance even before the Lords of the
Isles. As you leave Finlaggan, notice the smooth, rounded **standing stone** [214
E3] of about 6ft. Mentioned by Martin Martin in 1695, it is thought to be one
of a pair and, after a more recent geophysical survey, there is suggestion of it
being part of a more complex 164ft-wide monument that has so far only been
partially excavated.

North from Port Askaig
The ferry terminal at **Port Askaig** [214 F3] has an
excellent view across to the Paps of Jura. From here you can travel further up the
coast to the three distilleries: Caol Ila, Ardnahoe and Bunnahabhain.

Caol Ila Distillery
[214 F3] ☏ 01496 302769; w malts.com/en-gb/distilleries/
caol-ila; ⊕ 10.00–17.00 Mon–Sat) This distillery offers a classic tour for £20 or a
cask-draw and tasting experience for £60; the latter includes the chance to sample
five unique cask-strength expressions only available at the distillery.

Ardnahoe Distillery
[214 F2] ☏ 01496 840777; w ardnahoedistillery.com;
⊕ 10.00–16.00 Tue–Sat; tours & tastings £12–120; ♿) A relative newcomer in the

scheme of whisky distilleries, Ardnahoe was established in 2018 by the Scottish blenders and bottlers Hunter Laing. As Ardnahoe's first single malt will not be released for some time, its tastings focus on Hunter Laing's single cask bottlings from different regions of Scotland. The distillery is distinctly modern in its exterior appearance, though traditional techniques and equipment are used in the process. Tours provide an insight on Ardnahoe's use of unusual 'Worm Tub Condensers' in the production process.

Bunnahabhain Distillery and around [214 F2] (📞 01496 840557; w bunnahabhain.com; ⏱ 10.00–17.00 daily; tours & tastings £15–275) One of Islay's traditional distilleries, Bunnahabhain was established in the late 19th century and is known for its delicate, fresh-tasting whisky. Tour options include straight from the cask tastings of non-peated and peated drams, and relaxed walks around the distillery with its views across the Sound of Islay.

From Bunnahabhain, you can walk just over 4 miles north along the coast to the elegant Rhuvaal Lighthouse [214 F1]. Most of the route has a grassy track, but you should go fully prepared for a day hike with an OS map (Explorer: 353 *Islay North*) for route finding. The whole route has great views of Jura's wild and uninhabited west coast; there are deer and wild goats in the area, and you should keep an eye out for porpoises and dolphins in the Sound of Islay.

The north coast

There's a beautiful, seemingly endless beach at **Killinallan** [214 D2], signposted from just east of **Loch Gruinart Nature Reserve** on the B8017. If you have a car, you can park it after Craigens Farm [214 D3], at the end of the road, where there is space just before a gate. From there, the beach is only 400yds north; starting out a little muddy on the banks of Loch Gruinart, it gets increasingly lovely towards Killinallan Point about a mile further north. Alternatively, a circular 7-mile walk from the car park begins by following the track past Killinallan Farm, heading northeast for 3 miles towards the abandoned settlement at Gortantaoid. You can then cut across to the beach just before the buildings and return to the start along 4 miles of sand.

Glorious in sunshine, this is a very exposed stretch in high winds, but good for beachcombing and watching seabirds. Cattle and bulls are usually kept here, so it might be more relaxing to walk along the beach rather than the track if you have a dog with you.

With picturesque white houses around a sandy bay, Port Ellen is Islay's second village. It is best known for its distillery (page 213), which restarted production in April 2024 after a long period of closure. The village also has its own ferry terminal and is the start of the 'Three Distilleries Path'. To the southwest is the Oa Peninsula, with some of Islay's most spectacular cliffs and coastline, eagles, wild goats and an RSPB reserve. In the opposite direction, heading northeast from Port Ellen, the road becomes incrementally worse until it dwindles to nothing at Ardtalla.

 WHERE TO STAY Some of Islay's most upmarket accommodation options are found in the south, but there are also quite a few B&Bs in Port Ellen and plenty of excellent, remote, self-catering properties. There's a motorhome service point and facilities at Port Ellen Filling Station (PA42 7DF; 📞 01496 302443; **£**).

Islay Rum (300yds),
Port Ellen Distillery (350yds),
The Balaclava Byre (0.7 miles)

N

Bradt

0 ————— 100m
0 ————— 100yds

For listings, see opposite

Where to stay
1   The Islay
2   Seasalt Bistro & Take-away
3   The Trout Fly

Where to eat and drink
4   Little Charlotte's Café

Three Distilleries
Path

Port Ellen
filling station

Motorhome
Service Point

Islay
E-Wheels

BAC-CNOC-NA-FAIRE

CHARLOTTE STREET

BACK RD

Port Ellen
Practice

The Blue Letterbox
(post office & shop)

Co-op

BACK ROAD

MANSFIELD ROAD

FREDERICK CRESCENT

Campbells
of Islay

LENNOX STREET

CHURCH WAY

Port Ellen
Harbour Association

SCHOOL ST

PIER ROAD

FREDERICK CRESCENT

TEXA CRESCENT

Copper Still
Coffee

Ferry
terminal

Kennacraig

PORT ELLEN

Glenegedale House [215 D6] (4 rooms)
Opposite the airport PA42 7AS; 01496 300400;
w glenegedalehouse.co.uk. More personal than
a hotel, this luxury B&B has every detail carefully
considered: wallpaper is hand-printed in Glasgow,
soft furnishings have touches of Islay Woollen Mill
tweed & home-baked cakes are provided on day
of arrival. Great pride & care goes into ethically
sourced dinner options, including local seafood
platters. Of Islay's high-end accommodation
options, Glenegedale House would be my
choice. **£££££**

The Islay Hotel [map, above] (13 rooms)
Charlotte St PA42 7DF; 01496 300109;
w theislayhotel.com; Comfortable bedrooms,
luxury en-suite bathrooms & sea views. The
'Platinum' room has a jacuzzi bath. **£££££**

The Machrie Hotel & Golf Links [215 D6] (45
rooms) Port Ellen PA42 7AN; 01496 302310;
w themachrie.com; The most obviously
luxurious hotel on Islay. Along with the golf
course (page 218), it has a gym, sauna & spa.
Views across the golf course & out to Laggan
Bay. **£££££**

The Trout Fly [map, above] (4 rooms)
8 Charlotte St PA42 7DF; 01496 302608;
w troutfly-islay.co.uk. This friendly B&B has
modern bedrooms, a communal dining/
sitting room with TV & good information about
Islay. **£££**

Self-catering
Ardtalla Cottages [215 G5] Ardtalla PA42
7EE; w ardtallacottages.co.uk. Ardtalla
Estate occupies the land on either side of
the road to nowhere but Ardtalla. They have
a couple of comfortable holiday cottages to
rent & if you are looking for a quiet getaway,
you'd be hard pushed to find anything more
secluded. £980–1,085/week.

The Dower House [215 F7] Kildalton PA42
7EF; w dowerhouseislay.com. This 140-year-
old house, with a beach at the bottom of the
garden, is split in 2 halves: one side (sleeps 8)
is luxurious self-catering, perfect for 1 large
family or groups of nature-loving friends; the
other is owned & lived in by my parents. Dogs on
site. £1,600/week.

✖ WHERE TO EAT AND DRINK The quantity and quality of Port Ellen eateries has increased over recent years. In addition to the sit-down establishments, in summer, you can also get coffee and take-away food from the shiny, blue **Copper Still Coffee** (PA42 7BQ) trailer by the pier, or buy Arran Dairy ice cream from **The Blue Letterbox** (see below). If you're looking for a drink, **Islay Hotel Whisky Bar** (page 225; ⊕ 11.00–late) has an excellent range of malts from all the Islay distilleries, including Port Ellen, as well as live music on Thursdays and Saturdays in summer.

Seasalt Bistro & Take-away [map, page 225] 57 Frederick Cres, Port Ellen PA42 7BD; ☏ 01496 300300; w seasalt-bistro.co.uk; ⊕ 10.00–11.30, noon–14.30 & 17.00–20.30 Tue–Sun. Serving b/fast, lunch & dinner to eat in or take away, this modern bistro on the seafront specialises in seafood & pizza. Popular with locals & visitors alike. ££
Old Kiln Café & Ardstream Trailer [215 F7] Ardbeg PA42 7EA; ☏ 01496 302244; w ardbeg.

com; ⊕ hours vary; check website. High-ceilinged, modern café inside Ardbeg Distillery, serving light lunches & hearty meals. Ardstream Trailer outside the distillery serves soup, sandwiches & hot lunches from the wood-fired oven. £–££
Little Charlotte's Café [map, page 225] By No 1 Charlotte Street Hotel, Port Ellen PA42 7DF; ⊕ summer 08.30–16.30 daily, reduced in winter. Light lunches, fresh cakes & coffee in stylish café. £

SHOPPING There is a small **Co-op supermarket** (75 Frederick Cres; ☏ 01496 302446; ⊕ 07.00–22.00 daily; ♿), but there are also a couple of different options supporting the local economy.

The Balaclava Byre [215 E7] Port Ellen PA42 7DB; m 07778 279124; w thebalaclavabyre.co.uk; ⊕ 11.00–14.00 & 17.30–21.00 Fri–Mon, 18.00–21.00 Wed, 18.00–20.30 Thu. Farm shop attached to restaurant just outside Port Ellen selling local meat, eggs & vegetables.
The Blue Letterbox 66 Frederick Cres, Port Ellen PA42 7BD; ☏ 01496 300123; w theblueletterbox. co.uk; ⊕ 09.00–17.30 Mon–Sat. Along with

the usual services, this post office has a carefully curated range of local arts, crafts & gifts.
Campbells of Islay 19 Charlotte St, Port Ellen PA42 7DF; ☏ 01496 302264; ⧉ ; ⊕ 08.30–18.00 Mon– Wed & Fri–Sat, 11.15–18.00 Thu, 16.00–18.00 Sun. Previously Lauries, this shop was 'zero waste' before the craze began. Take your own containers & fill up with everything from dried fruit to porridge oats. Also a newsagent, & has groceries & an ATM.

OTHER PRACTICALITIES
Banks There is an ATM at Campbells of Islay (see above)
Fuel Port Ellen Filling Station, Charlotte St PA42 7DF; ☏ 01496 302443; ⊕ 08.00–17.30 Mon–Sat. Community-owned fuel station.

Health Port Ellen Practice, Geirhilda, Back Rd; ☏ 01496 302103; ⊕ 08.00–18.00 Mon–Tue & Thu–Fri, 08.00–13.00 Wed
Post office The Blue Letterbox (see above)

WHAT TO SEE AND DO
Port Ellen Sheltered in every direction apart from the southwest, Port Ellen has a perfect, horseshoe-shaped harbour, traditional cottages lining the bay and two lovely beaches. It's worth making time to walk the Three Distilleries Path while here (see below). **Islay Rum** [215 E7] (☏ 01496 302679; w islayrum.com), who bought and renovated the old lemonade factory on the outskirts of Port Ellen, are also happy to show you around if you give them a call first.

East from Port Ellen
Walk: Three Distilleries Path
Distance: 4 miles; time: 2 hours, but allow all day to visit the distilleries; start: Port Ellen; end: Ardbeg; OS Explorer map: 352 Islay South; ♿

This easy walk, which visits the distilleries of Laphroaig, Lagavulin and Ardbeg, can be co-ordinated with the bus schedule; you could also choose to cycle or allow extra time to hitchhike back. There is an ongoing joke that this path is surfaced better than the car road; although it has been built to be accessible for someone using a wheelchair, note that there are steeper sections where some assistance might be required.

Start in the east of Port Ellen, pass the Co-op on your left and then take the left-hand turning just before the closed Macaulay & Torrie's shop to go up the hill, passing the school. You will find the path (signposted) shortly afterwards on the right-hand side of the road. It meanders along the coastline, with rewarding views even for those who are not whisky enthusiasts.

After around 1½ miles, **Laphroaig** [215 E7] (✆ 01496 302418; w laphroaig.com; ⊕ Mar–Oct 09.45–17.00 daily, Nov–Feb 09.45–16.30 Mon–Fri; tours & tastings £18–90), pronounced 'la-froyg', is the first distillery you will come to. Founded in 1815, Laphroaig uses traditional process methods such as floor maltings, hand-cut peat and a cold smoking process. The distillery offers a range of tours and tastings, ranging from 1½ hours around the distillery with a dram to try afterwards, to a more extensive tour with the chance to fill your own bottle straight from the cask. You can also just pop into the Lounge Bar (⊕ Mar–Oct 10.00–16.30 daily, Nov–Feb 10.00–16.00 Mon–Fri) for a dram.

A little further on is the small settlement and distillery of **Lagavulin** [215 F7] (✆ 01496 302749; w malts.com/en-row/distilleries/Lagavulin; ⊕ Mar–Oct 10.00–17.00 daily, Nov–Feb 10.00–16.00 Mon–Sat; tours & tastings £22–105). Traditional in appearance and one of Islay's oldest distilleries, Lagavulin officially dates from 1816, but it is thought that, like in many remote spots in the Hebrides, illicit distilling was carried out on the site from as early as 1742. The modern distillery is owned by the British multi-national company Diageo, who also own Caol Ila (page 223) and Port Ellen Distillery (page 213). Lagavulin is known for its full-bodied, smoky-tasting whisky, rich in the peaty flavours that Islay is famous for.

Continuing a little further along a section of the route with no pavement, you will notice a turning to the right, just as you come out of the village. This steep side road leads down 500yds to the remains of **Dunyvaig Castle** [215 F7]. Standing on a rocky promontory, overlooking the sea, this strategically defensive spot was the namesake and stronghold of the MacDonalds of Dunyvaig intermittently from the end of the 14th century. It is a curious and overgrown ruin, surrounded by small, pebbly beaches, with an excellent view back to Lagavulin across the bay.

Returning to the path that follows the main road, it is a further half a mile to reach the final distillery of the walk: **Ardbeg** [215 F7] (✆ 01496 302244; w ardbeg.com; ⊕ hours vary, check website; tours & tastings £10–75; ♿). From the Gaelic An Àird Bheag, meaning 'a small promontory', Ardbeg Distillery is an extensive collection of attractive white buildings. It produces distinctly smoky whiskies, known for their light and complex flavours. Astonishingly, in 2022, an Ardbeg cask from 1975 sold for a record-breaking £16 million. From Ardbeg, you can either hitchhike, walk or catch a bus back to Port Ellen, or continue along the ever-deteriorating road north. If you are walking back in the evening, look out for owls and bats.

Ardbeg to Ardtalla The road north from Ardbeg is a fun route to cycle. The beach at Loch an t-Sàilein, with its stretching skerries and tiny islets, is also known as **Seal Bay** [215 F7]. For immediately obvious reasons. Along with Portnahaven (page 235) it is among the best places on Islay for *almost* guaranteed sightings of common seals. Depending on the tide, they are usually either lazing on the rocks or bobbing around

11

in the sea. Unfortunately this beach collects a lot of rubbish from the tide, so it's a good place for a beach clean if you're looking to do a holiday good deed.

Around 4½ miles from Ardbeg, down a short road on the right-hand side, is the famous **Kildalton Cross** [215 G6]; part of the Iona group of ring crosses, with the only other examples being the three on Iona itself (page 178). Combining Irish, Pictish and Northumbrian features, it is carved with intricate reliefs including interlacing spirals, serpents, lions and birds, as well as biblical scenes: Mary, Jesus and angels together, David killing the lion, Cain murdering his brother Abel with the jawbone of an ass or camel, and Abraham preparing to sacrifice Isaac; all rather weathered. In common with those on Iona, it dates from the second half of the 8th century. The small ruined chapel here was built in the 12th or early 13th century, but has been subsequently restored. There are also around 17 West Highland grave slabs both inside the church and around the graveyard, showing Kildalton's importance from early Christian times to the medieval period.

Continuing along the road, archaeology enthusiasts can walk through the field down to the shore and find a **vitrified fort** [215 G6] at Trudernish Point (✪ 55°42'04"N 6°01'54"W). Look out for otters among the rocks and seaweed. Just a little further is **Claggain Bay** [215 G6], a long, peaceful pebbly beach in the shadow of Beinn Bheigier, Islay's highest hill.

From the north end of Claggain, a substantial track leads some of the way up 1,610ft **Beinn Bheigier** [215 F5], with the final ascent being an intermittent path over rough ground. Though it does not sound particularly high, there are stunning views from here across the whole island and out to Jura. The easiest route down is to return the same way you came up.

If you are still energetic and well prepared (page 37), you can instead hike from the summit down the northern slopes to the old shepherds' cottage at **Proaig Bay** [215 G5], now a bothy; from here, the return to Claggain follows boggy tracks towards Ardtalla farmhouse.

From Proaig, more serious walkers can continue as far as the remote lighthouse at **McArthur's Head** [215 G5] (constructed in 1861 and automated 108 years later), or even further north to An Cladach bothy [214 F4]. This is unforgiving boggy terrain, with a bad reputation for ticks and adders, and you would most likely have to camp somewhere.

Keep an eye out for any instructional signs from Ardtalla Estate relating to deer stalking (page 219) in the area.

Back on the 'main road' near Claggain Bay, you can continue north to the wild beach and skerries near the end of the road at **Ardtalla** [215 G5]. The road is so terribly surfaced that it is probably better to leave your car in the car park at the

THE LOST VILLAGE OF SOLAM

With use of an OS map (Explorer: 353 *Islay North*), you can walk up the track opposite the turning to Ardbeg Distillery (page 227) to find the traces of a township called Solam [215 F7]. According to legend, it was abandoned in the 18th century as a result of an outbreak of the plague. Shipwrecked sailors are thought to have brought the disease, leaving the villagers a pearl necklace as a thank you for their kindness and thus infecting them all. The wider community brought food for the villagers and left it on a rock to avoid infection. Once the food was no longer being eaten, the settlement was burned down. You can contact Callumkill Estate (page 219) to check they are not deer stalking.

north end of Claggain Bay before making the final half a mile on foot. Before you reach the farmhouse, cut across the second field diagonally and walk down towards the sea, where there is a lovely, if rather seaweed-covered, beach with rocky islets offshore, resident swans and rock pools full of little fish and prawns at low tide. This secluded stretch of coastline provides a valuable marine habitat with lush kelp forests hidden under the water; look out for seals, otters and bottlenose dolphins, which pass occasionally.

West from Port Ellen Pleasant and sandy **Kilnaughton Bay** [215 E7], west of Port Ellen, is barely outside of the village. It looks back towards Port Ellen and out to **Carraig Fhada** [215 E7], an attractive, square-based lighthouse built in 1832. It's possible to walk out and right around it, or turn off the track to the right just before the lighthouse along a path signposted for '**Singing Sands**' [215 E7], which is a short walk away. This perfect spot, with protruding lumps of rock emerging from the yellow sand, is a favourite with wild goats and otters. It is a lovely, sometimes sheltered, place for family picnics and diverting streams, so take along a couple of spades if you have children.

The Oa My personal favourite part of Islay, the Oa Peninsula has spectacular cliffs, beautiful beaches and unique wildlife. The OS map for this area (Explorer: 352 *Islay South*) will help you find some of the more remote beaches.

The **RSPB reserve** [215 D8], which covers the most southwesterly half of the Oa, was originally set up to preserve choughs, a type of crow with red legs; now that there are only 46 breeding pairs left in Scotland this work is more important than ever. More dramatic inhabitants are the birds of prey: golden eagles, especially in spring and summer, hen harriers and peregrine. Autumn and winter are a good time to see twite. A marked, 2-mile circular walk from the RSPB car park at Upper Killeyan visits the **American Monument** [215 C8] (page 217) and then follows the cliffs to the east, before heading north to return. Dogs should be kept on leads and greater care should be taken to stick to paths between March and June when ground-nesting birds are breeding.

You can also walk down a steep, unmarked path to the spectacular rocky beach at **Port nan Gallan** [215 C8], with the dramatic backdrop of cliffs and a slender waterfall.

Like a scene from a fantasy novel, **Lower Killeyan Beach** [215 C7] has towering rocks emerging from the sea and seals sleeping on skerries. There is a small parking area at the settlement of the same name; the beach is less than a mile northwest.

The standing stone **Carragh Bhan** [215 D7] (⊕ 55°39'00"N 6°14'54"W) stands on the west side of the road that leads to Kintra and, according to tradition, marks the grave of King Godred Crovan who died in 1095, in exile from the Isle of Man. At the end of the road is Kintra Farm; go through the gate on the right to find the small car park (do not park in the farmyard). From here you can walk a couple of minutes down to **Laggan Bay** [215 D6] or 'The Big Strand'. Backed by dunes, this windswept beach stretches nearly 5 miles north and is the longest beach on Islay. It also collects a lot of plastic, so if you have a car, please take some away with you.

Walk: Abandoned settlements and Soldier's Rock
Distance: 5 miles; time: 4 hours; start/end: Kintra; OS Explorer map: 352 Islay South
Starting at Kintra [215 D7], this triangular walk starts on a good track and visits the ruined settlements of Frachdale, Ghrasdail and Tockmal; the path eventually dwindles to lumpy grassland as it approaches the coast. The majestic Soldier's Rock

11

sea stack is just part of the dramatic scenery to be found as the route follows the rough coastline in this part of north Oa. Be prepared to get wet feet unless the weather has been particularly dry.

Walk along a track from the car park that initially heads west towards the sea before it curves around to the left; follow it in a generally southerly direction for roughly a mile until you reach the ruins at **Frachdale**. Once bustling with communities living off its fertile lands, the Oa was cleared in the 1860s. This is the remains of a farmstead; the curious round building on the eastern side is a kiln (⊕ 55°38'29.7"N 6°15'59.3"W).

The track turns a corner here and runs roughly west, through a gate and then begins to disintegrate as the next set of ruins comes into view. Head towards the ruins; you will come to another kiln (⊕ 55°38'43.0"N 6°17'00.2"W), this one thought to have been used for lime and now overgrown with heather and nettles inside, though it is well preserved, like a rocky igloo. This first set of buildings is thought to have been called Cnoc Mor Ghrasdail, with **Grasdale** some 700yds up ahead, towards the sea, and Tockmal across from it on the other side of the valley to the south. Take some time to look around the ruins of the first settlements, before continuing to Grasdale where the path dwindles away to almost nothing. From there, it is easy to walk the 300yds across the small valley to reach Tockmal.

Some 40yds east of Tockmal is a large boulder with cup markings (⊕ 55°38'37.1"N 6°17'25.5"W), small bored holes thought to have been from prehistoric times, but of unknown purpose. From **Tockmal**, head about 150yds northwest to a pile of stones that show where a small chapel once stood, of which very little remains. Cross the stream around this point and find the easiest sheep path down through the valley, following the stream northwest towards the sea. Look out for choughs and golden eagles as you pick your way through the heather and grassy tussocks, and in summer you can admire the orchids.

Less than a mile from Tockmal, the stream begins to hurtle down a chasm into the sea. Cross carefully where you can find a sensible option (⊕ 55°38'52.5"N 6°18'06.5"W) and walk a few yards around the coast to the south to see the towering sea stack of **Soldier's Rock**. There are guillemots and fulmars nesting on the cliffs here around May and June, along with shags on rocks further out and the possibility of spotting basking sharks or porpoises. The coastline is a splintered series of grassy pinnacles, natural arches and towering cliffs of pink and white Dalradian schist, colonised by thrift and lichens.

To return to Kintra, you can follow the coast north and then east, keeping the sea on your left. Intermittent goat trails will help you along the way and you have a good chance of bumping into a herd. The going is rough and boggy in places, with clumps of willow to find your way through and plenty of bracken. After about a mile and a half you will come to a couple of beautiful sandy beaches, good places to stop for your picnic. Following the higher ground, you should come across a sporadic gravel track, which eventually leads you to a shallow ford and back on to the more substantial track you started the walk on.

THE RHINNS OF ISLAY

The Rhinns peninsula, Islay's western lung, is an undeniably picturesque part of the island with arguably some of the best beaches. The Rhinns are a delight for archaeology enthusiasts and could be a good starting place for anyone searching for their Ìleach ancestors. **Port Charlotte** is the main hub, with good provisions for visitors as well as a thriving local community.

WHERE TO STAY AND EAT
Most of Islay's affordable accommodation options are in this part of the island.

Port Charlotte Hotel [215 C5] (10 rooms) Port Charlotte PA48 7TU; ✆01496 850360; w portcharlottehotel.co.uk. Right on the seafront, with tastefully traditional Scottish finishings & luxurious bathrooms. The hotel's restaurant (⊕ noon–14.00 & 18.00–21.00 daily; ££–£££) is in a light conservatory with a view of Port Charlotte Lighthouse. Favourites include local scallops & Argyll venison, & there's live traditional Scottish music every Wed & Sun through the summer. £££££

✳ **Loch Gruinart House** [214 C3] (4 rooms) Gruinart PA44 7PW; ✆01496 850212; w lochgruinart.co.uk. Catherine & Jack, who also works for the RSPB, run this down-to-earth bed &'get your own b/fast'. It is a smart, white building at the head of Loch Gruinart & within the boundaries of the nature reserve. A great option for birdwatchers, outdoor people & anyone on a budget who would like a private room. Jack makes fresh bread every morning & is a wealth of information. They also have a cosy 1-bedroom, self-catering studio for weekly rental (£360–400). ££

Port Charlotte Youth Hostel [215 B5] (30 beds) Port Charlotte PA48 7TX; ✆01496 850385; w hostellingscotland.org.uk/hostels/port-charlotte; ⊕ Mar–Sep. Housed in a former distillery warehouse, this Hostelling Scotland accommodation is the only one of its type on Islay & thankfully great. Near a beach, with views out to sea, it has large communal areas & kitchen, bike storage, board games & laundry. Karl & Lorna have been running the hostel for well over a decade & are friendly & helpful. £

Port Mòr Centre & Campsite [215 C5] Port Charlotte PA48 7UE; ✆01496 850441; w islandofislay.co.uk; ⊕ Mar–Nov; ♿. Modern & well-equipped community-owned campsite with access near the shore for people using wheelchairs. An excavated Neolithic chambered cairn lies unassumingly between the centre building & the sea.

Port Mòr Centre Community Café [215 C5] The café at the centre (see above); ✆01496 850121; w port-mor-community-cafe.co.uk; ⊕ late-Mar–mid-Apr 10.00–19.00 daily, mid-Apr–mid-May 10.00–20.30 daily, mid-May–Sep 08.30–20.30 daily; ♿. Good-value, tasty food such as haddock & chips or Scotch pie. £

SHOPPING
Mini Market Bruichladdich PA49 7UN; ✆01496 850319; ⊕ 09.00–18.00 daily. A little of everything including groceries & a small café.

Port Charlotte Store 10 Main St, Port Charlotte PA48 7TL; ✆01496 850232; 🖪; ⊕ 09.30–12.30 & 13.00–17.30 Mon–Sat; ♿. Groceries & essentials.

Tormisdale Croft Crafts South of Kilchiaran PA48 7UE; ✆01496 860239; 🖪; ⊕10.30–16.30 daily. Hand-spun wool & knitwear, plus staghorn sticks.

OTHER PRACTICALITIES
Fuel Port Charlotte Store (see above)
Health The Rhinns Medical Centre, Port Charlotte PA48 7UD; ✆01496 850210; ⊕ 08.30–18.00 Mon & Wed, 08.30–13.00 Tue & Thu, 08.30–17.00 Fri

Post office Mini Market, Bruichladdich (see above; ⊕ 09.30–17.30 Mon–Fri, 09.30–17.00 Sat); Port Charlotte Store (see above; ⊕ 08.30–12.30 & 13.30–17.30 Mon–Fri)

WHAT TO SEE AND DO
Port Charlotte [215 C5] Port Charlotte is a pretty village made up of several terraces of traditional white cottages overlooking Loch Indaal. The new **Loch Indaal Way** (♿), a shared cycle and walking path joining the communities of Port Charlotte and Bruichladdich, makes this stretch of coastline more accessible for everyone and provides a gentle afternoon stroll or family bike ride. In the village, you cannot fail to notice the lovely Port Charlotte Lighthouse, but there are a couple of less obvious attractions.

Islay Nature Centre (Main St PA48 7TX; ☎ 01496 850288; w islaynaturalhistory. org; ⊕ Apr–May 13.00–16.00 Mon–Fri, Jun–Sep 10.00–16.00 Mon–Fri; adult/ concession/child/family £5/4/2/12; ♿) Celebrating its 40th year in 2024, this small but informative centre is run by the Islay Natural History Trust. It is of interest to both adults who wish to know more about Islay's natural heritage and children, who might enjoy the fish tanks with various rock pool creatures and the owl pellets filled with tiny bones that they are allowed to dissect and examine.

Museum of Islay Life ✳ (PA48 7UA; ☎ 01496 850358; w islaymuseum.org; ⊕ Apr–Oct 10.30–16.30 Mon–Fri; adult/concession/child £5/4/free) Housed in the restored Kilchoman Free Church, which was bought in 1976 for £100 and restored by the community, the Museum of Islay Life is a treasure trove of archaeological artefacts and historical information.

I had expected to find a cramped and dusty ensemble of traditionally dressed mannequins with threadbare eyebrows and gormless expressions, the men holding scythes and the women sat down sewing, but I was very much mistaken. With 3,000 objects and 5,000 photos, the carefully selected exhibits are arranged in a logical and eye-pleasing manner. There are sections for the Stone and Bronze ages, a late 19th-century croft house, a well-to-do Victorian bedroom and tools. A substantial exhibit on the tragic US shipwrecks *Otranto* and *Tuscania* includes both ships' bells, which were recovered by divers.

Toothache Stone [215 B5] (✛ 55°44'23"N 6°24'36"W) Of unknown antiquity and a little tricky to locate, the Toothache Stone is found in a small valley below the pump house at the back of Port Charlotte, about 1½ miles west of the village, between the southern bank of Abhainn Gearach and the road, just north of Gleann Cnoc a' Chrochaire (marked on OS Explorer map 353, *Islay North*). You will know you are approaching the right place when you notice a small white shed, which is located some yards behind the rock itself. Toothache sufferers are said to have gone (or maybe go?) to visit this boulder and hammer nails into the cracks on its surface. Whether effective or not, the action must have been cathartic as there are countless rusty nails jammed into every perceivable crack. Some recent coins are also stuck into the rock but, as nails rust quickly and eventually disappear, it is difficult to tell how long this site has been used.

Bruichladdich and around [214 C4] In Bruichladdich village is **Bruichladdich Distillery** (☎ 01496 850190; w bruichladdich.com; ⊕ Apr–Oct 10.00–17.30 daily, Nov–Mar 10.00–17.30 Mon–Sat; tours & tastings £15–35). Bruichladdich distils three single malts: an unpeated Bruichladdich, the heavily peated Port Charlotte and the super heavily peated Octomore, as well as **The Botanist** (w thebotanist. com) dry gin, which is made using 22 locally hand-foraged botanicals.

Following the main A847 road 3 miles northeast from Bruichladdich, **Uiskentuie** [214 D4] has a gigantic, 9ft-tall standing stone (✛ 55°47'15"N 6°19'06"W) presiding over Loch Indaal. It is visible for miles around, but its original purpose isn't known; a navigation tool is one seemingly sensible suggestion. If you want to look more closely, there is easy parking on the A847 across from a building with a caved-in roof, and a gate in the fence for access.

West of Loch Gruinart
RSPB reserve [214 C3] (☎ 01496 850505; w rspb.org.uk/days-out/reserves/ loch-gruinart; visitor centre ⊕ 10.00–17.00 daily; ♿) This RSPB reserve is 6 square

miles and includes a working farm. Cows and sheep are used to manage the land, demonstrating how farming and wildlife can coexist successfully; choughs, for example, rely on cowpats in order to find worms to eat. Roughly a third of the reserve comprises farmland; the rest is mostly heather moorland with an additional square mile of mudflats and salt marsh. It is a rewarding place to visit at any time of year, but especially in late April and May when the corncrakes are making their distinctive calls.

Towards the end of October, tens of thousands of barnacle geese and thousands of Greenland white-fronted geese fly in from further north and rest on the mudflats before dispersing elsewhere. Around this time, whooper swans and Brent geese also drop by on their way from Iceland to Ireland. Autumn is a good time to see birds of prey such as hen harriers, sparrowhawks, merlin and peregrine. You can still see the geese throughout winter, especially in the evening as they come back to roost on the flats. Looking out from the bird hide between flooded fields, you can spot exotic-looking ducks such as teal, goldeneye and shoveler.

In spring, all the animals are having young. Roe and red deer are raised on the reserve, as well as young wading birds and hen harriers. Lapwings and redshanks dive-bomb intruders to keep them away from their nests. By late summer, the migrating birds are ready to leave again. The **visitor centre** has more information and there is wheelchair access from the car park to a viewing platform over the reserve.

Kilnave Chapel [214 C3]

Kilnave Chapel [214 C3] In a desolate location, overlooking the sands of Killinallan, Kilnave Chapel dates from the 12th century. The MacLeans are thought to have been burned to death here by the MacDonalds after the Battle of Traigh Ghruinneart in 1598. The chapel is more or less complete, apart from the roof, and there are several interesting artefacts around the site. Missing part of its arms and so thin that it seems likely that it'll be worn away completely by the rain over the next few hundred years, the 8th-century **Kilnave Cross** is older than Kildalton Cross by around half a century, but still impressive and decorated with patterns on its eastern side. By the door of the chapel is a prehistoric saddle quern and stone for grinding grains.

Walk: Ardnave

Distance: 4–5 miles; time: 2 hours; start/end: Ardnave Loch; OS Explorer map: 353 Islay North

At the most northerly point of the Rhinns is Ardnave, which has an easy circular walk from Ardnave Loch to Ardnave Point. The track follows easy ground, which becomes muddy after rain, while the coastal route is slightly longer and less well defined. It is one of the best places on Islay to spot choughs and there are lapwings and skylarks singing in summer.

Starting in the car park at **Ardnave Loch** [214 C2], make your way along the track leading away on the right-hand side of the farm buildings. Keep right at the next fork; this track leads most of the way to **Ardnave Point**. The final section is pathless, but you can make your way down to the beach opposite tiny Nave Island; look out for seals and otters, and there is also a good view out to Colonsay in clear weather.

From the point, follow the coast, with the sea on your right, until you reach the old, concrete lobster pens on the shore, before heading inland and rejoining the track. It will bring you to the farmyard; walk past a cow barn before continuing back to Ardnave Loch and the car park.

The northwest

The northwest On the B8017, just after the turning to Culbuie, **An Sithean** [214 C3] (⊕ 55°48'47.3"N 6°23'14.5"W) is an unexcavated archaeological site showing evidence of an ancient settlement. Thought to be over 3,000 years old, there are at least eight roundhouses between 29ft and 49ft wide; four of these are easily distinguishable in the brown or purple heather by the bright, green turf growing on top of them.

Travelling west along the B8017, **Loch Gorm** [214 B3] soon comes into view. One of the tiny islands is a crannog (page 263), with the now severely ruined remains of a later castle built on top. This is also a good spot to look out for golden eagles.

Turning right on to the B8018 at the T-junction and continuing to the north coast, **Sanaigmore** [214 B2] is a beautiful sandy beach surrounded by rocks, delicate machair and wildflowers. If you prefer, you can take the turning heading southwest past Loch Gorm to visit **Ballinaby** [214 B3] (✪ 55°49'03"N 6°26'33"W), Islay's tallest standing stone, before reaching **Saligo Bay** [214 B3], a small sandy beach with handy rocks to picnic on around its edges. Then there is **Machir Bay** [214 B4], over a mile of sand dunes and clean, empty beach: another great place to spot choughs. Exposed to the full force of the Atlantic, it can get pretty windy down there and you should watch out for the currents if you're brave enough to go swimming.

The derelict church in the small village of **Kilchoman** is striking in the distance, but sadly access is restricted due to the building's instability. The site was once the residence of the Lord of the Isles and is thought to be the burial place of Lachlan MacLean of Duart, who died in the Battle of Traigh Ghruinneart. Some archaeological artefacts have been preserved in the Museum of Islay Life (page 232).

To the southwest of the church is a later cemetery where the victims of the shipwrecked *Otranto* (page 217) were initially laid to rest, before many of the bodies were taken home across the Atlantic.

Also in Kilchoman, but accessed more directly from the B8018, **Kilchoman Distillery** [214 B4] (☏ 01496 850011; w kilchomandistillery.com; ⌚ Mar–Oct 09.45–17.00 daily; Nov–Dec & Feb 10.30–15.30 daily; tours & tastings £10–40) is the only independently owned distillery on Islay. Established in 2005, it was the island's first new distillery since 1881, as well as Islay's only farm distillery; Kilchoman has a distinctly different aesthetic from the historical coastal buildings of other distilleries. They also have a café serving lunches, cake and hot drinks (£).

The southwest To travel further down the west coast by car, you need to return to Port Charlotte to find a turning marked to Kilchiaran. Just after Kilchiaran Farm, on the coast overlooking Kilchiaran Bay, the roofless medieval **Kilchiaran Chapel** [214 B4] has been somewhat restored to showcase a medieval font and grave slabs. One has a cross entwined in intricate foliage, two kneeling figures and a large sword; there should also be a small man and barrel, but this is difficult to make out. Outside, some 25yds closer to the sea on the southwest, is a slab with round, prehistoric cup markings, one of which has been ground right through to form a hole (✪ 55°45'11.7"N 6°27'26.3"W). The dramatic and rather exposed **Kilchiaran Bay** [215 B5] would make a lovely lunch stop on a calm day. In 1826, 25 families were removed from Kilchiaran by Walter Frederick Campbell in order to make room for a larger-scale farm and steading thought to be more profitable.

Four miles further south, oval in shape and 115ft wide at its narrowest point, **Coultoon** [215 B5] (✪ 55°43'31.5"N 6°28'05.7"W) would be one of the most formidable Bronze Age sites in the UK, if only they had managed to stand the stones up. Excavation in the 1970s reported that although sockets had been dug, most of the rocks were never actually erected and only a couple are still standing now. Though the rocks are horizontal, their placement is still alien in the landscape and the sheer scale of the site makes for mind-boggling further consideration as to what purpose these prehistoric people had in mind.

At the most southerly point of the Rhinns are the conjoined townships of **Portnahaven** and **Port Wemyss** [215 A6], looking out to the island of Orsay and its attractive lighthouse. With the feeling of a storybook beach town, small, white cottages line the harbour; this is one of the easiest places on Islay to see common seals.

Returning northeast, at **Nerabus** [215 B5], there is a group of five medieval West Highland grave slabs including one of a priest and four with claymores. There is parking down a small track opposite Nerabus Farm, towards the graveyard. Find the medieval site beyond the far side of the modern graveyard, following signs to 'Ancient Burial Ground of Clan Donald'.

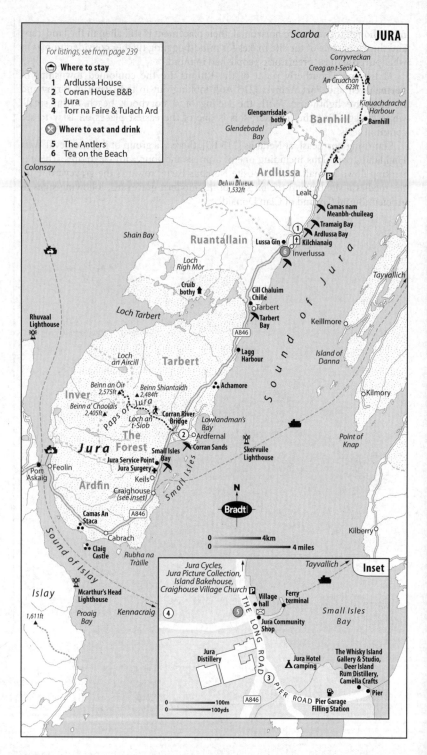

JURA

Scarba

Corryvreckan
Creag an t-Seoil
An Cruachan
623ft

Kinuachdrachd
Harbour
Barnhill

Glengarrisdale
bothy
Barnhill

*Glendebadel
Bay*

For listings, see from page 239

Where to stay
1 Ardlussa House
2 Corran House B&B
3 Jura
4 Torr na Faire & Tulach Ard

Where to eat and drink
5 The Antlers
6 Tea on the Beach

Colonsay

Benn Bhreac
1,532ft

Ardlussa

Lealt

Camas nam
Meanbh-chuileag
Tramaig Bay
Ardlussa Bay
Kilchianaig

Shain Bay

Ruantallain

Lussa Gin
Inverlussa

*Loch
Righ Mòr*

Taynvallich

*Cruib
bothy*

Cill Chaluim
Chille
Tarbert
Tarbert
Bay

Loch Tarbert

Keillmore

Rhuvaal
Lighthouse

A846

*Island of
Danna*

Lagg
Harbour

Tarbert

*Loch
an Aircill*

Beinn an Òir
2,575ft
Beinn Shiantaidh
2,484ft
Beinn a' Chaolais
2,405ft

Achamore

Kilmory

Inver

Paps of Jura

Corran River
Bridge

*Lowlandman's
Bay*
Ardfernal

*Loch an
t-Siob*

The
Forest

*Point of
Knap*

Jura

Small Isles
Bay

Corran Sands

Skervuile
Lighthouse

Port
Askaig

Feolin

Jura Service Point
Jura Surgery

Keils

Ardfin

Craighouse
(see inset)

Small Isles

N

Kilberry

Camas An
Staca

A846

Bradt

Cabrach

*Rubha na
Tràille*

0   4km
0   4 miles

Claig
Castle

Sound of Islay

Islay

Mcarthur's Head
Lighthouse

Kennacraig

*Proaig
Bay*

1,611ft

Inset

Taynvallich

Jura Cycles,
Jura Picture Collection,
Island Bakehouse,
Craighouse Village Church

Village
hall

Ferry
terminal

Small Isles
Bay

THE LONG ROAD

5

Jura Community
Shop

Jura
Distillery

Jura Hotel
camping

The Whisky Island
Gallery & Studio,
Deer Island
Rum Distillery,
Camella Crafts

3

PIER ROAD

A846

Pier Garage
Filling Station

Pier

0   100m
0   100yds

12

Jura (Diùra)

Studying the map, it's easy to assume that Jura could be Islay's sibling: similar in size and separated only by the narrow Sound of Islay. But while Islay has the Inner Hebrides' second-largest population, Jura is predominantly a red-deer-grazed wilderness.

Dwarfed by its Paps – the three mountains that dominate the skyline of the southern Hebrides – Jura is well known for having more deer than people. Though it's one of Scotland's largest islands (at 142 square miles it ranks eighth in size), it has a population of about 260. Historically, along with the exposed mountainous areas, much of the island has always been uninhabitable due to vast expanses of blanket bog. Where humans struggled to settle, nature has thrived and the entire north and west coasts, as well as the interior moorland and forests, have been left entirely for wildlife.

In 1695, Martin Martin described the island as 'perhaps the wholesomest plot of ground either in the isles or continent of Scotland, as appears by the long life of the natives and the state of their health, to which the height of the hills is believed to contribute in a large measure'; one such long-lived islander was Gillour MacCrain who apparently lived to 180. Though Martin's claim that the constant air flow blew away diseases and kept the population healthy is now viewed rather dubiously, there is no doubt that Jura is rich in wide-open spaces and there is still something to be said for the mental and physical benefits of battling high winds across exposed moorland.

GETTING THERE AND AWAY

Outside of the summer months, you will most likely have to travel via Islay. There's a **car and passenger ferry** from Port Askaig on Islay to Feolin in Jura run by Argyll and Bute Council (◊ 01496 840681; w argyll-bute.gov.uk/port-askaig-islay-feolin-jura-ferry-timetable; ⊕ every 30–60mins 07.35–18.30 Mon–Sat & 08.30–18.30 Sun; foot passengers/car £2.20/10.80). Pre-bookings are only necessary on specific early/late sailings displayed on timetable, otherwise you just turn up and pay on the ferry. Campervan drivers should contact the ferry office to check if their vehicle will clear the ramp. **Jura Passenger Ferry** (m 07768 450000; w jurapassengerferry.com; ⊕ Apr–Sep 4 times/day Sun–Mon, Wed & Fri; £27.50; children under 5, dogs & bikes free) runs from Tayvallich on the mainland to Craighouse in under an hour.

There are visitor **moorings** in the bay beside Craighouse (Jura Development Trust; ◊ 01496 820161; w juradevelopment.co.uk/about-jura/getting-to-jura).

You can also reach Jura by **air**, on a day trip with Loch Lomond Seaplanes (page 239).

GETTING AROUND

BY CAR Jura is 29 miles long and, as its single-track A road wins the prize as the worst in the Inner Hebrides, journey times should not be underestimated. As you drive further north, there are savage pot-holes and the sides of the roads are sunken from the tyres of previous travellers; at a certain point, grass starts to grow in the middle. In many places, the road is quite unsuitable for large vehicles, especially those with low clearance; note that there are no facilities for campervans. The nearest car hire is on Islay (page 218) or in Lochgilphead (page 41).

BY BUS Garelochhead Coaches/Argyll and Bute Council 🔍 01436 810200; w garelochheadcoaches.co.uk) operate the 456 bus (Feolin–Craighouse–Inverlussa) from Monday to Saturday. Services between Feolin and Craighouse run roughly once an hour between 08.05 and 17.50, but less regularly between Craighouse and Inverlussa.

BY BIKE Bicycles can be hired from Jura Cycles (Craighouse; m 07562 762382; e uracycles@icloud.com). They offer a variety of Ridgeback Meteor Hybrid bikes, as well as Ridgeback Dimension bikes for children (adult £25/100 day/week; child £15/45 day/week). They also have helmets, some panniers and provide a puncture-repair kit with every hire.

TOURIST INFORMATION AND TOUR OPERATORS

Jura does not have an official tourist information centre, but the **Jura Service Point** (Craighouse; 📞 01496 820161; w juradevelopment.co.uk; ⏲ 09.30–12.30 Mon–Fri) is run by the Jura Development Trust and has some local information as well as genealogy records. In addition, you'll find that the friendly staff at **Jura**

FESTIVALS AND EVENTS

MAY
Isle of Jura Fell Race Craighouse; w isleofjurafellrace.co.uk. This event has been going since 1973. Only for serious fell runners, this 28km race features 7 summits, including the Paps of Jura, & an intimidating 7,775ft of ascent. It's unmarked & over rough terrain so, in addition to fitness & fell-running technique, you'll also need navigation skills. It is said to be one of the toughest challenges in British hill racing; regardless, the 250 places fill up fast.

JULY
Ardlussa Sports Day Contact Ardlussa Estate: 📞 01496 820323; e enquiries@ardlussaestate.com. Visitors are welcome to just turn up & join in with sports & games on Ardlussa lawn field. Last Sat afternoon of the month.

AUGUST
Jura Regatta Stone pier, Craighouse. On the 1st Sat of the month this event includes sailing, rowing & swimming races. Spectators & visiting competitors are welcome: just show up on the day & put your name down if you want to join in. Concert & dancing in the village hall afterwards.

SEPTEMBER
Jura Music Festival Craighouse; 📞 01496 820362; w juramusicfestival. com. Now in its 30th year, this is a well-established favourite for traditional-music lovers. From the locals' Fri night cèilidh right through to Final Fling on Sun night, it's a w/end packed with fantastic performances & workshops. Tickets range from free to £45 depending on which events you attend & can be bought online from end of Jul.

Community Shop (page 240) are happy to help point visitors in the right direction. Information is also available online from **Explore Islay & Jura** (w islayjura.com). For tours, try:

Discover Jura   m 07884 024777; w discoverjura. co.uk. Choice of 2 minibus day trips including visits to historical & natural sites, Jura's main settlements & Lussa Gin distillery. More expensive option also includes lunch, wildlife boat trip & Jura Distillery tour. £95–225 pp.
Jura Boat Tours   m 07976 280195; w juraboattours.co.uk. Jura-born Robert Henry offers various trips (£30–80 pp) on an open RIB,

including out to Corryvreckan, Lowlandman's Bay & Brosdale Island, or a 4hr circumnavigation of the whole of Jura. This is definitely the easiest way to visit Jura's unique raised beaches.
Loch Lomond Seaplanes   Cameron House, Duck Bay, Alexandria G83 8QZ; 01436 675030; w lochlomondseaplanes.com. Provides day trips to Jura, flying from the Cameron House hotel on Loch Lomond to Craighouse, giving you 2 hours ashore.

WHERE TO STAY AND EAT   *Map, page 236*

With one hotel (which also hosts the campsite), a couple of B&Bs and about 20 self-catering properties, Jura has a range of accommodation options. In addition to those listed here, further options can be found on the Jura Development Trust website (w juradevelopment.co.uk/about-jura/where-to-stay).

The west coast of Jura is the perfect place for **wild camping** (especially as there is no other accommodation option in this part of Jura). The island also has two Mountain Bothies Association bothies (page 44): **Cruib** and **Glengarrisdale**. Please check up-to-date information online (w mountainbothies.org.uk).

There is only one place to get a main meal on Jura other than the Jura Hotel (see below), and it's also in Craighouse.

Ardlussa House   (10 rooms) Ardlussa Estate PA60 7XW; 01496 820323; w ardlussaestate.com. In Jura's northeast, a 10-bedroom property, with owner's home occupying a separate wing, Ardlussa House can be booked as either self-catering (£2,500/week) or on a dinner, B&B basis (£150 pp).
Jura Hotel   (17 rooms) Craighouse PA60 7XU; 01496 820243; w jurahotel.co.uk. Originally an 18th-century inn, Jura's only hotel also runs as a pub, restaurant & campsite. Dbl rooms have sea view. No TVs in bedrooms, but copies of Orwell's *Nineteen Eighty-Four* & photography books. The cheap camping (Apr–Sep; ; £) is on a grassy field, right on the seafront, with plenty of space for tents. No car park, but there are toilets, showers & laundry. The hotel's restaurant (summer noon–23.00 Mon–Thu, noon–midnight Fri–Sat, winter times reduced & variable; ££) serves hearty food & seasonal seafood with daily specials. ££££
Corran House B&B   (2 rooms) Small Isles Bay PA60 7XZ; 01496 820374; e fionajwalton@hotmail.co.uk. Owners Steve & Fiona are friendly & knowledgeable about Jura. Large, comfortable en-suite bedrooms with lovely sea views. The

location, on a long, empty sandy beach, is hard to beat. Hearty cooked Scottish b/fast. Resident dog & cat; dogs welcome, but call ahead. Lower end of this price range. £££
The Antlers   Craighouse PA60 7XS; 01496 305317; ; hours vary; check Facebook. Relaxed, community-run place with outside seating in good weather, serving warm drinks, b/fasts, hot lunches & cake. Fish & chips available for take-away on Fri evening. ££
Tea on the Beach   Inverlussa Beach, Ardlussa PA60 7XW; ; Apr–Aug, hours vary. Help-yourself hot drinks & cakes. It is run by local young people when they have time, with payment/donations via an honesty box. £

SELF-CATERING

Torr na Faire & Tulach Ard   (2 houses, each sleeps 4) Ballard, Craighouse; 01496 820222; w juraselfcatering.com; . Clean & modern, these 2 identical houses are surprisingly spacious & comfortable inside. The best thing about them is their elevated position & great view over the Small Isles Bay. Well-behaved pets welcome. £525/week.

SHOPPING

The community-owned **Jura Community Shop** (Craighouse; ☎ 01496 820231; w juracommunityshop.co.uk; ⏱ 09.00–17.00 Mon–Wed & Fri–Sat, 09.00–11.00 & 14.00–17.00 Thu) has all the basics, including groceries, toiletries and cleaning products. There is a decent selection of fresh fruit and vegetables (mostly unpackaged) and a small bookshop upstairs with a good range of local-interest books, OS maps and map sections of the Paps of Jura. Additionally, look out for honesty box stalls including the **Island Bakehouse** (Craighouse PA60 7XR; e islandbakehouse@icloud.com; ⏺; ⏱ Easter–Oct, restocked 11.00 Wed–Fri) a bright pink shed selling sourdough loaves, pastries and cakes – you can also email ahead to order.

There is a **Craft Fair** in the village hall from 10.30 to 16.30 most Wednesdays in summer (check noticeboards or ask locally to confirm dates), selling local crafts, framed photos and home-baked cakes. **Camella Crafts** (Unit 1, The Pier, Craighouse PA60 7XF; m 07769 851351; w camellacraftsjura.com; ⏱ summer, flexible) sells handmade gifts and cards. **The Whisky Island Gallery and Studio** (Unit 4, The Pier, Craighouse PA60 7XF; m 07786 352568; ⏱ Apr–Sep 11.00–16.30 Mon–Fri, noon–15.30 Sat; hours flexible & can sometimes open on request; ♿) shows the work of award-winning local photographer Konrad Borkowski.

OTHER PRACTICALITIES

Fuel Pier Garage Filling Station, Craighouse PA60 7XF; ⏱ 11.00–16.00 Mon–Wed & Fri
Health Jura Medical Practice (Glencairn Surgery, Craighouse PA60 7XG; ☎ 01496 820218; w juramedicalpractice.co.uk; also has a small dispensary); basic painkillers & over-the-counter medicines, first-aid supplies & cold remedies can be bought in Jura Community Shop (see above)
Post office Jura Community Shop (see above); ⏱ 09.00–13.00 Mon–Sat. Cash withdrawal available.

WHAT TO SEE AND DO

FROM FEOLIN TO CRAIGHOUSE From Feolin, where there is a very small ferry terminal and one house, the road runs perilously along the bottom of the cliffs as it follows the rocky shoreline, which is frequented by otters. Look out for your first red deer as the view opens up to expansive moorland. After about 3 miles, just after a patch of woodland, 300yds southwest of the road, is a huge, intentionally placed upright rock. At over 11ft tall **Camas An Staca**, a Gaelic name relating to the bay, is the tallest standing stone on Jura. Looking to the southwest from here, you can just about see the remains of **Claig Castle**, a sea fortress defended by the MacDonald Lords of the Isles until they were crushed in the 17th century. McArthur's Head Lighthouse (page 228) and its complex array of white walls can be seen clinging to the cliffs over on Islay.

CRAIGHOUSE Jura's tiny capital is home to most of the island's amenities, including its only shop, pub and campsite, as well as the famous Jura whisky distillery (see opposite) and a community-focused **Deer Island Rum Distillery** (Unit 3, The Pier Garage, Craighouse; w deerisland.co.uk; ⏱ check online), which opened in 2021, producing spiced Scottish rum – you can pop into the shop or arrange a private tasting here. Also setting it apart from the island's other small villages is the wonderful view over **Small Isles Bay**.

There are about 6,000 red deer on the island, which means you only need to leave Craighouse in order to see some of them. Not just a noble part of the island's fauna, these deer actually account for the majority of Jura's economy. Jura's seven estates own and manage most of the island's land and, counting them as one employer, they are also the biggest provider of jobs. Deer populations are managed, so it's important for hikers and wild campers to be aware of the deer stalking season and the island's estates. Stalking runs annually from 1 July to 15 February, and during these months it is sensible to call the estate whose land you want to walk over in advance. These are the phone numbers for each estate; their boundaries are marked on the map on page 236, or see w juradmg.co.uk.

Ardfin \ 01496 820396
Ardlussa \ 01496 820323;
e ardlussaestate@gmail.com
Barnhill \ 01496 820327
The Forest \ 01496 820217

Inver \ 01496 820223;
e ghayes@inverfarmers.co.uk
Ruantallain \ 01496 820287;
e fishing@ruantallain.co.uk
Tarbert \ 01496 820207

From north to south these uninhabited Small Isles, not to be confused with the ones detailed in *Chapter 5*, are Eilean Bhride (Bridget's Island), Pladda (Flat Island), Eilean nan Coinein (Rabbit Island), Eilean Diomhain (Useless Island) and Eilean nan Gabhar (Goat Island). The last of these, appropriately, is home to a herd of wild goats that was running amok in Craighouse around 20 years ago – rather than shoot them, they were relocated to Eilean nan Gabhar. There were originally just five goats but they have subsequently (and unsurprisingly) tripled in number.

Too far offshore to make out properly, the Small Isles' presence lends a mystical element to the bay. Some trips with Jura Boat Tours (page 239) run past the islands, allowing you to get a closer look.

Jura Distillery (Craighouse; \ 01496 820385; w jurawhisky.com; ☉ 10.00–16.30 Mon–Fri) Originally founded by the Laird of Jura, Archibald Campbell, in the early 19th century, Jura Distillery could reportedly produce 720 gallons of whisky each week when it was first built. The establishment has gone through several long spells of disrepair before being rebuilt in its present form in 1963, with some subsequent additions. Tours start from £15 for 45 minutes – for £50 you can learn about and try some of Jura's limited releases and single-cask distillery exclusives.

Jura Picture Collection Attached to Craighouse Village Church, towards the northern end of Craighouse, this historical photo collection shows life on the island from as early as 1854. The space is tiny, but the exhibition is particularly notable for its unusual inclusion of photos showing normal village life. There is 'Kate Buie at her spinning wheel' and 'Off to Islay' – depicting women on a small boat going for a 'cruise' and men heading over to the neighbouring island for a drink. There are also many labelled images of Jura's older houses, which make for an interesting comparison with the modern day. The door is left open and the exhibition is free, but donations to the church are welcome.

Jura   WHAT TO SEE AND DO

12

241

CORRAN SANDS At the northern end of Small Isles Bay is the idyllic Corran Sands, arguably Jura's finest beach. Once the island's main deep-water anchorage, this was where emigrants waited for ships to take them away in the 18th and 19th centuries. (The island's population had dropped to just a few hundred by the 1900s – not due to forced evictions as elsewhere but rather most of Jura's residents seemingly left by choice, with hopes of escaping their impoverishment.) These days, if winds are favourable, it is a lovely place for a picnic.

PAPS OF JURA Visible on the horizon from as far afield as Mull and even Northern Ireland, the Paps of Jura are three mountains: **Beinn an Òir** (Mountain of Gold; 2,575ft), **Beinn Shiantaidh** (Sacred Mountain; 2,484ft) and **Beinn a' Chaolais** (Mountain of the Sound; 2,405ft). Climbing them is undoubtedly one of the main reasons people come to Jura and, on a clear day, the views are difficult to beat.

To climb all three takes about 10 hours and is a serious expedition that should only be done after checking the weather forecast and with proper clothing and supplies, including navigation tools. The scree slopes are relentless and, with weather likely to change fast, you must be prepared for all conditions. As winter sees more extreme weather conditions (including the possibility of snow) and shorter hours of daylight, it's generally better to attempt the Paps between April and September. Climbing just Beinn an Òir, the highest of the peaks, is a more manageable hike of around 5 hours, but the same preparation instructions apply.

Walk: Climbing Beinn an Òir

Distance: 8 miles; time: 4½–6½ hours; start/end: Corran River Bridge; OS Explorer map: 355 Jura & Scarba

This hike has an ascent and descent of 2,487ft. There is not a lot of scree to tackle, but the ground is very boggy for the first few miles. These instructions are only meant for general route finding; you must also have a proper map and compass or offline navigation (and know how to use them).

JURA, SCARBA AND THE GARVELLACHS SPECIAL PROTECTION AREA FOR GOLDEN EAGLES

Dark brown with golden plumage at the napes of their necks, the golden eagle is possibly Scotland's best-loved bird. As persecution and disturbance from humans are the main threats to golden eagles, the Jura, Scarba and the Garvellachs Special Protection Area (SPA) has been created in recognition of its important population. As well as the uninhabited islands of Scarba and the Garvellachs (to the north of Jura), this conservation area includes the entirety of Jura, excluding a narrow strip following the road along the eastern coastline.

The rocky outcrops on Jura's Paps provide the perfect breeding grounds, while eagles can hunt small and medium-size animals and birds such as grouse, hares or rabbits on the surrounding molinia grassland and heather moorland, as well as young deer and carrion, particularly in winter. Although wildlife spotting is always unpredictable, Jura is one of the best places in Scotland to see these majestic birds. Look out for them soaring above the Paps; apart from their large size, eagles are easily identified from more common buzzards by the long, finger-like feathers extending from the tips of their wings.

Start just over 3 miles north of Craighouse at Corran River Bridge, a three-arched structure over the Corran River, built by Thomas Telford in 1810. If you have a car, park on the north side and then walk back across the bridge to find a stile and path leading northwest. The path starts near the river before climbing up to higher ground across the corner of a hill. Soon you will have an excellent view of all three Paps: Beinn Shiantaidh is the closest and largest-looking of the three, with Beinn an Òir behind it and Beinn a' Chaolais on the left. When you see Loch an t-Siob, head towards the river running off it to find the substantial stepping stones and cross it.

The path then runs around the northern side of the loch, below Beinn Shiantaidh. Begin to climb up when you are level with the gap between Beinn Shiantaidh and Beinn an Òir; here the path disappears. You should soon find yourself on a beautiful triangular plateau (obvious from the contour lines on your map). From here, head west for a few hundred yards, towards the south of Beinn an Òir, where you should be able to find a path leading up directly north, before it heads northwest for the final ascent.

The remains of stone buildings at the top were once Colby Camp, used for triangulation and mapping of the area. The summit is a little further south, with superlative views across to Islay and over to Beinn Shiantaidh and Beinn a' Chaolais. Don't forget to look out for eagles. Return along the same route.

FROM CORRAN RIVER BRIDGE TO ARDLUSSA Heading north from Corran River Bridge, after about a mile the road passes **Lowlandman's Bay**, where the old cottages of Skervuile Lighthouse's keepers occupy the headland that reaches around to the east. The lighthouse itself, a small white tower, was constructed in the mid 19th century to mark dangerous rocks near the southern end of the Sound of Jura.

A little further north, **Achamore** (between ✪ 55°55'01.4"N 5°52'34.3"W and ✪ 55°54'59.9"N 5°52'28.9"W) is the remains of a small settlement of stone-walled huts on the edge of a ravine. One for real archaeology enthusiasts, they are on the opposite side of the road from a patch of woodland and the small hill Cnoc na Fritheilt. Not particularly easy to find, once you have spotted the remains of one house you will realise that there are many in the same area. The origin of the buildings is something of a mystery as they are smaller than permanent residences usually are, but the rig and furrow, lazy beds and field walls suggest that farming definitely took place here. A post-medieval settlement, it was already abandoned by the end of the 18th century. This peaceful spot seems idyllic in good weather, but it would have been a tough and exposed place to grow crops. Although the ruins are not far from the road, an OS map or GPS device is probably needed to locate them.

Lagg Harbour The well-preserved pier and walled cattle slipway in Lagg Harbour were both built around 1810; the farmhouse at Lagg was built around the same time as an inn for the cattle drovers to drink in while they waited for (frequently delayed) ferries – it is now a private residence. For the nearby islands of Islay and Colonsay, Jura was often used as a stepping stone to the mainland. This ferry carried incoming and outcoming cows for all three islands, in addition to being the official postal route for Jura and mail on its way to Islay. This was a hazardous crossing, made in open boats with both livestock and drovers vulnerable to large waves and currents. You can walk down the track to the curved pier and slipway, which remains an impressive site with an interesting perspective over the bay. Be very careful if you walk on either as there are many loose rocks, holes and algae to potentially slip on.

EASGA BHUIDHE NA FÈIDH

A story recounted by Heather Dewar in *Seanchas Ìle: Collecting, Recording and Preserving Islay's Gaelic Heritage* (page 267) refers to the postal route, from a time when mail had to travel through Jura before being delivered to Islay. Two women had gone from Islay to Jura to collect whelks, when one asked the other to look after her baby while she worked. Returning, she immediately noticed something was wrong; not only would her friend not tell her where the baby was, but there was also a terrible smell coming from the fire. Going to check in the pot, she was terrified to discover her baby had been cooked and ran away as fast as she could – but the cannibalistic woman caught her and ate her too. Thrown into a rage, the mad woman fell to all fours; her nails grew long like the 'claws of an eagle' and her hair grew long like a beast. Anyone who went too close was also killed and eaten.

Too scared to travel their normal route through Jura, the Islay mail came to a halt until one day when two Ìleach men with dogs and guns decided to find and kill her. One of the men climbed Beinn an Òir and, after some struggle, managed to kill her with the stock of his gun. Sgrìob na Caillich ('the scrape of the old woman'), a geological feature on the southwest flank of Beinn an Òir known as a medial moraine, is supposed to have been where she fell down and died. This woman, recorded in folk tales as 'Easga Bhuidhe na Fèidh' was used for generations as a scare tactic to stop young islanders from staying out late. Kelp on the beaches was said to be her hair and Clach an Daormunn, a huge stone close to Ardnahoe on Islay, is said to be a stone she threw across in rage.

While most of this folk tale is fantastical, it probably reflects to some extent an unfortunate woman with mental health problems who was villainised by the community and considered to be a witch.

Tarbert About 2 miles north of Lagg Harbour, and easily recognisable by a standing stone next to the road, is the small settlement of Tarbert, which overlooks Tarbert Bay. Meaning 'a place to carry your boat across the land from sea to sea', you will find Tarberts and Tarbets all over the west coast of Scotland, something that can cause major confusion on the mainland. Here, the name refers to the short distance between the settlement of Tarbert and Loch Tarbert, which cuts into Jura from the opposite (west) coast. At this point, Jura is nearly cut in half and the walk across the island from Tarbert on the east coast to Loch Tarbert on the west is only 1 mile.

About 80yds after the standing stone is a parking place on the right-hand side of the road; you can follow the track leading east towards Tarbert and Tarbert Bay on foot from here. After about 200yds, cutting across the field south towards the bay, you will reach **Cill Chaluim Chille** (⊕ 55°58'23"N 5°50'01"W), a walled graveyard that stands conspicuously in an otherwise clear grassy field, surrounding the remains of a medieval chapel. As well as the lower walls of the chapel, there is also a tall stone, which, underneath the crusty lichen, has sunken Latin crosses on both faces. This stone may be prehistoric, but is believed to have been moved, with the cross a later addition.

If you would like to walk across the island to **Loch Tarbert**, an easy 2-mile return route begins on the opposite side of the main road, 150yds southeast of the standing stone. A track (⊕ 55°58'23"N 5°50'21"W) leads all the way across to the loch. The shore of Loch Tarbert is a peaceful place with a small boathouse. Look out for wading birds and sit quietly for a while in the hope of seeing otters.

INVERLUSSA AND ARDLUSSA Five miles north of Tarbert are the small settlements of Inverlussa and Ardlussa, named after the Lussa River. Just south of Ardlussa a turning to the right, marked for Inverlussa, follows the river down to **Inverlussa Beach**, passing the graveyard at **Kilchianaig** where Mary MacCrain, a descendant of the even longer-lived Gillour MacCrain (page 237), was buried after dying at the grand age of 128 in 1856. Inverlussa and its sandy, grass-bordered bay, is just 400yds further; you can get 'Tea on the Beach' (page 239) in summer months. Signs of human habitation in the form of small flint artefacts from over 8,000 years ago have been found here. Today, you are just as likely to share the beach with cows.

Lussa Gin (The Stables, Ardlussa; ☎ 01496 820196; w lussagin.com; tours £10; book online) Lussa Gin, north of Inverlussa, is distilled and bottled by Jura residents Georgina, Alicia and Claire. What started in a kitchen has now grown into an award-winning business. Their giant copper contraption, Hamish, makes a smoother version of the same recipe they first crafted five years ago. The gin is distilled with 15 botanicals, giving it a pleasantly complicated taste with hints of citrus from the lemon thyme and balm. They grow some of the plants themselves, while others, such as water mint, are picked wild from the island. As the space is small, tours are relatively concise.

NORTH OF ARDLUSSA The road, steep in places, continues along the coast, past small beaches and ancient oak woods until eventually you will come to **Lealt**, where in order to proceed you will have to open a gate before driving a further ¾ mile to the end of the public road. Those wishing to walk to see Corryvreckan and the very north end of Jura should find somewhere to park here: don't attempt to drive down the track at the end of the road, as it isn't suitable for vehicles, even those with 4x4 capability.

Gulf of Corryvreckan The name Corryvreckan comes from the Gaelic Coire Bhreacain ('cauldron of the speckled seas'). As the flood tide enters the gulf

Jura WHAT TO SEE AND DO

THE TRAGIC TALE OF PRINCE BRECKAN

A natural phenomenon as impressive and intimidating as Corryvreckan has its fair share of folk stories. One of these tells the tale of a Scandinavian prince called Breckan, who wanted to marry a daughter of one of the local lords. The latter agreed on the condition that Breckan would anchor his galley in the Hag, as the whirlpool is also called, for three days and three nights. Breckan went home to make ready his galley, and was advised by wise men to take three anchor ropes: one of the best wool, one of hemp grown in a graveyard, and one of pure maidens' hair. He followed the instructions, but as you might expect, the first night the wool rope broke. During the second night the hemp rope also gave way, and finally on the third night the maidens' hair rope broke too, because one of them had lied about her virginity. Breckan was drowned. He was pulled ashore by his dog, and buried in Breckan's Cave (Uamh Bhreacain), in Bagh Gleann nam Muc, north Jura. The dog died in the sound to the north of Scarba, which is now called the Grey Dogs Race.

12

Once known to Jura locals by his real name, Eric Blair, George Orwell lived on Jura from 1946 to 1948. During this time he was seriously ill with tuberculosis but, with a typical writer's stubbornness, insisted on living in the badly equipped, damp house at Barnhill until he was no longer physically able to. Government surveillance, propaganda and the perpetual war suffered by the characters in his dystopian novel *Nineteen Eighty-Four* may seem far away from life on Jura, but it would be hard to find a more isolated spot to find the time and concentration required to write such a masterpiece. In the charming booklet *Jura and George Orwell*, written by Gordon Wright in 1983, Mrs Nelson of Ardlussa explains how Orwell was a 'tall, gaunt and sad-looking man' who she worried would not manage on his own. In fact, he did not live alone for long and, reading between the lines, was only able to concentrate on his great novel through the tireless efforts of his sister Avril who dug the garden, cooked and kept the house going. There were also several other people around to help, as well as his three-year-old son, who he nearly lost in the Gulf of Corryvreckan on a camping trip. A booklet with more information and Mrs Nelson's personal account is available in several places on Jura including from Fiona, Gordon Wright's daughter, at Corran House B&B (£2.50; page 239).

between uninhabited Scarba and Jura, it speeds up to 8½ knots and races through various underwater rocky features to create the third largest whirlpool in the world. Corryvreckan is at its best during spring tides: these occur during times when there is a full or new moon and are nothing to do with the seasons. You can check the dates at w tides.willyweather.co.uk. For walking beyond Corryvreckan, to Jura's wild and uninhabited west coast, Peter Edwards's book *Walking on Jura, Islay and Colonsay* (page 268) is the best resource.

Walking to Corryvreckan The walk to see the very northern end of Jura and Corryvreckan is a long and boggy, but not particularly difficult, 13 miles return – though it can take more than 7 hours. You should be prepared for hiking in wet weather, and have the means of navigation for the final stretch as there is no path. A good track runs as far as the turning to **Barnhill**, where George Orwell wrote *Nineteen Eighty-Four*. Located a couple of hundred yards from the walking track, the owners ask that you observe from afar as it is not open to the public.

Just north of Barnhill the track meets a junction, where you should choose to go left, following the track north for about half a mile. Passing through some protected woodland, you will reach a junction with a short sidetrack to **Kinuachdrachd Harbour** and its small jetty, which once served a ferry route to the mainland. Returning to the main path and continuing north past the bay, take a fork on to a grassy path going left just before the last house at Kinuachdrachd.

Keeping on higher ground, with the coast on your right, the path begins well, but soon disintegrates into bog and sheep tracks for the final mile and a half. The flat rock platforms between **An Cruachan** and **Creag an t-Seoil** (✦ 56°08'48"N 5°42'29"W) make a good spot for a picnic and are the best place to observe Corryvreckan when the whirlpool is swirling. Look out for gutsy porpoises or dolphins, swept along in the current of the channel. Return along the same route.

13

Gigha (Giogha)

Gigha (pronounced 'Gee-a') sits at a jaunty angle off the Kintyre Peninsula and is the most southerly of the Inner Hebrides. Owned by the community, the island is run by the Isle of Gigha Heritage Trust. With just 177 residents, and at just 6 miles long and no more than 1½ miles wide, Gigha is the epitome of small-island life; literally everybody knows everyone and, if you are friendly, it will only take a few days for a lot of them to know you too. The community holds meetings to decide the best way forward for the island, whether it's a serious discussion about finances or to debate the fate of the island's peacocks. As the fire engine whizzes up and down Gigha's only road, trying to rack up the 200 miles of practice required for the island's voluntary firefighters to be fully qualified to use it, it becomes obvious why mainland logic doesn't and shouldn't always apply here.

Ardminish is the only settlement that can be defined as a village on the island and, approaching on the ferry, it's hard to believe that this is Gigha's 'capital'. With whitewashed walls and grey slate roofs, it's barely a sprinkling of houses, the grandest of which is Gigha Hotel. Ardminish is where you will find all the island's amenities, places to eat and much of its accommodation. Though it has a pleasant beach of its own, to visit Gigha without exploring further than Ardminish would be doing yourself and the island a great disservice. The wild, uninhabited north coast has an iconic, double-sided beach and a wealth of ancient sites to be found among the heather, while the cliffs and bays to the south are home to colonies of seals and squawking seabirds.

Gigha's warm microclimate, due to the surrounding Gulf Stream and a lack of any large hills, encourages an unusual array of plants. Larger mammals such as deer are absent and the introduction of new, innocuous-seeming animals can cause real havoc to the island's ecosystem. Invasive hedgehogs, for example, are captured and taken to a mainland sanctuary before they devour the eggs of native ground-nesting birds. Around Easter, the whole island bursts into colour with a profusion of wildflowers. Thrift, orchids, bluebells, yellow iris and grass of Parnassus are all widely distributed across Gigha's plentiful wild areas. Both the air and surrounding bodies of water, coming straight from the Atlantic, are refreshingly clear and clean.

HISTORY

Rev R S G Anderson, writing in his 1939 book *The Antiquities of Gigha* describes Gigha's history as: '...the scattered links of a broken chain, most of which are lost and the others mixed.' However much you try to smooth it over, there is no getting away from the fact that the island's written history is sporadic; before Clan MacNeill came on the scene in the 15th century, we have mostly only place names and archaeology to rely on. Prehistoric archaeological sites on Gigha, including Bronze Age burial cists (page 252) and mysterious standing stones like the small but

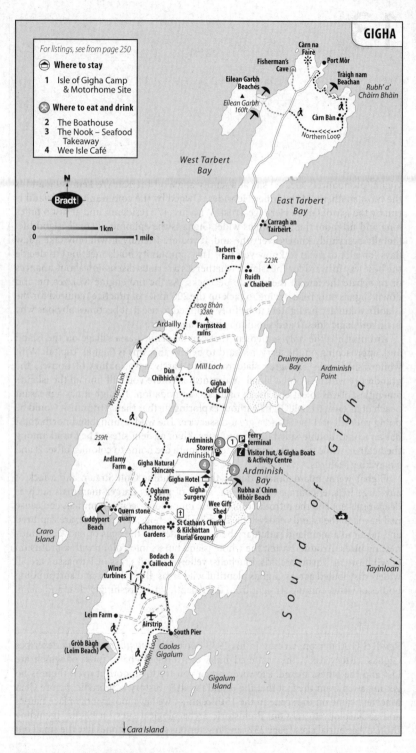

GIGHA

For listings, see from page 250

Where to stay

1　Isle of Gigha Camp
　　& Motorhome Site

Where to eat and drink

2　The Boathouse
3　The Nook – Seafood
　　Takeaway
4　Wee Isle Café

Bradt

0 — 1km
0 — 1 mile

N

Càrn na Faire
Port Mòr
Fisherman's Cave
Eilean Garbh Beaches
Tràigh nam Beachan
Eilean Garbh 160ft
Rubh' a' Chàirn Bhàin
Càrn Bàn
Northern Loop

West Tarbert Bay

East Tarbert Bay

Carragh an Tairbeirt

Tarbert Farm
223ft
Ruidh a' Chaibeil

Creag Bhàn 328ft
Ardailly
Farmstead ruins

Mill Loch
Druimyeon Bay
Ardminish Point

Dùn Chibhich
Gigha Golf Club

259ft

Ardlamy Farm

Ardminish Stores
Ferry terminal
Visitor hut, & Gigha Boats & Activity Centre
Ardminish
Gigha Natural Skincare
Gigha Hotel
Ogham Stone
Gigha Surgery
Ardminish Bay
Rubha a' Chinn Mhòir Beach

Quern stone quarry
Cuddyport Beach
Craro Island
Achamore Gardens
Wee Gift Shed
St Cathan's Church & Kilchattan Burial Ground

Western Link

Bodach & Cailleach
Wind turbines

Leim Farm
Airstrip
South Pier

Gròb Bàgh (Leim Beach)
Caolas Gigalum
Southern Loop

Gigalum Island

Sound of Gigha

Tayinloan

Cara Island

distinctive Bodach and Cailleach (page 254), are inconspicuous, but well indicated with signs and information boards thanks to recent work done by the Isle of Gigha Heritage Trust.

The Vikings started their raids on the southern Hebrides at the end of the 8th century and the name 'Gigha' itself most likely comes from the Old Norse Guðey meaning God or possibly 'good island'; there are various other place names and some archaeological sites left by the Norse. Evidence for Viking visits include a grave that was found in East Tarbert Bay, which hoarded held treasures including a bronze weighing balance from the 10th century. Additionally, one of the first written references to Gigha comes from the Icelandic book *Haakon's Saga*, which mentions King Haakon IV of Norway visiting the island, after bad weather delayed his 100 ships on their way to the Battle of Largs in 1263 (where he was defeated).

In the 14th century, Gigha came under the control of the Lords of the Isles who, in 1449, granted part of Gigha to Torquil MacNeill of Taynish, a clan chief from the mainland; by 1493 the MacNeills had control of the whole island. Excluding a few short periods, the MacNeills kept control of the island for the next 372 years. Seemingly consistent in retrospect, it was not a peaceful time and though the following history reads like the squabbles of petulant children, clan warfare wreaked havoc, massacre and destruction on the people of Gigha. The best surviving archaeological relics from these times can be found at St Cathan's Church and Kilchattan Burial Ground (page 253).

In 1792 Gigha's population peaked at 614 but, like most of the Inner Hebrides, was almost halved over the following century owing to the economic hardships around the time of the Clearances (page 15). The MacNeills sold up the island in 1865 and in the 20th century Gigha saw several owners including Sir James Horlick, 4th Baronet and chairman of Horlicks Ltd, the malted-milk drink company. Although some lairds showed generosity, the people of Gigha saw their lives and property passed from one man to the next. The community lacked agency and the quality of social housing was poor; some houses still had dirt floors in the 1970s. By the turn of the millennium Gigha's population had dwindled to around 90 people.

On 15 March 2002, after being put on the market again, the community voted to buy out the island. With the help of grants and loans from the National Lottery and the Highlands and Islands Enterprise, the Isle of Gigha Heritage Trust purchased Gigha for £4 million. Through selling Achamore House, although not the gardens, and huge fund-raising efforts from the people themselves, the Trust then managed to pay off the short-term loan of £1 million they had taken from the Scottish Land Fund within two years of purchasing the island.

At the end of 2023, the Isle of Gigha Heritage Trust finally managed to clear their debts. The population has risen to 177, the school has dramatically increased in size and many small businesses have sprung up on the island, but perhaps their most inspiring success has been in setting up Gigha Renewable Energy. Their wind turbines, known locally as the Dancing Ladies, produce an excess of electricity, which provides the main source of income for the island, as it's sold back to the National Grid.

GETTING THERE AND AROUND

Only a short **ferry** ride from the mainland, Gigha is surprisingly accessible in comparison with many of the Inner Hebrides' islands. Services from Tayinloan on the mainland are run by CalMac (page 30; foot passengers/car £2.90/8.40). The

13

JUNE

The Sound of Gigha w thesoundofgigha.co.uk. Intimate traditional Scottish music festival, with dancing, workshops & family entertainment.

JULY

Gigha Raft Race Contact the Boathouse restaurant (see opposite). Competitors race home-built rafts. Usually held on the last Sat, this is entertaining to watch even if you haven't sculpted your own craft. There's also a BBQ & live music.

journey takes around 20 minutes, with ferries running between six and ten times a day, and tickets can now be bought in advance.

The ferry over to the island is an enjoyable trip and the only plausible option for the vast majority of visitors, but those with their own **boat** or **aircraft** are also catered for; information about these options can be found at w visitgigha.co.uk.

Gigha's main road is single track and is regularly used by tractors and trucks, so if you bring a **car**, be careful not to park blocking passing places or gates. Caravans are not permitted, but campervans are welcome if they are booked into the campsite (see below) in advance.

After a community consultation in 2019, the Isle of Gigha Heritage Trust launched the Gateway to Gigha project with the aims of reducing car traffic, improve island access and conserve historical sites. Two years were spent building an extensive network of **foot and cycle paths**, as well as information boards and signage. With bike hire also available from Gigha Boats and Activity Centre (near the ferry terminal; f; e-bikes/bikes £30/20 a day) and an interactive map (found at w visitgigha.co.uk/Interactive-Map), no Inner Hebridean island is easier to explore without a car.

TOURIST INFORMATION

Near the ferry slip, a small visitor hut provides information about the island, including maps and event posters. Online, the Visit Gigha website (w visitgigha. co.uk) is a helpful source of information.

WHERE TO STAY AND EAT   *Map, page 248*

Gigha has a handful of accommodation options. For self-catering, contact Gigha Holiday Lets (m 07538 435628; w gigha-holidaylets.co.uk; 5 cottages, sleeping 2–6). At the time of writing, Gigha Hotel was closed for extensive refurbishment, but it was hoped would reopen under new management in 2025 – see w visitgigha. co.uk for updates. If you have a large motorhome, you can also stay at Ferry Farm (\ 01583 441141; £) in Tayinloan next to the ferry port and come across as a foot passenger.

Isle of Gigha Camp & Motorhome Site
Ardminish PA41 7AA; w gighacampsite.co.uk; &. This community-owned campsite, opened in 2022, is conveniently located by the ferry pier. The site is clean & well thought-out, with good facilities for campervans, motorhomes & tent campers. Secluded tent pitches are mown into a wild area, which is hidden from the car park. There are size restrictions on both motorhomes & tents, & it's important to book in advance. **£**

The Boathouse Ardminish; ☎ 01583 505123; w boathouseongigha.com; ⏰ Apr & Sep noon–23.00 Wed–Sun, May–Aug noon–23.00 Tue–Sun. High-quality restaurant with excellent local seafood, right on the beachfront. Book in advance. ££–£££

The Nook – Seafood Takeaway Ardminish Stores, Ardminish PA41 7AA; m 07557 277735; fi; ⏰ check Facebook. Fresh seafood take-away with everything from beer-battered haddock to a crayfish cocktail. £

Wee Isle Café Craft Unit 3, Ardminish PA41 7AA; m 07467 449613; fi; ⏰ check Facebook. B/fast rolls, burgers, coffee & creamy ice cream from Gigha's Wee Isle Dairy. Eat in or take-away. £

SHOPPING

Ardminish Stores (Cnr of the main road & the ferry port; ☎ 01583 505251; fi; e tealejc@yahoo.co.uk; ⏰ Apr–Sep 09.00–18.00 daily; reduced in winter) has all your absolute essentials under one roof: Joe and Hannah sell groceries, gifts and souvenirs, with a good range of local products, plus there's a post office and a petrol/diesel filling station.

Look out, too, for honesty box stalls along the main road.

Gigha Natural Skincare (Unit 2, Ardminish PA41 7AA; m 07881 426616; fi; ⏰ 09.30–17.00 Mon–Sat, but hours flexible) sells a large range of natural oils and creams, as well as offering alternative therapies by appointment. A little further south, whether you're looking for a knitted chicken, woolly hat or handmade necklace, Caroline's **Wee Gift Shed** (Calag Ruadh, North Drumachro PA41 7AB; ☎ 01583 505151; e caroline_mcvean@yahoo.co.uk; ⏰ Apr–Oct 11.00–16.00 daily) has souvenirs and presents crammed into every inch of available space. She makes many of the things herself.

OTHER PRACTICALITIES

Information about **medical services** available from Gigha Surgery (top row of Ardminish Village) can be found online (w gigha.org.uk/Visitor-Information; drop-in clinic ⏰ 09.30–10.30 & 12.30–13.30 Mon–Fri at the time of writing). There's a **post office** at Ardminish Stores (see above).

LOCAL PRODUCE

As a visitor, choosing to buy local produce is a positive contribution to Gigha's economy, plus the carbon footprint of your food will be small and the quality is excellent. Honesty box stalls around the island sell a variety of seasonal produce, while there are also a couple of more established businesses.

Emma, of the **Wee Isle Dairy** (☎ 01583 505033; fi), calls her herd of free-range cows the Liquorice Allsorts – a mixture of breeds for the best-quality milk. You can buy their glass-bottled milk, ice cream and sauces from Ardminish Stores or visit the Wee Isle Café.

Gigha's clean water is perfect for oysters and in high season, Tony and Cat Walker run **Gigha Oysters** (☎ 01583 505237), which can be found on the menu of the island's restaurants. You can also usually buy them directly by phoning.

You can also buy fresh bread loafs and rolls from micro-bakery **Sunshine Bread** (w sunshine-bread.square.site); place orders online on Tuesdays for pickup on Saturdays 10.00–noon.

THE NORTH Easily found at the summit of Gigha's most northerly point is **Càrn na Faire** (the 'Watch Cairn'). There is a waymarked path, which leads off to the left just after the small ruined building on the other side of the road. This spot was used for centuries during clan times, and probably by the Norse, as a smoke-signalling beacon. Anderson (page 247) suggests that it is 'practically certain' to be late Bronze Age and that excavations would uncover burial cists. In its current state, there is not a lot to see other than a large pile of rocks, but it is a fantastic viewpoint for the surrounding coastline and the Paps of Jura, with the possibility of seeing large marine mammals such as seals or occasionally dolphins, and well worth the short walk in any weather conditions.

At the very northern end of the island's road is **Port Mòr**, the old ferry port; it's possible to park here. A sign indicates '**Northern Loop**/Càrn Bàn' at the start of a 2-mile waymarked path leading to a string of sandy beaches at Tràigh nam Beachan. This beautiful, low-lying stretch of coastline is home to many species of seabird, including oystercatchers and cormorants.

Continuing to follow the waymarkers brings you to the late Bronze Age **Càrn Bàn** (the 'White Cairn'). The burial site was discovered accidentally by dyke builders in 1792, who found chambers, a complete skeleton and 'an intolerable stench'. The whole cairn was apparently a complicated structure of 49ft diameter, with four cists.

Eventually the Northern Loop trail ends at the road, half a mile south of Port Mòr.Back on the main road, some 200yds southwest of the turning to Càrn na Faire, there is a sign for the short path to **Fisherman's Cave**. Located between a small inlet called Bàgh Beag and the hill Cnoc An Itch, this dank cavern has been inhabited at several times throughout history, something which must have been a miserable existence as the only truly sheltered, dry area is extremely small. Bored inhabitants have carved the walls and you can find engravings from as far back as 1735. From here, you can clamber south round an unpathed 700yds of coastline to Eilean Garbh, or return to the road.

Half a mile south of Port Mòr, where there is a car park at the southern end of the Northern Loop walking trail, a signpost pointing west indicates the beginning of a shared walking/cycling track to **Eilean Garbh Beaches**. Here, a tombolo – a double stretch of white sand separated by a few yards of coastal grasses – connects Gigha to the tied island of Eilean Garbh. The summit of the rocky island has unparalleled views down Gigha's western coastline and across to Islay and Jura.

CENTRAL GIGHA Continuing south along the main road brings you to **Carragh an Tairbeirt** (the Stone of Tarbert), on the east side. Also known as the Hanging Stone, Druid's Stone or Spitheag an Fhamhair (the Giant's Chip/Pebble), this is a distinctive cleft standing stone, which you will most likely recognise from the Gigha Heritage Trust's logo. Horrifically, it was once used for hanging people condemned at the nearby Hill of the Assembly, but this was not its original purpose, which has now been forgotten.

About 600yds further south, in the field opposite Tarbert Farm, is **Ruidh a' Chaibeil** (Field of the Chapel; ⊕ 55°42'03.9"N 5°44'02.3"W). Though this is an ancient burial site, which once had stones to mark the graves, the battered remains of a Celtic cross are all that is now distinguishable to an interested novice. Apparently the graveyard had originally been larger but was destroyed by a farmer who wanted to make more use of his field. The graveyard's date is unknown, but it certainly pre-dates Kilchattan (see opposite).

Just south of Tarbert Farm, the waymarked **Western Link** walking route is indicated by a signpost. This route, which is just over 3 miles, rambles along Gigha's wild west side, passing the ruins of a farmstead at **Ardailly** and Creag Bhàn before climbing above the island's western sea cliffs and eventually coming out near Achamore Gardens – it's a great way to connect the north and south if you're on foot.

In the centre of the island, it's an easy clamber up to **Creag Bhàn**, Gigha's highest hill at 328ft, which is a good vantage point to spot hen harriers and provides unrivalled views across the island, including down on to the farmstead ruins at **Ardailly**. To get there from the road, take the rough road west towards Ardailly; opposite Mill Loch, on the right-hand side, you'll find a path that leads to the summit. There is a small place here where it is possible to park without blocking the passing place.

Returning to the main road, half a mile south of the turning to Ardailly is **Gigha Golf Club** (PA41 7AA; w visitgigha.co.uk/Golf; adult/child £15/10), which has a nine-hole course. From here, a 1½-mile circular, waymarked path leads to the ancient fort of **Dùn Chibhich**. The name is said to derive from Chibhich or Keefie, the Norse King of Lochlin's son, and is tangled with the Irish legend of tragic lovers of Diarmuid and Grainne. The fort is overgrown, but has spectacular views over Mill Loch, Creag Bhàn, the Paps of Jura and Islay.

THE SOUTH Back in Ardminish, **Rubha a' Chinn Mhòir Beach** is signposted from the main road just south of the Gigha Hotel. It only takes a couple of minutes to walk to this beach and, although it's small, the sand and water look as tropical as anywhere on the island.

Half a mile south of the Gigha Hotel is a turning to the right marked to Achamore Gardens (page 254). Just 300yds up the track, past the village hall (on your right), **St Cathan's Church and Kilchattan Burial Ground** is the perfect place to ponder on previous generations of island inhabitants. Now an atmospheric ruin with some elaborate window frames intact, the church is thought to have been built in the 13th century. Among the more obvious and interesting graves are those of Malcolm MacNeill (in a walled enclosure to the east of the church), who died in 1493 and is depicted as a warrior, and an elaborately carved grave slab in the southeast corner of the church, thought to be from the 14th century.

Continuing along the track, at its highest point, before you reach the houses, there is a short path up to the **Ogham Stone** (⊕ 55°40'10.8"N 5°44'56.7"W). This proud pillar, presiding over the burial ground, is inscribed in Ogham, an early medieval alphabet from Ireland. The translation is disputed and the stone is currently coated in crispy lichen, making it difficult to distinguish anything at all, but it's thought to be a gravestone around 1,400 years old and mentions the name of the man buried there and his father.

Cuddyport Beach and the **quern stone quarry** (⊕ 55°40'07.7"N 5°45'49.9"W) are further along the main track that passes the burial ground and the path to the Ogham Stone; the bay is best reached on foot or by bike as there is no parking. Follow the track and bear left past a couple of houses at the top of the hill, heading towards Ardlamy Farm. When you reach a junction, follow the sign for Cuddyport and a track leading northwest through the fields.

Stop some 200yds before you reach the farm to pass through the gate on your left. Follow this next track southwest until it dwindles to nothing around a gateway where you should walk straight on, across the field, to a gate and a boggy path down to the shore. From the shore, turn right and walk 200yds west to Cuddyport Beach.

Sometimes referred to as Ardlamy Bay by locals and Port Na Cathrach on the OS map, this is an attractive sandy beach with an old rocky pier and a small boathouse – a perfect spot for a picnic. The quern quarry, with its many distinctive 20-inch-wide, round marks, can be found on the western side of the headland on the beach's east (Port nan Each), though it can be easier to approach them from the back, rather than following the slippery rocks at the water's edge. The site probably dates from the 18th century; quern stones were used for grinding corn.

Achamore Gardens The Gigha Heritage Trust decided to sell the mansion at Achamore, but keep possession of the garden, which is open to visitors one mile south of Ardminish, just west of the main road (w visitgigha.co.uk/Achamore-Gardens; adult/child/family £7.50/5/20). When I first looked around in 2019, the rambling 54 acres were more of a Hebridean jungle exploration than the finely manicured grounds one might imagine of a stately home, but the difference on my second visit was remarkable. An extensive restoration programme began in 2020 and is well on its way to restoring the gardens to their former glory.

Achamore Gardens were originally created in 1944 by the laird Colonel Sir James Horlick and his gardener Kitty Lloyd Jones. Over the last 80 years Gigha's warmer microclimate has ensured the survival of many plants that would not usually be found in Scotland; gigantic Brazilian rhubarbs, rare species of colourful rhododendron and delicate, spring blooming trout lily have been uncovered from the brambles as part of an extensive restoration programme.

Walk: The Southern Loop with Bodach and Cailleach
Distance: 3 miles; time: 2 hours; start/end: South Pier; OS Explorer map: 357 Kintyre North
This great walk takes in the best of Gigha's far south. Starting at South Pier (the very southern end of the main road; parking is possible here), begin by walking back up the road, past the grassy airstrip on the left, until you reach a gravel track signposted to 'Southern Loop and paths north' that heads towards the wind turbines.

Follow this track, ignoring a left turn towards a house, until you are level with the turbines; here you will see a gateway on the right. Go through this gateway and follow a path 250yds north to the rocky hillock Cnoc a' Bhodaich ('Hill of the Old Man'). At the top of the hillock are **Bodach and Cailleach** ('the old man and woman', or 'hag' to be more precise; ✛ 55°39'41.8"N 5°45'19.5"W), two very curiously shaped stones that appear to be linked to other sites in Scotland. For example, Tigh nam Bodach ('house of the old man') in central Scotland has a Cailleach, Bodach and a whole family of their smaller stones. On Gigha itself, a folk tale talks of how they prowl the moorland after dark.

Return the way you came, back to the gate on the south side of the field. From here, walk straight ahead (continuing south) to a second small gate, passing the most southerly of the wind turbines on your right. Go through the gate and follow a path through a patch of woodland with rocky knolls on your right and a fenced field on the left. When the path ends at a T-junction, go through the gate here and turn right on to a track. Follow the track west for about 100yds, then turn left on to a muddy track leading south (a wooden arrow indicates the direction for 'beach'). Go through a gate and follow yellow stick markers bearing right down to the wide, sandy **Gròb Bàgh** (also known locally as **Leim Beach**), with Leim Farm on your right. Take some time to enjoy the beach and its rocky headlands, looking out for boulders of white quartzite, basking seals, seabirds and more elusive otters.

Continue to follow the yellow markers southeast along the beach and go through a small gate at its far end. Walk up a set of stone steps and follow the markers as they bear right towards the top of a small hill where there is a cairn. From here there are great views over the small uninhabited island of Cara and further south along Kintyre towards Northern Ireland.

Continue to follow the yellow markers as they lead south and then turn sharply northeast heading towards a walled field and the distant South Pier. Upon reaching the wall, follow the path on its shore side as it descends to the raised shore platform where there is a gate. Go through the gate and head northeast along the shoreline of Caolas Gigalum back to South Pier. Gigalum Island is just offshore.

OBAN

Corran Halls ●

CORRAN ESPLANADE

→ Oban Airport
(5 miles)

No 26 By The Sea (½ mile),
Barriemore Oban (½ mile),
Dunollie Castle &
1745 House Museum
(1 mile)

DUNOLLIE RD

DUNOLLIE ROAD

CORRAN ESPLANADE

BREADALBANE STREET

ALBERT LANE

ALBERT ROAD

NURSERY LANE

GEORGE STREET

Bradt!

N

0 ⊢——— 100m
0 ⊢——— 100yds

Oban Phoenix
Cinema

Oxfam
Books ●

Oban War &
Peace Museum

Oban
Cycles 🚲

7 ●

Oban Whisky &
Fine Wines Shop

CRAIGARD ROAD

DALRIACH ROAD

ARDCONNEL ROAD

LAUREL ROAD

DUNCRAGGAN ROAD

McCaig's
Tower ⛰

*Oban
Bay*

Lismore, Mull,
Colonsay, Islay,
Coll, Tiree

2 ●
6 ●

GEORGE STREET

4 ●

ARDCONNEL TERRACE

ARDCONNEL ROAD

ARGYLL ST

TWEEDALE STREET

TAYLOR'S BRAE

ROCKFIELD ROAD

P

✚ Boots
$ Royal Bank
of Scotland

West Coast
Motors ●
● Waterstones
Jackson
Butchers

HILL STREET

STEVENSON STREET

3 ●

$ TSB

Outside
Edge ●

AIRD'S PLACE

AIRD'S CRESCENT

QUEEN'S PARK PLACE

STATION ROAD

Oban Station
Square bus stop 🚌
$

Railway
station

Argyll
Square

5 ●

Food from Argyll
at the Pier

Ferry
terminal 🚢

P

SHORE STREET

CAMPBELL STREET

HIGH STREET

COMBIE STREET

LOCHSIDE STREET

Oban Holiday
Park (3 miles)

ALBANY STREET

CREAG AN AIRM

GLENSHELLACH ROAD

DRIMVARGIE RD

Halfords
Autocentre ●

Glen Sonas
Campsite
(2½ miles)

GLENCRUITTEN ROAD

SOROBA ROAD

SOROBA LANE

Tesco
✉

Lidl
Oban

Lorn & Islands
Hospital (½ mile)

P

For listings, see page 258

🏠 **Where to stay**
1 Oban Backpackers
Off map
   Barriemore Oban
   No 26 By The Sea

🍴 **Where to eat and drink**
2 Ee.usk
3 George Street Chip Shop
4 Hinba
5 Oban Seafood Hut
6 Piazza
7 The Pokey Hat

14

Gateway Towns

OBAN

Oban is by far the biggest and most exciting of the ports serving the Inner Hebrides. Home to over 8,000 people, a population that more than doubles with visitors in the summer months, the waterfront town maintains its charm through a thriving community, as well as the historic buildings and characterful boats of its harbour. Ferries leave from here to Mull, Coll, Tiree, Lismore, Colonsay and Islay; and, with a train station, bus connections and even an airport, the town is well connected to the rest of the mainland. There is plenty to detain you in Oban for a couple of days, which is particularly fortunate in bad weather when you might not have any other option. Those doing extended trips in the Hebrides might be pleased to have a break from the restrictions of island life; of all the places featured in this book, Oban has by far the best shopping and eating opportunities. For information and listings beyond what is included here, check w oban.org.uk.

GETTING THERE AND AWAY
By bus or rail   Oban is well connected to Glasgow; those wanting to travel to/from Mallaig will usually need to change in Fort William or Crianlarich. Oban Station Square bus stop, the West Coast Motors ticket and tour office, and the train station are within 500yds of the ferry terminal. For route planning and connecting bus and train services, use w traveline.info.

By ferry   CalMac (page 30) run services between Oban and the islands of Mull, Coll, Tiree, Lismore, Colonsay and, less frequently, on to Islay. The ferry terminal is near the centre of town.

By air   Oban has a small **airport** (North Connel PA37 1SW; ℂ 01631 572910; w obanandtheislesairports.com), which is only open during the daytime. Services from here are operated by the equally small **Hebridean Air** (ℂ 08458 057465; w hebrideanair.co.uk), which runs flights to Coll, Colonsay, Tiree and Islay, as well as charter flights.

FESTIVALS AND EVENTS

Check Oban What's On (w obanwhatson.co.uk) for event listings around the time of your visit. In September, the **Argyll Food Festival** (The Corran Halls, 54 Corran Esplanade PA34 5AB; ℂ 01631 567333; w wildaboutargyll.co.uk) showcases local produce.

14

GETTING AROUND Oban is easy to wander around on **foot**. There are a few outlying attractions, such as Dunollie Castle, which are quicker to reach on the **bus** (see w westcoastmotors.co.uk/timetables/oban-isle-of-mull for route map & times), or by cycling or driving. Note that parking (mostly pay and display in the centre) in Oban is in high demand during the busy summer season and as a result can be difficult at times.

If you prefer cycling, **hire a bike** from Oban Cycles (87 George St PA34 5NN; w obancyclescotland.com; ⏰ 10.00–17.00 Tue–Sat); they also offer sales and repairs.

🏠 WHERE TO STAY *Map, page 256*

Whether you're looking for luxury on the seafront or a lively backpackers' hostel, Oban has a full range of accommodation options and good choices to make within each. There isn't a campsite right near town, but **Glen Sonas Campsite** (Glencruitten PA34 4QB; ☎ 01631 710478; **£**) 2½ miles east of town, provides a basic but friendly hardstanding option for campervans, with toilet and no shower, while **Oban Holiday Park** (Gallanachmore Farm, Gallanach Road PA34 4QH; ☎ 03331 881930; w highlandholidays.com/parks/oban; **£–£££**), 3 miles southwest, can accommodate everything from small tents to caravans with more modern facilities, as well as offering a range of self-catering options, from basic pods to lodges with hot tubs. Should you need them, paid toilets and showers are available in Oban behind the white buildings with red roofs on the harbour.

No 26 By The Sea (9 rooms) Corran Esplanade PA34 5AQ; ☎ 01631 705178; w no26bythesea.com. Small, luxurious hotel with spectacular sea views. Carefully considered décor is individual to each room, with fluffy bathrobes & a sun terrace with firepit for when the weather allows for outdoor relaxation. **£££££**

Barriemore Oban (14 rooms) Corran Esplanade PA34 5AQ; ☎ 01631 566356; w barriemore.co.uk. On the seafront a short walk northwest of the town centre, this guesthouse offers friendly & comfortable room-only accommodation. **£££**

Oban Backpackers (55 beds) Breadalbane St PA34 5NZ; ☎ 01631 562107; w obanbackpackers. com; ⏰ Apr–end Oct. Colourful hostel with wonderful painted map on the wall in communal area. Kitchen would be rather lively if fully booked, but communal seating is pleasant & relaxed. **£**

✕ WHERE TO EAT AND DRINK *Map, page 256*

Ee.usk North Pier PA34 5QD; ☎ 01631 565666; w eeusk.com; ⏰ noon–14.30 & 17.30–21.00 daily; ♿. This modern white building with a red roof on the harbourfront serves reliably good local seafood, including lobster from Luing. Surrounded by glass for harbour views. **£–££**

George Street Chip Shop 13–15 George St PA34 5RU; ☎ 01631 566664; w georgestreetfishrestaurant.co.uk; ⏰ noon–22.00 daily. Fish & chips with crispy batter, plus a great vegetarian haggis. Take-away only. **£**

Hinba 62 George St PA34 5SD; m 07956 734913; w hinba.co.uk; ⏰ 09.00–16.00 daily. Coffee shop run by Hinba Coffee Roasters, who roast their single-origin coffee on Seil. They also sell sandwiches & cakes; very popular with both locals & visitors. **£**

Oban Seafood Hut Railway Pier PA34 4DB; m 07881 418565; 🖪; ⏰ mid-Mar–Oct 10.00–18.00 daily (reduced in shoulder seasons). This green shed with 'Local Shellfish' painted above the doorway is right next to the ferry terminal & usually buzzing with customers. All sorts of local fish & shellfish including lobster, oysters & a famous prawn sandwich. **£**

The Pokey Hat 13 Stafford St PA34 5NJ; ⏰ flexible. Pink building with lime-green sign & model cows outside, serving Italian ice cream that's homemade on the premises daily. **£**

Piazza North Pier PA34 5QD; ☎ 01631 563628; w piazzaoban.com; ⏰ 10.00–15.00 & 17.30–21.00 daily; ♿. Spacious family restaurant serving pizza & pasta. Next to Ee.usk, with views over the harbour. **£**

SHOPPING Oban has a decent range of standard high-street shops for clothing and other things you might have forgotten. Although most of the islands have grocery stores and it is good to support the local economy there, it's generally worth taking at least some food across with you for self-catering holidays, and Oban is by far the best place to stock up.

Food from Argyll at the Pier The Ferry Terminal, The Railway Pier PA34 5DB; 📞 01631 563636; 📘 🕐 08.45–15.30 Mon–Sat, 08.45–14.00 Sun. Shop, café & take-away (£) with a good selection of local produce.
Jackson Butchers 2 George St PA34 5RX; 📞 01631 562016; 🕐 08.00–17.00 Tue–Fri, 08.00–16.00 Sun. Traditional butchers established in 1932.
Lidl Oban Soroba Rd PA34 4HY; w lidl.co.uk; 🕐 08.00–22.00 Mon–Sat, 08.00–20.00 Sun. Probably the cheapest & best value for money of the large supermarkets.
Oban Whisky & Fine Wines Shop 19 Stafford St PA34 5NJ; 📞 01631 570586; w whiskyfix.com; 🕐 10.00–20.00 Mon–Sat, noon–18.00 Sun. Independent whisky experts specialising in rare &

interesting bottles of single-malt scotch whisky. Friendly & welcoming shop.
Outside Edge 6 MacGregor Court PA34 4DJ; 📞 01631 566617; w outsideedgeoban.com; 🕐 09.00–17.30 Mon–Sat. Outdoor gear & local tide-table booklets.
Oxfam Books 107/109 George St PA34 5NT; 📞 01631 566465. Notably large selection of secondhand books, including local interest.
Tesco Lochside St PA34 4HP; w tesco.com; 🕐 07.00–23.00 Mon–Sat, 08.00–20.00 Sun. Jarringly enormous supermarket.
Waterstones 12 George St PA34 5SB; 📞 01631 571455; w waterstones.com; 🕐 09.00–17.30 Mon–Sat, 11.00–17.00 Sun. Oban branch of the nationwide bookshop chain.

OTHER PRACTICALITIES If you're in need of a **mechanic**, try Halfords Autocentre (McConechys, 21 Lochside St PA34 4HP; 📞 01631 570047; 🕐 08.00–18.00 Mon–Sat). Oban also has a good independent and community-owned **cinema** (Oban Phoenix Cinema, 140 George St PA34 5NZ; 📞 01631 562905; w obanphoenix.com; ♿).

Banks Bank of Scotland (Station Rd, Oban PA34 4LL; 📞 03457 213141; 🕐 09.00–15.30 Mon–Fri); Royal Bank of Scotland (26 George St PA34 5SB; 📞 03457 242424; 🕐 09.30–15.30 Mon–Tue & Thu–Fri, 10.00–15.30 Wed); TSB (31–35 Airds Cres PA34 5SQ; 📞 01631 399998; 🕐 10.00–16.00 Mon–Fri)
Fuel Tesco Petrol Filling Station, Lochside St PA34 4HP; 📞 03456 779519; 🕐 06.00–20.00 daily

Health Lorn & Islands Hospital (Glengallan Rd PA34 4HH; 📞 01631 789000; w obanhospital. com); Boots Pharmacy (34–38 George St PA34 5NL; 📞 01631 562517; w boots.com; 🕐 09.00–17.30 Mon–Sat)
Post offices 128 George St (PA34 5NT; 🕐 08.00–20.00 Mon–Sat, 08.00–18.00 Sun); in the Tesco (Lochside St PA34 4HP; 🕐 09.00–17.30 Mon–Sat)

WHAT TO SEE AND DO There's plenty to fill a day or two in Oban. This is just a small selection, but pick up a copy of the *Oban Times* or find more on w oban.org.uk.

The **Oban War & Peace Museum** (Old Oban Times Bldg, Corran Esplanade PA34 5PX; 📞 01631 570007; w obanmuseum.org.uk; 🕐 Mar–Nov 10.00–16.00 Sat–Thu, 10.00–14.00 Fri; free) is a good introduction to Oban's history, including the town's role in World War II.

Just a little north of the town is **Dunollie Castle** and the **1745 House Museum** (PA34 5TT; 📞 01631 570550; w dunollie.org; 🕐 Apr–Oct; adult/concession/child £9/7.50/4.50; ♿). While the ruined castle itself is small, it is spectacularly positioned with views across to Kerrera (page 191). The museum, set in an 18th-century house about 100yds away, gives a more balanced account of history than most castle museums, with space and consideration given to servants and normal people from the 18th century. The restored Dunollie weaving loom is a real highlight. The castle has wonderful leafy grounds with pathways through mature deciduous trees as well as a giant redwood sequoia. The on-site **Kettle Garden Café** sells soup, proper coffee, homemade cakes and ice creams to be eaten outside or under a marquee. Weekly piping performances, guided tours and seasonal events are listed online.

MALLAIG

The only other substantial port town serving the Inner Hebrides is Mallaig, which has ferries running to Skye and the Small Isles. Little more than a village, it is mostly made up of B&Bs, fish and chip shops, fishing boats and seagulls, with a backdrop of pretty hills and an interesting boatyard. There are limited shopping opportunities, but they are still probably more extensive than those on the Small Isles or Sleat.

GETTING THERE AND AROUND By both rail and road the journey to Mallaig follows two of the most beautiful routes in Scotland. The West Highland Line runs arguably the most picturesque railway journey in the UK, crossing the unforgettable Glenfinnan Viaduct, famous for its appearance in the *Harry Potter*

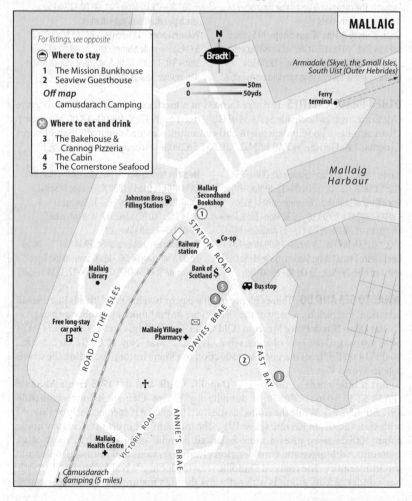

MALLAIG

For listings, see opposite

🛏 **Where to stay**
1 The Mission Bunkhouse
2 Seaview Guesthouse
Off map
    Camusdarach Camping

✖ **Where to eat and drink**
3 The Bakehouse &
    Crannog Pizzeria
4 The Cabin
5 The Cornerstone Seafood

N

Bradt

0 ———— 50m
0 ———— 50yds

Armadale (Skye), the Small Isles,
South Uist (Outer Hebrides)

Ferry
terminal ●

Mallaig
Harbour

Mallaig
Secondhand
Bookshop

Johnston Bros
Filling Station

①

● Co-op

Railway
station

STATION ROAD

Bank of
Scotland $

⑤

④

🚌 Bus stop

Mallaig
Library

ROAD TO THE ISLES

Free long-stay
car park
🅿

Mallaig Village
Pharmacy ✚

✉

DAVIES BRAE

②

EAST BAY

③

✝

VICTORIA ROAD

ANNIE'S BRAE

Mallaig
Health Centre
✚

Camusdarach
Camping (5 miles)

films. Travelling by road, the A830, which starts just north of Fort William, forms part of the well-known Road to the Isles, passing mountainous scenery, lochs and parts of the coast.

By **rail or bus**, the easiest and quickest journeys from the rest of the UK to Mallaig usually pass through Glasgow. Check w traveline.info to plan all connecting rail/bus journeys. West Coast Railways (03339 966692; w westcoastrailways.co.uk) run the picturesque *Jacobite* steam train from Fort William to Mallaig; the fare is relatively expensive compared with the distance covered and booking in advance is recommended. The train station is opposite the ferry terminal.

By **ferry**, CalMac (page 30) runs services to Armadale on Skye (page 89), the Small Isles (page 102) and South Uist in the Outer Hebrides. The ferry terminal is on the western side of the harbour.

Mallaig is a small town and is easy to explore **on foot**. There is a free long-stay car park, but make sure you allow plenty of time to find a space before your ferry.

WHERE TO STAY *Map, opposite*

For additional accommodation and options for eating out, have a look at w road-to-the-isles.org.uk.

Seaview Guesthouse (4 rooms & 1 annex) Main St PH41 4QS; 01687 462059; w seaviewguesthousemallaig.com. Spotlessly clean & tastefully decorated in greys & blues. 3 en-suite dbls; 1 twin with private bathroom, 1 self-catering annex. **£££**

The Mission Bunkhouse (10 rooms) Station Rd PH41 4QA; m 07765 013817. A friendly little hostel with private rooms above the bookshop & café. Bedrooms are small, but there is a comfortable communal lounge & the kitchen does not feel crowded. Door on to large flat roof gives extra space & is a novelty in good weather. **£**

Camusdarach Camping PH39 4NT; 01687 450221; w camusdarach.co.uk; ⏲ Apr–Sep. Located 5 miles south of Mallaig on the way to Arisaig, this is a lovely campsite near a huge sandy beach. Small shop selling fresh coffee, croissants, cold drinks & snacks. Free Wi-Fi & phone charging, plus laundry, kettle & microwave. **£**

WHERE TO EAT AND DRINK *Map, opposite*

The Cornerstone Seafood Restaurant Davies Brae PH41 4PU; 01687 462306; w seafoodrestaurantmallaig.com; ⏲ noon–14.30 & 17.30–20.30 Mon–Sat. Good, locally landed seafood in small restaurant. **££**

The Cabin Davies Brae PH41 4PU; 01687 462207; ; ⏲ noon–20.00 daily. Fish & chips to take away or sit-down meals in relaxed restaurant, specialising in seafood. **£–££**

The Bakehouse & Crannog Pizzeria The Old Quay PH41 4QF; 01687 462808; ⏲ Bakehouse summer 09.00–15.00 Tue–Sat, winter 09.00–15.00 Tue, Fri–Sat; pizzeria Apr–Oct 16.00–20.00 Fri–Sat. Coffee, fresh bread & excellent pastries from the Bakehouse; hand-stretched sourdough pizzas from Crannog Pizzeria. No tables, but decking outside on the harbourfront. **£**

SHOPPING

Co-op Station Rd PH41 4PY; 01687 462240; w coop.co.uk; ⏲ 07.00–22.00 daily. Medium-size grocery shop.

Mallaig Secondhand Bookshop Station Rd PH41 4PU; ⏲ hours vary; &. Old history books including some local & of the isles; also fiction. Proceeds go to local charities.

OTHER PRACTICALITIES

Bank Bank of Scotland, Station Rd PH41 4PZ; 03457 213141; ⏲ 10.00–14.00 Mon–Fri

Fuel Johnston Bros Filling Station PH41 4QD; 01687 462215; ⏲ 10.00–17.00 Mon–Fri, 10.00–14.00 Sat

Health Mallaig Health Centre (Victoria Rd PH41 4RN; ☎ 01687 462202); Mallaig Village Pharmacy (Davies Brae PH41 4QY; ☎ 01687 462209; ⏰ 09.00–17.30 Mon–Fri, 09.00–13.00 Sat)
Library Mallaig Library, Mallaig & Morar Community Centre, West Bay PH41 4PX; ☎ 01687

460097; ⏰ 10.30–14.00 Tue, 13.00–17.00 Wed, 17.00–20.00 Thu, 10.00–14.00 Fri, 10.00–noon Sat
Post office 1 Davies Brae PH41 4PU; ☎ 01687 460257; ⏰ 09.00–13.00 Mon–Fri, 14.00–17.00 Mon, Wed & Fri

OTHER PORTS AND CONNECTIONS

Although Oban and Mallaig serve the majority of the Inner Hebrides, there are several other small ports. The following port towns have small villages and a couple of limited amenities: **Kyle of Lochalsh** for the Skye Bridge (page 55); **Arisaig** for the Small Isles (page 105); **Kilchoan** for Tobermory on Mull (page 153); **Lochaline** for Fishnish on Mull (page 153); and **Tayinloan** for Gigha (page 249).

Port Appin, where you can catch a short passenger ferry to Lismore (page 187), has certain amenities that are missing on Lismore: a doctor (Port Appin Surgery PA38 4DE; ☎ 01631 730271) and somewhere to get evening meals (Pier House Hotel PA38 4DE; ☎ 01631 730302; w pierhousehotel.co.uk; ⏰ 12.30–14.30 & 18.30–21.30 daily). Nearby **Castle Stalker** (PA38 4BL; w castlestalker.com), a spectacularly positioned fortress on a tiny island, could also technically be counted as one of the Inner Hebrides.

Kennacraig, where ferries leave for Islay (page 217), and **Gallanach**, for Kerrera (page 32), are both just ferry ports with nothing else around them.

Appendix 1

Bard A poet. Historically, bards were employed by clan chiefs to tell their family history; they were professional storytellers, oral historians and genealogists who composed poems and songs.

Broch A specific term for a round Iron Age fortification with wide, double dry-stone walls that contained galleries, cells and a stairway.

Cairn Referring to a stony mound, this word comes from the Scottish Gaelic *càrn*. While more modern cairns can be used as waymarkers or are the result of collective efforts to indicate the end of a journey, often to the top of a hill or mountain, in archaeology these piles of stones often conceal deliberately deposited human remains dating from prehistoric times. They are often found in dramatic positions and sometimes have individual chambers.

Cenél An Old Irish word meaning kinship or family group in the time of Dál Riata (page 14).

Cist A burial method; generally rectangular and formed from stone slabs, set on an edge and covered by one or more horizontal slabs or capstones to make a coffin shape. They might be above or below the ground and can be from as early as Neolithic times.

Clan A Scottish group whose leaders claim descent from a common ancestor. Following Dál Riata, various family groups established territories across the islands. Lower-class people who lived on the ruling families' lands were also considered to be part of the clan.

Corrie A bowl-shaped geographical feature found among hills, usually formed by glaciation.

Cottar Relating predominantly to the 17th and 18th centuries, this is a Scottish term for a tenant on a farm who occupied a cottage, which may or may not have had a small piece of land attached. Comparable in meaning to the word peasant.

Crannog A small artificial or partially artificial island built within a loch or wetland and dating from anywhere between prehistoric and medieval times.

Croft In the Highlands, islands and west coast of Scotland, a croft is a small piece of agricultural land, which often has an accompanying dwelling and access to grazing rights in an area of common land. Subject to special protective legislation since 1886, crofts were originally a form of rented land; however, since 1976 tenants have had the option to buy and become owner-occupiers. Working crofts are common in certain parts of the Inner Hebrides, most noticeably on Tiree.

Cup-marked stones Somewhat mysterious, this term is used in archaeology to describe a rock bearing one or more obviously artificial, small, round depressions. In certain cases this is thought to be prehistoric art, but other examples seem more likely to indicate some sort of grinding for practical or superstitious reasons.

Dùn A Scottish Gaelic word meaning fort; often Anglicised to 'dun'. In archaeology, it refers to a rounded building or settlement enclosure with a thick dry-stone wall, often found in an elevated position. Generally, they are small structures that would have been able to protect a family group.

Firth A coastal inlet similar to a fjord, but with a less constrained definition; generally the result of glaciation and often associated with a large river.

Fish trap In the context of this book, a fish trap is an archaeological term relating to a substantial ring of rocks intended to catch fish as the tide goes out.

Fort A fort is a defensive enclosure, often in an elevated position, with one or more banks, ditches, ramparts or walls. Generally distinguished from a dùn by being big enough to house a small community.

Hut circle An archaeological term to describe the remains of a roundhouse, often only visible as a raised circle with an indented centre.

Lazy beds Parallel banks of rig and furrow dug by spade for cultivation purposes.

Loch Scottish Gaelic and Scots word for a lake or a sea inlet.

Machair A Gaelic word for a fertile low-lying area of grass; used more specifically to describe the place where sand and shells have been colonised by plants along the edge of a beach.

Malt Germinated grain that has been dried in a process called 'malting'.

Midden An ancient rubbish dump, which can be as old as the Mesolithic era.

Mill stone Large, disc-shaped stones used in a mill for grinding grain. They originally would have come as a pair.

Pictish stone Decorative stones engraved by the Picts.

Ppm phenol Often used as a measure of the 'peatyness' of whisky, this term specifically refers to the parts per million of phenols, a group of aromatic chemical compounds, found in malted barley after they come out of the kiln and before being used in the rest of the whisky-making process.

Quern stones, saddle querns and quern quarries Quern stones are rocks used for grinding food such as corn from Neolithic times up until the 19th century. A saddle quern is usually thought to be the earliest incarnation, later being replaced by round rotary quern stones. At various points in the 18th and early 19th centuries, landowners banned quern stones and built mills with the intention of charging tenants to use them. Quern quarries are easily distinguished by their obviously artificial succession of roughly 60cm circular indentations, often in difficult-to-access locations, begging the question as to whether they were made in secret.

RIB A rigid inflatable boat, usually 13–28ft long, with one or two motors.

Roundhouses In Britain, circular or oval-plan roundhouses were the standard type of dwelling between the Bronze and Iron ages.

Saga Icelandic literature written in the 12th and 13th centuries to record the historical or legendary figures and events of Norway and Iceland.

Shielings Upland pastures used for grazing in summer; shieling huts are usually smaller than regular houses and were often inhabited by women and children or used for storing dairy. Most common in the 16th, 17th and 18th centuries.

Skerry A word originating from the Old Norse *sker*, meaning a small rocky island or reef.

Souterrain An underground chamber or passage, not found to contain human remains and often associated with an above-ground structure such as a roundhouse. There is some speculation that they were used for storing food. Generally thought to be from the Iron Age.

Standing stone Stones that have been deliberately set upright in the ground. These are of mysterious origin, but usually thought to be prehistoric, often Neolithic or Bronze Age.

Stone circle A circular or oval formation of multiple standing stones.

Ungulate A zoological term for a large group of hooved mammals.

Appendix 2

BASIC PLEASANTRIES

Hello/welcome	Fàilte (fahl-tche)
Goodbye	Beannachd leat (benn-ichk let)
Please	Ma's e do thoil e (mass eh doh holl eh)
Thank you	Tapadh leat (ta-pa let)

COMMON WORDS IN PLACE NAMES

Beag	Small	Cnoc	Hill	Mar	Sea
Beinn	Mountain	Dubh	Black	Mòr	Big
Bhaile	Town/village	Dùn	Fort	Taigh	House
Bùth	Shop	Eaglais	Church	Tràigh	Beach
Chlach	Stone	Eilean	Island		

266

Appendix 3

FURTHER INFORMATION

Many works, both factual and fictional, have been written about the Inner Hebrides. While the list below is far from exhaustive, the following publications are valuable in their specific areas of expertise and have been instrumental in the research for this guide. For literature, including children's books, see page 21.

GEOGRAPHY, GEOLOGY AND NATURAL HISTORY The following books and websites are essential for identification and, in some cases, for developing a wider understanding of the Inner Hebrides' natural environment.

Buczacki, Stefan *Collins Fungi Guide* HarperCollins, 2013
Chinery, Michael *Collins Complete Guide to British Insects* HarperCollins, 2009
Horne, D J *The Geology of Jura* D G B Wright, Craighouse. Part of a series of booklets available to buy on Jura (page 240).
Oldham, Tony *The New Caves of Scotland* 2004. A *very* extensive record of Scotland's caves.
Sterry, Paul *Collins Complete Guide to British Coastal Wildlife* HarperCollins, 2012
Streeter, David *Collins Wild Flower Guide* HarperCollins, 2016
Svensson, Lars *Collins Bird Guide* HarperCollins, 2022
Tolman, Tom *Collins Butterfly Guide* HarperCollins, 2009
Watson, Jeff *The Golden Eagle* T & A D Poyser, 2010

Websites

Hebridean Whale & Dolphin Trust
w hwdt.org
Lochaber Geopark w lochabergeopark.org.uk
Royal Society for the Protection of Birds
w rspb.org.uk

Scottish Geology Trust
w scottishgeologytrust.org
NatureScot w nature.scot
Scottish Raptor Study Group
w scottishraptorstudygroup.org

HISTORY, ARCHAEOLOGY AND HISTORICAL TRAVELOGUES Many of these books or publications are more suited to academic research and would be a good starting point for anyone interested in studying the islands' history in more depth.

Anderson, R S G *Antiquities of Gigha* The Galloway Gazette, Newton Stewart, 1936. A dated but extensive guide to Gigha's archaeological sites.
Argyll: An Inventory of the Monuments, Volume 5: Islay, Jura, Colonsay & Oronsay The Royal Commission on the Ancient and Historical Monuments of Scotland, 1984. An enormous tome of a book, full of invaluable archaeological information.

Boswell, James *The Journal of a Tour to the Hebrides with Samuel Johnson* (4th edition) The Temple Classics, 1903. Boswell's account of his journey with Johnson in 1773. Johnson's book (see below) is more informative and easier to digest.

Caldwell, D H *Islay, Jura and Colonsay: A Historical Guide* Birlinn, 2001. Useful guide for discovering archaeological sites.

Caldwell, D H *Islay: The Land of the Lordship* Birlinn, 2008. An exploration of Islay's history.

Cameron, Archie *Bare Feet and Tackety Boots: A Boyhood on Rhum* Luath Press, 1988. A valuable first-hand account of social history on Rùm before World War I.

Campbell, J L *Canna: The Story of a Hebridean Island* Oxford University Press, 1984

Hardy, K and Wickham-Jones, C R (eds) *Mesolithic and Later Sites around the Inner Sound, Scotland: the Scotland's First Settlers project 1998–2004* SAIR 31 (Scottish Archaeological Internet Reports), 2009

＊ Hunter, John *The Small Isles* Historic Environment Scotland, 2016. The most in-depth study of the Small Isles' archaeology, this book is also full of incredible aerial photographs and is aesthetically pleasing enough to keep on the coffee table.

Hutchinson, Roger *Calum's Road* Birlinn, 2008. The incredible story of Calum MacLeod, resident of northern Raasay.

Johnson, Samuel *A Journey to the Western Islands of Scotland* Cassell & Company Ltd, 1886. Johnson's account of his and Boswell's trip in 1773.

Lamont, W D *The Early History of Islay* Burns & Harris Ltd, 1966

Macaulay, Margaret *The Prisoner of St Kilda – The True Story of the Unfortunate Lady Grange* Luath Press Ltd, 2009. An interesting revised history of Rachel Chiesley (page 79).

Macculloch, J A *The Misty Isle of Skye: Its Scenery, its People, its Story* Oliphant, Anderson & Ferrier, 1905

McDonald, Andrew *The Kingdom of the Isles: Scotland's Western Seaboard, c110–1336* Tuckwell Press, 1997

Maceacharna, Domhnall *The Lands of the Lordship: The Romance of Islay's Names* Argyll Reproductions Ltd, 1976

Martin, Martin *A Description of the Western Islands of Scotland, circa 1695: A Voyage to St Kilda* Birlinn, 1999

Meek, Donald *Seanchas Ìle: Collecting, recording and preserving Islay's Gaelic heritage* Argyll Publishing, 2007

Miers, Mary *Western Seaboard: An Illustrated Architectural Guide* The Rutland Press, 1998

Omand, Donald (ed) *The Argyll Book* Birlinn, 2004. An introduction to Argyll, with sections written by different experts covering history, folklore, literature and a range of other topics.

Wilson, Les *The Drowned and the Saved: When War Came to the Hebrides* Birlinn, 2018. History of the shipwrecked SS *Tuscania* and HMS *Otranto* in World War I.

Wright, Gordon *Jura and George Orwell* D G B Wright, 1993

Wright, Gordon *Jura's Heritage: A Brief History of the Island* D G B Wright, 1994

Website Historic Environment Scotland Canmore (w canmore.org.uk) is an amazing resource containing more than 320,000 records and 1.3 million catalogue entries for archaeological sites across Scotland.

WALKING AND GENERAL GUIDES

Edwards, Peter *The Hebrides* Cicerone, 2020. An inspirational walking guidebook to both the Outer and Inner Hebrides, with glorious photos.

Edwards, Peter *Walking on Jura, Islay and Colonsay* Cicerone, 2019. Details serious hikes in the southern Hebrides, including the entire west coast of Jura.

Edwards, Peter *Walking on Rum and the Small Isles* Cicerone, 2024. For exploring the Rùm Cuillin and other exciting hikes in the Small Isles; Peter and I worked on this second edition of the book together.

Edwards, Peter *Walks in the Inner Hebrides: Skye* Pocket Mountains, Moffat, 2024

Fairweather, Nick *Exploring Raasay: 20 Walking Routes* Thirsty Books, 2015

Marsh, Terry *Walking the Isle of Mull* Cicerone, 2017

Orr, Willie *Discovering Argyll, Mull & Iona* John Donald Publishers, 1990. A dated guidebook but full of fascinating anecdotes.

Welsh, Mary *Walks on the Isle of Islay* Clan Walk Guides, 1996

Youngson, Peter *The Long Road: A Driver's Guide to Jura* D G B Wright, 2005

Website **Walkhighlands** (w walkhighlands.co.uk) is an extensive website dedicated to Scottish walks.

Index

Page numbers in **bold** indicate main entries; those in *italics* indicate maps

INDEX OF ADVERTISERS